The Literary Institution in Portugal since the Thirties

D1789317

Margarida Rendeiro

The Literary Institution in Portugal since the Thirties

An Analysis under Special Consideration of the Publishing Market

PETER LANG

Bern · Berlin · Bruxelles · Frankfurt am Main · New York · Oxford · Wien

Bibliographic information published by Die Deutsche Nationalbibliothek
Die Deutsche Nationalbibliothek lists this publication in the Deutsche
Nationalbibliografie; detailed bibliographic data is available on the Internet
at ‹http://dnb.d-nb.de›.

British Library Cataloguing-in-Publication Data:
A catalogue record for this book is available from The British Library,
Great Britain.

Library of Congress Cataloging-in-Publication Data

Rendeiro, Margarida.
The literary institution in Portugal since the thirties : an analysis under
special consideration of the publishing market / Margarida Rendeiro.
p. cm.
Includes bibliographical references.
ISBN 978-3-0343-0050-6 (alk. paper)
1. Literature publishing-Portugal-History-20th century. 2. Literature
publishing-Portugal-History-21st century. 3. Literature and state-Portugal. 4.
Portugal-Intellectual life. 5. Books and reading-Portugal. 6. Literary prizes-Por-
tugal. 7. Portuguese fiction-Translations-History and criticism.
8. Saramago, José-Appreciation. 9. Peixoto, José Luís, 1974-Appreciation.
10. Canon (Literature) I. Title.
Z421.R46 2010
070.509469'0904-dc22
                                        2009050187

CEPESE

Cover design: Eva Rolli, Peter Lang AG

ISBN 978-3-0343-0050-6

© Peter Lang AG, International Academic Publishers, Bern 2010
Hochfeldstrasse 32, CH-3012 Bern, Switzerland
info@peterlang.com, www.peterlang.com, www.peterlang.net

All rights reserved.
All parts of this publication are protected by copyright.
Any utilisation outside the strict limits of the copyright law, without
the permission of the publisher, is forbidden and liable to prosecution.
This applies in particular to reproductions, translations, microfilming,
and storage and processing in electronic retrieval systems.

Printed in Germany

Table of Contents

Acknowledgements

There are many people I would like to thank for a variety of reasons. Firstly, I would like to thank my Supervisor, Dr. Juliet Perkins. I could not have imagined having a better advisor and mentor for my PhD, and without her common sense, knowledge, perceptiveness and cracking-of-the-whip I would never have finished. I would also express my gratitude to Professor Salvato Trigo, Rector of Fernando Pessoa University, for having encouraged me to start my research in the Portuguese literary field and take a wholly different perspective of Portuguese literature. I am grateful to Mr AbdoolKarimVakil for managing to read the dissertation so thoroughly and give precious advice; to Professors Helder Macedo and Malyn Newitt for their insightful comments; to Dr Rui Vinhas da Silva for revising the final text so accurately; to Mr José-António Carochinho for helping me tackle my survey on Portuguese purchasers of Portuguese fiction and to all my friends who helped me distributing it nationwide. Thanks to my parents, Natália, Rute, and Miguel: your friendship and support kept my head above water. I am more than grateful to Luís and Martim: without you, I would not have made it.

I would also like to thank all the people who agreed to be interviewed by me for this thesis: Zeferino Coelho, António Lobato Faria, Maria do Rosário Pedreira, Margaret Jull da Costa, and Paul Langridge. Also thanks to those people who provided me with valuable information whether they know it or not, especially to: Maria Teresa Santos, Ilídio Matos, and Carola Hermelin.

Thank you all.

Abstract

The dissertation aims to show that the Estado Novo (1933-1974) influenced the constitution of the Portuguese literary canon and the positioning of Portuguese literary producers in the domestic and foreign book markets. Despite the numerous studies of the politics, economy, culture, and society of the Estado Novo, the development of the Portuguese publishing market, the relations established between publishers, authors, and Governmental institutions and their contribution to the making of the literary canon are still marginal subjects of analysis.

The research is based on the systems theories developed by Pierre Bourdieu, Jacques Dubois, and Itamar Even-Zohar and it makes use of a survey on habits of purchase of Portuguese fiction, interviews with publishers, original statistical analyses, and takes a new approach to the study of Portuguese literature. I suggest that the degree of autonomy of the Portuguese literary field has been compromised due to its close dependence on the political, economic, and social fields.

The Estado Novo moulded the Portuguese readership through the implementation of an educational policy that met the Regime's needs of emasculation of subversive thinking. This purpose had an effect on Portuguese publishing and on the positioning of Portuguese literature abroad, and this influence continued after 1974. Despite literary consecration being fundamentally oriented towards the Neo-Realist literature and towards authors who were not approved of by the Estado Novo, the Revolution did not introduce greater autonomy into the Portuguese literary field.

Editorial Caminho's skilful use of contexts and management of the social trajectory of José Saramago, the Nobel Prizewinner in 1998, confirms the systemic relations of the Portuguese literary field, despite being a non-typical case of literary consecration. José Luís Peixoto whose prestige was influenced by Saramago's stature, is pinpointed to show that, present-day literary field is as dependent on the environment as it was in 1933.

List of Acronyms

APE	Associação Portuguesa de Escritores [Portuguese Association of Writers]
APEL	Associação Portuguesa de Editores e Livreiros [Portuguese Association of Publishers and Booksellers]
CADC	Centro Académico para a Democracia Cristã [Academic Centre for Christian Democracy]
CDS	Centro Democrático Social [Social Democratic Centre]
FAOJ	Fundo de Apoio a Organizações de Juventude [Fund for Youth Organizations]
FNAT	Fundação Nacional para a Alegria no Trabalho [National Foundation for the Joy at Work]
ICAP	Instituto de Cultura e Arte Portuguesa [Portuguese Institute of Arts and Culture]
ICALP	Instituto de Cultura, Arte e Língua Portuguesa [Portuguese Institute of Arts, Culture and Language]
IPLB	Instituto Português do Livro e das Bibliotecas [Portuguese Institute of the Book and Libraries]
MFA	Movimento das Forças Armadas [Movement of the Armed Forces]
MUD	Movimento de Unidade Democrática [Movement for Democratic Union]
MUNAF	Movimento de Unidade Nacional Anti Fascista [Movement of Anti Fascist National Union]

PCP	Partido Comunista Português [Portuguese Communist Party]
PDC	Partido da Democracia Cristã [Party of Christian Democracy]
PEN	Poets, Essayists and Novelists
PVDE	Polícia de Vigilância e Defesa do Estado [Police of Vigilance and Defence of the State]
PIDE	Polícia Internacional de Defesa do Estado [International Police for the Defence of the State]
PPD	Partido Popular Democrático [Democratic Popular Movement]
PREC	Plano Revolucionário em Curso [Ongoing Revolutionary Plan]
PS	Partido Socialista [Socialist Party]
RTP	Rádio Televisão Portuguesa [Portuguese Broadcasting Authority]
SEIT	Secretariado de Informação e Turismo [Secretariat of Information and Tourism]
SNI	Secretariado Nacional de Informação [National Secretariat of Information]
SPA	Sociedade Portuguesa de Autores [Portuguese Society of Authors]
SPE	Sociedade Portuguesa de Escritores [Portuguese Society of Writers]
SPN	Secretariado de Propaganda Nacional [Secretariat of National Propaganda]

Introduction

This thesis will set out to show that the Estado Novo (1933-1974) coordinated its educational and cultural policies with the purpose of implementing a pre-defined political strategy. This influenced the constitution of the Portuguese literary canon and had effects on canon revisions between 1974 and 2004.[1] This authoritarianism was particularly felt in the consecration of the Portuguese novel, in view of the associated financial rewards and the struggles for legitimacy based on compromise and opposition that involved the Government as instance of consecration and reproduction and Portuguese novelists. Moreover, the novel has played the most important role in the promotion of contemporary Portuguese literature worldwide. The fact that the Nobel Prize for Literature was given to José Saramago, for his work as a novelist, is evidence of that promotion. The number of Nobel Prizes given to novelists, media exposure given to national and international literary prizes for fiction and the importance of the novel in the worldwide book trade were also reasons for focusing this thesis on the constitution of the Portuguese canon novel within the wider struggles for literary legitimacy and consecration.

Since literature is regarded as a valuable asset, the aesthetic value is assessed, consecrated, or rejected by the valuing community, understood as the dominant group within a political, social, and cultural context. 'Valuing community' is used in this thesis to refer to the persons and institutions involved in the appraisal of a literary work, that is, publishers, editors, fellow-writers involved in reviewing and consecrating it, the media, governmental institutions, purchasers and readers. I will also borrow the term 'intellectual' from Pierre Bourdieu for operational purposes; according to Bourdieu, intellectuals are cultural producers who use their skills and legitimacy (acquired in the literary field) in the political field (albeit not becoming politicians because they con-

---

1   As discussed below.

tinue being cultural producers).[2] As far as Portuguese secondary education is concerned, there are writers that have been included and excluded from the curriculum of Portuguese language and literature disciplines. Nevertheless, this does not imply that their literary value is volatile. Reception is contextually developed with particular purposes and canon formation is not free from ideology. However, we should not discuss it in elegiac terms, as did Harold Bloom in 1994.[3]

Canon formation can be discussed within systems theory, in particular the conceptual contributions of Pierre Bourdieu and Jacques Dubois. The constitution of the valuing community and reception of literary works are carried out within time and place. Assuming the complex relations developed in the contemporary Portuguese literary field, consecration of writers by Portuguese people and the accumulation of prestige do not follow some principles stated by these scholars, in particular as far as the distinctions between commercial and symbolic recognition and between best-sellers and classics are concerned. Academic research, especially that undertaken by Frank de Glas, Hugo Verdaasdonk and Wouter de Nooy, is helpful to explain that Portuguese literary consecration is not unique and positions held by Portuguese publishing houses, critics and writers are also common to those held in different political, social and cultural contexts.

This thesis also looks into José Saramago's canonicity established on unparalleled grounds, in view of the fact that he was not

---

2   'Eles são, assim, seres bidimensionais. [...] têm de aplicar as competências e autoridade específicas que detêm na sua esfera intelectual própria numa actividade política fora dela. Têm de permanecer produtores culturais a tempo inteiro sem se transformarem em políticos', in Pierre Bourdieu, 'The Corporativism of the Universal: The Role of Intellectuals in the Modern World', Telos, 81, 99-110 (99). Cited in ' A relação entre o escritor e a sociedade mantém-se, neste aspecto, marcada por descoincidências várias e pela correlativa dificuldade em encontrar a identidade dada por uma função social'. Quoted from António Sousa Ribeiro, 'Configurações do Campo Intelectual Português no Pós-25 de Abril: O Campo Literário', in *Portugal: Um Retrato Singular*, ed. by Boaventura de Sousa Santos (Lisbon: Edições Afrontamento, 1993), pp. 483-512, (484).

3   Harold Bloom discussed canon formation in his *The Western Canon – The Books and The School of The Ages* (New York: Harcourt Brace & Company, 1994).

part of the literary opposition against the Estado Novo and became involved in the aftermath of the Revolution in 1974. Literary legitimacy after 1974 was particularly directed to Portuguese writers who opposed the Estado Novo. Nevertheless, Saramago's symbolic capital was gained through a combination of factors, among them, Editorial Caminho's decision to publish his works opportunely, considering that they focussed on political and cultural issues debated at that time both in Portugal and foreign countries; the constitution of the writer's social trajectory; and the fact that his translated works were published by key publishing houses in the world book market, which gave him international visibility.

This research started with my critical reading of contributions about systems theory applied to literature, led by the scholars mentioned above. Purchase of fiction and reading of fiction are two different decisions that are not necessarily complementary and publishing houses play a decisive role behind the literary scene. Therefore, in 2001, I submitted a survey to Portuguese purchasers of fiction to learn what were the motivations that influenced their purchasing decisions. The results of this survey were complemented with my analysis of Portuguese best-sellers' lists between 1980 and 2004 and also with my analysis of the publishers and translations of the Nobel Prizewinners between 1947 and 2004 before they were awarded this prize on the assumption that the Nobel Prize for Literature is the highest level of literary consecration. In 2004, I also interviewed the publishers of Editorial Caminho, Temas e Debates and Oficina do Livro, three publishing houses with different policies, whose success has to be measured through distinct criteria. Although this thesis is centred on the consecration of novelists, I decided not to interview them. The writers whose novels were examined in my research have frequently been interviewed by different media. On the assumption that their statements contribute to their making of public personae, I believed that this contribution was enough for my research. In the course of my research on José Saramago, I interviewed (2005) Margaret Jull da Costa, his British translator since 1999 and, in order to better understand the British market, I interviewed (2004) Paul Langridge, a former director of A & C Black, Publishers. My various attempts to contact publishers or editors at Harvill were unsuccessful.

I came across unexpected difficulties derived from the constitution of the Portuguese literary field. Unlike in other European countries access to statistical data about the Portuguese book market is not easy. Statistics on the ranking of Portuguese publishers and other aspects related to publishing are non-existent or unavailable to the public. My efforts with the Associação Portuguesa de Editores e Livreiros, the institution that represents Portuguese publishers and booksellers, also proved unsuccessful as they claim that publishers resent publicising their volumes of sales and, consequently, that constrains official studies. Moreover, an analysis of the reading and purchasing habits of the Portuguese communities abroad, in particular of the second generation of Portuguese emigrants, would have been valuable for the discussion of the results of the promotion of Portuguese literature abroad. However, these studies are also non-existent, as confirmed by the APEL and by the North-American Embassy in Lisbon.

This thesis is organized into eight chapters. In Chapter 1, the theories of the Literary Field developed in the seminal works by Pierre Bourdieu, Jacques Dubois and Itamar Even-Zohar are discussed, with special emphasis on Bourdieu's construction of a space of positions and the struggles for legitimacy in the distribution of recognition and stature, understood as symbolic capital. Canon formation within a political, social, and cultural context is also the object of study, focusing on the contributions of Frank Kermode, John Guillory and Andrew Milner.

Chapter 2 analyses the educational purposes for Portuguese primary and secondary schools led by the Estado Novo to show the priority given to the shaping of way of thinking. This chapter also looks at Portuguese reading patterns to show that they were constrained by political ideology, social patterns that emerged from ideology, high rates of emigration, illiteracy and the Colonial War. My analysis of facts and events will focus on the period that comprises the establishment of the Estado Novo, formally elected in 1933, and the Revolution on 25 April 1974.

Chapter 3 will examine the results of the Estado Novo's most powerful instrument of propaganda to create the cultural establishment, the SPN/SNI/SEIT. This institution launched several initiatives with the aim of normalizing literary production and publishing, such as national prizes and international events to promote Portuguese books. I have included five tables in which I organized publicly available information about prizes, prizewinners, works and their publishing houses chronologically in order to show that the Regime was determined to reward and encourage works whose literary content illustrated the Government's ideology and educational policy. Furthermore, the Government's action in the promotion of Portuguese literature worldwide, enhanced by the country's geographical peripheral position and political alliances, limited the visibility of Portuguese writers abroad. Portuguese writers did not participate massively in the SPN/SNI/SEIT's prizewinning competitions, especially after the Sociedade Portuguesa de Escritores set up its own literary prizes in 1961. The SPE, together with the Academia das Ciências de Lisboa, challenged the Government in its role as consecrating agent.

Chapter 4 will measure the literary prizes set up by the Academia das Ciências de Lisboa and the SPE. The relations between the political and cultural fields did not always imply a full opposition to the Regime and that institutional compromise was the cornerstone of consecration and recognition.

Chapter 5 will establish that, despite the changes in readership and in the book market carried out between 1974 and 2004, the Revolution did not introduce radical changes into schools' curricula. Raising the State's expenditure on Portuguese education had an effect on reducing the level of illiteracy and on restructuring the educational system but it was not of particular relevance to redefining the literary canon as studied at secondary school level.

Chapter 6 will see the Revolution did not provide the cultural field with more autonomy. Dominating and dominated strata reversed positions efforts were oriented towards consecrating writers and literary trends disregarded by the Government during the Estado Novo and targeting to achieve literary autonomy.

Chapter 7 will examine how the Portuguese Government was led to consecrate Saramago due to internal and external pressure, since consecration also benefits those who have the power to consecrate. Saramago was canonized through an established structure of literary consecration and a mechanism of social recognition, enhanced by the fact that his publishing house struggled to legitimize its business, with the traditional establishment and efforts to consecrate Neo-Realist literature. I will also examine José Luís Peixoto, whose works started being published in the late 1990s and whose literary legitimacy was achieved through his positioning in relation to Saramago, a process which was mainly led by critics and by the media and which Peixoto tacitly accepted. Peixoto was regarded as a control writer in my research into José Saramago's consecration, in particular, and of the development of the Portuguese literary field between 1974 and 2004. The expression 'control writer' in this thesis is referred to a Portuguese writer whose literary career and its recognition are developed according to what, in the present dissertation, are considered to be the Portuguese patterns of literary production and popularity between 1974 and 2004. 2004 was the *terminus ad quem* to limit my comprehensive analysis because it coincides with the beginning of the international promotion of José Luís Peixoto. In view of the fact that it was carried out in several European countries, I decided to compare it with José Saramago's early international promotion.

Chapter 8 will show how finding the right publisher and getting reviewed by the right reviewers is fundamental when it comes to acquiring legitimacy. The management of the publication momentum of Saramago's works in Brazil, Spain, the United States and the United Kingdom was essential to enhance consecration: publishing novels at the moment their stances and topics engaged with the political, social and cultural debate in those countries. Inevitably, this also implied a different management of the sequence of the works published in each country. The relevance of the publishing houses in their respective publishing markets and their communication skills played a significant role in attaining a desired impact. History shows that the Nobel Prizes are recurrently given to writers who are published by the same publishers in certain key countries, which also publish several works of literary critique about those writers, strengthening their literary legitimacy.

The Conclusion will examine my findings and the extent to which the theoretical systems models fully address my hypothesis.

CHAPTER 1
Literature as an Institution: Systems Theory

This chapter will establish that Literature has thoroughly been studied as a social construct and that canon formation and revision can be understood within the framework of systems theory. Systems theory enables us to understand the complex relations that involve writers, publishers, translators, critics, booksellers and readers, who operate as agents of (re)production and consecration when certain texts are chosen, read and rewarded against others in a particular political, social and cultural context. This stance does not imply that aesthetic valuing is irrelevant and that it is not inherent to literary writing. As Andrew Milner pointed out, 'value is a transitive term' and this means that literary writing is valued by a community in a specific context.[1] As far as systems theory is concerned, this thesis will particularly focus on Bourdieu's seminal work on the Theory of the Literary Field (*champ littéraire*) in the early 1970s.[2] This theory influenced the academic work of scholars and researchers who published in the 1980s and 1990s.[3] Moreover, Bourdieu's theoretical postulates have also encouraged socio-

---

1   Andrew Milner, *Literature, Culture and Society* (London: University College London Press, 1996), p. 22.
2   Some of Pierre Bourdieu's early works are 'Le marché des biens symboliques', L'année sociologique, 2 (1971), 49-126 ; 'Champ du pouvoir, champ intellectuel et habitus de classes', Scolies, Cahiers de recherches de l 'École normale supérieure, 1 (1971), 7-26 ; 'La production de la croyance : contribution à une économie des biens symboliques', in *Actes de la recherche en sciences sociales*, 13 (February 1977), 3-43 ; *La distinction, Critique sociale du jugement* (Paris, Minuit, 1979).
3   Sigfried J. Schmidt, *Foundations For The Empirical Study of Literature: The Components of A Basic Theory*, trans. by R.de Beaugrande (Hamburg:Helmut Buske, 1982); Robert Estivals, ' Les Sciences de L'écrit ', *Encyclopédie Internacionale de Bibliologie*, ed. by Robert Estivals and others (Paris : Retz, 1993); Niklas Luhmann, *Social Systems*, trans. by John Bednarz, Jr., and Dirk Baecker (Stanford: Stanford UP, 1995).

logical approaches to literary output, such as the studies developed by Frank de Glas, Hugo Verdaasdonk in the Netherlands and Lewis Coser in the United States.

According to Bourdieu, the Literary Field is a social microcosm that has its own structure and laws; it is a space of objective relationships among positions and each position exists only in relation to the others. Political, social, economic and cultural circumstances exert pressure and have effect through transformations in the structure of the field. Pressure drives the relations of power among agents, viz. producers, and their struggle for the preservation or transformation of the order. Studying these transformations enables us to understand both the relations among writers, critics, and publishers and the importance a specific genre acquires at a given period. Bourdieu pointed out that the principle of legitimacy in the field of power is based on possession of economic or political capital. Within this field, the cultural dimension is in a dominated or subordinated position because of its low degree of economic capital and, thus, intellectuals belong to the dominated fraction of the dominant class. Bourdieu also stated that the cultural field possesses relative autonomy with respect to its political and economic determinations. The value which the symbolic capital of intellectuals represents to the dominant class (old/new bourgeoisie, aristocracy) is dependent on the struggle to conserve the established order and, more specifically, on the struggle between fractions aspiring to domination within the field of power and on the production and reproduction of economic capital.

Bourdieu based struggling for the preservation or transformation of the established order on two important concepts: position and taking position. He defined 'position' as 'the one which corresponds to a genre such as the novel or, within this, to a subcategory such as 'the society novel' and is 'subjectively defined by the system of distinctive properties by which it can be situated relative to other positions'.[4] Positions are defined by their degree of recognition within the structure. 'Taking position' (originally '*prise de position*') in the literary field implies developing strategies

---

4   Pierre Bourdieu, *The Field of Cultural Production: Essays on Art and Literature*, ed. and trans. by Randal Johnson (Cambridge: Polity Press, 1993), p. 30.

to acquire legitimacy and can be defined as 'the structured set of the manifestations of the social agents involved in the field – literary or artistic works, of course, but also political acts'.[5] Those strategies should be understood as practices specifically oriented towards recognition and which result from education. Taking a position is defined in relation to the position a specific genre holds in the literary field. The work of art is, thus, identified as a 'symbolic capital' because it is the symbol of accumulated prestige and honour in the dialectical relations between knowledge and recognition. It is subjected to the laws of the market, with the irruption of techniques borrowed from the economic field (collective production, advertising, etc.).

Jacques Dubois, who followed Bourdieu and developed the Theory of the Literary Institution (*L'institution littéraire*) in 1978, pointed out that literary creation is held back by market constraints and that sometimes writers participate in the system in order to achieve legitimacy. This is also shown in Richard Peterson's article on the production of literary works.[6] According to Peterson, there are six constraints that alone, or in combination, influence the development of literary work: technology, law, industry structure, organizational structure, occupational career and the market. This thesis will claim that legal constraints, such as the censorship implemented during the Estado Novo, the structure of the Portuguese book markets, writers' jobs and their political involvement and the understanding of the market both by the State and by book professionals, played decisive roles in the development of the Portuguese market and, especially, in consecrating some Portuguese novelists.

Bourdieu distinguished between two different forms of capital: symbolic and cultural. Symbolic capital refers to accumulated prestige, consecration and honour and is established upon the dialectic between knowledge and recognition, whilst cultural capital

---

5   Bourdieu, p. 30.
6   Richard Peterson, 'Six Constraints on The Production of Literary Works', *Poetics* 14 (1985), 45-67.

involves a form of cultural knowledge which equips the agent with competence to appreciate the cultural works and relations.[7]

In other words, Bourdieu insisted that texts should be analysed in relation to other texts, in relation to the structure of the literary field and in relation to the agents operating in it. The agents of production position their texts in relation to the Establishment, reproducing it or rebelling against it. This position may be overtly or covertly taken not only by writers, but also, for example, by publishers and critics who play a decisive role when they present the texts and their authors to the public.

Taking position in the literary field is competing for legitimacy and Bourdieu has differentiated three competing principles: first, recognition granted by producers who produce for other producers, their competitors; second, 'taste' consecrated by the dominant class and the latter includes academies that sanction literary production; and third, popular consecration, viz. the one bestowed by readers.

Jacques Dubois classified authorities that confer legitimacy to literary production: literary movements, in view of the fact that new writers, viz. initiators, position themselves in relation to a legitimated authority; publishers and booksellers, considering that their position in the literary institution enables them to select and promote literary production; academies, because they use literary awards as promotional strategies and position themselves in the field as official commentators; and, finally, the educational system that integrate literary practices into a set of norms and regulations (prescribed reading). A selection of a corpus of literary texts creates a pre-designed image of literature.[8] Dubois's taxonomy is very helpful in defining the establishment of legitimacy and consecration in the Portuguese literary field. Although neither author defines these agents in relation to hierarchical positions, the fact is that Bourdieu has recognized that the State has the widest range of possibilities for conferring legitimacy, in view of the fact that cul-

---

7 Pierre Bourdieu, *Distinction: A Social Critique of The Judgement of Taste*, trans. by Richard Nice (London: Routledge, 1986), p. 2.

8 Jacques Dubois, *L'Institution littéraire : Introduction à une sociologie* (Bruxelles: Labor/ Paris : Fernand Nathan, 1986), pp. 81-102.

tural policies include subsidies, commissions, and honours; that the educational system inculcates oriented reading; and that the State also has ways to implement overt and covert censorship.

Bourdieu also differentiated the field of restricted literary production (highbrow literature) from the field of large-scale literary production (mass or popular literature). As far as restricted literary production is concerned, the system of relations between different instances functionally is divided according to their role in production, reproduction and promotion of symbolic goods. They develop their own criteria of assessment so that they achieve the recognition of the elite. Hierarchy is dependent on success (volume of sales, prizes and reputation). As far as large-scale literary production is concerned, recognition is entirely defined by the public because this field is dominated by the quest for maximum profitability. The product is aimed at various 'targets' and involves 'brand-name' culture.

Therefore, Bourdieu divided literary business into 'commercial' and 'cultural'. A commercial business corresponds to pre-existent demand and usually involves short-production cycles in order to minimize financial risks. It uses marketing techniques, such as eye-catching dust jackets, signing-sessions, advertising and public relations, and uses short-term authors, such as journalists and celebrities. A cultural business is associated with long production cycles and does not have a pre-defined market. It is a future-oriented production and its stocks may either relapse into the status of material or rise to the status of cultural objects. It depends heavily on the activity of publishers as talent-spotters.

De Glas and Verdaasdonk suggested that Bourdieu's clear-cut division between 'commercial' and 'cultural' businesses no longer holds. They studied the Dutch literary market in the late 1980s, in particular, the activity of leading Dutch publishers, and concluded that the division between 'commercial' and 'cultural' business should not be taken in an absolute sense. De Glas studied the status of Dutch publishers and he found that debutant writers often used their first work as a sort of training ground.[9] The productivity of authors varied constantly and many of them did not produce more than one title. If the debut was taken as a seedling, this meant that the publisher's initial investment was not returned. Fiction debut also became the training ground for writing in another genre and only in a quarter of these cases, did the debut grow into maturity production. Authors who produced only a limited number of fiction books contributed to the cultural prestige and economic success of a publisher by writing in other literary genres. The cooperation between publishers and writers was strongly influenced by commercial interest and mutual loyalty. The Dutch dominating publishers took by far the most initiatives when it came to publishing debuts.

Developments in book markets, and particularly in the Portuguese book market in the late 1990s, show that the publishing houses that were committed to publishing highbrow literature have also published popular literature to overcome financial problems, and that consecrated writers also agreed to some promotion associated with popular literature, such as carefully designed covers and media exposure.[10]

De Glas also concluded that publishers, like writers, were subject to social ageing and often had uncertain relations with many debutants whose future as writers was unclear. This conclusion disputed Bourdieu's suggestion of publishing as talent spotting. After analysing the literary programmes of the leading Dutch publishers, Verdaasdonk concluded that the literary programme is the

---

9   Frank de Glas, 'Literature, 'In-House' writers and processes of success in publishing', *CLCWeb: Comparative Literature and Culture* 1.4 (1999): http://docs.lib.purdue.edu/clcweb/vol1/iss4/3v [accessed in December 2009].

10   After being taken over by Planeta Publishers, Dom Quixote has published some titles, often commissioned, that are clearly identified with 'popular literature'; equally relevant is the fact that other publishing houses, that are more committed to popular literature, have also felt the need to publish titles that could be associated with 'highbrow literature', such as the historical novel (an example is Oficina do Livro's *Equador* (2003) by Miguel Sousa Tavares).

result of a number of choices, which are restrained by market demand for some literary works and by competitors' analyses.[11]

The concept 'gatekeeping' is important to analyse the relations established between publishers, writers and public within the cultural field. It is associated to the process of decision-making and, according to Lewis Coser's study of the North-American book market, it implies 'operating a 'sluice gates for ideas', deciding which will be offered and which will be excluded'.[12] De Glas also suggested that we should see publishers as 'gatekeeping'. Deciding what to publish at the right time makes the difference between the bestseller and the commercial flop. Lewis also extended 'gatekeeping' to book reviewing, bookselling and working as literary agent. There are many examples in Portuguese literature where recognition and commercial success occurred because certain books were published at the right time, examples being José Cardoso Pires's successful *Dinossauro Excelentíssimo* in 1972 and Saramago's earlier works which were commercial flops unlike their multiple reprints after his consecration, ten years later.

Commercial success and legitimacy are also determined by writer profile. Bourdieu pointed out that the perception of the space of possible positions depends on what he called 'social trajectories', that is constructed biographies, considering that literary genres, schools, styles and subjects have a specific value attached to them. Similarly, Dubois suggested that the establishment of writers' profiles is determined by the stages of their career; their participation in groups; the literary genre they have chosen; their relation with other literary producers; their rewards; their attitudes towards aesthetic programmes; their stances; and the image their publishers promote of them. He also added that these pro-

11 H. Verdaasdonk, 'The Influence of Certain Socio-Economic Factors on The Composition of The Literary Programs of Large Dutch Publishing Houses', *Poetics* 14 (1985), 575-608 (p. 602).

12 Lewis A. Coser, Charles Kadushin and Walter W.Powell, *Books: The Culture and Commerce of Publishing* (Chicago & London: The University of Chicago Press, 1982), p. 4. Equally relevant is Frank de Glas, 'Authors' oeuvres as the backbone of publishers' lists: Studying the literary publishing house after Bourdieu', *Poetics* 25 (1998), 379-97.

files are complemented by their family and academic background; jobs; and political and ideological stances.[13]

Writer profile is helpful in understanding the positions they take in the literary field and this can be shown in interview transcripts and in the way publishers promote their writers. This thesis will endeavour to show that profiles of Portuguese writers during the Estado Novo and between 1974 and 2000 enact mechanisms of recognition and prestige, especially as far as their consecration is concerned. In other words, family and social background, employment and ideological stances enhance the social value attached to a particular literary genre and to particular writing styles. As far as Portuguese literature is concerned, it is worthy of note that publicized biographies of most consecrated writers after 1974 share several aspects in common, such as their opposition to the Estado Novo, their working-class or lower middle-class background, and the fact that they were brought up in rural areas. These aspects strengthened their writing in terms of enhancing them with 'publicized' experience and also influenced the promotion of writers consecrated more recently.

Systems theory enables us to recognize dialectical relations between individuals and institutions in the constitution of what has been called national literature. Itamar Even-Zohar proposed that Literature is dynamic and heterogeneous and that these features ensure its vitality when the dominating classes, such as Governments or literary institutions, introduce new norms and models.[14] He first suggested the Polysystem Theory in 1969 and 1970, subsequently reformulating and developing it in the early 1990s. It was designed to deal with multi-lingual literary communities and, to be more accurate, to discuss the historical structure of Hebrew Literature. According to the Polysystem Theory, Literature is a complex whole of systems, bound by history, and, thus, open to interpretation. Tension between canonized and non-canonized literary praxis ensures the vitality and balance of the systems. The absence of any pressure causes their collapse, motivated by a revo-

---

13   Dubois, pp. 109-10.
14   Itamar Even-Zohar, 'Introduction to Polysystem Studies', *Poetics Today* 11.1 (1990), 1-6.

lution such as the overthrow of a Regime, and the total disappearance of a hitherto preserved model.

The definition of national literature is worth discussing because it raises complex interpretations. Does it refer only to a set of texts written in the official language, reflecting the official culture? Does it correspond only to the inside view of intellectuals? What does the collocation *national literature* imply as far as its suitability to the literary promotion led by official agents of consecration are concerned? The constitution of the valuing community is very heterogeneous, and encompasses academic institutions, critics, publishers, booksellers, political and cultural authorities, literary associations and writers producing in particular circumstances.

This also raises the question of how the work of art is received in a particular context, an issue that has been debated within the framework of literary work, particularly that developed by Pierre Macherey.[15] *National literature* is constructed upon value judgements by the dominating class. Reception Theory, as developed by Hans Robert Jauss, Tony Bennet and Steven Mailloux, among others, is a valuable contribution to the debate on national literature.

Reception theorists hold that the interpretative activity of readers explain the text's aesthetic value. Jauss emphasized that the reader has an 'horizon of expectations'; in other words, this 'stipulates that, to interpret a text or a society readers bring to bear the subjective models, paradigms, beliefs and values of their necessarily limited background'. According to him, texts serving political ends can demonstrate aesthetic value.[16] Steven Mailloux took a more radical stance as far as Reception Theory is concerned. He held that a text is interpreted differently by different communities of readers and acknowledges the existence of political divisions.[17] The importance of politics in Reception Theory was also endorsed

---

15   A relevant contribution for this debate is Pierre Macherey, *A Theory of Literary Production*, trans. by Geoffrey Wall (London: Routledge & Kegan Paul, 1978).

16   In Hans Robert Jauss, 'The Identity of the Poetic Text in the Changing Horizon of Understanding' and Toward an Aesthetic of Reception (1977), rephrased and ed. by James Machor & Philip Goldstein, *Reception Theory: From Literary Theory to Cultural Studies* (New York & London: Routledge, 2001), p. 2.

17   In Steven Mailloux, 'Interpretation and Rhetorical Hermeneutics' (1982), rephrased by James Machor & Philip Goldstein, pp. 3-4.

by Tony Bennet. He claimed that reception study is a political intervention in cultural affairs; in other words, institutional structures encourage interpretation with their justifying ideologies.[18]

This is particularly relevant for the analysis of the literary canon, consecrated by the educational system, in relation to the inclusion and removal of several literary texts following curricula revisions. In Portugal, these revisions show that authors, such as Camões and Fernando Pessoa, have been studied with different emphases and objectives. Moreover, the fact that many literary texts associated with the foundation of Portugal and with the Discoveries, were studied at secondary education level during the Estado Novo and removed from the curriculum after 1974, indicates that aesthetic valuing contributed to shaping the mind of the Portuguese within certain 'horizons of expectations'.

In the 1970s, history revisions were encouraged by the academic work of scholars such as Hayden White, Kiernan Ryan and A. Aram Veeser, which has become known as New Historicism. The New Historicist perspective claims that history is a construct, a selection of facts made by historians who rearrange them according to a point of view:

> New Historicism can be distinguished from 'old' historicism by its lack of faith in 'objectivity' and 'permanence' and its stress not upon the recreation of the past, but rather the processes by which the past is constructed or invented. Unsettling, transgressive, at times contradictory, new Historicism tends to regard texts in materialist terms, as objects and events in the world, a part of human life, society.[19]

> So, too if we recognized the literary or fictive element in every historical account, we would be able to move the teaching of historiography onto a higher level of self-consciousness than it currently occupies.[20]

---

18 In Tony Bennet, 'Texts in History' (1987), rephrased by James Machor & Philip Goldstein, p. 5.
19 *New Historicism and Cultural Materialism: A Reader*, ed. by Kiernan Ryan (London: Arnold, 1996), p. 4.
20 Hayden White, *Tropics of Discourse: Essays in Cultural Criticism* (Baltimore and London: The Johns Hopkins University Press, 1978), p. 99.

History revisions can be understood as constructs in the sense that they serve the purpose, institutionally defined, of showing the past as an orientation or an explanation for political policies. This is not far from Reception Theory, in particular Tony Bennet's stance, and is relevant when analysing cultural and ideological paradigms held during the Estado Novo. Moreover, the New Historicist tenets are also relevant when reading the novels of Saramago, in particular his novels such as *Memorial do Convento* and *História do Cerco de Lisboa*, in which he approaches certain periods of Portuguese history.

The concept of *national literature* is rooted in consecration; nowadays, the word 'consecration' has become a useful catchphrase to refer to those texts and writers who achieve the highest degree of legitimacy and are widely appraised as part of a cultural heritage. Nevertheless, it was an interesting expansion of the original meaning that referred, according to Christian theology, to that which was genuine and divinely inspired; the term 'canon' referred to a set of sacred texts of the Bible officially recognized by the Church. However, when used within literary studies, this does not mean that writers were gods. It means, by analogy with the biblical texts, that the literary canon is deemed 'authentic' and 'inspired' by legitimate literary authorities in ways that other texts are not. The canonized or consecrated texts constitute the literary establishment, the fundamentals of which should remain unquestioned. The authorities who form the valuing community decide on the basis of judgement of taste defined by context.

Sociological approaches to Literature challenge stances that claim that the literary canon is dependent only on aesthetic value. Harold Bloom is a staunch supporter of literary studies as a search for a kind of value that transcends particular prejudices and needs of societies at a particular time.[21] Frank Kermode, John Guillory and Andrew Milner developed studies that challenge Bloom's *Western Canon* and defined premises that support systems theory. Kermode assumed that history is manageable for literary periods and has pointed out that the association between canon and au-

---

21   Harold Bloom, *The Western Canon – The Books and The School of Ages* (New York: Harcourt Brace & Company, 1994).

thority is ingrained in us.[22] This means that the canon is a selective instrument used by authorities, themselves complicit with power. The canon, he claimed, 'shapes the past and makes it humanly available, accessibly modern' and this is effected through periodization.[23] I consider that their contributions are very valuable for understanding the establishment of the Portuguese literary canon, especially when assessing the definition of aesthetic values inherent to canon formation.

This stance is not far from Even-Zohar's definition of the canon because authority is vested in the dominant circles. Kermode explained that the consensus around the canon is perpetuated through institutional control of interpretation, such as academic curricula. Students are trained to make certain interpretations of the favoured texts. Guillory's study of the canon was influenced by Bourdieu's theory but he pointed out that the literary canon has more complex social contexts than the immediate response of readers and that the institutional context shapes and moulds judgements in such a way that the canon cannot be considered as a representation of the dominant community.[24] This was true, Guillory claimed, at least in the United States because there was no real national cultural school programme. This should constitute ground for allowing for countries' differences to be scrutinized. Unlike the United States, Portugal lived through a repressive Regime. The Portuguese Government was the hegemonic consecrating authority and repressive methods were used to shape literary production as part of the nationwide project to educate the Portuguese way of thinking. In view of the fact that dynamic and heterogeneous relations are essential to preserve the system's vitality, the institutions that competed with the Government as far as consecration was concerned, played the role of counter-hegemonic forces within the literary field. They consecrated alternative narrative representations and, thus, ensured restricted le-

22 Frank Kermode, 'Canon and Period', in *History and Value – The Clarendon Lectures and the Northcliffe Lectures 1987* (Oxford: Clarendon Press, 1988).
23 Kermode, pp. 116-17.
24 John Guillory, 'Canonical and Noncanonical: The Current Debate' in *Cultural Capital: The Problem of Literary Canon Formation* (Chicago and London: The University of Chicago Press, 1993), p. 29.

gitimacy. By compromising with the Regime, they also ensured their literary legitimacy. The present thesis will argue that commitments taken by literary producers have affected the literary field's autonomy and that they continued between 1974 and 2004.

Milner also disagreed with Bloom's stance and has defined the 'literariness' of literature as a 'function of the ways in which different kinds of writing are socially processed, both by writers themselves and by readers, publishers, booksellers, literary critics and so on'.[25] Literature is a social construct and social studies and cultural studies have to be interrelated for it to be understood in-depth. The aesthetic value is identified by the valuing community in specific contexts, according to particular criteria and with defined purposes. The fact that some texts are better than others are becomes a relevant assumption only when the valuing communities of different generations are able to sustain the same judgement over time. Studying the literary field during the Estado Novo and its developments after 1974 exposes the diversity of criteria used to establish the literary canon, and the vested interests that resulted in successive revisions of the Portuguese literary canon over decades.

Whether taking more traditional or radical approaches to Reception Theory, the question is that the interpretative community determines the validity of the interpretation of a particular text and this becomes especially relevant when considering the establishment of the literary canon. This links with conclusions drawn by Milner and Kermode as regards value judgements by a community at a particular time. Assuming that the interpretation, and especially its communication, is influenced by the political, social and cultural environment, it follows that canon revision is influenced by the dominant ideology and that the canon is formed with the purpose of representing the nation, something that is clear in representation of national history.

---

25   Milner, p. 22.

CHAPTER 2
Education and Readership at the Service of Politics during the Estado Novo (1933-1974)

This chapter will aim to show: first how the Estado Novo enforced education and moulded a Portuguese literary canon that met the requirements of its political strategy; and second, how education influenced readership in a country with economic and social problems, such as poverty and massive illiteracy. The contribution of Itamar Even-Zohar's work on the Polysystem Theory will be of particular relevance to the understanding of the Estado Novo's disregard for the systematicity of Portuguese society.

Immediately after the Portuguese Government was appointed on 19 March 1933, António de Oliveira Salazar defined that education should serve the wide-ranging purpose of re-defining national identity.[1] The 1933 Constitution guaranteed that public opinion was a fundamental instrument and that the State was responsible for defending it from every subversive factor.[2] When the Revolução Nacional was implemented, opposition was only theoretically possible because Salazar wanted to make sure that it would not affect his reforms. The União Nacional, set up in 1930, aggregated the civilian forces which supported the Estado Novo. The Regime was strengthened through the assimilation of certain ideological stances and vocabulary used by nuclei and institutions

---

1   'Mas a posse do Estado, que é condição necessária para salvar a Nação da ruína total e da desordem, não é factor suficiente de renovação material ou moral nem por si só pode garantir a estabilidade, o futuro da obra realizada. Esta há-de firmar-se na reforma da educação', António Ferro, *Salazar – O Homem e a sua obra*, *Oliveira Salazar* (pref.) (Lisbon: Empresa Nacional de Publicidade, 1933), p. xxxiii.
2   Constitution, Title VI, 'Da Opinião Pública', Art. 20: 'A opinião pública é elemento fundamental da política e da administração do País, incumbindo ao Estado defendê-la de todos os factores que a desorientem contra a verdade, a justiça, a boa administração e o bem comum'.

that had been set up before 1933, such as the Integralismo Lusitano, the Centro Académico de Democracia Cristã and the Centro Católico Português.[3] Moreover, and as indicated by António Costa Pinto's study on contemporary Portugal, early on the establishment of the Estado Novo, Salazar created institutions that aimed at subduing opposition: the Acção Escolar de Vanguarda, set up in 1933, replaced by the Mocidade Portuguesa in 1936, was used to hold back the Nacional Sindicalismo; and the Legião Portuguesa, set up in 1936, was an anti-communist militia. The Acção Católica Portuguesa, structured in 1933 within the wide-range promotion of Catholicism led by the Holy See, followed the dissolution of the CCP, and involved the Church in the role of strengthening Roman Catholicism in Portugal. This was useful to strengthen the values defended by the Estado Novo, as discussed below.[4]

The Portuguese Government also created institutions, such as the Obras das Mães para a Educação Nacional, the Fundação Nacional para a Alegria no Trabalho and the Casas do Povo, that endorsed the values of the Revolução Nacional. These institutions were effective in the process of accepting the Regime because the Portuguese people were strongly encouraged to take part in the activities organized.[5] Outlawing political movements and parties

---

3   The Integralismo Lusitano was a political and social movement set up in 1913. It aimed at the regeneration of Portugal. It was nationalist, monarchical and anti-liberal. The death of António Sardinha in 1925 contributed to this movement's dissolution in 1933; the CADC was a students' nucleus set up at Coimbra University in 1901 with the purpose of discussing political, economic and social issues from a Christian point of view. It was discontinued in 1971; the CCP was a nucleus set up in 1917 and stood for the need to preserve the Portuguese's Christian values which, the CCP claimed, were menaced by the First Republic. It had been supported by Salazar and Cardinal Cerejeira before the Estado Novo. The CCP was replaced by the Acção Católica Portuguesa in 1933.

4   António Costa Pinto, 'Portugal Contemporâneo: Uma Introdução', in *Portugal Contemporâneo*, ed. by António Costa Pinto (Lisbon: Dom Quixote, 2005), pp. 11-50.

5   The OMEN was set up through Decree-Law No.26 893 on 15 August 1936 with the purpose of 'estimular a acção educativa da família'; and the FNAT was set up through Decree-Law No.25 495, on 13 June 1935 with the aim of promoting 'o aproveitamento do tempo livre dos trabalhadores portugueses'.

such as the Communist Party hit opposition, although the Estado Novo did not succeed in dissolving it completely, as will be shown below. The formation of the Polícia de Vigilância e Defesa do Estado (PVDE) in 1933, subordinated to the Ministry of the Interior, aided the Prime Minister in controlling oppositionist and subversive movements. It was specially oriented towards prevention and repression of political and social crime and also towards the fight against illegal emigration.[6]

As far as the education of the Portuguese was concerned, the major objective of the Estado Novo, as established in the revised Constitution, was to deal with illiteracy *in strictu sensu*, that is, children should be able to read and write at a basic level at the end of their primary education.[7] National education was to be run according to basic values: the cult of the family; religious faith; respect for authority and hierarchy; and love for literary and scientific culture. These principles were rooted in five values that Salazar considered unquestionable: God, Homeland, Authority, Family and Work.[8] The Government was assigned, in Salazar's own words, the mission of national regeneration, saving the Nation from chaos and disorder through the indoctrination of principles and good education.[9] Preserving the legacy of Portuguese

6   PVDE was renamed PIDE in 1945. In 1969, Marcello Caetano's Government changed its name to DGS-Direcção Geral de Segurança in an attempt to reduce the extremely negative connotation to this institution.

7   Decree-Law No.27603 of 29 March 1937: 'escrever uma cópia, redigir um telegrama, preencher um questionário, fazer um requerimento, passar um recibo ou um vale do correio'.

8   '[...] temos respeitado a consciência dos crentes e consoladdo a paz religiosa. – Não discutimos Deus. [...] Sem receio colocámos o nacionalismo português na base indestrutível do Estado Novo; [...] Não discutimos a Pátria. Não discutimos a autoridade. Ela é um facto e uma necessidade. [...] Não discutimos a família. Aí nasce o homem, aí se educam gerações, [...] Não discutimos o trabalho nem como direito nem como obrigação'. Speech delivered on 26 May 1936. António de Oliveira Salazar, *Antologia – Discursos, Notas, Relatórios, Teses, Artigos e Entrevistas* (Lisbon: Editorial Vanguarda, 1954), pp. 52-7.

9   'A obra educativa a realizar, mormente nesta época de renascimento nacional, tem de partir dum acto de fé na Pátria portuguesa e inspirar-se num são nacionalismo. É preciso amar e conhecer Portugal – no seu passado de grandeza heróica, no seu presente de possibilidades materiais e morais,

history and tracking the roots of popular culture were essential steps to achieve national regeneration. This stance was not new because it used some of the Republican propaganda about Portuguese nationalism whose theoretical principles had been developed by Teófilo Braga at the end of the 1880s. Braga had pinpointed collective beliefs, cultural symbols and rituals as ways to build national identity. As shown in Nuno Monteiro's and António Costa Pinto's study on Portuguese national identity, the Estado Novo approached the concept of Nation, bestowed it transcendental value and promoted it in the political and ideological fields.[10]

Salazar believed that the major objective of the government's educational policy should be the constitution of elites.[11] The masses should receive instruction which enabled them to perform daily chores, whereas the pursuit of higher education should more accessible to the upper classes. Philippe Schmitter's study on the social basis of the Portuguese authoritarian rule has shown that the highly qualified deputees served more terms at the Assembleia Legislativa and Câmara Corporativa: between 1934 and 1938, workers, landowners and military officers did not serve more than one term, whilst professors and educators, lawyers, judges and physicians were amongst those who served more than five terms.[12] The gap between the population and the Government was self-consciously arranged.[13] By respecting authority, the Estado Novo

---

adivinhá-lo no seu futuro de progresso, de beleza, de harmonia', Ferro, pp. xxxv-xxxvi.

10 Nuno G. Monteiro and António Costa Pinto, 'A Identidade Nacional Portuguesa', in *Portugal Contemporâneo*, pp. 51-65.

11 Considero [...] mais urgente a constituição de vastas elites do que ensinar o povo a ler. É que os grandes problemas nacionais têm de ser resolvidos, não pelo povo, mas pelas elites enquadrando as massas', Anais da Revolução Nacional, Vol. IV, p. 259, Cited in Maria Filomena Mónica, *Educação e Sociedade no Portugal de Salazar* (Lisbon: Editorial Presença/ Gabinete de Investigações Sociais, 1978), p. 116.

12 Phillipe Schmitter, "The Regime d'Exception That Became The Rule: Forty-Eight Years of Authoritarian Domination in Portugal", in *Contemporary Portugal – The Revolution and Its Antecedents*, ed. by Lawrence Graham and Harry Mackler (Austin & London: University Texas, 1979), pp. 3-41 (p. 12).

13 Our regime is popular, but it is not a Government of the masses, being neither influenced nor directed by them. These good people who cheer me one

aimed at the maintenance of hierarchical social positions in order to ensure social order: children should follow in their parents' footsteps within foreseeable horizons of social expectations.[14]

Salazar's stance, shared by the supporters of the Estado Novo, revived the discussion on (il)literacy that dated back to the nineteenth century and had opposed nationalists, such as Ramalho Ortigão, and Republicans, who had blamed the Church for encouraging illiteracy.[15] The Church in turn had accused the State of being the authority responsible for massive illiteracy due to the state monopoly of education. In 1927, other personalities, such as Virgínia de Castro Almeida, João Ameal and José de Sá Pereira Coutinho, advocated traditionalist and conservative stances, similar to those of Salazar, and glorified illiteracy, seeing in it traces of genuine Portuguese qualities.[16] In 1938, the Reform of Primary Education headed by the Minister of Education Carneiro Pacheco was discussed at the Assembleia Nacional and Câmara Corporativa and deputees, such as Moura Relvas, Correia Pinto, and Querubim Magalhães, revived some of those arguments published in

---

day, may rise in rebellion the next day [...]'. Cited in *The Observer*, Sunday, 29 August, 1954.

14 'A organização, a defesa dos interesses colectivos e a conciliação dos interesses individuais, a ordem, a paz, a definição dos fins a atingir pelo agregado social, a preparação dos meios necessários, o impulso no sentido do melhor são ainda sua obra e fruto', Salazar, *Antologia*, pp. 54-5.

15 The Decree-Law no.36969 (27 October 1952) stated that the Portuguese people 'não sentia necessidade de aprender'. Ramalho Ortigão's political ideas were studied by Vasco Pulido Valente, in *O Tempo e o Modo*, no.47/48, 1967. In 1927, Aquilino Ribeiro, who opposed the republicans' claim that education encouraged progress, wrote in *O Século* that 'em toda a aldeia qu não seja servida, ao menos, pelo macadame, a escola é vã e absurda'.Cited in Mónica, p. 110.

16 Virgínia de Castro Almeida (1874/1945; author of children's literature): 'A parte mais linda, mais forte e mais saudável da alma portuguesa reside nesses 75 por cento de analfabetos', *O Século*, 5 February 1927; João Ameal (1902/1982; historian and essayist): 'Portugal não necessita de escolas' [...] 'Ensinar a ler é corromper o atavismo da raça'; J. Pereira Coutinho (1896/1969; novelist): 'Felizes aqueles que não sabem ler!'. Cited in Mónica, pp. 119 and 123. Literacy was linked to the possibility of being in contact with new and potentially subversive literature. As will be shown in Chapter 3, the personalities mentioned above were among those who received the SNI prizes.

the Portuguese press, such as *Diário de Notícias* and *Século*, in 1927.[17] They legitimized the Reform of Primary Education which reduced compulsory education from five to four years.[18] As far as secondary education was concerned, the Regime set up two strands of school system: the 'ensino liceal' and the 'ensino técnico' (subdivided into 'escola técnica elementar', 'escola comercial' and 'escola industrial'). The former was more general and aimed at pupils who pursued higher education, whereas the latter gave youngsters enough skills to get a job in trade and industry. Rural areas were deprived of schools because most of these were located in urban centres, such as Lisbon, Porto, and Coimbra.[19]

It was on 11 April 1936 that the Ministry of Public Instruction was renamed the Ministry of National Education; the new designation reflected the Government's policy for framing Portuguese education within the ideals of the new Regime since early childhood. The name of this Ministry would be changed only after 1974. The assignments of the ten Ministers who were sworn into office up until the Revolution were always within the wide-ranging policy of educating the nation as a whole and also responded to the political debate on educating the nation.[20]

---

17 These deputees stated that instruction should not be reagarded a priority because the Portuguese were genuinely conservative, and their knowledge about practical aspects of life and Roman Catholicism was enough for their needs. Cited in Mónica, pp. 116-17, 123 and 125.

18 Compulsory education was divided into four years up till 1964 and between 1964 and 1973, it was extended to six years. Only in 1973, did Minister Veiga Simão carry out an educational reform that added two more years.

19 This situation did not change dramatically throughout the Estado Novo, despite some governmental investment in illiteracy campaigns and in infrastructure. For example, in 1951-1952, statistics on the national distribution of public schools showed that there were twelve Escolas Técnicas Elementares, 9 Comercial and 8 Industrial in the Lisbon district, whereas in rural districts, such as Bragança, Castelo Branco, Portalegre and Viseu, there was one of each. See Instituto Nacional de Estatística, *Estatísticas de Educação 1951-1952* (Lisbon, 1952).

20 There were several discussions at the National Assembly in 1937 and 1938, by the time the Minister of Education, Carneiro Pacheco, presented a bill to restructure nationwide primary education. They are referred to in Maria Filomena Mónica, *Educação e Sociedade no Portugal de Salazar* (Lisbon: Editorial Presença/ Gabinete de Investigações Sociais, 1978).

Although illiteracy was regarded as a way to favour the population's acceptance of the Revolução Nacional, literacy was used as a useful means to educate the Portuguese in the Regime's ideology, as indicated in Filomena Mónica's 1978 study on Portuguese primary education during the early years of the Estado Novo. Thus, literacy was employed to strengthen the Portuguese people's support to the Government. At the same time that the Government delayed industrialization, it invested in literacy campaigns.

The Government's campaigns against illiteracy, headed by Ministers of Education Pires de Lima and Leite Pinto between 1949 and 1955 were particularly active and produced results: in 1925-1926, there were 330,000 pupils enrolled in primary schools; in 1951-1952, there were 670,000; and in 1955-1956, there were more than one million. The number of enrolments in secondary schools and universities rose likewise.[21]

Consequently, the rate of illiteracy fell during the Estado Novo: in the 1930s, 61.8 per cent of the Portuguese aged over seven were illiterate; in the 1940s, this figure dropped to 49 per cent and again to 40.4 per cent in the 1950s; by the 1960s, it had dropped even further to 31.1 per cent. Despite this, it compared badly with the European average. Portugal's rate of illiteracy in the 1930s was higher than that of France, Italy and Finland in 1911: illiteracy affected only 24.1 per cent of the French, 46.5 per cent of the Italians and 19.8 per cent of the Finns in 1911.[22] Furthermore, the average expenditure on education during the Estado Novo was similar to that of other Southern European countries and lower than that of most northern European countries. The percentage of Portuguese public expenditure on education as a percentage of the GDP was 1.2 per cent in 1947 and 1.3 per cent in 1950. In the same years, the

21 There were 33,000 pupils attending secondary schools in 1926 and 73,000 in 1940. In 1950, there were already 100,000 pupils and more than 200,000 pupils in 1960. As far as higher education is concerned, the upward tendency is also a fact: 1926: 6,000; 1940: 9,000; 1950: 15,000; 1960: 38,000. Cited in Franco Nogueira, *O Estado Novo (1933-1974)*, pref. by Marcelo Rebelo de Sousa (Lisbon: Civilização Editora, 2000), p. 412.
22 Instituto Nacional de Estatística, Direcção Geral da Estatística, 'Analfabetismo em diferentes países', 1915.

percentage of Italy's public expenditure was 2.1 per cent and 2.8 per cent; Spain's public expenditure was 0.9 per cent in 1947 (no data available in 1950); France's public expenditure was 0.83 per cent and 1.68 per cent; and Finland's public expenditure was 2.5 per cent and 3.1 per cent.[23] As will be shown in Chapters 6 and 8, in the countries where the rate of illiteracy was lower and public expenditure on education was higher, there was a more complex book market network, whereas in Portugal, publishing houses were mostly small businesses. It is noteworthy that Portugal, Spain and Italy all experienced authoritarian Governments during that period, but it was in Portugal that the investment in education remained lower for a longer period. It was also in Portugal, that an authoritarian Government lasted the longest.

The introduction of the subject Moral and Civic Education into the primary and secondary school curriculum in 1936 became central to the moulding of the Portuguese mindset.[24] The Ministry of Education's imposition of the 'livro único' was very important to orient education; in other words, primary and secondary public schools used the same schoolbooks, which made it easier for the Government to guide education. Itamar Even-Zohar pointed out that the imposition of official ideology hides the dynamic tensions that make culture evolve:

> The ideology of an official culture as the only acceptable one in a given so-
> ciety has resulted in massive cultural compulsion affecting whole nations

---

23 Data available in *The Public Expenditure on Education, a Preliminary Statistical Report* prepared by the Department of Social Sciences, Statistical Divisions in 1953, Available on http://unesdoc/unesco/org [Accessed in March 2007]. This report also indicates that in 1947 public expenditure on education was 2.8 per cent of the total British income; 2.9 per cent of the Dutch national income and that in 1949, it was 3.7 per cent of the West German national income.

24 Carlos Reis discussed the relevance of this discipline in 'A Produção cultural entre a norma e a ruptura', in *Portugal Contemporâneo (1928-1958)*, ed. by António Reis, 5 vols (Lisbon: Alfa, 1990), V, p. 208. This discipline completed individual education and was framed within the concept of Portuguese citizenship as defined by Salazar: 'A Constituição de 1933 [...} permitiu atribuir à Igreja, na constituição dos lares e na formação da juventude [...] não ir até ali seria igualmente ter em menos conta o que é exigência de justa liberdade e necessidade da estrutura cristã da Nação portuguesa', Salazar, p. 42.

through a centralized educational system and making it impossible even for students of culture to observe and appreciate the role of the dynamic tensions which operate within the culture for its efficient maintenance.[25]

The school syllabuses for primary and secondary education during the Estado Novo showed two complementary aspects of traditionalism: on the one hand, the belligerent and heroic nationalist tradition; on the other hand, the rural and popular tradition.[26]

The imposition of a Portuguese official culture was defined by patterns of social behaviour and legitimized by literature approved of by the Government.[27] The purpose of official syllabuses was to inculcate respect for Portuguese values and history. Historical and cultural interpretation was based on three periods: the Foundation of the Nation, the Discoveries, and Restoration. Viriato, D. Afonso Henriques, Santo António, D. Nuno Álvares Pereira, D. João I, Camões, D. João II, D. João V, Gago Coutinho and Sacadura Cabral, and the Estado Novo leaders were set up as examples of the belligerent and heroic tradition. They symbolized nationalism, devotion to the Catholic Church, past glories and contemporary achievements. Rurality, associated with physical and mental health and happiness, completed the Portuguese character.[28] The majority of writers and poets that studied at school belonged to the nineteenth and early twentieth centuries. Teachers presented them as landmarks of the Portuguese literature. Their

---

25   Itamar Even-Zohar, 'Polysystem Theory', *Poetics Today*, 11:1 (1990), 9-26 (p. 16).
26   Apart from the work by Mónica (1978), other important studies on the syllabuses of the primary and secondary education during the Estado Novo are by Irene Maria Fialho, 'Popular e Popularizante nos Manuais Escolares do Estado Novo'(unpublished master's thesis, Universidade Nova de Lisboa, December 1993) and Paulo Jorge Lampreia Costa, 'Construção do Cânone Literário Escolar – Uma Análise de Textos Programáticos para o Ensino Secundário'(unpublished thesis, Évora University, 1997).
27   This was what Even-Zohar has defined as uni-system, (p. 14).
28   Citing Eric Hobsbawm,'"Invented tradition" is taken to mean a set of practices, normally governed by overtly or tacitly accepted rules and of a ritual or symbolic nature, which seek to inculcate certain values and norms of behaviour by repetition, which automatically implies continuity with the past. In fact, where possible, they normally attempt to establish continuity with a suitable historic past', in *The Invention of Tradition*, ed. by Eric Hobsbawm and Terence Ranger (Cambridge: Cambridge University Press, 1992), p. 1.

reading of the chosen literary texts substantiated that education was to be run according to Portuguese cultural and historical 'invented tradition' and thus legitimized the Regime through literature and history.[29] Schoolbooks referred to Afonso Lopes Vieira's work as 'tradicional e *saudosista*'; João de Deus as 'escritor espontâneo e popular'; Júlio Dinis's novels were studied as 'modelos de simplicidade e espontaneidade com fins educativos'; António Correia de Oliveira was studied as a writer who wrote a work 'de inspiração religiosa e popular relevante para a terra e para o orgulho nacional'. Guerra Junqueiro and Gomes Leal were 'contemplativos e crentes na natureza'; Augusto Gil was a 'escritor popular e descritivo'; Garrett was pinpointed as 'percursor do movimento Romântico e da literatura dramatúrgica'; Camilo Castelo Branco was 'um génio habilidoso' and António Sardinha was 'um poeta nacionalista, com orgulho nacionalista genuíno'; António Nobre's and Antero de Quental's works showed 'pessimismo e da saudade portuguesa'; Fernando Pessoa's 'O Mostrengo' was a 'poema complexo' and Eça de Queirós's A *Cidade e as Serras* was an 'eulogia à vida rural'.[30]

The choice of the writers reflects a pattern: their texts were selected according to the State's best interests and, thus, certain writers' overt positions were ignored, such as Afonso Lopes Vieira, who supported the Integralismo Lusitano and did not support the Estado Novo in its early years.[31] Some novels by Eça de Queirós, such as *O Crime do Padre Amaro, O Primo Basílio, A Capital, Uma Campanha Alegre, Os Maias, O Conde d'Abranhos* and *Alves & Ca*

---

29   The 1936 syllabus for secondary education aimed at 'promover a ilustração do espírito e também da educação cívica dos alunos, por meio da ilustração metódica da história da literatura portuguesa, à luz de numerosos documentos que permitam acompanhar a evolução dos sentimentos, das ideas e da arte, bem como da linguagem, numa síntese da vida mental da Nação'. Cited in Lampreia, p. 103.

30   References collected by Fialho, pp. 120-30.

31   National Syndicalism, or Os Camisas Azuis, was a movement rooted in the Integralismo Lusitano. Despite being a right-wing movement that emerged in 1932, several members, such as Dutra Faria and Ramiro Valadão, were won over to Salazar's Regime and that movement eventually collapsed due to lack of national support

were not included in school libraries because the Regime found them morally degraded. These were major works focusing on social, cultural, and political criticism. Exceptions were his A *Cidade e as Serras, O Mandarim, A Ilustre Casa de Ramires, As Minas de Salomão, Cartas Familiares, Bilhetes de Paris (1893-1896), Correspondência* and *O Egipto*.[32]

Portugal's isolation from Europe, in particular up until the 1960s, was decisive for the effectiveness of the Estado Novo's educational policy because it enabled the State to control access to information.[33] Official neutrality during the Second World War had spared Portugal from acute deprivation and destruction, but it also made isolation a useful tool for perpetuating the Portuguese Regime's ideology.

The Estado Novo resisted change and progress and built up an image of Portugal that did not reflect the real country, especially between the 1950s and the early 1970s. In 1979, Eduardo Lourenço's study on Portuguese culture during the Estado Novo pointed out:

> Todavia a glosa do relativo sucesso dessa tentativa é que não foi nada modesta e breve redundou na fabricação sistemática e cara de uma *lusitanidade* exemplar, cobrindo o presente e o passado escolhido em função da sua mitologia arcaica e reaccionária que aos poucos substituiu a imagem mais ou menos adaptada ao país real dos começos do Estado Novo por uma ficção ideológica, sociológica e cultural mais irrealista ainda do que a proposta pela ideologia republicana, por ser ficção oficial, imagem sem controlo nem contradição possível de um país sem problemas, oásis da paz, exemplos das nações, arquétipo da solução ideal que conciliava o capital e o trabalho, a ordem e a autoridade com um desenvolvimento harmonioso da sociedade.[34]

---

32   Daniel Melo, *A Leitura Pública no Portugal Contemporâneo 1926-1987* (Lisbon: Imprensa de Ciências Sociais, 2004), pp. 154-56.

33   Portugal joined the European Free Trade Association in 1960, after having joined the OECD in 1948. These organizations fomented the industrialization process in Portugal and economic exchanges with other European countries. These trade relations boosted Portuguese emigration flows to EFTA countries.

34   Eduardo Lourenço, *O Labirinto da Saudade – Psicanálise Mítica do Destino Português* (Lisbon: Gradiva, 2000, 1st edn, Lisbon: Dom Quixote, 1978).

Portuguese education was based on the same values between 1933 and 1974. Official school manuals extolled the virtues of family life associated with rural life, inherent to genuine Portuguese qualities: essentially rural, mostly employed in agriculture, poor, with modest life expectations. Salazar eulogized these virtues setting up his own family background as an example.[35]

Educating to mould the Portuguese mind was less straightforward in higher education. The Ministry of Education did not interfere directly in the choice of books at university. However, the Government controlled higher education. There was some investment in infrastructure: certain universities, such as Coimbra University, Lisbon University and the Faculties of Medicine and Engineering in Porto, were refurbished. Nevertheless, Salazar ostracized various eminent liberal and humanist scholars, such as António Sérgio, António José Saraiva, António Henriques de Oliveira Marques, Vitorino Magalhães Godinho, Mário de Azevedo Gomes, Mário Silva, Aurélio Quintanilha, Bento de Jesus Caraça and Rodrigues Lapa.[36] These professors, such as Vitorino Magalhães Godinho, António Sérgio and Oliveira Marques, had developed work that challenged the Regime's ideology and pursuit of legitimacy of the Government's mission of national regen-

---

35 In his interviews with António Ferro, Salazar mentioned these virtues several times. Equally relevant of this ideology were Pacheco de Amorim's words at the National Assembly on 1 April 1938: 'Tanto debaixo do ponto de vista do sentimento como do da cultura, a família da aldeia é, incontestavelmente, superior à da cidade, digam os pedagogos o que disserem". Cited by Carlos Reis, 'A Produção cultural entre a norma e a ruptura', in *Portugal Contemporâneo (1928-1958)*, ed. by António Reis, 5 vols (Lisbon: Alfa, 1990), V, p. 207. In 1938, the Ramalho Ortigão Prize rewarded Luís Teixeira's *Perfil de Salazar*: Elementos para a história da sua vida e da sua época. This biography was published by the SPN in Portuguese, French and English in 1940 and presented the Prime Minister as a hardworking and isolated man.

36 Hugo Gil Ferreira & Michael W.Marshall refer to 'twenty-two of the best professors in the universities'. Cited in *Portugal's Revolution: Ten Years On* (Cambridge: Cambridge University Press, 1986), p. 25. Carlos Reis refers to 'universidades foram afectadas sobretudo por purgas que arrastaram do ensino ou reduziram ao silêncio', p. 204.

eration based on historical legitimacy.[37] Certain professors, such as Azevedo Gomes, António Sérgio and Bento de Jesus Caraça, participated in the Movimento de Unidade Democrática (MUD) in 1946 and were dismissed by the Government in 1947.

The inadequacy of the reality approved of by the State from the real country showed signs of petrification, a term borrowed from Even-Zohar in his study on the relations between canonized and non-canonized literature:

> The first steps towards petrification manifest themselves in a high degree of boundness and growing stereotypization of the various repertoires. For the system, petrification is an operational disturbance: in the long run, it does not allow it to cope with the changing needs of the society in which it functions.[38]

The studies of academics, such as Sérgio, Magalhães Godinho and Oliveira Marques, undermined the Government's building of legitimacy for the Estado Novo and their writings represented challenging agents of consecration. Their contribution to the building of Portuguese national identity lay in discussing it in the light of social and economic development. As António Sérgio explained, 'não escondendo as misérias das *pedras vivas* humanas por detrás dos muros de *pedras mortas* de *obras*'.[39] The solidity of the Government's legitimacy depended on the moulding of Portuguese minds and, thus, on education based on history revision and the establishment of cultural symbols. The corpus of consecrated literary texts was legitimized by the Estado Novo's ideology and official

---

37 In his *Documentos sobre a Expansão Portuguesa* (3 vols, 1943-1945-1956) and *A Economia dos Descobrimentos Henriquinos* (1962) Vitorino Magalhães Godinho analyses the economic and social motivations of the Discoveries; António Sérgio's social criticism and support of cooperativism were represented in works, such as *Ensaios III* (1932), *Ensaios IV* (1934), and *Democracia* (1934); Oliveira Marques's historical research on the Middle Ages (including his *História de Portugal* (1972)) does not support the nationalist interpretation of the Cruzades or the foundation of the nation (published in works by the historians Joaquim Bensaúde, Manuel Heleno and Mário Albuquerque). See António José Saraiva and Óscar Lopes, *História da Literatura Portuguesa*, 14th edn, rev. (Porto: Porto Editora, 1955; repr.1987), pp. 1084-5.

38 Even-Zohar, p. 17.

39 António Sérgio, *Democracia*, (Lisbon: Sá da Costa, 1974), p. 146.

interpretations referred to an outdated country, disregarding the fact that the country did not continue to be the same rural and poor country throughout the Estado Novo. In primary and secondary education especially, values were simply decanted and given without questioning.

The fact that Portugal was not a bi- or multilingual society, unlike other European countries, such as Spain and the Netherlands, enhanced the Estado Novo's perception of a homogeneous society, that did not include more than one literary system, and its assumption that the dominating view was also the view of the people-in-the-culture. The media, in particular television, were also important in promoting the Estado Novo's ideology. As the introduction of television into Portugal was signalled as an important landmark of modernization, it served the purpose of the Government to control information.[40]

Portugal in 1973 was not the same country as at the beginning of the Estado Novo as far as social patterns were concerned. In the early 1930s, the country had 6,825,883 inhabitants, was underdeveloped and the living standards were below the European average. Up to the late 1950s, 48.4 per cent of the Portuguese workforce was employed in the primary sector. This percentage showed that, despite significant employment in agriculture, an equally relevant percentage of the Portuguese workforce was employed in the secondary and tertiary sectors.[41] After the Second World War,

40 Statistics showed a gradual increase in the number of televisions owned by the Portuguese families. Data included in Barreto, Table 8.7, p. 146. See also Francisco Rui Cádima's study on the introduction of television in Portugal and its 'pedagogic purposes', especially as far as news editing and broadcasting were concerned: *Salazar, Caetano e a Televisão Portuguesa* (Lisbon: Editorial Presença, 1996).

41 In the 1930s, the primary sector employed 56.5 per cent of the Portuguese and the secondary and tertiary sectors employed 20.5 per cent and 23 per cent respectively. In the 1950s, only 48.4 per cent of the Portuguese worked in the primary sector, whereas 24.9 per cent worked in the secondary sector and 26,7 per cent worked in the tertiary sector. In the 1970s, the percentages confirmed the tendency showed in the 1950s: 29.8 per cent were employed in the primary sector; 36.7 per cent worked in the secondary sector and 33,5 per cent worked in the tertiary sector. As regards demography, the population rose significantly to 8,648,369 in the 1970s, according to António Barreto

Lisbon's population increased significantly: in the 1940s, it had around 700,000 inhabitants, and twenty years later, it had 800,000. The outskirts also increased dramatically. Between the 1950s and 1960s, Amadora, Queluz, Baixa da Banheira, Cova da Piedade, Moscavide and Almada more than doubled their populations. For example, those of Baixa da Banheira and Cova da Piedade increased from 5,119 and 3,066 to 12,525 and 15,720 inhabitants, respectively. Urban centres could not cope with the phenomenon of sudden overcrowding. The housing shortage was so acute that about 40 per cent of the population lived in 10,000 slum dwellings in the Lisbon area in 1960.[42]

Despite lagging behind the rest of Europe, the Estado Novo worked to modernize the country's infrastructure. Economic reconstruction was strengthened through three Planos de Fomento launched between 1953 and 1973. Among priorities, there were public services, school facilities, ports, the restoration of national monuments, energy and power networks and water for agricultural purposes. As far as communications were concerned, the road network increased from 13,000 km in the 1920s to 32,000 km in 1970.[43] Several bridges were built, especially in the 1960s, such as the one over the Douro (Porto) in 1963 and another over the Tagus (Lisbon) in 1966; port facilities, particularly in Lisbon and Leixões, were also improved.

Delaying the economic development up until the 1950s had long-term consequences for Portuguese standards of living. In addition to political repression, economic difficulties aggravated by de-

(ed.). *A Situação Social em Portugal, 1960-1995*, 3rd edn (Lisbon: Inst. de Ciências Sociais da Univ. de Lisboa, 1997), p. 221.

42   Statistical data included in A.Sousa Franco, "A População de Portugal: notas para um estudo da estrutura demográfica portuguesa", in Boletim do BNU (75-76, Lisbon, 1968). Cited in Maria Filomena Mónica, 'A Evolução dos Costumes em Portugal, 1960-1995', in Barreto, p. 221.

43   R.A.H. Robinson, *Contemporary Portugal – A History* (London: George Allen & Unwin, 1979), p. 137.

pressed prices for raw materials, incipient industrialization and insufficient exports boosted internal migration and emigration.[44]

Migration shaped the country and constituted one of Portugal's features, especially during the Estado Novo. As far as internal migration is concerned, it was stronger during the 1950s. When industries developed in the 1950s, there was demand for labour in the cities, which depleted the rural labour force. Politicization of agricultural workers, who had had little access to information as they mixed with their industrial counterparts, was an important consequence of migration.

Opposition to the Regime was essentially developed in the political field. Political elections, such as those held in 1949, 1958, 1965 and 1969, were used by intellectuals to express their disagreement with Salazar's policies. Despite having been outlawed in 1927, Portuguese Communist Party's action (PCP) as a political organized opposition, in particular under the leadership of Álvaro Cunhal (1941), was important for attracting intellectuals, especially up until 1974. It was the best politically organized movement during the Estado Novo, particularly when compared with the Socialists. Communists supported Norton de Matos in 1949, General Humberto Delgado in 1958 and fomented university students' unrest in 1962.

The PCP had absorbed the claims presented by anarchist groups disseminated in Lisbon, Coimbra, Porto, Setúbal and in the Alentejo, among the rural workers, in the 1920s. These were also the areas with the highest records of voters against the Estado Novo in 1933. Lisbon, Coimbra and Setúbal were the urban centres where the major industrial companies were set up during the 1940s and 1950s. They were usually large-sized and were often the alternative to migrants coming from the rural regions. Social differences were most clear in cities, especially in the area of Lisbon. The north, except for Porto, was more traditional, conservative, and companies were mainly small and medium sized. The Communist influence was almost non-existent there and found it hard

---

44 The proportion of the national product of agriculture decreased from 32 per cent in 1953 to 18 per cent in 1969, although employing over 40 per cent of workers in 1950 and in 1960. Cited in Robinson, p. 136.

to collect support inside the corporations. Being a member of the PCP, above all, meant opposing to ideology of the Estado Novo.

Maria Ioannis Baganha's study on Portuguese emigration after the Second World War indicated that Portuguese emigration rose from 21,892 individuals in 1950 to 35,159 in1960. [45] The economic boom in European countries, such as France and Germany, in the 1950s and political persecution were not the only reasons for emigrating from Portugal. In the last three decades of the Estado Novo, about 1.8 million Portuguese left the country. The Colonial Wars boosted Portuguese emigration: from 38,572 individuals in 1961 to 155, 672 in 1969. Thousands emigrated, both legally and illegally, to avoid conscription. Between 1950 and 1959, of the 350,000 departures of Portuguese emigrants, 327,000 went to overseas countries, especially Brazil (absorbing 68 per cent of the global total). However, between 1960 and 1969, Portuguese emigration shifted towards European countries: for example, in 1963 there were 55,000 departures, of which 33,000 went to European countries. It is very difficult to track illegal emigration up until 1951 because there are no records. Nevertheless, between the 1950s and the 1970s, illegal emigration nearly equals legal emigration and this accounts for the workers' general desolation in not being able to improve their living conditions. As far as the percentages of emigrating flows distributed per Portuguese districts are concerned, in the 1950s, Aveiro, Viseu and Porto accounted for the highest records, with 10.74, 10.59 and 10.47 per cent of global flows; in the 1960s, emigrants mainly came from Braga (9.31), Porto (8.55) and Lisbon (8.10); and in the 1970s, the majority came from Lisbon (12.14), Porto (7.73) and Aveiro (7.32). On the whole, Porto (8.79), Aveiro (7.84) and Lisbon (7.78) recorded the highest rates of emigrating flows between the 1950s and 1970s. Moreover, the coastal regions contributed more than half of total emigrants. The interior, the Alentejo and the Algarve were poor sources of emigration. The highest record of emigration from Beja was in the

---

45   Maria Ioannis B.Baganha, 'Portuguese Emigration After World War II', pp. 1-19. The statistical data were also included in this article and the source is SECP, *Boletim Annual*, 1980-1981 and 1988.Statistical information on Portuguese emigration taken from this study.

1970s with 2.04 per cent; Évora did not supply more than 0.73 per cent of total emigration in the same period and Faro accounted for 3.69 per cent of total emigration in the 1960s; Santarém accounted for 3.79 per cent in the 1960s and Setúbal accounted for 3.08 in the 1970s. Statistics also show that when directed overseas (Brazil, United States and Canada), migration was from rural areas and when directed to Europe (mainly France and Germany), it was from the most urban and industrial areas.

As far as the profile of the Portuguese legal emigrant is concerned, Baganha's study showed that, before leaving Portugal, 43.63 per cent, 50 per cent and 32.39 per cent of the emigrants had been employed in the primary sector in the 1950s, 1960s and 1970s. Only in the 1970s were the majority of the Portuguese emigrants originally employed in the secondary sector (50.29). Furthermore, the overseas flow was more male dominated and tended less toward family reunification. The European flow was male-dominated, both single and married, and tended to family reunification, especially in the 1970s.[46] Family reunification became a trait of Portuguese emigration because of the proximity of destination countries, improved means of transportation and labour opportunities for women.

It is ironical that a regime, which boasted to have put so much effort into providing for its people and igniting patriotic love, brought about the perfect conditions for losing such a relevant percentage of the workforce due to the excesses of its repressive practices and to the deficient capacity in generating national wealth. Eduardo Lourenço commented that:

Deste processo, e como coroamento dele, constituirá a emigração em massa dos nossos aldeões a simbólica e dura expressão final. O nacionalismo

---

46 Emigration became a key topic in Portuguese Literature. An example is the fictionalized account of emigrants' living and working conditions in Portugal before emigrating and in their host country, in Olga Gonçalves, *A Floresta em Bremerhaven*, 4th edn (Lisbon: Editorial Caminho, 1992; 1st edn, Lisbon: Seara Nova, 1975), especially pp. 17-18 and pp. 45-47. The APE awarded novel by Paulo Castilho, *Fora de Horas* (Lisbon, Contexto, 1989) focuses on emigrating flows to the U.S. in the 1960s, also driven by ideals.

orgânico do antigo regime favoreceu a objectiva desnacionalização de milhares de portugueses.[47]

In the late 1960s, Portugal was going through a deep crisis that affected the political, economic and social sectors. As Monteiro and Costa Pinto's study has shown, the political instability produced by the Colonial Wars, which had started in 1961, had effects on ideological reassurances which had been built since the 1930s. The definition of the concept of Nation was associated with the idea of empire and this dichotomy linked to the historical legacy of the Portuguese Discoveries. Patriotism and Colonialism merged into the definition of Portuguese national identity. The Portuguese territory was unified with the 'províncias ultramarinas' and the Estado Novo's ideology excluded the existence of any racial discrimination.[48] When Marcello Caetano replaced Salazar in 1968, his motto 'uma ideia de movimento, de sequência e de adaptação' appealed to national unity:

> Temos de cerrar fileiras, aquém e além-mar, para avançarmos juntos com prudência, sim, mas seguramente. A divisão pode-nos ser fatal a todos. A dispersão enfraquecer-nos-á sem remédio.[49]

The Government used the Colonial Wars in their appeal to patriotism, pointing out that the Portuguese Nation was in danger. The late years of the Estado Novo showed that the Regime failed to see that the political and social changes that had occurred in Portugal could not have been tackled with the same ideological approach used in the Government's early years underestimating tensions as dynamic factors in the evolution of the Portuguese society. The Revolution in 1974 bears out what Even Zohar suggested as the inevitable consequence of allowing no pressure to be released from the system:

> As with a natural system, which needs, for instance, heat regulation, cultural systems also need a regulating balance in order not to collapse or disappear.

---

47 Eduardo Lourenço, p. 33.
48 Monteiro and Costa Pinto, p. 61.
49 Cited by Nogueira, pp. 452 and 454.

> [...] when no pressures are allowed release, we often witness either the gradual abandonment of a system and movement to another (e.g., Latin is replaced by its various Romance vernaculars), or its total collapse by means of a revolution (overthrow of a regime or the total disappearance of hitherto preserved models, etc.).[50]

The emasculation of potentially subversive thinking, the delays in radical educational reforms and the use of literacy as a means to endorse the Regime were of significance for the constitution of Portuguese readership. Considering that the Estado Novo's priority was focussed on the education of the Portuguese within the established ideological principles, with special attention on the school curriculum; that political, economic and social conditions did not encourage the promotion of diversified reading and, above all, did not encourage the enlargement of readership; and that Portugal remained politically isolated for a considerable period, the Estado Novo's aims to mould the Portuguese way of thinking were achieved with long-term effects. Developments and applications of the cultural policy as a reflection of the official ideology are expanded in the next chapter.

---

50   Even-Zohar, p. 16.

CHAPTER 3
Literary Canon and Ideology in the Formation of Cultural Identity during the Estado Novo (1933-1974)

This chapter will seek to establish that during the Estado Novo the Government coordinated the educational and the cultural policies and oriented consecration of literary authors and texts with the purpose of creating a corpus of national literature, representative of the Regime's ideological principles. It will also discuss to what extent the Government's construction of cultural identity interfered with the promotion of Portuguese literature in worldwide book markets. This chapter will focus on the role of the Government as consecrating agent.

Since Government-sponsored literary prizes rewarded works that reflected the Regime's promotion of cultural regeneration of the nation, my analysis focuses on writers, texts rewarded and financial rewards and systematized this information in five tables. Data were first published by the SNI and have been differently compiled by historians.[1] My tables also include the prizewinners' publishing houses and, thus, this facilitates an examination of the profile and prestige of publishers of the SNI prizewinners, crossing them with data of prizewinners and works. I compared literary prizes with the Government's official speeches and facts and figures on the Portuguese book trade, in order to consider the following: the extent to which financial rewards indicated a scale of im-

---

1   For information on prizewinners, works and financial rewards, see António Ferro, *Prémios Literários (1934-1947)* (Lisbon: SNI, 1950); João Medina, ed., *História Contemporânea de Portugal*, 2 vols (Lisbon: Multilar, 1990), I: *Ditadura: O Estado Novo – Do 28 de Maio ao Movimento dos Capitães*. Since information on publishers was not published, I researched the bibliographical details of every Secretariado's literary prizewinner between 1933 and 1973 in the database of the National Library, in Lisbon.

portance given to different literary genres; how the texts and writers rewarded expressed the values of the União Nacional; the extent to which writers' legitimacy was acquired through those prizes; and, finally, how publishing houses managed the prestige generated by the Regime's cultural initiatives. I also examine *A Exposição do Mundo Português*, in 1940, and *30 Anos de Cultura Portuguesa 1926-1956*, in 1956, and the SNI mobile library service organized by the Regime between 1945 and 1949, with the purpose of showing that the Government's cultural policy, particularly literary promotion, was ineffective because of it being ideologically driven.

3.1 SPN/SNI/SEIT

Jacques Dubois's Theory of the Literary Institution highlighted that culture is tailored to the Government's objectives of shaping the mind of the population when national politics are constructed on ideological grounds:

> Précisement, l'effet imaginaire initialement évoqué porte sur ces contradictions et permet de les 'résoudre' à l'intérieur de représentations en les dissimulant en fait par reconstitution d'un discours cohérent servant d'*horizon* au vécu des individus. En dernier recours, il s'agit toujours de justifier des inégalités économiques, sociales et politiques en leur conférant la transparence du naturel; il s'agit, par le dispositif idéologique, d'assurer la domination d'une classe ou fraction de classe sur d'autres sans recourir à la force ou à la violence. Ainsi l'idéologie de la classe dominante opère insidieusement en se constituant en discours général, en discours de tous, même si les groupes dominés infléchissent et réinterprètent ce discours suivant leurs propres positions.[2]

As regards the Estado Novo, accomplishing the Government's mission required arranging horizons of expectations that appeased the population and encouraged the Portuguese to accept it. I will

---

2   Jacques Dubois, *L'institution de la littérature* (Brussels: Editions Labor/Ferdinand Nathan, 1986), p. 63.

aim to establish that decentralizing consecration would have made implementation of the Revolução Nacional less effective because legitimacy would not have been wholly controlled by a major agent.

On 26 October 1933, the Government set up an institution that answered directly to the Prime Minister and was assigned the mediation of domestic relations between the press and the State. It was responsible for encouraging publication on the work of the Regime; organizing a service of information on national propaganda and public rallies; preventing subversive ideas from penetrating the country; collaborating with Portuguese artists and writers; and establishing prizes to award national art and literature. Externally, it had to collaborate with Portuguese institutions of propaganda abroad; supervise official press services abroad; promote press conferences with Portuguese and foreign personalities; establish contacts between Portuguese writers and journalists and their foreign counterparts; and clarify international public opinion on the Portuguese civilising mission in the colonies and in the Portuguese empire.[3] Other contemporary authoritarian regimes also set up cultural institutions with similar hierarchical dispositions, such as the Brazilian *Departamento de Informação e Propaganda*, the Spanish *Departamento de Prensa y Propaganda* and the German *Reichsministerium für Volkaufklärung*.

The Portuguese institution was restructured three times during the Estado Novo: it was called the Secretariado de Propaganda Nacional (SPN) between 1933 and 1944; in 1944, the name was changed to Secretariado Nacional de Informação, Cultura Popular e Turismo (SNI) and in 1968, it was changed to Secretaria de Estado de Informação e Turismo (SEIT). The change of name in

---

3   'Corrigir a ideia que cada um involuntariamente forma das realidades nacionais, filosofando à soleira da porta, com o que todos devem conhecer dos mesmos factos no conjunto da vida da Nação. E no plano externo, propiciando aos que falam e escrevem sobre Portugal, elementos bastantes para que inconscientemente não deturpem a verdade e se não dê o caso de até a doce amabilidade com os que recebemos aparecer nos seus escritos como prova de inferioridade moral'. Quoted from SNI, *Catorze Anos de Política de Espírito: Apontamentos para uma exposição apresentados no SNI* (Palácio Foz) em Janeiro de 1948 (Lisbon: SNI, 1948), [n.p.].

1944 shifted the emphasis on objectives, removing the 'propaganda' part of its official name that stressed the authoritarian role of the State. In 1968, the Colonial War was more intense. The opposition's demands for giving independence to the African colonies, civilian unrest and economic hardship introduced instability into the Portuguese cultural identity as it had been built since 1933: the historical civilizing mission of the Portuguese empire centred on deep cultural and moral regeneration. The SEIT's emphasis on information and tourism indicated the priority given to external promotion of the country and to information control. These were two basic functions which the SPN had been assigned in 1933 with the purpose of constructing the Portuguese identity.

Between 1933 and 1973, several persons were in charge of that institution: António Ferro (1933-1950), António de Eça de Queirós (1950-1951), José Manuel da Costa (1951-1956), Eduardo Brazão (1956-1958) and César Moreira Baptista (1958-1973).

The historian Jorge Ramos do Ó pointed out that much of the work developed by Ferro between 1933 and 1950, such as the establishment of literary prizes, was discontinued by the directors who followed him because they were placemen, bureaucrats and they were not deeply connected with the intellectual millieu.[4] Ferro's admiration for Salazar and belief in his Government as enabler of the regeneration of the nation were not the only reasons for his commitment to the Estado Novo between 1933 and 1950. His policy was motivated, within the framework of his intellectual background as editor of *Orpheu* in 1915 and commitment to the ideals of Modernism. Ferro yearned to boost literary production and involve every literary producer in the construction of Portuguese cultural identity and, thus, his cultural experience helped gaining the momentum of the Estado Novo. Ferro's cultural activities were needed to legitimize the Estado Novo's political and social programme, particularly at its outset, in the 1930s. In his *Decálogo do Estado Novo*, published in 1934, Ferro expanded the strategy of the SPN within the framework of the Regime:

---

4   Jorge Ramos do Ó, 'Salazarismo e Cultura', in Joel Serrão and A.H. De Oliveira Marques, eds., *Nova História de Portugal. – Portugal e o Estado Novo (1930-1960)*, 12 vols (Lisbon: Presença, 1992), XII, pp. 391-454 (p. 454).

Mas que se faça uma política de Espírito, inteligente e constante, consolidando a descoberta de Portugal pelos portugueses!, dando-lhe altura, significação e eternidade [...] O Espírito, afinal, também é matéria, uma preciosa matéria, a matéria-prima da alma dos homens e da alma dos povos [...][5]

The expression 'Política de Espírito' put across the spiritual commitment demanded from the Portuguese, stimulating their awareness and pride in their historical heritage. The Portuguese cultural policy did not result in the Estado Novo's fully-fledged consecration of Portuguese Modernist writers.[6] Cultural regeneration, as stated by Salazar in his speeches in 1933, was to be managed within observance to Portuguese historical tradition and detached from the cosmopolitan European environment of which Portuguese Modernism had been influenced in the mid-1910s.

The glorification of certain historical personalities was clear in the educational policy of the Estado Novo. The SPN, in its manifold activities (for example, the literary prizes and the *Exposição do Mundo Português* in 1940), picked up certain historical periods, for example the foundation of Portugal and the Discoveries, which were to be representative of the Portuguese historical past and mission in the world.[7]

---

5   Secretariado de Propaganda Nacional, *Decálogo do Estado Novo* (Lisbon: Ed. SPN, 1934), p. 79.
6   1934 was the only year when the Antero de Quental Prize rewarded a Modernist writer, (Fernando Pessoa, *A Mensagem*, 1934). According to José Blanco's study on this literary prize, this was given after Ferro putting effort into having the work of his friend rewarded by the SPN. See José Blanco, 'A Verdade sobre A Mensagem' <www.portalpessoa.org> [accessed September 2007].
7   António de Oliveira Salazar, *Antologia – Discursos, Notas, Relatórios, Teses, Artigos e Revistas* (Lisbon: Editorial Vanguarda, 1954), p. 54: 'Vocação missionária se tem podido chamar a esta tendência universalista, profundamente humana do povo português, devido à sua espiritualidade e ao seu desinteresse'. The Exposição do Mundo Português celebrated the eighth centenary of the foundation of Portugal (1140) and the third centenary of Portuguese Restoration (1640).

3.2 The Secretariado's Literary Prizes

On 10 August 1933, the Academia das Ciências set up a literary prize to stimulate 'a cultura e a produção literária nacional'. It rewarded fiction or poetry.[8] Within the framework of the Literary Institution, Jacques Dubois referred to panels of literary prizes as institutions whose structure enables it to define publicly acknowledged mechanisms of consecration.[9] Dubois's Theory helps us to understand the SPN's decision to establish its own literary prizes. Having supporters of the Regime among the panels of the Ricardo Malheiros Prize would not have strengthened the Government's role as distributor of symbolic capital. Thus, the SPN's literary prizes ensured the public acknowledgement of the Government as consecrating agent and its dominating position in the literary field. The SPN's objectives were made quite clear both by Salazar and by Ferro in the 1930s:

> Impossível nesta concepção de vida e da sociedade e indiferença pela formação mental e moral do escritor ou do artista, e pelo carácter da sua obra; é impossível valer socialmente tanto o que edifica como o que destrói, o que educa como o que desmoraliza, os criadores de energias cívicas ou morais e os sonhadores nostálgicos do abatimento e da decadência.[10]

---

8   The name of that prize is due to the fact that, when Ricardo Malheiros, financier and editor of the *Diário da Tarde* newspaper, died in 1932, he left a substantial amount of money to the Academia das Ciências for the setting up of a literary prize. It rewarded 'literatura de ficção, romances, novelas, contos, poesias, teatro em prosa e verso'. See Prémio Ricardo Malheiros: Regulamento.
<http://www.acadciencias.pt/html/menuacademiadigital/premioricardomalheiros/premio.pdf > [accessed September 2007]

9   'Un comité de prix littéraire ou un organe de presse consacré à la critique sont détenteurs en général d'une meilleure définition structurelle et juridique qu'un groupe d'écrivains. [...]Elles sont dépositaires d'une orthodoxie qui permet de délimiter le champ du littéraire et qui oriente les sanctions en matière de reconnaissance, de consécration et de classification.' See Dubois, pp. 86-7.

10   Salazar, p. 41.

Como escritores podemos ler, admirar certas obras literárias inconformistas, que consideramos dissolventes e perigosas quanto mais fortes. Como dirigentes de um organismo que se enquadra dentro do Estado Novo, não podemos aceitar nem premiar certas obras.[11]

The SPN would reward only those writers whose work best expressed the concept of the Portuguese nation and values.[12] Writers sent their works to be accepted but, according to rules, those writers rewarded three times in previous years could not be admitted to competition. The director of the SPN chaired the four-member panels of all literary prizes. Despite the fact that some of the prizes were discontinued and others were changed throughout the Estado Novo, they remained the Government's most important form of literary consecration and support.

As shown in Tables 1A-5, the SPN/SNI/SEIT named the literary prizes after Portuguese writers.[13] As pointed out by Andrew Milner in his study on the literary canon, valuing a writer means that the institutions which are responsible for rewarding literary work acknowledge that he or she belongs to the literary canon and recognize his or her position in the literary field at a given time within a particular political and cultural context.[14] This was not the only form of literary consecration; Naming libraries, schools and streets after writers during the Estado Novo were complementary ways of consecrating writers in Portugal and resulting, to a great extent, from Government and municipal decisions and this practice has continued since 1974 and present-day.

The names of prizes and their monetary value are indicative of some of the purposes of the SPN. Names confirm that the Government's literary canon was chiefly oriented towards nineteenth-century literature (the Antero de Quental, Eça de Queirós, Alexan-

---

11 António Ferro, *Prémios Literários (1934-1947)* (Lisbon: SNI, 1950), p. 30.
12 Immediately after the SPN announced the establishment of the literary prizes, Albano Nogueira published an article in *Presença*, in which he accused the SPN of affecting 'direitos do Espírito e a inalienável liberdade do Artista' and of reducing the artist to a 'servidor de qualquer doutrina ou seita'. See Albano Nogueira, 'Uma iniciativa cultural', *Presença*, 40 (1935), 15.
13 See Tables 1A-5 on pp. 272-9.
14 Andrew Milner, *Literature, Culture & Society* (London: University College London Press, 1996), p. 22.

dre Herculano, Fialho de Almeida and Ramalho Ortigão Prizes). Others, such as the Camões and the Gil Vicente Prizes, evidenced the writers who were also studied at school as landmarks of Portuguese literature. The specific names of the SPN's literary prizes were replaced by the term 'Prémio Nacional' in 1966. Towards the latter years of the Estado Novo, the concepts Nation and Empire were questioned by the rise in emigration, social unrest, growing opposition, in particular since the defeat of General Humberto Delgado in 1958 presidential elections, economic problems and the Colonial Wars. The Regime celebrated the 40th anniversary of the Revolução Nacional and appeals to the Nation and to the importance of the Portuguese Empire were used to maintain national unity.[15] Cultural activities were, as they had been in 1933, used to strengthen the cultural identity. The speech delivered by Moreira Baptista on 17 December 1964 is illustrative of the Government's views on the prizes and of the emergence of the crisis in cultural identity at the beginning of the early 1960s:

> Estamos há 36 anos a fazer uma Revolução; temos uma doutrina, defendemos valores morais e regras jurídicas que temos vindo a institucionalizar [...] Estamos a viver um momento em que os conflitos ideológicos integram praticamente todas as formas do pensamento [...] parece que é absolutamente correcto que o Regime se defenda e com tanto maior vigor quanto é certo que estamos a viver um período anormal que é o da guerra que de fora nos movem e que de dentro, uns quantos – ainda que poucos apoiam.[16]

The designation 'Prémio Nacional' pointed out the value of national representation over literary diversity, despite the fact that

---

15 On 30th December 1966, the deputee José Hermano Saraiva's speech at the Assembleia Nacional, was reproduced on Portuguese television: 'A unidade da Nação Portuguesa tem sido afirmada, desde o século XVI, e por todas as formas e até nos pregões reais que sempre situaram Portugal aquém e além-mar.[...] independentemente das interpretações no plano do direito constitucional, no plano da integração económica, no plano da consciência colectiva dos valores e no da solidariedade do sangue e do sacrifício, a Nação foi restituída às dimensões verdadeiras e ao sentido de sempre'. See Francisco Rui Cádima, *Salazar, Caetano e A Televisão Portuguesa* (Lisbon: Editorial Presença, 1996), p. 185.

16 César Moreira Baptista, *Informação, Cultura Popular, Turismo – Discursos Pronunciados* (Lisbon: SNI, 1965), p. 45.

the Government did not change the basis of the Portuguese literary canon.

Marc Verboord's study on the literary prestige of Dutch prizewinners between 1980 and 2000 showed that monetary values were valid indicators to evaluate literary prizes' prestige and that they influenced the making of the literary canon as a social construct.[17] Given this conclusion, I decided to examine whether the monetary value attributed to the SPN/SNI/SEIT literary prizes could be an indicator of literary prestige and, thus, have an effect on the Portuguese literary canon and on the literary prestige associated to different literary genres. The highest amount (20,000$00) was given to the Camões Prize that rewarded foreign authors who wrote best about Portugal, published in Portuguese, English, German, Spanish or Italian. This showed the SPN's concern with the promotion of Portugal abroad, within the framework of its effort to coordinate this promotion with journalists, academics and writers. These books were promoted in international book fairs that the SPN/SNI participated in, particularly in Spain and Brazil.[18]

The second highest amount (10,000$00) was given to the Eça de Queirós and the Alexandre Herculano Prizes, which rewarded novels and works on history respectively. Since the Revolução Nacional was planned to change the nation through education and patriotism, the Alexandre Herculano Prize was given to a work that served 'um firme critério patriótico' and its high monetary reward was meant to convey prestige to revision of Portuguese history ('evolução, análise ou rectificação histórica'). The Govern-

---

17 'What it does show, however, is that at the heart of the 'canon' debate lies a social embeddedness. Choices made in the selection and classification of books are socially constructed.' Marc Verboord, 'Classification of authors by literary prestige', *Poetics*, 31 (2003), 259-281 (p. 261).

18 SNI, [n.p.]. References include participation in the cultural events in Madrid, Barcelona, Lausanne, Rome, Rio de Janeiro, S.Paulo. The State's promotion of literature included the promotion of Portuguese language; the António Vieira Prize, not included in Tables 1-5, rewarded those writers who wrote in Portuguese 'no melhor português, no português mais português' (See António Ferro, *Prémios Literários (1934-1947)* (Lisbon: SNI, 1950), p. 33, my italics). This followed some initiatives to safeguard the language, such as the setting up of the Sociedade de Língua Portuguesa, in 1949, by Vasco Botelho do Amaral.

ment's perception of the novel's potential readership might have been influential in deciding to reward the Eça de Queirós Prize generously. In his study of the Field of Cultural Production, Bourdieu concluded that the novel's central position in the literary space is due to its readership's expansion since the nineteenth-century: popular audience, through serialization in newspapers, and bourgeois audience, through official honours and academic appraisal, especially with the society novel.[19] The rule that prize-winning novels should be constructive ('uma intenção ampla-mente construtiva') indicated the novel's inherent feature as a lit-erary and social construct. In other words, the novel's literariness enabled it to represent Portuguese society, as the Regime believed it should be made available to the public.[20]

If one takes the monetary value as indicator of literary pres-tige, poetry, short stories, essays and drama were potentially less prestigious because they were rewarded with 5,000$00 each. Es-says on politics and economy were more influential in view of the fact that the Anselmo de Andrade Prize was rewarded with 6,000$00. Children's fiction was rewarded slightly less (4,000$00).[21] The Government was more committed (and attributed more pres-tige) to educating Portuguese adults' reading habits, especially relating to political issues and novels, than to boosting children's reading, a task that was assigned to the Ministry of Education.

The process of literary consecration based on prizewinning production failed its initial purpose because it was ideologically rooted. As José Martins Garcia put it:

O provincianismo português – que não necessita, para uma definição, de abundantes exemplos nem de pesadas invectivas – reduz-se, no plano do produto interno, à obediência incondicional a um cânone. O cânone impõe-se, divulga-se, multiplica-se, vulgariza-se. O leitor 'canónico' aprecia um es-

---

19 Bourdieu, *The Field of Cultural Production* (Oxford: Polity Press, 1993), p. 51.
20 *Diário de Lisboa*, 29 November 1933, p. 16.
21 The Maria Amália Vaz de Carvalho Prize was rewarded with the same amount as the Afonso de Bragança Prize, which rewarded news reports. This latter prize was excluded from my tables since they concern literary production only.

tereótipo. E o produtor de cultura, se não quer ficar à margem, engendra um estereótipo consumível.[22]

The Alexandre Herculano prizewinners focussed on historical figures, institutions and periods also taught at school as landmarks of the establishment of the Portuguese nation: D. Maria I, D. Sebastião, Infante D. Henrique, Cardeal D. Henrique, the Catholic Church, the religious Orders and the Portuguese achievements in Brazil and in the East. The SPN/SNI's reward was illustrative of the Government's role as distributor of symbolic capital. Alexandre Herculano prizewinners received the symbolic capital the Government needed to grant to works which, in turn, legitimised the ideological and historical bases of the Regime. Portuguese cultural identity was constructed on history revision. The historical narrative was organized around the concept of Portugal's predestined civilizing mission in the world. Hayden White's study on history revision is helpful to understand the Estado Novo's interpretation of Portuguese history:

> The narrative itself is not the icon; what it does is *describe* events in the historical record in such a way as to inform the reader *what to take as an icon* of the events so as to render them 'familiar' to him. The historical narrative thus mediates between the events reported in it on the one side and pregeneric plot structures conventionally used in our culture to endow unfamiliar events and situations with meanings, on the other.[23]

This also shows Tony Bennet's claim that reception was determined by political context.[24] Literary historians have associated the

---

22 José Martins Garcia, 'Introdução', in Vitorino Nemésio, *Obras Completas*, 21 vols (Lisbon: Imprensa Nacional-Casa da Moeda, 2002) VIII: *Mau Tempo no Canal*, pp. 14-5.

23 Hayden White, 'Historical Text As Literary Artifact' in *Tropics of Discourse – Essays in Cultural Criticism* (Baltimore and London: The Johns Hopkins University Press, 1985), p. 88. Author's italics.

24 'The relations among literary texts, other ideological phenomena, and broader social and political processes can be determined or specified for all time by referring such texts to the conditions of production obtaining at the moment of their origin.': Tony Bennet, 'Texts in History: The Determinations of Readings and Their Texts', in Machor & Goldstein, *Reception Theory*, pp. 65-74 (p. 65).

writers rewarded with the Alexandre Herculano Prize between 1934 and 1948 to conservative and Catholic sectors, such as Padre Miguel Oliveira, João Ameal and Queirós Veloso.[25] The fact that this prize was discontinued after 1950 shows its relevance in forming the bases to legitimize the Estado Novo during its first decade. My conclusion is strengthened by SNI's establishment of the Ocidente Prize in 1963. In 1964, Moreira Baptista announced that it rewarded those works (poetry and prose) which 'melhor sirvam o conceito do viver português e cristão'.[26] This was the Government's response to signs that the Estado Novo's ideological and cultural bases were challenged. The prizewinning writers rewarded for their prose were historians only (Francisco Caeiro, Torquato de Sousa Soares and Cruz Pontes) who reviewed different periods of Portuguese history.

The changes of the SNI literary prizes indicate that the Regime strove to consolidate itself as consecrating agent within the framework of the evolving political and social context. In 1961, the SPE also set up literary prizes. The Government's dictation of the SPE's closure in 1965, following the Sociedade's award of the Grande Prémio de Novelística to Luandino Vieira's *Luuanda*, a work which the Regime considered subversive and its author a terrorist, strengthened the Government's consecrating position in the Portuguese literary field up till 1974.

The prizes were awarded more or less regularly despite some gaps. The Alexandre Herculano Prize was the most regularly awarded prize: there was a new prizewinner every year, between 1934 and 1948. In addition, the Ocidente Prize also rewarded works on Portuguese history between 1963 and 1965. The Eça de Queiroz Prize was the prize which awarded the fewest writers:

---

25 The Anselmo de Andrade Prize is also worthy of mention because, despite having rewarded two authors only (1945 and 1946), the prizewinning texts focussed on what was accepted by the Regime as the nation's world importance; it is equally relevant that in 1946, it rewarded José Nascimento Ferreira, Under Secretary for Trade and Industry. The fact that the Regime rewarded work produced by members of the Government enhanced its prestige, and thus its symbolic capital, as both producer and consecrating agent.

26 César Moreira Baptista, p. 30.

fewer than ten prizewinning novels between 1934 and 1961.[27] Between 1934 and 1948, the Gil Vicente Prize was not awarded four times, whereas the Antero de Quental and the António Enes Prizes were not given twice.

The winning novels illustrated several issues which served the Government's values: conservative, traditional and Catholic, for example in *A Garça e a Serpente*, 1944, and *Companheiros*, 1961; *Diário de Um Emigrante* (1936) dealt with Portuguese emigration within the framework of the Portuguese empire, and *A Toca do Lobo* (1948) was influenced by Camilo Castelo Branco's novels.[28] The novels written by writers, such as Ferreira de Castro and Aquilino Ribeiro who participated in the *Presença* movement and in Neo-Realism in the 1930s and 1940s were not rewarded by the SNI, despite having been so by the Academia das Ciências. The literary production socially committed and aesthetically innovative was not officially approved of by the Government. It is worthy of mention that a significant part of Portuguese writers who authored these works were politically committed (for example, through their involvement in the MUNAF and in the MUD).

As far as unpublished work is concerned, the SPN also established the Inéditos Prizes in 1935 with no monetary value to encourage new literary producers. This prize only rewarded debutants's poetry, drama and essays in 1935. Prizewinning texts were

---

27 On 31 December 1934, the *Diário de Lisboa* reported that the Eça de Queirós Prize did not reward any novel because the jury 'embora reconhecendo notáveis qualidades em algumas das obras que lhe foram submetidas', considered that 'em nenhuma delas ter encontrado todos os requisitos exigidos pelas bases do concurso e pelas altas exigências e finalidades a que deveria corresponder a sua escolha' (p. 16).

28 These values were also found in several Fialho de Almeida prizewinning short stories, such as: *Litoral a Oeste* (1940) which focuses on local customs and traditions; and *Neve sobre o Mar* (1942) narrates travel stories. Similar values are also evident in Gil Vicente Prizewinning works, such as *Tá Mar* (1936), *Telmo o Aventureiro* (1937), *Camaradas* (1938) and *Pátria* (1939); and in the Maria Amália Vaz de Carvalho Prizewinning children's fiction, for example, *Viagem à Roda de África* (1938), *História Extraordinária de Iratan e Iracema* (1939) and *História do Coelho Kalulu* (1948).

published by the SPN's *Panorama* journal.[29] Between 1960 and 1973, the SNI/SEIT's Manuscritos Prizes rewarded five new writers of fiction and twelve new poets. In 1961, the SPE also set up its own prizes for unpublished work (Prémio de Revelação de Prosa and Prémio de Revelação de Poesia). The Government's rewarding of new literary production, and fiction in particular, was more *reaction* than real *action* in the literary field. During the Ferro period, and as seen in his statements in the early 1930s, there was an intention of spotting new talents, whilst after the 1940s, the purpose was to consecrate published writers and talent spotting was reconsidered only when the Regime's literary consecration was challenged by the SPE literary prizes in 1961. These and the Ricardo Malheiros Prizes will be examined in Chapter 4. The Manuscritos de Poesia Prize rewarded new poetry (like the Antero de Quental Prize), whilst, the Manuscritos de Prosa rewarded new fiction (like the Eça de Queirós Prize).

The SPN/SNI's literary prizes did little to encourage new literary production, especially fiction. According to Ramos do Ó, during the 1940s, the Regime did not succeed in establishing a publishing policy that met its ideological principles.[30] The SPN/SNI found it easier to consecrate poetry than fiction, both published and unpublished. Those prizewinning works had rarely more than one edition and most writers rewarded with the Inéditos did not produce regularly. They were frequently published by small-sized regional publishing houses.[31] The Secretariado focussed its efforts, in particular in the 1940s and 1950s, into consecrating writers by

---

29 *Panorama* represented 'popular culture'. It illustrated the Estado Novo's purpose of rooting literary production to the nineteenth century literary canon in view of the fact that it was also the name of a journal published in the mid 1800s, whose contributors included Alexandre Herculano and Luís Augusto Rebelo da Silva.

30 Ramos do Ó, p. 416.

31 Some of the publishing houses which published António Cabral, prizewinner in 1960, subsequently, included Setentrião (Vila Real) in 1965; Nova Realidade (Tomar) in 1967; Razão Actual (Porto) in 1971, Centelha (Coimbra) in 1977) and Livros do Nordeste (Vila Real) in 1983 and 2003. Maria Ondina Braga, who was rewarded with the Manuscritos de Prosa Prize in 1967, was one of the few exceptions.

exploring literature as didactic material. Those works illustrated social representations approved of by the Estado Novo.

This strategy was intensified in the late 1960s and in the early 1970s. An example was the trial that involved Maria Velho da Costa, Maria Isabel Barreno and Maria Teresa Horta, following the publication of *Novas Cartas Portuguesas* in 1972. Taking the *Cartas Portuguesas*, written by Soror Mariana Alcoforado in the seventeenth century as its starting-point, the book dealt with the desire of women's social, religious and social emancipation, raising questions that had to do with their personal identity.[32] This collided with the representation of Portuguese society, in particular the role of Portuguese women, officially promoted since 1933.[33] It warranted the Regime's accusations of pornography and immorality. The trial of those writers showed the Government's inability to cope with debate on cultural patterns. The SPN/SNI's use of literary prizes substantiates Dubois's claim that literary prizes legitimize promotion strategies of accepted literary production.[34]

---

32 'Se a mulher se revolta contra o homem nada fica intacto, para a mulher, o chefe, a polícia, o negócio, a propriedade, o lugar, o prazer (bem viciado) só existem através do homem [...] por enquanto nada há onde a mulher possa firmar-se e compensar-se das suas lutas. Chegará o dia? Até lá fica sem sentido a vida da mulher como eu'. See Maria Isabel Barreno, Maria Teresa Horta, Maria Velho da Costa, *Novas Cartas Portuguesas* (Lisbon: Moraes Editores, 1980), p. 182.

33 According to Maria Teresa Horta, this trial was motivated by Moreira Baptista's personal hostility against her being a professional. Teresa Horta had written *Minha Senhora de Mim* (1971), which was also censored. Horta headed the literary supplement of *A Capital* between 1970 and 1974 and had been the first woman to head the ABC (Lisbon cinema club). Thus, she misrepresented the ideal Portuguese woman, as approved of by the Estado Novo, as shown in Marcello Caetano's statement on those writers. See 'Senhora de Si' in <http://www.spautores.pt/revista.aspx?idContent=776&idCat=189> [Accessed January 2008]. In his 'Conversas em Família', Marcelo Caetano referred to them as 'três senhoras que não são dignas de ser portuguesas'. See Cândido Azevedo, *A Censura De Salazar e Marcelo Caetano* (Lisbon: Editorial Caminho, 1999), pp. 138-149. Passage on Caetano cited on p. 148.

34 'De la sorte, le système des prix est immanquablement voué au simulacre: ce qu'il reconnaît est tantôt le dejà reconnu tantôt ce qui n'appelle qu'une reconnaissance temporaire (les produits de routine !), Dubois, p. 98. In the heart of Lisbon city, some streets are also named after those writers whose

3.3 Public Libraries and the SNI Mobile Library Service

Illiteracy constituted a serious hindrance to the expansion of Portuguese readership. The national libraries service did not cover the whole country. This fact compromised both the access of literates to books and any possibility of successfully encouraging illiterates to learn reading through close contact with books. In 1945, the mobile library service of popular culture ('bibliotecas ambulantes de cultura popular') was set up to 'familiarizar as [...] populações rurais com as grandes figuras nacionais e os grandes problemas da cultura nacional'.[35] This service visited 63 towns in the coastal districts of Lisbon, Porto, Setúbal, Braga, Faro and Viana do Castelo. This service was operational for four years and the SNI claimed having recorded a total of 13,796 readers, that is, an average of 220 readers per town between 1945 and 1947.[36]

One of Salazar's priorities was to control Governmental expenditure all throughout his dictatorship. The establishment of the Gulbenkian Foundation in Portugal, in 1956, was an opportunity to economize efforts in culture.[37] The Foundation also created a mobile library service headed by Branquinho da Fonseca. He had been the curator of the library of the Museum of Condes de Castro Guimarães, in Cascais, between 1941 and 1956 and, due to his work this library expanded its book collection and number of

---

SPN/SNI literary prizes were named after and those writers studied at school. As far as writers whose production was first consecrated by the SPN/SNI are concerned, only a handful received similar honours, including Júlio Dantas, Joaquim Paço d'Arcos and Olavo d'Eça Leal.

35   SNI, [n.p.].
36   SNI, [n.p.].
37   The Gulbenkian Foundation was officially set up on 18 July 1956 through the Decree-Law 40690 andthe former MUD subscriber Azeredo Perdigão was its trustee. For a study on the Gulbenkian mobile library, see Tiago Santos, 'As Bibliotecas Itinerantes da Fundação Calouste Gulbenkian', in Diogo Ramada Curto, ed., *Estudos de Sociologia da Leitura em Portugal no Século XX* (Lisbon: Fundação Calouste Gulbenkian and Ministério da Ciência e do Ensino Superior, 2006), pp. 239-260. Data on the Gulbenkian mobile library service are cited in this article.

readers' passes during that period.[38] According to Daniel Melo's study, Fonseca's understanding of the library as a cultural institution at the service of its community was central in his success. His involvement in the *Presença* movement was indicative of his awareness of contemporary literature and that library strengthened his collection of contemporary literature (fiction, poetry and drama). Moreover, he also developed a successful pilot experiment of mobile library service of the Museum's library in 1953. The Fundação Calouste Gulbenkian set up this service, with 15 vans in 1958. In 1960, 29 Gulbenkian vans carried around 2,000 books and offered reading on a monthly or fortnightly basis. Writers, such as Herberto Hélder, Alexandre O'Neill and Tomás Kim, were involved in this project, since they travelled around the country, in the vans, to encourage mass reading. Twenty-three libraries with more than 445,000 items and 151,000 enrolled borrowers all over the country complemented that initiative.

Between 1933 and 1974, Portuguese public libraries were either national, district (built in district capitals), governmental, corporative (*grémio, casas do povo, casas de pescadores*), popular and municipal, school (primary, technical, secondary and university), local or subsidized by associations and companies. In 1937, there were about 50 municipal libraries and this increased to 84 in mainland Portugal in 1958.[39] Municipal libraries were the oldest type of library (dating back to 1852) and their name was due to the fact that they were set up by city halls.[40] They were called popular libraries because since the early 1930s, Portuguese Governments considered them to be the most suitable for the provision of public service. The Government's investment in reading was concentrated in the most productive and populated areas. Moreover, it officially 'transferred' to the Gulbenkian the responsibility of providing reading to the interior of the country. This collaboration between the Foundation and the Government implied the Foundation's tacit support of the

---

38 A study on Branquinho da Fonseca's work at the Cascais Municipal Library was published in Daniel Melo, *A Leitura Pública No Portugal Contemporâneo 1926-1987* (Lisbon: Imprensa De Ciências Sociais, Instituto De Ciências Sociais, 2004), pp. 98-109.

39 Daniel Melo, p. 87.

40 They were officially set up in 1852. See Melo, p. 87.

Regime in economic hardship, despite challenging the Regime as dominating consecrating agent, especially after the Gulbenkian sponsored SPE's literary prizes in the 1960s.[41]

The distribution of the public libraries was unbalanced, suggesting that considerations about their financial impact were more important than cultural promotion. This is strengthened by the fact that migrations towards the main cities along the coastline soared significantly after the SNI discontinued the mobile library service in 1949. The Government did not invest in another similar service that competed with that developed by the Gulbenkian. Moreover, when the Gulbenkian service was established, the Ministry of Education launched a campaign against illiteracy, whereas the SNI had withdrawn from promotion of popular culture.

The official book list of the SNI mobile libraries included a total of 103 writers, of whom 88 were Portuguese, and 309 titles, of which 195 were Portuguese and foreign fiction books. Those included 16 writers of the nineteenth century and 18 SPN/SNI prizewinners.[42] As far as foreign writers are concerned, they featured in the 'Travel and Adventure' collection, and included Jane Austen, Salgari, Daniel Defoe, Jonathan Swift, the Countess of Ségur, Vicente Ibañez and Madelena Genestoux. Many medieval and contemporary writers were also neglected: Fernão Lopes, Gil Vicente, Camões, Bernardim Ribeiro, Pe António Vieira, Mário de Sá-Carneiro, Almada Negreiros, amongst others.

---

41 According to José Cardoso Pires, when the PIDE closed down the Sociedade Portuguesa de Escritores in 1965, the Gulbenkian Foundation overtly supported this decision and withdrew financial support from the Sociedade for initiatives such as their literary prizes. See 'Técnica do Golpe de Censura', in *E Agora José?* (Lisbon: Edições Dom Quixote, 1997), pp. 181-2.

42 According to the book lists of the SNI's mobile libraries, the writers included were Camilo Castelo Branco, João da Câmara, Castilho, Pinheiro Chagas, João de Deus, Malheiro Dias, Júlio Dinis, Arnaldo Gama, Almeida Garrett, Alexandre Herculano, Pedro Ivo, Ramalho Ortigão, Alberto Pimentel, Silva Pinto, Eça de Queiroz, Teixeira Queiroz, Virgínia de Castro e Almeida, João Ameal, Caetano Beirão, Mário Beirão, Fernanda de Castro, António Ferro, Antero Figueiredo, Olavo de Eça Leal, João da Costa Leite Lumbrales, Domingos de O. Martins, Manuel Múrias, Leopoldo Nunes, António Correia de Oliveira, Teotónio Pereira, Oliveira Salazar, Luís Teixeira and Afonso Lopes Vieira. Cited in Ramos do Ó, p. 419

The SNI worked as a gatekeeper of literary production. The absence of works, such as Eça de Queirós's *O Crime do Padre Amaro* and *O Primo Basílio*, showed the Secretariado's strict criteria for book-listing, especially as far as fiction was concerned. Since the aim was to introduce the population to major national cultural topics, the Secretariado included only fiction books whose plots fitted official social and individual representations; this aim had publicly been defined in 1934, when setting up the Eça de Queirós Prize. Therefore, raising subjects that involved the Roman Catholic dogma or family representation introduced the debate which the Government was determined to erase.[43]

3.4 SNI Exhibitions

A Exposição do Mundo Português (1940) and *30 Anos de Cultura Portuguesa: 1926-1956* (1956) were planned to promote Portuguese culture and are suggestive of Government's management of Portuguese fiction in the construction of the national cultural identity.

The organization of *A Exposição do Mundo Português* strengthened the concept of empire and nation promoted among the Portuguese. Initiatives were directed towards the celebration of national cultural symbols, examples being the construction of monuments celebrating the Discoveries and the promotion of historical personalities.[44] The Secretariado published the monthly journal *Revista dos Centenários* to inform the Portuguese about the

---

43 In 1933, Salazar told Ferro that attacking the Government was damaging welfare. Thus, censorship was 'uma questão de decôro e dignidade pública' because it prevented attacks to the Government's work based on ignorance and perfidy. See António Ferro, *Salazar: O Homem e A Sua Obra*, pref. Oliveira Salazar (Lisbon: Empresa Nacional de Publicidade, 1933), p. 46.

44 The SNI published a séries of publications on 'Grandes Portugueses', targeting youngsters and promoted wooden statuettes of Camões 'destinada sobretudo a tornar mais próxima do povo a figura do grande poeta'. Cited in SNI, *Catorze Anos de Política de Espírito*, [n.p.].

work developed by the Regime.[45] Contributors included António Ferro, Júlio Dantas (chairman of the Comissão dos Centenários), Vitorino Nemésio, Aquilino Ribeiro, Hernâni Cidade and Manuel Múrias. The Secretariado organized conferences and book fairs abroad, in particular in Brazil. In 1941, the Portuguese and Brazilian Cultural Agreement, signed by SPN and the DIP, had the purpose of strengthening Luso-Brazilian cultural relations. It motivated the bi-annual publication of *Atlântico* between 1942 and 1945, with Brazilian and Portuguese contributors and, among them, were Fernanda de Castro, Almada Negreiros, Luís Forjaz Trigueiros, José Régio, Jorge de Sena and Natércia Freire. The Gil Vicente prizewinner Carlos Selvagem went with Júlio Dantas to Brazil to participate in literary lectures, within the framework of the Agreement. The SPN and the DIP rewarded Hernâni Cidade with the Pero Vaz de Caminha Prize in 1945 for his *A Literatura Portuguesa e a Expansão Utramarina*. According to Heloísa Paulo's research, the Luso-Brazilian Agreement did not achieve its aims, due to the Brazilian participation in the Second World War, the Portuguese Section of the DIP did not promote Portugal in Brazil effectively, whereas the SPN's promotion of Brazil was successful in Portugal.[46]

The SPN strengthened the symbolic capital of its prizewinners, such as Carlos Selvagem and Manuel Múrias, through their involvement in the Estado Novos's official cultural events between 1939 and 1945. However, the notoriety of writers, for example José Régio, Aquilino Ribeiro and Jorge de Sena, who had acquired prestige in the literary journals *Presença* (1927-1940) and *Revista de Portugal* (1937-1940), was also strengthened. Setting up those journals, especially *Presença*, was motivated by some disbelief regarding the Republican ideals and by the yearning to produce literature, devoid of any political and religious stances (unlike the *Seara Nova*). Modernist writers and artists, such as Almada Negreiros,

---

45 The purpose of the articles was 'traduzir, se não criar, o estado de vibração da consciência de um povo que celebra os seus oito séculos de história' (SPN, *Revista dos Centenários* (Lisbon: SPN, 1939), p. 1. Quoted in Heloísa Paulo, *Estado Novo e Propaganda em Portugal e no Brasil – o SPN/SNI e o DIP* (Coimbra: Livraria Minerva, 1994), p. 164. This journal was published between 31 January 1939 and 31 December 1940.
46 Heloísa Paulo, p. 174.

strengthened their prestige through those journals which played a role in their academic consecration.[47] The literary contribution of those writers to *Revista dos Centenários* and *Atlântico* is suggestive of how their position in the Portuguese literary field tailored the Government's needs of cultural legitimacy and this was enabled by the fact that António Ferro headed the SPN between 1933 and 1950. The Secretariado's use of those writers in the early years of the Estado Novo did not prevent those writers from having problems with the Government, as for example the lawsuit against Aquilino Ribeiro in 1958 and Jorge de Sena's exile to Brazil in the 1950s.

According to Ramos do Ó, *30 Anos de Cultura Portuguesa: 1926-1956* was one of the few cultural events in which the Government could display a production of the Regime.[48] It exhibited literary production (poetry, children's fiction, periodicals, literary criticism, fiction, short stories, essays, and works on history and linguistics) by SNI prizewinners and consecrated writers, including Camilo Castelo Branco, Ramalho Ortigão, Almeida Garrett, Antero de Quental, António Nobre and Cesário Verde on bookstalls.[49] The SNI made the criteria of selection clear:

> Apenas alguns livros aparecem em cada sector, escolhidos entre os muitos que se publicaram, a título permanente, representativo e levando em conta o aspecto gráfico. De cada autor não se expôs mais do que uma obra em cada secção e não figuram livros publicados antes de 1926, salvo reedições de especial significado.[50]

---

47 António José Saraiva and Óscar Lopes, História *da Literatura Portuguesa*, 14th edn rev. (Porto: Porto Editora, 1987), pp. 1056-7.

48 Ramos do Ó, pp. 413-4.

49 Some writers who opposed the Regime, such as Adolfo Casais Monteiro, did not agree to participate in official events. In 1956, he suggested that 'O que o Estado tem feito para suprimir a inteligência nacional' should be an alternative exhibition to Trinta Anos de Cultura Portuguesa, with the aim of pointing out the effects of censorship on Portuguese literary production. Cited in Jacinto Baptista, 'À Procura do Espírito na 'Política do Espírito' do Estado Novo', *in História de Portugal*, ed. by João Medina, 15 vols (Lisbon: Ediclube, 1998), XIII, pp. 63-113 (p. 110).

50 SNI, *Roteiro da Exposição 30 Anos de Cultura Portuguesa: 1926-1956* (Lisbon: SNI, 1956), [n.p.]. This catalogue refers to major Portuguese literary movements, in particular after 1926, when Salazar was assigned to the Ministry of

3.5 Censorship

The difficulty in regulating Portuguese and translated literature, especially fiction, is also shown in prior censorship that lasted until 1974.[51] Fiction was not subject to prior censorship but both publishers and writers were obliged by law to inform the Censorship Committee about the titles they planned to publish. The Committee would then decide to impose or not prior censorship on those titles. When procedures were not observed, books could be banned after publication which meant huge losses with the total waste of whole print-runs of books, together with the risk of arrest of both publishers and writers.[52] Censors usually intervened after accusations against some books by either individuals or PIDE agents. Some booksellers or newsagents collaborated with the PIDE in order not to have their shops closed or incur heavy fines. Moreover, they were urged to collaborate with the Regime and threatened with repression.

Criteria for censoring fiction could be extremely diversified and censors (as well as the Government) believed that certain statements hit the Regime and the Revolução Nacional: a comment against the Regime or Salazar or challenging conservative moral values; a report or a description of characters whose lives were morally dubious; economic and social details from which the reader could surmise that Portuguese living standards were below the average; references to social unrest; criticism of the Church, the army and conditions in Portuguese colonies. Some problems were that censors had no literary background experience and reasons for banning books varied. Censorship was a restraint on literary

---

Finance: Portuguese symbolism and 'neo-lusitanismo', 'futurismo', 'exotismo' and 'supra-realismo', literary movements which had emerged in the *Orpheu*.

51 Prior censorship was institutionalized on 29 July 1926 as a provisional measure but the 1933 Constitution approved it definitely through Decree-Law No.22469 on 11 April 1933.

52 An example was the arrest of Luís de Sttau Monteiro after the publication of *Peças de um Acto: A Guerra Santa, a Estátua,* that also resulted in the closing of the publishing house Minotauro in 1966.

creation and publication, once legitimacy depended heavily on conformation to ideological standards.[53]

Statistics show that between 1932 and 1960, 1,174 individuals working in the cultural and intellectual field (including 21 writers, 160 teachers, 97 journalists and 477 students) were arrested and this figure corresponds to 6 per cent of total arrests, estimated to have been 19, 224 individuals.[54] 8,293 of those arrests (43%) were carried out between 1936 and 1939, that is, when the Regime was going through consolidation. The same sources highlight that the number of arrests decreased significantly in the 1950s. This does not mean that censorship was less intense. As referred to in Chapter 2, the rate of Portuguese emigration rose in that decade and also in the 1960s. Not only did economic hardship influence the decision to emigrate; repression was also a motivation to leave the country both legally and illegally. Nevertheless, the point to be made here is that censorship shaped Portuguese literary production by restraining writers, publishers and booksellers. Censors were assigned the mission of authorizing the publication of works that were not considered potentially harmful to the Regime's ideology.

Statistics also demonstrate that the Estado Novo's cultural policy did not produce substantial results as regards book production. The rise in number of books that were published in the Portuguese book market between 1930 and 1960 was very uneven. Up until 1941, annual figures were roughly around 3,000 first editions. Be-

---

53   For a complete list of censored titles, see João Mascarenhas, ed., *Relação das obras, cuja circulação esteve proibida em Portugal durante o Regime de Salazar/ Marcello Caetano* (Lisbon: Câmara Municipal de Lisbon/Biblioteca República e Resistência, 1996). In 1974, Adolfo Casais Monteiro summed up the Regime, summing up the generalized tension among all those who participated in the literary field: 'Cada um tem medo do outro, e todos juntos têm medo do Poder. Fazem censura à toa porque [...] têm medo de ser censurados. Têm medo às reclamações da Igreja, que tem a força da lei, e às do primeiro salazarista bronco que possa denunciá-los. ' Cited in Cândido Azevedo, *Mutiladas e Proibidas. Para a História da Censura Literária em Portugal nos tempos do Estado Novo* (Lisbon: Editorial Caminho, 1997), p. 170.

54   Data published in António Pedroso, 'A Polícia Política', in *História de Portugal*, ed. by João Medina, 15 vols (Lisbon: Ediclube,1998), XIII: *Opressão e Resistência*, pp. 11-38.

tween 1942 and 1943, the number of first editions topped 4,000 but fell immediately to fewer than 3,000 titles by the end of the Second World War. Figures rose again only in the mid 1950s to more than 4,000 and reached a peak of 6,000 first editions towards the end of this decade.[55] In the United Kingdom, the significant decrease in the number of titles published, including first editions, was only reverted in the 1950s with a steady rise in numbers of new editions.[56] Portuguese neutrality apparently protected the domestic books market and this can account for the rise seen between 1941 and 1942. Nevertheless, whereas the increase in number of books in the United Kingdom was steady after the War, in Portugal, this was more irregular up until the 1950s. The percentage of books classified as 'Literature' (which includes fiction, children's fiction, poetry and drama) gradually decreased in Portugal between the 1930s and the 1950s. It was the third largest percentage in the 1930s, the second in the 1940s and the fourth in the 1950s. British fiction alone also fell slightly during the period between 1937 and 1950, but retained a comfortable margin of more than 20% of the total books published whereas other categories barely reached 10%.[57]

---

55   Instituto Nacional de Estatística, *Anuário Estatístico de Portugal* (Lisbon, INE). Ramos do Ó concluded that the Estado Novo was unable to train a significant number of intellectuals to communicate the Regime's principles effectively. See Ramos do Ó, p. 414.

56   Figures included in Ian Norrie, *Mumby's Publishing and Booselling in the Twentieth Century*, London: Bell and Hyman, 6th edn, 1982 (Mumby, Frank, *Publishing and Bookselling*, London: Jonathan Cape Ltd, 1930). The fact that the United Kingdom was one of the belligerent countries aggravated problems related to the shortage of paper. Rationing was introduced in April 1940 and publishers were forced to introduce drastic reductions in paper consumption.

57   Portuguese statistics are given by Ramos do Ó, op. cit, p. 301. British statistics are given by Marjorie Deane, *United Kingdom Publishing Statistics* (Rpt. *The Journal of the Royal Statistical Society*, Vol.CXIV, Part IV, 1951), [n.p.].

3.6 Prestige of Publishers of Prizewinners

As far as book promotion in the domestic and international markets is concerned, the Estado Novo's cultural policy was not entirely effective. One of the indicators of prestige for publishers is the amount of literary prizes included in their book lists. The literary prizes promoted by the SPN/SNI/SEIT were important to the accumulation of symbolic capital of prizewinning writers and also for their publishers. Those prizes could associate writers and their publishing houses with the Regime, in view of the purposes defined in the prize's regulations. Tables 1A-5 show that it is possible to pinpoint some publishing houses which benefited from the Estado Novo's consecration. Between 1934 and 1973, Parceria A.M.Pereira published 8 prizewinning writers. It was followed by Império (5); Europa, Livraria Tavares Martins and Empresa Nacional de Publicidade (4 each); and Gama and Agência Geral das Colónias (3 each). Ática, Verbo and Portugália published 2 prizewinning writers each. It is possible to identify the category which benefited these publishing houses: Parceria A.M.Pereira published 2 prizewinning poets, 3 prizewinning playwrights and 1 novelist. It also had 1 prizewinning essayist and 1 writer of short stories. Ática was the only publishing house to have 2 prizewinning novelists; Europa published two rewarded short stories; Empresa Nacional de Publicidade and Agência Geral das Colónias published two prized works on history each.

If we exclude the Inéditos and Camões prizes, Tables 1-5 show that five out of eight categories benefited some publishers: poetry and drama (Parceria A. M. Pereira); novel (Ática); works on history (Empresa Nacional de Publicidade and Agência Geral das Colónias) and short story (Europa). No publishing house benefited substantially with the prizes for children's fiction and essays. When cross-analysing prizewinning works and the number of times a publishing house published prizewinning works, results are not very significant. As far as the Eça de Queirós and the Alexandre Herculano prizewinning works are concerned, publishing houses varied: only two out of six prizes rewarded novels published by the same publishing house and only four out of fourteen prizes rewarded historical works of two publishing houses. As far as poetry is concerned, variation is wider: two out of thirteen prizes were given to poems published by the same publishing house. Despite results not being very significant, these publishers became associated to the Estado Novo and only a few, for example, Ática and Verbo, continued business after 1974.[58]

An indicator of success in book promotion is the possibility of the writer's work being translated. The potential interest of the topics discussed in books is a major condition for arousing the interest of foreign publishers. The works rewarded by the Regime were those which served their interest, that of building a corpus of ideologically representative literary works. There were several events organized to present them abroad. The Portuguese repre-

---

58 Parceria A. M. Pereira's, book lists were mainly composed of nineteenth-century writers, such as Latino Coelho, Oliveira Martins, Pinheiro Chagas, Camilo Castelo Branco and Raúl Brandão. When the SNI prizes were set up, Parceria also published its prizewinning writers, such as Maria Archer, Luís Forjaz Trigueiros, Joaquim Paço d'Arcos, Virgínia Vitorino and Olavo d'Eça Leal. In the late 1940s, Parceria introduced moderate left-wing writers, such as Artur Portela, Urbano Tavares Rodrigues and Carlos Ferrão. At first, the new book releases sold well but, as time went by, this policy nearly drove Parceria to bankruptcy because these writers were not among the readers' preferences and their promotion involved costs that the publisher could not afford. Taking into consideration that the publisher's book lists had been concentrated on works that preserved the dominant ideology and that this publishing house had been operating for a century, the State provided a subsidy at António Maria Pereira's request. This money was not sufficient and the publishing house did not live through the Revolution. See Pereira, António Maria, *Parceria António Maria Pereira, Crónica de Uma Dinastia Livreira* (Lisbon: Pandora Edições, 1998). The Agência Geral das Colónias was set up in 1924 and was used by the Government to promote the Regime's work through the Missão Cinegráfica às Colónias de África (for example, *O Feitiço do Império*, 1940) and publications on different subjects of the colonies (history and geography). The Agência served the concepts of empire/colonization and the SPN/SNI prizes strengthened its legitimacy (for example, it published *A Literatura Portuguesa e a Expansão Utramarina*, Pero Vaz de Caminha Prize, serving the wide-ranging concept of Portuguese-speaking world). After the independence of the colonies in 1974, it closed business. For a detailed list of the works published by the Agência Geral das Colónias, see http://memoria-africa.ua.pt/Digital_Coleccoes.aspx [accessed October 2007].

sentations at international exhibitions in Paris, Nice, New York and Seville were managed as cultural promotion and included the work of contemporary writers and presented current literary trends. The Grémio Nacional de Editores e Livreiros, which represented Portuguese publishers and booksellers, received subsidies from the SNI to organize book displays at Madrid Book Fairs between 1945 and 1953. Claims that subsidies were not enough to cover expenses involved in the organization of these events led the Grémio to consider more cost-effective alternatives for promoting Portuguese books abroad.[59]

3.7 International Promotion of Portuguese Novels

The SPN/SNI did not consider major cultural events, such as the Frankfurt Book Fair before 1970. It privileged historical bonds and, thus, it directly targeted the Portuguese local communities in India, Macau, Cape Verde and Guinea Bissau, and also Brazil.

The Portuguese-Brazilian Agreement in 1941 postulated the exchange of publications, of propaganda, and cultural contacts among Portuguese and Brazilian writers and artists. Nevertheless, despite this Agreement, the penetration into the Brazilian book market found a significant obstacle when in 1948 the Brazilian Government issued Decree-Law no.25 442 which stipulated that the translation and originals by Brazilian writers required official authorization before entering Brazil. This restriction was not applied to texts by Portuguese writers.[60] Moreover, delayed bank

---

59 Grémio Nacional de Editores e Livreiros, *Relatório de Contas do ano de 1946* (Lisbon: Grémio Nacional de Editores e Livreiros, 1946), p. 3. The Grémio's yearly Relatórios de Contas published up till 1974 show that the promotion of Portuguese Books abroad was restrained by tight budgets.

60 Grémio Nacional de Editores e Livreiros, *Relatório de Contas do ano de 1947 e 1948* (Lisbon: Grémio Nacional de Editores e Livreiros, 1948), p. 14. This problem is also referred to in Grémio's *Relatório de Contas do ano de 1949* (Lisbon: Grémio Nacional de Editores e Livreiros, 1949), p. 5 *Relatório de*

transfers of Brazilian payments to Portuguese publishers aggravated the Portuguese-Brazilian book trade. The Portuguese Government did little to tackle this problem which annoyed the Grémio Nacional de Editores e Livreiros . The official agreement guaranteed that the books exported from Portugal were those the Regime agreed with. The promotion of Portuguese books was, thus, ensured through official book fairs but they did not prevent publishers from running clandestine book exchanges. In 1953, the Government appointed a Committee composed of Government delegates and the chairman of the Grémio to supervise book promotion in the Portuguese colonies.[61]

The Portuguese economic situation did not encourage an effective expansion of the publishing business. Portuguese publishing houses were small-sized businesses and proved incapable of tackling that business problem, as pointed out by the Grémio:

> A pequena dimensão da empresa portuguesa, não lhe permite e não lhe permitirá que a abordagem do mercado internacional se processe como estímulo saudável, em termos, pelo menos, de não pôr em causa os resultados que se desejam.[62]

The Portuguese small-sized publishing business encouraged close relations between writers and publishers. However, scouts and literary agents were almost non-existent in the Portuguese publishing industry. Writers gave their manuscripts personally to publishers or sent them by post; advances were decided in face-to-face conversations. Personal relations often favoured an environment of complicity at a time of repression but the absence of business specialists who could decide on the best ways to promote books internationally made it impossible to encourage an effective

---

Contas do ano de 1952 (Lisbon: Grémio Nacional de Editores e Livreiros, 1952), pp. 3-4.

61 Grémio Nacional de Editores e Livreiros, *Relatório de Contas do ano de 1953* (Lisbon: Grémio Nacional de Editores e Livreiros, 1953), p. 5.

62 Grémio Nacional de Editores e Livreiros, *Relatório de Contas do ano de 1972* (Lisbon: Grémio, 1973), p. 19.

visibility of Portuguese literature by using major international publishers.[63]

A comparison between the work developed by the SPN/SNI and the British Council provides evidence for the dependence of the Portuguese institution on the political, economic and social environment. The British Council administered the English Language Book Society, a Governmental scheme for providing subsidized and low-priced books for foreign markets. This organization was set up on the assumption that literature was essential to promoting Britain and the British way of life to the world at large, separating it from politics and ensuring the autonomy of the literary field.

Very few prizes given by the Secretariado were translated abroad. According to the Portuguese publishers interviewed by me, an important reason was the fact that the books rewarded were oriented to Portuguese readers and were shaped by the Portuguese reality.

One of the few exceptions of translations of the Secretariado's literary prizewinning books was Joaquim Paço d'Arcos's novels. *Neve sobre o Mar* (Fialho de Almeida Prize, 1942) was published in Spain (Ediciones Ambo) in 1944; *Diário de um Emigrante* (Eça de Queirós Prize, 1936) was published in Finland (Suomen Kirja Ed.) in 1944.[64] This novel was also translated into French (Robert Laffont), Spanish (Planeta) and Italian (Fratelli Bocca) in the 1950s. There are no studies on the international recognition of Joaquim Paço d'Arcos's literary production. However, and in view of my

---

63 There is not any information available on the work of Portuguese literary agents. According to my interviews with Portuguese publishers, Portuguese writers do not have any literary agents to promote their work in Portugal. Ilídio Matos, literary agent, confirmed to me by e-mail on 3 May 2005 that his work with Portuguese writers mainly consisted of promoting them abroad during the 1950s and 1960s and that he only worked with foreign writers nowadays. He was the only cited Portuguese literary agent in the *Writers' & Artists' Yearbook 2005* (London: A& C Black, 2004), p. 431.

64 *Ana Paula: Perfil de Uma Lisboeta* (Ricardo Malheiros Prize, 1938) was published in Spain (Miracle Ed.) in 1942. For complete list of Joaquim de Paço d'Arcos's translations, see Projecto Vercial's database, available on <http://alfarrabio.di.uminho.pt/vercial/parcos.htm > [accessed in October 2007].

interviews conducted with Portuguese publishers, there are three factors that might have enabled the internationalization of Paço d'Arcos books in 1944: he was a three-time prizewinner in 1944; the issues he dealt with in those works; and he was published by Parceria A.M.Pereira. The first book to be translated was a Ricardo Malheiros Prize. The fact that he turned this prize down must have contributed subsequently on increased awareness of his *Ana Paula*. Nevertheless, it is worthy of mention that this book was only published in Spain, indicating that the fact that it dealt with particular aspects of Lisbon was potentially interesting for a readership whose social and cultural experience was closer to the Portuguese than that in France, Italy and Finland. *Neve sobre o Mar* and *Diário de um Emigrante*, translated two years after *Ana Paula*, dealt with Portuguese emigration and with life abroad, an issue potentially interesting for foreign readership. Parceria A.M.Pereira, Paço d'Arcos's publishing house, was the publishing house with the highest number of literary prizes in the early 1940s: two SPN's literary prizes and two Ricardo Malheiros Prize in 1942 and in 1944, it published two other prizewinning books. Paço d'Arcos was the prizewinner of three out of Parceria's six rewarded books. This is indicative of the symbolic capital acquired by both the writer and his publishing house corroborating this with literary prizes as far as translation is concerned.[65]

None of Paço d'Arcos's translations had more than one print-run each, but they were important to the writer's literary prestige in Portugal. His books were commercially successful in Portugal and Parceria A.M.Pereira publicized the fact that he was a writer translated abroad. The publishing houses which published Paço d'Arcos abroad are also relevant for discussing acceptance of Portuguese literature. Ediciones Ambo and Suomen Kirja Ed. are small publishing houses. Planeta, Fratelli Bocca and Robert Laffont are publishers oriented to commercial success. Pierre Bourdieu's study on Laffont between the 1950s and the early 1970s showed

---

65 For example, Francisco Costa's *A Garça e a Serpente* (Eça de Queirós Prize, 1944) was not translated. This shows that Costa's only literary prize contributed to Parceria A.M.Pereira's prestige, although it did not warrant him being translated.

that it is a large publishing house which spent considerable amount in advertising, that up until 1975, its lists consisting of translations of works already successful abroad and bestsellers. Thus, according to Bourdieu, it favoured short-cycle book production.[66] Translations published by small publishing houses and those oriented to short-cycle book production have a low potential in attracting foreign academic reviews, as shown in the example of Paço d'Arcos.

Miguel Torga and Aquilino Ribeiro were proposed to the 1960 Nobel Prize for Literature and, in 1968, the Brazilian Academia das Letras proposed Ferreira de Castro as a candidate for the 1969 Nobel Prize. Although the Government did not publicly endorse those candidatures, those writers had little chance of being rewarded because promotion was insufficient.

Miguel Torga's books were published by Presença in the 1930s. The *Edições de Autor* had a fundamental role of ensuring the circulation of books, relieving publishers from the risk of potential losses, since Torga was arrested in 1939 following the publication of his *O Quarto Dia*.[67] His short story 'Vicente' was translated into German in 1943. Several other of his short stories were published by small publishing houses, in eastern European countries, in Italy and in the United Kingdom in the 1950s and in Germany in the 1960s. In 1959, Torga was proposed by Professor Aquarone, at Montpellier University, as a candidate for the 1960 Nobel Prize for Literature. In that same year, José Régio, Ferreira de Castro, Carlos de Oliveira, José Gomes Ferreira, José Cardoso Pires, Manuel Mendes and Fernando Namora (headed by Manuel Mendes), lobbied the Portuguese Society of Writers to sponsor the candidature of Aquilino Ribeiro. However, due to the ongoing trial against this writer after the Government having charged him

---

66 Pierre Bourdieu, pp. 98-101.
67 *O Quarto Dia* refers to the Civil War in Spain, describing the devastation that war caused to that country. The PIDE censors wrote that Torga was an 'escritor de forte poder de aceitação por leitores de deficientes recursos espirituais'; that he 'procura motivos sugestivos, em prol da descrença, da aversão ao dirigente ou ao afortunado, fomentando o desrespeito social'. Cited in Cândido Azevedo, p. 98.

for slander following the banning of *Quando os Lobos Uivam*, the Society ended up not supporting the writers' plea.

It is a fact that the Regime did not endorse any of these proposals. This writers' literary production did not serve the Regime's purposes. Nevertheless, none was published by major foreign publishing houses. Appendix 6 shows the list of all Nobel Prize-winners between 1947 and 2004, their original publishers, countries and publishers that translated their books. A close examination reveals that publishers and countries formed some kind of network that ensured visibility of writers before they received the Nobel Prize. Being published by major publishing houses is not enough, because symbolic capital is obtained by being published simultaneously in at least five key countries that operate as a network of hubs and spokes of symbolic capital: the United States, the United Kingdom, Sweden, France and Germany. Amongst these, the English-speaking countries are extremely important, because it is very difficult to be translated in these countries. Some of France's prestige goes back to its relevance in the book market before the Second World War. Being published in Sweden is also very important, though not a requirement, because the Nobel Committee members may read translations as long as members are proficient in the languages used. After 1945, as the United States's economy prospered and academic studies developed, American publishers became important channels of distribution for British publishers. It is not easy for foreign writers to be translated in the United States and the United Kingdom because translations do not sell in these countries. Nevertheless, it is easier to publish a foreign writer in the United Kingdom if he or she was previously published in the United States.

Being published by major publishing houses, such as Gallimard, Secker & Warburg Ltd, Farrar, Straus & Giroux, and Harcourt Brace & Company strengthens a writer's symbolic capital, because the work gets widespread readership (book promotion skills are often more effective), and that includes the possibility of drawing the attention of academics of those countries. This fact encourages the publication of critical reading on those works, which is very important for literary consecration. An isolated or less consensual nomination may be understood as having been driven by political, ideological and nationalistic reasons.[68]

One cannot know whether the nominations of the Portuguese writers mentioned above were seriously regarded by the Nobel Committee. Nevertheless, despite the enthusiasm that these nominations aroused among Portuguese intellectuals, the reality is that they were not sufficiently promoted and studied abroad and, thus, their literary geniuses were essentially respected in Portugal, but ignored in hubs of international visibility.

To sum up, the SPN was the Estado Novo's most powerful instrument of propaganda and its initiatives were aimed at regulating literary production and publishing: literary prizes and international events to promote Portuguese literature within the framework of defined cultural and ideological standards.

These initiatives did not encourage either the publication of fiction or the expansion of readership. Constraints related to illiteracy, censorship, definition of economic priorities and the subordination of aesthetic values to ideological stances led to a gradual abandonment of many intellectuals and to the inability of Portuguese publishers to develop efficient businesses. Geographic periphery, an ineffective international cultural policy based on political and historical alliances, and the unwillingness to cope with literary trends that did not conform to official stances, compromised the accumulation of prestige and recognition of writers and, thus, the visibility of Portuguese literature in the world.

---

68   According to information sent to the author by Carola Hermelin, of the Swedish Academy, by e-mail on 18 November 2004.

CHAPTER 4
Compromise and Autonomy in Consecration during the Estado Novo

This chapter will examine the literary prizes set up by the Academia das Ciências de Lisboa and the Sociedade Portuguesa de Escritores, which competed with the Government as consecrating agents during the Estado Novo. The aim is to show that, although they challenged the Government's ideology (particularly the SPE), the Government's pursuit of being the sole consecrating agent restrained those institutions' rewarding of Portuguese fiction. Table 6 shows the Ricardo Malheiros Prize (1933-1973) and Table 7A and 7B list the SPE Literary Prizes (1961-1965). I included their prize-winning writers, works and their publishing houses with the aim of showing that the cultural opposition led by certain writers and publishers had significant impact in the constitution of the Portuguese canon between 1974 and 2004.[1] I will examine literary prizewinning and complement it with my study on the booklists and readership of the Gulbenkian mobile libraries (and contrast it with the SNI mobile libraries). My purpose is to illustrate that the struggles of legitimacy in the literary field involving the establishment of the SPE, the Gulbenkian and, to some extent, the Academia das Ciências, as alternative agents of consecration, aimed at

---

1   Information on the Ricardo Malheiros Literary Prize was taken from <http://www.acadciencias.pt/html/menuacademiadigital/premioricardomalh eiros/premio.pdf > [accessed September 2007]; Information on the SPE Literary Prizes was taken from João Pedro George, *O Meio Literário Português (1960/1998) – Prémios Literários, Escritores, Acontecimentos* (Lisbon: Difel, Difusão Editorial S.A, 2002). This book is based on George's M.A. Thesis presented to the Universidade Nova de Lisboa in 1998.; as with the SNI-sponsored prizes, information on publishing houses of the Ricardo Malheiros and the SPE Prizewinners was not published. Thus, I researched the bibliographical details of every prizewinner between 1933 and 1973 in the database of the National Library, in Lisbon. See Table 6 on pp. 278-80 and Tables 7A and 7B on pp. 281-2.

the autonomization of the field. The analysis that was conducted of prizewinners' publishing houses will determine that they were influenced by the Estado Novo's ideology and that their profile also contributed to the way culture was disseminated. I will also try to establish that the political and economic environment did not enable them to develop radically different strategies of international consecration of Portuguese fiction.

Publishers and booksellers joined in an organization to better defend their interests before 1933. The Grémio Nacional de Editores e Livreiros was restructured in 1939 and adopted a name which corresponded to the ideological principles of the Regime.[2] Members were classified according to three categories: publishers, booksellers and the joint category of booksellers/publishers. The last category integrated those publishers who published more than 30 books annually and sold their books in their own bookshops, and also books published by other publishers who paid them a production tax.[3]

According to the Grémio's documents, in 1946, there were 231 booksellers, 35 booksellers/ publishers and 83 publishers. They were distributed as follows: 80 booksellers, 22 booksellers/publishers and 65 publishers altogether in Lisbon; 22 booksellers, 10 booksellers/publishers and 12 publishers in Porto; 9 booksellers, 1 bookseller/publisher and 1 publisher in Braga; and 5 booksellers, 2 booksellers / publishers and 3 publishers in Coimbra. This means that slightly more than half of the booksellers were concentrated in Lisbon, Porto, Braga and Coimbra; the booksellers/publishers were concentrated only in these cities and there were only 2 publishers that were not located in those urban centres: there was 1 in Barcelos, in the north, and another in Montijo, on the south bank of the

---

2   In 1927, Lisbon booksellers set up an association called Associação de Classe dos Livreiros de Lisbon, a sub-section of the Associação dos Lojistas de Lisbon. At the beginning of 1939, this was named Associação de Classe de Editores e Livreiros de Portugal and, in June 1939, it was again renamed the Grémio Nacional de Editores e Livreiros according to the Decree-Law 24.715.

3   Jorge Ramos do Ó, 'Salazarismo e Cultura', in Joel Serrão and A.H. De Oliveira Marques, eds., *Nova História de Portugal. – Portugal e o Estado Novo (1930-1960)*, 12 vols (Lisbon: Presença, 1992), XII, pp. 391-454 (pp. 415-7).

Tagus. Braga was the third city with more booksellers and a small publishing niche. It was an archbishopric centre and, thus, it had a strongly implanted Catholic and conservative community.[4] All the other booksellers were distributed in 74 cities, especially in those along the coast, although some inland municipal centres also had bookshops, such as Beja (4), Bragança (3), Castelo Branco (3), Chaves (1), Covilhã (1), Évora (3), Fundão (1), Gouveia (1), Guarda (1), Lamego (2), Lousã (1), Montemor-o-Novo (1) and Viseu (7). Out of 74, 43 municipal centres had only 1 bookshop. This means that many villages and towns had neither libraries nor bookshops within walking distance, which held back expansion of readership.

According to the Grémio's statistics, Lisbon accounted for an average of 41.5 per cent of the books published and sold in Portugal between 1939 and 1960. The number of members of the Grémio rose steadily up until 1974. In 1939, there were 164 associates and this number rose to 510 in 1960. By 1974, the Grémio had about 1,312 associates.[5]

The Grémio's organization up until 1974 shows that nearly half of all publishers and booksellers were concentrated in Lisbon. This fact reflected the importance of the Portuguese capital as the country's political and business centre. Furthermore, the absence of publishers and, particularly, booksellers in most interior cities and also in some coastal cities, favoured the impact of cultural initiatives, such as the SNI mobile libraries in the 1940s and also the Gulbenkian's mobile libraries in the 1950s. Information was

---

4   The list of the SNI literary prizewinners confirm the geographic distribution of publishers. Most were based in Lisbon (for example, Parceria A.M.Pereira, Império, Europa, Gama, Agência Geral das Colónias and Portugália). A significant number of publishers was located in Porto (for example, Liv. Tavares Martins, Imprensa Portuguesa, Tip. Sequeira, Domingos Barreira and Ibérica). Only a few SNI prizewinners were published by publishing houses based in Coimbra (Tip. Atlântida). Braga had important publishing houses, such as Editora Pax and Braga Editora (although they did not publish SNI prizewinners). In addition, the Editora A Educação Nacional, which published primary school books and dictionaries, was set up in Porto in the 1930s.

5   *Anuário Comercial* (1930 a 1960); *Livros de Portugal* (1939 a 1975); *Relatório de Contas da Direcção e Parecer do Conselho Fiscal* (1945 a 1973). Figures cited in Ramos do Ó, p. 417.

controlled by the Government and a significant part of the population was vulnerable, in view of the high rates of illiteracy and deprived social conditions. Thus, the Regime's educational policy became more effective because it offered the Portuguese, their major source of information. These factors altogether strengthened the population's passiveness towards information.

The fact that Portuguese publishers and booksellers were jointly organized also deterred them from developing separate business strategies.[6] Between the 1940s and the early 1970s, the major issues under discussion were: the status of translation; the expansion of Portuguese literature to Brazil and Portuguese-speaking African countries; participation at national and international book fairs; shortage of paper, especially in the years following the Second World War; censorship; and the organization of school textbooks.[7] The problems discussed at the Grémio concerned the basic survival of the book trade in Portugal, which affected both publishers and booksellers: sales, circulation of books and literacy. Its subsidies given to the SPE's literary prizes aimed at enhancing print-runs and, thus, maximizing profits in a country where readership was limited.

The Grémio's relations with the Government showed that it was mainly an organization that represented Portuguese publishers and booksellers at an institutional level. Dialogue between institutions was ensured by the fact that the Grémio's chairmen were supporters of the Estado Novo: men, such as António Maria Pereira (1944-1953; publisher of Parceria António Maria Pereira)

---

6 Separation of interests was achieved only in 1999, when several publishers set up the União de Editores Portugueses. In the United Kingdom, booksellers and publishers were organized separately: the Publishers Association was set up in 1896 and the Associated Booksellers has existed since 1895. Publishers were able to muster strength for joint action after 1896. In 1950, young publishers organized their own association, the Society of Young Publishers. For further information on British publishing, see Ian Norrie, *Mumby's Publishing and Booselling In The Twentieth Century*, London: Bell and Hyman, 6th edn, 1982 (Mumby, Frank, *Publishing and Bookselling*, London: Jonathan Cape Ltd, 1930).

7 See Grémio Nacional de Editores e Livreiros, *Relatório de Contas* (Lisbon: Grémio Nacional de Editores e Livreiros). This refers to the years 1944, 1946, 1947, 1948, 1950, 1951, 1952, 1953, 1970, 1971, 1972 and 1973.

and Fernando Guedes (1970-1971; publisher of Editorial Verbo). These were also among those who most frequently published SNI prizewinning books. It is indicative of the institutional communication that the Grémio was informed of arrests of publishers, booksellers and writers before they took place. Nevertheless, the fact that the Grémio could do very little to influence a decision illustrates its limited range of action.[8]

The only known survey on the publishing market was developed by Irene Lisboa, commissioned by Seara Nova in 1944. She was involved in Seara Nova and before 1944, her published work focuses on documenting urban life.[9] The Política de Espírito celebrated its tenth anniversary and the SPN was restructured and renamed SNI. The Government-sponsored literary prizes also celebrated its tenth anniversary. In view of the relative success of the literary prizes and of the growing opposition (through political movements, such as the MUNAF), the Government invested in initiatives to promote culture and gain popular support. Seara Nova's concern for the state of the publishing market is illustrative of its examination of Portuguese society, which had been among

---

8   The Portuguese Government never rewarded publishers and booksellers for their services, unlike, for example, in the United Kingdom, where Geoffrey Faber was knighted for his service to British publishing in 1954. British booksellers and publishers were organized in separate organizations that made some important achievements, such as the Charter Bookselling Group, in 1964, that laid down the standards about minimum stocks, floor space, training and stock control; Equally relevant was the fact that, due to the proposal of a wartime sales tax in 1940, the Publishers' Association rallied public support and managed to exclude books from that tax. The Portuguese Grémio's range of action and negotiation skills was subdued by the State's authority.

9   Seara Nova appealed to reform through pedagogy, responding to the integralist and traditionalist Nação Portuguesa. It was in this journal that José Régio and Álvaro Cunhal were involved in a political-literary discussion on aesthetics.Among Irene Lisboa's works, Esta Cidade!, published in 1942 documents life of middle and working classes in Lisbon. Her literary merit was praised in the 1940s by José Régio in Presença, by Vitorino Nemésio in Revista de Portugal and by João Gaspar Simões in the cultural supplement of Diário de Lisboa.

its priorities when it was set up in 1921.[10] The Government did not commission any extensive studies on the Portuguese book trade, showing that the Portuguese authorities were less concerned with the book business than on its use for political motivations, disregarding the literary system's dynamic nature. As Itamar Even-Zohar pointed out in his Polysystem Theory, within the framework of a unisystem, the 'inside view' of 'the people-in-the-culture' who implement an official culture regard other institutions as 'peripheries' and, therefore, 'extra-systemic' and are unaware of any 'tensions between strata' and the 'value', in other words, the meaning of concurrent items.[11]

Irene Lisboa surveyed booksellers and publishers, including Parceria António Maria Pereira, Livraria Portugália, Livraria Lello, Editorial Cosmos, Editorial Gleba, Editorial Miverva, Livraria Guimarães, Livraria Sá da Costa and Seara Nova. Although she does not refer to the Government's cultural policy directly as Seara Nova's motivation to survey publishers, their answers prove publishing strategies were non-existent, and ineffective in breaking through the constraints of Government's cultural policy and the country's peripheral condition.[12] As far as publishing strategies were concerned, they were mainly based on the publishers' 'nose for business' and the 'readers' preferences'.[13] Their inability to organize a joint strategy also deterred them from tackling international markets effectively. Portuguese-speaking countries and Spain remained unexplored markets.[14] That was aggravated by the

---

10 In 1921, Seara Nova was published with the aim of 'intervir activamente na vida política do país, sem se transformar em partido político', Irene Lisboa, *Inquérito ao Livro*, 2 vols (Lisbon: Seara Nova, 1944), I – *Editores e Livreiros*, p. 213.

11 Itamar Even-Zohar, 'Polysystem Theory', *Poetics Today*, 11:1 (1990), 9-26 (p. 14).

12 'Ficar-se-á assim com um painel de juízos sobre o livro, numa época em que a leitura tanto se intensificou e o comércio livreiro tão grande expansão obteve', 'Explicação', in Lisboa, [n.p.].

13 [António Maria Pereira, Parceria António Maria Pereira] 'A escolha dos originais baseia-se muitas vezes em palpites, num *faro* do que mais interessa [...] ' (author's italics), in Lisboa, p. 7; [Manuel Rodrigues, Editorial Minerva] ' Há uma espécie de olfacto, uma perspicácia que me serve', p. 74.

14 António de Sousa Pinto (Casa Livros de Portugal) pointed out that the expansion of Portuguese written books to the United States was under

fact that publishers had to cope with economic restrictions, such as taxes on paper in the late 1940s, despite the Grémio's efforts to persuade the Government to reduce them.[15]

There are thus few opportunities to publicize writers and books in the media, as António Maria Pereira concluded, 'A opinião pública forma-se sobre desportos, mas não sobre livros'.[16] His statement is indicative of the Government's priority in involving the Portuguese in entertaining activities that diverted their attention from any subversive thoughts.

There are two aspects mentioned by Portuguese publishers that are worthy of note, because they convey the publishers' position in the literary system during the Estado Novo. Running a publishing business was limited by several legal constraints mentioned above and, thus, the risk of losses dissuaded publishers from developing wide-ranging strategies. Publishing tactics were mostly based on safe, economical investments, such as following readers' preferences, and publishing well-known novels because fiction was more in demand.[17] The objectives defined by publishers and literary directors were decisive in their organization of booklists. There were those, such as Parceria António Maria Pereira, Sá da Costa, Bertrand, Gama, Lello, and Guimarães who created 'classics series' with Portuguese and foreign nineteenth-century writers.[18] These included the writers whose works were

---

Brazilian publishers' responsibility and recalled that in Brazil, writers were carefully publicized whereas Portuguese publishers were disorganized: 'O editor português, por via de regra, é pobre, e a sua acção é sempre limitada e tímida. [...] Todos gemem – os autores, os editores....É uma barafunda! É a casa onde todos ralham e ninguém tem razão'. In Lisboa, p. 16.

15 Grémio Nacional de Editores e Livreiros, *Relatório e Contas do ano de 1949* (Lisbon: Grémio Nacional de Editores e Livreiros), pp. 3-4.

16 Lisboa, p. 8.

17 Some relevant answers are given by publishers of Editorial Gleba: Lisboa, p. 42; Livraria Portugália: Lisboa, p. 69; Casa Livros de Portugal: Lisboa, p. 136.

18 In 1944, Parceria António Maria Pereira's booklist included Camilo Castelo Branco, Ramalho Ortigão, Guerra Junqueiro, Oliveira Martins, Raul Brandão, Maria Archer, Virgínia Vitorino, João de Almeida, Luís Forjaz Trigueiros, Francisco Costa, Joaquim Paço d'Arcos, Maria da Graça Azambuja, Natércia and João Gaspar Simões. Guimarães published Silva Gaio,

studied at school and those who were most acclaimed at official ceremonies. Other publishing houses and their literary directors in particular, also gave some priority to the promotion of contemporary writers: for example, Portugália's booklist included Mário Beirão, Hernâni Cidade, Manuel da Fonseca and Alves Redol.

Promoting writers whose work was not fully endorsed by the Regime was a difficult assignment. Certain publishers transferred these difficulties to the writers, blaming them for poor writing standards.[19] To claim that this was the writers' fault was simplifying the literary system and denying that the imposition of an authoritarian regime based on ideological standards compelled publishers to be gatekeepers of literary creation. They read manuscripts and decided who was part of the scene according to what could best be promoted without compromising business, and that often implied endorsing the Estado Novo's ideology.

Between 1933 and 1974, certain publishers, such as Parceria António M.Pereira and Livraria Tavares Martins, published those writers who were legitimated by the Government; others, including Dom Quixote and Arcádia, who set up their business in the 1960s, offered reading that challenged the Government's literary canon. Taking this position in the Portuguese literary field did not enable publishers to develop business strategies oriented towards business expansion and sales boosting. Publishing and writing were ways of actively contributing to education; even those who opposed the Regime worked to convey their own 'sentimento de elevado nacionalismo'.[20] Certain publishing houses, such as Publi-

---

Alberto Pimentel and André Brun and Lello reprinted Eça de Queirós and Teófilo Braga.

19 'Para falar a verdade, exclama o Dr. Vilela [Lobo Vilela, Editorial Gleba], todos nós somos, afinal, escritores das horas vagas, escritores de ócio, e não profissionais. E é possível que o romance careça de constância de trabalho, de um certo profissionalismo literário! Os portugueses têm sido mais ou menos insuficientes escritores ficcionistas', in Lisboa, pp. 44-5.

20 Quoted in Carneiro Pacheco, *Portugal Renovado (Discursos)* (Lisbon: Bertrand, 1940), p. 86. Pedro Jorge de O.Pereira Leite has differentiated the strategies used by Portuguese publishers between the 1930s and the 1960s. Whereas in the 1930s and 1940s, 'a actividade do editor uma forma de actividade política no interior de um projecto de divulgação cultural, enquanto parte integrante deo projecto de alteração de mentalidade', in the 1950s, he was 'mais

cações Europa-América, gave special relevance to national and foreign left-wing writers. Francisco Lyons de Castro, a PCP member in the 1930s, and publisher of Europa-América since 1945, created strategies to publish books without them being pre-viewed by censors. Publishing particular writers was a way of taking a political stance for or against the Regime. The distinction between 'commercial' and 'cultural' businesses introduced by Bourdieu is not applicable in the Portuguese literary system because investment decisions were risky, depending on the publishers' and literary directors' ideological stances driving their commercial or cultural projects.

During the Estado Novo many Portuguese publishers and literary directors were writers, unlike what happened, for example, in the United Kingdom, where publishing houses were set up by businessmen and writers were often employed as literary advisors.[21] There were problems of distribution of books that were not tackled in a business-like way, such as the penetration of books into the inland areas and the international promotion of writers. Therefore, educating people equated to promoting certain values, disregarding business issues that involved the penetration of the book and the expansion of readership.[22] Publicizing writers corre-

---

discreto politicamente, não abandonando os projectos editoriais as suas características educacionais'. In the 1960s, publishers' strategies were more active and fighting-like. *Mercadores de Letras: Rumos e Estratégias dos Editores e Livreiros na Divulgação Cultural durante o Estado Novo (1933-1974)*, (published M.A.Thesis in Contemporary History, Lisbon: Faculdade de Letras da Universidade de Lisboa, 1998), p. 157. Manuel Rodrigues de Oliveira, of Editorial Cosmos, told Irene Lisboa in 1944 that ' O livro é útil, é até já indispensável. Tem uma função social determinada: educa, contribui para a formação do indivíduo, e, por intermédio deste, da comunidade a que pertence. O editor, para honrar o seu comércio, tem de possuir esta consciência'. See Lisboa, p. 14.

21 Some of them were António Alçada Baptista and Pedro Tamen (Editora Moraes); José Marmelo e Silva (Portugália); Natália Correia (Estúdios Cor); and Fernando Guedes (Editorial Verbo).

22 'Há muitos casos curiosos, que despertaram no seu tempo a atenção de editores e de livreiros, mas que nunca foram resolvidos. O de Bragança, por exemplo, uma cidade que mal consome livros! [...] Ninguém arrisca afinal o seu tempo e o seu dinheiro a sondar problemas deste teor'. Cited in Lisboa, p. 8.

sponded to taking a political stance. In 1958, Lyons de Castro organized a book-signing session for *A Barca dos Sete Lemes* by Alves Redol without first requesting censors, who then found it difficult to ban the book due to its commercial success.[23] Lyons de Castro's isolated participation at the Frankfurt Book Fair between 1959 and 1970 shows that, despite this book fair's importance this was neglected by the State and the Grémio during that time.

The fact that Portuguese publishing houses were small-sized businesses, coping with problems that involved their survival in the field, deterred them from hiring specialized staff and operating a whole structure that could expand the book trade inside and outside the country. As regards countries where Portuguese writers were translated, there was a difference between those who received Government-sponsored literary prizes and those who did not and opposed the Regime. Fiction written by Joaquim Paço d'Arcos (one the few Portuguese Government-sponsored prize-winners worldwide translated during the Estado Novo) was published in Spain, France, Italy, Sweden and Finland. Miguel Torga's, Fernando Namora's and Urbano Tavares Rodrigues's works were also translated before 1974: Miguel Torga's short stories and poems were published in Germany in 1943, 1964 and 1972; in Yugoslavia in 1952; in the United Kingdom in 1955; and Italy in 1954. Fernando Namora's novels were published in Spain in 1954; in Romania, Poland, France and the U.S.S.R in the 1960s and early 1970s. Urbano Tavares Rodrigues's novels were published in Czechoslovakia in 1967; and in France in 1969.[24] This shows that

---

23 Cited in Cândido de Azevedo, *A Censura de Salazar e Marcelo Caetano* (Lisbon: Editorial Caminho, 1999), pp. 541-2.

24 Fernando Namora's international promotion and commercial success benefitted from the publicity gained with Jorge Brum do Canto's film, adapted from his *Retalhos da Vida de Um Médico* (1948 and rewarded with Vértice Prize in 1949), shortlisted to the 1962 Berlin Cinema Festival; Manuel Guimarães's film, adapted from his *O Trigo e O Joio* (1954) *in 1965; and António Macedo's film, adapted from* Domingo à Tarde (1962) in 1966, shortlisted to the Venice Cinema Festival. He was also consecrated with Mário Sacramento's *Fernando Namora: A Obra e o Homem* in 1967. Information on Torga, Namora and Tavares Rodrigues available at <http://www.instituto-camoes.pt/ escritores> [accessed in December 2004].

Portuguese writers (especially prizewinners) were published abroad: France, Spain and Italy. However, translations were usually published by small-sized publishing houses and thus, the visibility that might be generated by big publishing houses (with a more complex organizational structure) was reduced.

A different case was Ferreira de Castro's novels. Despite the fact that *A Lã e a Neve* was rewarded with the Ricardo Malheiros Prize in 1934, *Emigrantes* and A *Selva* were Ferreira de Castro's best translated novels; they were published in London in 1934, in New York in 1935, in Paris in 1938, in Bratislava in 1949, in Warsaw in 1950, in Oslo in 1953 and in Bremen in 1955. They were also translated in Eastern Europe (such as in Poland, Yugoslavia and Romania), U.S.S.R., Italy and Switzerland, and in South America (such as in Brazil and Argentina). These novels and his *Missão* were also published in relevant local journals (such as *Revue des Deux Mondes, Point de Vue, Atlas, The London Magazine, and Portugiesische Erzähler*). Unlike what happened to most Portuguese writers' novels, Ferreira de Castro's were published by relevant publishing houses, such as Grasset (Paris), Hamish Hamilton (London) and The Viking Press (New York), in the late 1930s.His literary quality and the cosmopolitanism of the topics (including emigration) covered by his novels contributed to his widespread promotion.

On the contrary, promotion of Portuguese literature (and fiction in particular) was mostly limited to several events organized by the Government and, thus, promotion led by publishers was scarce. Those writers who opposed the Regime were also published in Eastern Europe and that was a cultural book market unexplored by the Portuguese Government. Political affiliations must have been the reason why the Estado Novo did not consider that market, and also the reason why its opponents (publishers included) chose to invest in it. However, and in view of the countries that map the most relevant book trade exchanges (as shown in Appendix 6), Eastern European countries are not among the most influential countries as far as accumulated symbolic capital (that is, prestige generated by literary reviewing and print-runs in the countries where books are published) is concerned.[25] Consequently, tackling the problem of international promotion of Portuguese literature during the Estado Novo was not easy, as this would have required sophisticated business organizational structures.

Tables 6, 7A and 7B list the Ricardo Malheiros Prize and the SPE literary prizes and the current analysis will establish that, although those prizes rewarded works and writers whose literary aesthetics were not particularly favoured by the Estado Novo and, thus, implied a certain degree of challenge to the Government's consecrating role, the consecrating strategies were not radical enough to implement a different approach to literary consecration, with effects after 1974.

As far as the Ricardo Malheiros Prize was concerned, the analysis covers the period between 1933 and 1971, because there were no prizes in 1972-1973. Some of the members of Classe de Letras of the Academia de Ciências de Lisboa were: Júlio Dantas who chaired the Academia up till the late 1950s, Joaquim Leitão, Queirós Veloso, Luís Forjaz Trigueiros and Augusto de Castro. This institution was subsidized by the Ministério da Educação Nacional. The financial reward of the Ricardo Malheiros Prize was less than that of the SNI prizes rewarding fiction. However, the 6,000$00 prize was more appealing for many writers who did not want to receive a SNI prize and wanted to avoid being associated with the Regime.

Broadly speaking, and especially between the 1930s and the 1940s, the prizewinning works served the Regime's ideology.[26] Augusto da Costa's *As Inocentes* is an example of how the Estado

---

25 Miguel Torga turned down the Almeida Garrett Prize in 1954 since he assumed an anti-prizewinning stance. Vergílio Ferreira's translated works (by Basilio Losada (José Saramago's Spanish translator) published by Seix Barral in Spain in 1972) could also be set as an example.

26 See Table 6 on pp. 279. Works, such as *Miradouro, Dona sem Dono, Ana Paula: Perfil de Uma Lisboeta, Aldeia das Águias, Novas Estrelas, As Inocentes, Calcanhar do Mundo, Maria da Lua and Entre Duas Labaredas* display regional environments and deal with Christian values and paternalist-based family structures. Information about Ricardo Malheiros prizewinning works and writers can be found in *Dicionário Cronológico de Autores Portugueses*, 6 vols (Lisbon: Europa-América, 2005).

Novo appeased supporters of the Integralismo Lusitano. Augusto da Costa had been the director of *A Monarquia* in 1918, Secretary of the Presidência do Conselho in 1933 and published several works on corporativism, Portuguese economy and history (one of them, *Portugal Vasto Império*, was rewarded by the António Enes Prize in 1934). The novel *As Inocentes* also reflect its writer's support of the Regime by supporting the values of family and work. Nevertheless, the Classe de Letras also rewarded works, such as *As Três Mulheres de Sansão*, *Terra Fria*, *Servidão*, *O Castigo de D. João*, and *Horizonte Cerrado*, which were aesthetically influenced by the Neo-Realist literature and expressed some social concerns such as the living conditions of the Portuguese working class. These works were important for the accumulation of symbolic capital of their writers; nonetheless, as far as Óscar Lopes and António José Saraiva are concerned, they are not their writers' most representative works. In fact, their examination of the literary production of writers, such as Aquilino Ribeiro and Ferreira de Castro, which had started before 1933, and also Fernando Namora, look at their Ricardo Malheiros prizewinning fiction as minor works.[27]

The valuing of certain works not representative of the Regime's principles was more recurrent after Júlio Dantas left the Academia de Ciências's chairmanship and it coincided with the period when Salazar's Government went through more difficult times.[28] *Uma Pedrada no Charco*, *O Livro das Sombras*, *O Signo da Ira*,

---

27 Óscar Lopes and António José Saraive have reviewed Portuguese literary history in the late 1950s and, within the context of growing opposition to the Regime, have earned authority as academics. *História da Literatura Portuguesa* does not mention Aquilino Ribeiro's *As Três Mulheres de Sansão* and Alves Redol's *Horizonte Cerrado*; Ferreira de Castro's *Terra Fria* is referred to as a novel in which he 'manteve e aperfeiçoou o tipo de romance de inquérito aos meios e problemas sociais' (p. 1073). In 1934, the Academia rewarded *Terra Fria* for being a tribute to regional environments: 'embora não isenta de defeitos, releva qualidades apreciáveis de romancista, poder de observação, propriedade de linguagem, conhecimento das paixões humanas e cuidadoso estudo dos tipos e dos costumes da paisagem barrosã'. Namora's *As Minas de S.Francisco* is also pointed out by Saraiva and Lopes as an example of this writer's 'romance-inquérito' (p. 1090).
28 It is worthy of mention that between 1933 and 1974, Júlio Dantas was the only chairman of the Academia de Ciências de Lisboa who was a novelist.

A Hora di Bai, As Boas Intenções and *A Torre de Barbela* are examples of the Academia's consecration of literary currents, such as the return to Neo Realism in the 1950s, Surrealism, and Existentialism, which emerged in Portuguese literature in the early 1960s. Orlando da Costa's *O Signo da Ira* deals with Goa's conflicts during the Portuguese rule and Manuel Ferreira's *A Hora di Bai* focuses on life in Cape Verde and Cape Verdian emigration to Lisbon. These works were published during the Colonial War and the Goa conflict and only a few years before José Luandino Vieira's *Luuanda*. Although they express social concerns, they do not take clear stances on political conflicts and oppose the Regime's sovereignty over the Colonies. Other works, such as *Jerónimo e Eulália* and *Canção diante de Uma Porta Fechada*, although acknowledging some decadence in the rural bourgeoisie, are expressive of a certain support of traditional religious values. A few members of the panels who sat for the Ricardo Malheiros Prize, such as Vitorino Nemésio and Jacinto do Prado Coelho, came from academia studies and were less supportive of the Regime. Therefore, they approved of Portuguese fiction that emerged from different literary influences and that differed from that rewarded with the SNI and SEIT prizes.

Although this prize gave certain publishing houses the possibility of gaining prestige, many of them, such as Parceria António Maria Pereira, Empresa Nacional de Publicidade and Portugália, were also those which also benefited from the Government's prizes. However, other publishers, such as Bertrand and Arcádia, published Ricardo Malheiros Prizes and did not publish any of the SNI prizewinning works. Bertrand published six Ricardo Malheiros Prizes, whereas Sociedade de Expansão Cultural published five. Parceria António Maria Pereira came third, having published three prizewinning works. Portugália, O Século, Arcádia and Empresa Nacional de Publicidade published two prizewinning works each. Bertrand, Empresa Nacional de Publicidade and Arcádia

---

Reynaldo dos Santos, Moses Bensabat Amzalak and Amorim Ferreira also had published work but were linked to sciences and economics. Dantas's support to the Regime's values, also visible in his fiction, might be relevant for the fact that the Academia did not reward different fiction.

were among the publishing houses out of this list which published more fiction representative of emerging literary currents which were not particularly favoured by the Regime. Bertrand was among those publishing houses showing some development in its booklist during the Estado Novo, ranging from Antero de Figueiredo's *Miradouro* in 1935 to Augusto Abelaira's *As Boas Intenções* in 1963.

Print-runs were not particularly boosted by the Ricardo Malheiros Prize. This fact did not make that prize more prestigious than the SNI prizes. The average number of prints of most prize-winning fiction was two and many rewarded titles, such as *Dona sem Dono, Aldeia das Águias, Novas Estrelas* and *As Boas Intenções* did not reach the second print-run. Some of the few exceptions were *As Três Mulheres de Sansão, Ana Paula: Perfil de Uma Lisboeta, Mau Tempo no Canal, As Minas de S.Francisco,* and *Uma Pedrada no Charco* were printed three or more times.[29] Nevertheless, not rarely did certain writers move to other publishing houses and, then, their prizewinning work was printed more than once; examples are Assis Esperança's *Servidão* printed twice by Guimarães in the late 1940s and Rúben A.'s *A Torre de Barbela,* printed three times by Parceria António Maria Pereira and prefaced by José Palla e Carmo in the mid 1960s.[30] In this case, the second publishing house benefited from the prize which enabled the writer to move to bigger publishing houses.

The Sociedade Portuguesa de Escritores was set up in 1956 with funds provided by publishers, the Grémio and the Gulben-

---

29 Aquilino Ribeiro's *As Três Mulheres de Sansão* was printed five times by Bertrand and Paço d'Arcos's *Ana Paula* was printed six times by Parceria António Maria Pereira. It is worthy of mention that the writer turned that prize down in 1938, arguing against the hesitation of the panel'(Information available at [http://blogdaruanove.blogs.sapo.pt/222251.html] accessed on 30 September 2007) Papers on the Ricardo Malheiros Prize mentions that it was decided unanimously. Paço d'Arcos never turned any of the SPN and SNI prizes. His decision might have contributed to the popularity of his novel, although Paço d'Arcos was a case of commercial success at that time, unlike most SNI and Ricardo Malheiros prizewinning writers.

30 José Palla e Carmo was an essayist and literary critic, and a regular contributor in *O Tempo e o Modo, Jornal de Letras e Artes* and *Colóquio-Letras*.

kian Foundation.[31] It was established by writers who opposed the Regime's ideological principles and its founders were writers, such as Aquilino Ribeiro, Assis Esperança (both Ricardo Malheiros prizewinning writers) and Branquinho da Fonseca, whose literary production had emerged from Modernism and Neo-Realism. The enthusiasm and encouragement shown in the competition for literary prizes in 1934 was clearly declining and the Estado Novo had faced harder opposition culminating with the presidential campaign contested by General Humberto Delgado in 1958. Political and ideological motivations were behind literary valuing for different reasons: whereas the SNI's major concern was to strengthen the Regime through a cultural strategy, the SPE strove to assert its literary autonomy through consecration of aesthetic and literary values, autonomous from the Regime's ideology.[32] Two hundred and seventy-three writers joined it. In the following year, this number rose to 358 and again to 479 in 1960.

Bourdieu claimed, within the framework of his Theory of the Literary Field, that cultural producers are more inclined to reject the judgements of the canonical institutions the more intensely the cultural field asserts its autonomy.[33] During the Estado Novo, the restricted field of literary production developed instances of legitimacy whose principles were grounded on political and aesthetic opposition to the dominating agents of consecration. When César Moreira Baptista reformulated the SNI literary prizes in 1961, the SPE also launched its own literary prizes. The Camilo Castelo Branco Prize, rewarding fiction annually, was the only

---

31   According to the SPE's Relatórios in 1958 and 1961, Pedro de Andrade (Portugália) and António de Sousa Pinto (Livros do Brasil) were among the publishers who were committed to sponsor the SPE Prizes.

32   'Estava, nesse sentido, delineado um programa de realizações várias, quer no plano da defesa da dignidade e dos interesses dos escritores, quer no da criação de condições e oportunidades de maior convívio e solidariedade entre eles', in *Relatório de 1973*, Associação Portuguesa de Escritores, Lisbon, p. 3. Statistical information on the SPE cited in its *Relatórios de Contas* between 1961 and 1973.

33   Pierre Bourdieu, *The Field of Cultural Production – Essays on Art and Literature*, ed. and introd. by Randal Johnson (Cambridge: Polity Press & Blackwell Publishers, Ltd, 1993), p. 123.

prize that was named after a writer.[34] All the other SPE literary prizes were biennial and competed with the SNI's for legitimacy using the alternative terminology 'Grande Prémio'.[35]

That the only prize with a specific name was the one rewarding fiction becomes relevant because it was the SPE's most important prize. However, the fact that the chosen name positions prizewinning writers in relation to a writer also consecrated by the Regime raises the question of the literary autonomy of these agents of production. The question is less important in terms of assessing the aesthetic and literary valuing decisions about Camilo Castelo Branco and Eça de Queiroz than in terms of the definition of the literary canon.

On discussing the literary canon, Frank Kermode pointed out that 'changes in the canon obviously reflect changes in ourselves and our culture'.[36] Kermode's statement helps us to understand how autonomy was established within the framework of the SPE: on the one hand, the SPE asserted its literary autonomy by consecrating works that expressed different literary trends; on the other hand, the constitution of certain panels also suggested a certain compromise with the official establishment.

Prizes rewarded published writers and debutants. Portuguese fiction, such as the one produced by Vergílio Ferreira and Almeida Faria in the 1960s, influenced by Existentialism and the *nouveau roman*, were given the literary legitimacy that was not rewarded by the Regime. Those who were awarded or sat on panels for the SPE were not given the SNI prizes. António Ramos Rosa turned down the Prémio Nacional de Poesia in 1971 and Vergílio Ferreira did the same with the Prémio Nacional de Novelística in 1972.[37] Their attitude shows an unequivocal rejection of the Government's cultural policy, positioning consecration within the framework of autonomous alternative instances of legitimacy. This stance was

---

34   See Table 7A on pp. 281.
35   See Table 7B on pp. 282.
36   Frank Kermode, *Pleasure and Change: The Aesthetics of Canon*, ed. by Robert Alter (Oxford: Oxford University Press, 2004), p. 36.
37   Vergílio Ferreira, *Conta-Corrente I* (Lisbon: Bertrand, 1982), p. 121. José Régio received the Prémio Nacional de Poesia posthumously, after Ramos Rosa's declining it.

not followed by every writer: David Mourão Ferreira and Fernanda Botelho received SEIT prizes in 1972. Esther de Lemos received the Eça de Queiroz Prize in 1961 and, as a member of the SPE, sat on the panel for the Prémio de Revelação de Prosa in 1965. Several SPE members also received the SNI prizes: Vitorino Nemésio (1966), Domingos Monteiro (1966), Agustina Bessa Luís (1968), and Rui Cinatti (1968), among others. I will endeavour to show in Chapter 6 that these writers' acceptance of the SNI/SEIT Prizes had small effects on their recognition after 1974.

There was relative stability in the constitution of panels, enhanced by the fact that prizewinning writers often sat on those panels. Mário Dionísio sat on the panel for the Camilo Castelo Branco Prize in 1961 and 1962, and won the Grande Prémio de Ensaio in the following year; David Mourão-Ferreira sat on the panel for the Castelo Branco Prize in 1961, 1962 and 1964; Jacinto do Prado Coelho sat on that panel four times between 1961 and 1964; Maria de Lourdes Belchior sat once on the panel for the Grande Prémio de Poesia and once for the Grande Prémio de Novelística; José Régio sat on the panel for the Castelo Branco Prize in 1965 and was a prizewinner in 1963; Fernanda Botelho received the Castelo Branco Prize in 1962 and sat on the panel for the Grande Prémio de Novelística in 1965; Vergílio Ferreira received the Castelo Branco Prize in 1961 and sat on the panel for the Grande Prémio de Ensaio in 1963; José Gomes Ferreira received the Grande Prémio de Poesia in 1962 and sat on the panel for the Prémio de Revelação de Poesia in 1965; José Cardoso Pires received the Castelo Branco Prize in 1964 and sat on the panel for the Grande Prémio de Ensaio in 1965.   Literary prestige can be measured according to the prizes received, the career developed in the literary field and the panels on which intellectuals sat. Wouter de Nooy suggested in his study of Dutch literary prizes that the literary prestige of the panel members can be evaluated according to some basic characteristics related to literary seniority, administrative experience and the continuous practice of literary criticism.[38] His research pro-

---

38   W. De Nooy, 'Gentlemen of the Jury… – The Features of the Experts Awarding Literary Prizes', *Poetics*, 17 (1988), 531-545.

vides helpful hints for analysing the SPE prizes, notwithstanding the fact that due to the abrupt closure of the SPE, the list of prizes is limited.

Nevertheless, almost every writer who was awarded the Camilo Castelo Branco Prize sat on panels for prizes related to different genres, a fact that enhanced the prestige of those prize-winners: Manuel da Fonseca sat on panels for prizes related to novellas and poetry; Vergílio Ferreira sat on a panel for essays; Augusto Abelaira sat on panels for novellas. This fact is relevant when a comparison with the other prizes shows that the same did not happen: José Gomes Ferreira and Eugénio de Andrade sat only on panels for poetry, showing that their literary prestige was essentially linked to this genre. University teachers, critics and novelists dominated these panels. Prizewinning writers sat on panels only after having received the prize. Mário Dionísio was the only exception because he sat on panels for the Camilo Castelo Branco Prize in 1961 and 1962 and was awarded the Grande Prémio de Ensaio in 1963. This suggests that literary seniority and long-standing practice of literary criticism enhanced literary prestige of someone before sitting on a panel. The relative stability of the valuing community also suggests that there was a concern to safeguard aesthetic and literary standards.

An analysis of the publishing houses which published the prizewinning works shows that most did not publish works rewarded by both the SNI/SEIT and the Academia de Ciências: Presença, Salamandra, Prelo and ABC. Portugália published seven out of fifteen SPE prizewinning works whereas the other six publishing houses published one rewarded work each.[39]

Portugália is worthy of analysis, considering that it also benefited from three Ricardo Malheiros and five SNI Prizes. It was set up at the end of the 1930s and João Gaspar Simões was literary editor up until 1958. Augusto da Costa Dias replaced him until the early 1960s. Jorge de Sena held office briefly in 1959. The participation of those, such as José Régio and Gaspar Simões, who had been involved in *Presença*, and of Fernando Namora and Sena in Por-

---

39   I could not find any indication about Ângela Caires's *As Pedras Envelhecem*'s publishing house at the Portuguese National Library's database.

tugália was important for the legitimacy of both. Régio's *Música Ligeira*, rewarded with a Prémio Nacional de Poesia in 1971, was also published by Portugália and represents the Regime's posthumous consecration of a member of the *Presença* group. Gaspar Simões's literary section 'Livros da Semana' in *Diário de Notícias* was decisive in the making of his prestige as literary critic and gave him the possibility of allowing new writers to be known to the public.[40] Portugália was important for writers who emerged from Portuguese Modernism and Neo-Realism because it gave them the opportunity to have their work published. The fact that Vitorino Nemésio and Jacinto do Prado Coelho sat on the panels for the Ricardo Malheiros Prize in the late 1950s and in the 1960s is also of relevance because it was then that new fiction produced by writers, such as Campos de Figueiredo and Manuel Ferreira, was first rewarded.[41]

In 1998, João Pedro George's sociological study of the Portuguese literary field during the Estado Novo showed that the Portuguese writers who acquired consolidated symbolic capital, through recognition and consecration, were predominately linked to an urban middle class environment; those with rural family background studied in a city and continued their activities there,

---

40 At the same time that Portugália, under Gaspar Simões's literary management, strengthened its prestige by publishing prizewinning works, Gaspar Simões, as literary critic, promoted Fernando Pessoa as persona non grata of the Regime, who was rewarded with the second Antero de Quental Prize in 1934. José Blanco's 'A Verdade sobre 'A Mensagem', focusses on what he has defined as one of the 'mitos pessoanos'. Similar historical approaches have been promoted after 1974 with the aim of positioning the Estado Novo as an adversary to the Portuguese writers who were consecrated by opponents to the Regime. One of them had to do with promoting Aquilino Ribeiro, Ferreira de Castro and Miguel Torga as candidates to the Nobel Prize who did not win that prize because the Regime did not support them. Intellectuals and politicians, such as José Manuel Mendes and Mário Soares, have publicly supported this stance. See Mário Soares, 'Prefácio', in *Em Defesa de Aquilino Ribeiro* (Lisbon: Terramar, 1994).

41 Campos de Figueiredo was first appraised by José Régio in *Presença* in 1935 as 'seguro talento de evocação e descrição'.

had higher education and most were left-wing affiliated.[42] Their university studies exposed them to ideas and beliefs considered subversive by the Regime, especially in the 1950s and in the 1960s. Political opposition was fundamentally developed in the cities; literary production emerged from an urban environment.

The tight political and ideological control wielded by the Regime through censorship, pressure on universities, political surveillance and consecration according to ideological conformity, encouraged certain Portuguese intellectuals to join opposition movements.[43] In the late 1940s, writers such as Alves Redol, Adolfo Casais Monteiro, Álvaro Salema, Ferreira de Castro, Vergílio Ferreira, Aquilino Ribeiro, Manuel Mendes, Mário Dionísio, Vitorino Nemésio, João Gaspar Simões, Armindo Rodrigues, Irene Lisboa and Rocha Martins, among others, endorsed the MUD.[44] This movement was divided into different professional sectors, one of which, the Comissão Específica de Escritores, Jornalistas e Artistas Democráticos, set up the Portuguese Section of the PEN Club with the purpose of supporting writers, encouraging literary production independent from the Government and promoting relations with foreign writers.

Moreover, intellectuals, and writers in particular, were also involved in the presidential campaigns led by adversaries. For example, José Régio openly endorsed Norton de Matos's campaign in 1949 when he published a text overtly accusing the Estado

---

42 João Pedro George, *O Meio Literário Português (1960/1998) – Prémios Literários, Escritores, Acontecimentos* (Lisbon: Difel, Difusão Editorial S.A, 2002). The study included in Chapter 2 was based on the profile of forty-one writers who have been prizewinners, sat on panels or been members of boards of literary institutions.

43 Before a publisher could start his activity, he had to be given prior authorisation, make a financial deposit equivalent to a six-month print of a newspaper or magazine in the censorship committee's accounts, sign a document denying any hostile stance against the Regime, inform the Government of: the printing house he was going to work with; employees; and print-runs.

44 The *República*'s edition of 10 November 1945 reported the intellectuals' criticism of the Government's cultural policy: ' extinta a liberdade, negou-se à inteligência criadora a sua maior força, faltou ao povo o esclarecimento dos seus próprios problemasm que deve ser a primeira missão dos intelectuais, como a estes faltou uma soberania justa que só o povo pode realizar'.

Novo of repression and intimidation.[45] In 1957, 1969 and 1973, intellectuals participated actively in the Congressos Republicanos de Aveiro and accused the regime of deterring their integration into society and treating them as outcasts.[46]

Many of the writers mentioned above as well as intellectuals were influenced by Marxism and were members of the Communist Party since the early days of the Estado Novo. Being a member of the PCP meant, above all, being against the Regime. Some writers, such as José Cardoso Pires, left the PCP after the Revolution when the party used coercive measures to impose discipline. Most Neo-Realist writers focussed on problems of families living in rural areas; a few, including Álvaro Cunhal and Soeiro Pereira Gomes, dealt with factory workers' difficulties. Writing was seen less as literary aestheticism than as a tool to portray this reality, which constituted the dark side of the Portuguese way of life as officially propagated by the Regime:

> Torna-se urgente que nos apercebamos de que aos novos escritores, integrados numa nova corrente histórica e iluminados por uma nova concepção da vida cumpre não se isolarem do grande combate corpo a corpo que se está

---

45 'O medo é que guarda a vinha [...] Em grande parte tem sido o medo que tem guardado a actual Situação. Pode, ainda, ser o medo quem melhor a defenda. Não só em Portugal como em quaisquer países onde um regime conquistou o poder pela força, e pela força impera, esse poderoso inimigo da alma se agigantou a ponto de tapar todo o horizonte', in José Régio, 'O Recurso ao Medo', in *Depoimento contra Depoimento*, in *Campanha Eleitoral da Oposição*, ed. by Serviços Centrais da Candidatura (Lisbon: 1949), p. 59. Quoted by Cândido Azevedo, *Mutiladas e Proibidas* (Lisbon: Caminho, 1997), p. 14.

46 Some of the papers delivered by writers were Ferreira de Castro's 'Pão e Liberdade'and Natália Correia's 'Política de Espírito Desnacionalisante' in 1957; in 1969, Ferreira de Castro's 'Mensagem', Urbano Tavares Rodrigues's 'Um Conceito de Liberdade', Óscar Lopes's, Maria Cristina Araújo's and Egito Gonçalves's 'Perspectivas Democráticas da Literatura Portuguesa'. The congress's final document included an appeal for wide access to education and culture; in 1973, José Saramago's 'Para um estudo da Situação da Cultura e da Informação em Portugal' and Urbano Tavares Rodrigues's 'Contribuições para uma análise da situação do Escritor em Portugal e da sua quase impossibilidade de comunicação com as Massas'. Cited in Marília de Assis Tavares, 'Os Congressos Republicanos de Aveiro' (unpublished thesis, Faculty of Letters, University of Coimbra, Coimbra, 1994).

travando em todas as frentes entre os interêsses antagónicos que exprimem a contradição irredutível da sociedade actual.[...] Romancistas, novelistas, ensaístas, críticos, polemistas, poetas, jornalistas e tradutores – é preciso que todos compreendam a missão que lhes incumbe.[47]

Literary creation was considered a tool to accomplish the mission of opposing the Regime. This was true in the late 1930s and when opposition and repression against adversaries, and writers in particular, was intensified, fiction was used to document Portuguese social conditions and standards of living, going against the ideology and aesthetics as endorsed by the Regime. The following texts were written in different periods of the Estado Novo and show how literary creation was closely linked to circumstantial constraints: the first, by Alves Redol in the late 1930s and the second, by Aguiar e Silva, deputy of the Assembleia Nacional [quoted by José Cardoso Pires] in the late 1960s:

> [...] publiquei crónicas e contos ribatejanos, confundindo rebuscamento com estilo, numa amálgama de poesia romântica e de Fialho, de barroquismo e de certo tom melodramático que correspondiam, por um lado, à falsa ideia de que "escrever difícil" seria o objectivo supremo de um verdadeiro escritor, e, por outro, à exaltação com que sentia os problemas das personagens a que aderira por origem familiar e por decisão de consciência premeditada.[48]

> [...] a censura obrigou o escritor a fazer da sua pena uma arma de subtileza, de acutilante subtileza. Por outro lado, sob o ângulo do leitor, obrigou-o a ler nas entrelinhas, nas meias palavras, a esforçar-se por apreender aquilo que o escritor quis mas não pôde dizer à vontade.[49]

---

47 Rodrigo Soares, 'A Missão dos novos escritores', *O Diabo*, 21 October 1939, p 1. Equally relevant is João Pedro de Andrade's 'O Problema do Romance Português Contemporâneo', published by Seara Nova, in 1942. This text, originally a paper delivered at A Voz do Operário, on 8 June 1942, claims that the novel should combine social concerns and aestheticism.

48 Alves Redol. 'Breve memória para os que têm menos de 40 anos ou para quantos já esqueceram o que aconteceu em 1939', in *Gaibéus* (Lisbon: Publicações Europa América, 1971), p. 13.

49 José Cardoso Pires, *E Agora José?* (Lisbon: Publicações Dom Quixote, 1999), p. 165.

Alves Redol's text taken from the preface to Europa América's edition of *Gaibéus* in 1971 and Aguiar e Silva's words both date from the late 1960s and point out inner conflicts on the relationship between writing as a learning process and its political, social and cultural environment; Alves Redol establishes this learning process as a development from reproducing literary predecessors' styles to his awareness of their unsuitability when using them to reflect the Portuguese reality of the 1930s. Aguiar e Silva generalises on Portuguese writing as self-conscious learning of how to oppose the Regime's ideology, at the same time it also contributed to the Portuguese writers' increasing literary complexity.

The reception of the SPE literary prizes was different from that of the SNI's and the literary debate took place in the field that was not dominated by the Government. SPE prizes were extensively publicized in the press, via interviews with the prizewinning writers.[50] This contrasted with very brief articles on the SNI prizes, published in the press that did not particularly support the Regime. The SNI praised the SPE prizes and this is relevant of the strategy for the SNI headed by Moreira Baptista in the 1960s.[51] Tight control of economic expenditure, the SNI's investment in control of information and the gradual disinterest among contenders in the SNI literary prizes led the SNI to discontinue some of their prizes. The Eça de Queirós was discontinued as the Camilo Castelo Branco Prize was set up. Apart from manuscripts, essays, poetry and short stories were rewarded by the SNI after the SPE was closed. In spite of the Gulbenkian's support to the SPE, literary valuing did not cease to be under close surveillance. Praising the SPE prizes meant that they were a more economical way to consecrate literature. However, when José Luandino Vieira was rewarded for his *Luuanda*, the members that sat on the panel were held by the PIDE because the writer had been in prison since 1961, charged for his participation in the Angolan nationalist movement. This is evidence for the fact that the Government retained its role

---

50 *Jornal de Letras e Artes*, '1962 nas Artes e nas Letras', 9th January 1963, last page; *Diário de Lisboa*, 25 May 1960.
51 SNI, *Informação Cultural Portuguesa*, no.1, Lisbon, 1960, p. 59: [Prémio Camilo Castelo Branco] o mais importante prémio literário português'.

as dominating agent of consecration, even at literary prizes it did not sponsor officially.

Unlike what happened with the SNI prizes, the SPE prizes generated literary critique. A relevant case was the debate that opposed Vergílio Ferreira and Alexandre Pinheiro Torres in 1963, following the prize given to *Rumor Branco*, opposing the approach of the nouveau roman to that of the Neo-Realist fiction.[52] The literary critique was completely atypical of what was common practice in the cultural establishment. Whereas the cultural field, and the literary field in particular, dominated by the Regime, did not allow space for debate because this was constrained by the imposition of ideology, the field that was opened by those who opposed the Regime was dominated by struggles for legitimacy to consecrate writers and works. Agents of production and consecration also strove for the survival of a literary system that was crystallized by the Regime's cultural standards. Institutions overtly asserted their autonomy through their refusal of the others' legitimacy.

The Gulbenkian libraries (permanent and mobile) were under the supervision of Branquinho da Fonseca up until 1974 and a specialized committee selected the stocks. This committee included essayists and literary critics: Orlando Vitorino, António Quadros, Almeida Langhans, Manuel Breda Simões, Antero Cochofel de Miranda Mendes, Monteiro Grillo, Patrícia Joyce, Maria João Allen de Vasconcelos, Maria de Lourdes Belchior and Natércia Freire. According to the Foundation's trustee Azeredo Perdigão, this committee represented several literary and aesthetic trends:

A Fundação organizou um Conselho de Leitura, composto por pessoas que há muito se impuseram, não só pelo valor da sua cultura, mas também pelo equilíbrio dos seus ideais, embora, como convém, para eliminar todo o risco

---

52 Alexandre Pinheiro Torres, 'Rumor Branco de Almeida Faria', *Jornal de Letras e Artes*, 30 January 1963, p. 3; Vergílio Ferreira, 'A propósito duma crítica. Vergílio Ferreira responde a Pinheiro Torres', *Jornal de Letras e Artes*, 6 February 1963, p. 4; Alexandre Pinheiro Torres, 'Alexandre Pinheiro Torres responde a Vergílio Ferreira. Na tenda de Abracadabra', *Jornal de Letras e Artes*, 13 February 1963, p. 10; Vergílio Ferreira, 'Palavras Finais. Tréplica de Vergílio Ferreira', *Jornal de Letras e Artes*, 20 February 1963, p. 9.

de proselitismo literário, filosófico, social ou político, representem vários correntes ou tendências do pensamento contemporâneo.[53]

The prestige of some of these members was strengthened by literary prizes given by the SNI/SEIT and the Academia das Ciências: Natércia Freire (1947 and 1972), António Quadros (1966); Maria de Lourdes Belchior sat on two panels for the SPE prizes before joining this Committee. This is indicative that literary prizes enhanced the symbolic capital of the consecrating agents and this, in turn, enhanced the recognition and prestige of the literary works. Moreover, the fact that the committee included individuals whose literary prestige was legitimized by Salazar and the SPE suggests that the Gulbenkian's stance endeavoured to combine innovative and conservative values in order to avoid repression. This is also shown in the catalogues of the libraries. Portuguese literature was represented through the following writers: Eça de Queirós, Camilo Castelo Branco, António de Campos Jr., Aquilino Ribeiro, Domingos Monteiro, Júlio Dinis, Branquinho da Fonseca, Alexandre Herculano, Ferreira de Castro, Manuel da Fonseca, Vergílio Ferreira, Mário Braga, Sophia de Mello Breyner, José Régio, and Fernando Namora.[54] José Cardoso Pires, despite the prestige, was not represented in the catalogue until 1970, when his *Jogos de Azar* was introduced. The fact that, following Cardoso Pires's overt protest against the Foundation's endorsement of the State's decision to close the SPE in 1965, he signed a contract with Moraes Editores prohibiting the sale of his books to the Gulbenkian, could explain the omission of this writer in the Gulbenkian catalogues.

The comparison with the stocks of the SNI's mobile libraries shows that the writers who endorsed the Regime were not included in the Gulbenkian's libraries. Both libraries coincide as far as the Portuguese nineteenth-century literature is concerned but diverge in terms of the promotion of reading of writers conse-

---

53   Fundação Calouste Gulbenkian, *Relatório do presidente. 20 de Julho de 1955-31 de Dezembro de 1959*, Lisbon, FGC, 1961. Cited by Daniel Melo, *A Leitura Pública no Portugal Contemporâneo 1926-1987* (Lisbon: Imprensa de Ciências Sociais, 2004), p. 319.
54   Melo, pp. 310-1.

crated by the SPE and those whose stance opposed the Estado Novo's ideology. Nevertheless, it is relevant that despite this, some of Eça de Queirós's works that were not included in the SNI's catalogues were also absent from those of Gulbenkian: Eça was only represented through *Os Maias*, *O Primo Basílio* and *A Capital*; works such as *O Crime do Padre Amaro* were neglected. Nevertheless, despite its connotations with the Regime, the Gulbenkian covered the gap left open by the Government's promotion of contemporary literature and enlarged the size of readership more effectively. Simultaneously, this Foundation also served the State's interests as far as becoming a more economical way to carry out a structured cultural policy. It is in these terms, that the link between both institutions should be understood.

The Government did not carry out any surveys on the reading of the books offered by the SNI mobile libraries. However, regular surveys organized by the Gulbenkian show that between 1958 and 1974, readers of its libraries were essentially young people: children (42.7 per cent), teenagers (36.6 per cent) and adults (20.7 per cent).[55] In 1962, the preferred writers were Júlio Dinis, Trindade Coelho, Camilo Castelo Branco and Alexandre Herculano. Aquilino Ribeiro was essentially read by children (*O Romance da Raposa*) whilst other writers (such as Jaime Cortesão and António Sérgio) were essentially read by teenagers on topics related to Portuguese history (*Crónica do Condestável de Portugal* and *História Trágico-Marítima*). In 1971, another survey showed slight changes: teenagers (48 per cent) and adults (45.6 per cent) read Júlio Dinis, Camilo Castelo Branco and Eça de Queirós. Fernando Namora, Ferreira de Castro, Alves Redol, Miguel Torga and Urbano Tavares Rodrigues were especially read by adults. The segmentation of adult readers according to professions shows interesting aspects: teachers read Fernando Namora, José Régio, Aquilino Ribeiro and Alves Redol; public servants read Fernando Namora, Ferreira de Castro, Domingos Monteiro and Branquinho da Fonseca; clerks read Fernando Namora, Ferreira de Castro, Aquilino Ribeiro, and Alves Redol; housewives and seamstresses preferred Fernanda de

---

55 *Boletim Cultural [do SBIF-FCG]*, série VII, no.5 (December 1991), p. 75. Cited in Melo, p. 343.

Castro, Sarah Beirão and António Campos Júnior.[56] These findings show that the least qualified workers preferred to read works that did not deal with social problems and they were also readers of writers whose work was consecrated by the Regime, whereas the highest qualified workers showed reading preferences that included writers taking critical stances against the Regime. Furthermore, these data also show the effect of the educational system as an instance of consecration and legitimacy. As Jacques Dubois pointed out:

> Cet ensemble de norms fonctionnelles est singulièrement manifesté et concretisé par cet instrument de l'école qu'est le manuel de littérature. Sous sa forme traditionnelle, ce manuel est le conservatoire ou le musée; il transmet l'heritage; il établit les découpages et les categories.[57]

Basic instruction dictated reading habits and preferences and this was only modified by higher studies and higher professional qualifications: students and less qualified individuals were the most vulnerable targets of the Regime's educational and cultural policies.

Reading preferences of the Portuguese in the 1960s and early 1970s show that the struggles for legitimacy and symbolic capital were fundamentally developed within the framework of the restricted field of literary production and that their impact on readership was constrained by the Government's cultural policy. Literary prestige was set up on the basis of the relations that the agents of production established and on their assertions of autonomy in relation to the Regime: literary prizes, panels, overt stances and their connections with various institutions. The fact that José Rodrigues Miguéis, Vergílio Ferreira and José Cardoso Pires were consecrated writers did not place them in the top ten of Portuguese readers' preferences. The relations established in the literary field contributed to this: especially those between the institutions that gave literary prizes, the Portuguese educational system and social

---

56   José Tengarrinha, *A Novela e o Leitor Português. Estudo de Sociologia da Leitura* (Lisbon: Prelo Editora, 1973). Cited in Melo, pp. 189-95.

57   Jacques Dubois, *L'institution de la littérature* (Brussels: Editions Labor/Ferdinand Nathan, 1986), p. 100.

conditions did not encourage mass reading, especially of writers who did not support the Estado Novo. The fact that the Portuguese book trade faced several obstacles to its national and international expansion also played a part in the constraints of the Portuguese reading preferences.

As far as opposition to the Regime is concerned, and the organization of literary prizes shows it, autonomy was not totally achieved. Certain compromises were vital for the maintenance of institutions that competed in terms of literary consecration and diluted their effective domination of the literary field. Nevertheless, symbolic capital of the agents of literary production that opposed the Regime was enhanced, with public exposure and some commercial success. This goes against what Bourdieu identified as the struggle between the autonomous principle, more concerned with art for art's sake, and the heteronymous principle, favourable to those who dominate the field politically and economically and, thus, with greater commercial success.[58] Symbolic capital was also strengthened by permanent panels and a relatively small group of prizewinners, which favoured the legitimacy of new aesthetic and literary works regularly produced by the same writers. The fact that some of them were consecrated by the SPE, the SNI and the Academia das Ciências is also relevant in terms of their prestige, albeit it constrained its acceptance among these instances of legitimacy.

Furthermore, it is also relevant that struggles for literary legitimacy and the influence of politics and the economy over the literary field introduced decisive developments into Portuguese fiction. Several factors competed in the shaping of fiction, and the novel genre in particular: it was more exposed to the public through literary critique involving the most prestigious literary specialists; fiction was rewarded with the most generous prizes; it was also under the close attention of censors and writers were thus encouraged to develop new literary representations, able to delude the committees which constrained wide readership, partly impaired by illiteracy and, thus, enhanced the prestige of Portuguese fiction; the stability of panels encouraged the valuing decisions over

---

58   Bourdieu, pp. 40-3.

certain literary works and the fact that members of these panels were overtly considered the ablest to value other literary genres.

In view of the fact that publishing and writing were viewed by their producers as part of an educational mission, I have also established that it is possible to differentiate publishing houses as far as ideological stances are concerned. Certain publishing houses, such as Presença and Salamandra, did not publish a single work rewarded by the Regime, whereas others, such as Parceria António Maria Pereira, did not publish a work rewarded by the SPE and regularly published SNI and Ricardo Malheiros prizewinning works. The fact that publishing was not essentially managed as business had consequences for their positioning in the Portuguese book trade as the Regime degenerated. A significant number of publishing houses, including Parceria António Maria Pereira, Livraria Tavares Martins, Europa, Império and Gama which supported the Estado Novo were unable to survive after 1974. Certain publishing houses, such as Verbo, continued business after the Revolution at the expense of exploring different market niches (reference books, school books), published series of writers who were prizewinners during the Regime and were identified as 'clássicos'. Publishing houses, such as Presença, were the ones that were able to strengthen their symbolic capital after 1974, as will be discussed in Chapter 6.

CHAPTER 5
Politics, Economy and Social Environment as Constraints on the Constitution of Readership between 1974 and 2004

This chapter sets to examine the extent to which the political, economic and social transformations between 1974 and 2004 shaped Portuguese readership and how the Governments' educational reforms influenced the Portuguese literary canon. The Revolution overthrew the Estado Novo and its institutions overnight: the President of the Republic was dismissed; the Government was exonerated; the National Assembly and the Council of State were dissolved; the PIDE and the Mocidade Portuguesa were extinguished. My aim is to establish that, despite the political, economic and social changes between 1974 and 2004, certain values supported by Salazar's Government continued to influence the Portuguese literary field, and particularly consecration and Portuguese readership during the period mentioned above.

Statistics show that Portuguese public expenditure on education more than doubled after the Revolution: in 1970, it corresponded to 1.5 per cent of the GNP, and it rose to 3.8 per cent in 1980 and again to 4.3 in 1990. Only in 1990 did it become closer to the average spends of other European countries. This was mainly due to the fact that public expenditure on education decreased or levelled off in those countries until the 1990s: according to the UNESCO statistics, the United Kingdom's public expenditure corresponded to 5.3 per cent in 1970 and to 4.9 per cent in 1990; Finland's public expenditure was 5.9 per cent in 1970 and 5.7 per cent in 1990. As far as other southern European countries are concerned, only Italy decreased its expenditure (as a percentage of the GNP) slightly: it was 3.7 per cent in 1970 and 3.2 per cent in 1990; in France, expenditure as a percentage of the GNP went from 4.8 per cent in 1970, to 5 per cent in 1980 and to 5.4 per cent in 1990; in

Spain it was 2 per cent in 1970, 2.3 per cent in 1980 and 4.4 per cent in 1990.[1] The significant increase in Portugal did not correspond to substantial changes in the way education was practiced.

According to Jacques Dubois's study on the Literary Institution, schools adjust literary interpretation to pre-defined established relations and categories.[2] Reforms in Portuguese education after 1974 denote that school curricula on the subjects of Portuguese language, literature and history continued to be oriented according to political values. Portuguese secondary education went through critical structural changes which aimed to dismantle the Estado Novo school structure. In 1975, the 'escolas técnicas' and 'liceus' were merged into secondary education. In 1977, the 'Serviço Cívico' was discontinued and replaced by the 'Ano Propedêutico' which was renamed 12th Grade in 1981. In 1986, the Lei de Bases do Sistema Educativo determined nine-years of compulsory schooling, divided into primary education (four years), and a two-cycle secondary education (three+ three years); the 12th Grade targeted those who wanted to go on to study at university.

The Portuguese school curriculum was repeatedly revised in 1978, in 1991 and 1997, and literary texts which were compulsory reading in the disciplines of Portuguese language and literature at secondary schools also altered. Although the Governments after 1974 swept away the Estado Novo's ideology from the Portuguese Language and Literature curriculum in primary and secondary education (such as texts on the value of the family, the nation, and on Salazar), the changes introduced in 1978 were not drastic. As regards secondary education, the study of Portuguese literature was organized according to literary periodization. Teachers taught a selection of texts and writers (chosen by the Ministry of Education) which were introduced to pupils as the most relevant examples of the Middle Ages, the Classical Age, Romanticism, Modernism and Neo-Realism. Carlos Ceia stated in his paper on the

1   Data available in UNESCO Statistics, Table D 'Public Expenditure on Education as A Whole',
     www.tfhe.net/report/downloads/Table%20D.pdf [Accessed May 2007]
2   Jacques Dubois, *L'institution de la littérature* (Brussels: Editions Labor / Ferdinand Nathan, 1986), p. 100.

practice of Portuguese literature teaching that, between 1974 and 1991, the discipline of Portuguese Language (and Literature) was taught as a 'disciplina *nacional* de conteúdos essencialmente historiográficos, com a exigência de promover o gosto e a competência de leitura das nossas obras literárias máximas'.[3] The methodological objectives were defined on the assumption that text reading was diachronical and, thus, it contributed to a 'desenvolvimento integral da personalidade'.[4] This indication was not too far from that before 1974. The aims of learning literature in secondary education in 1978 illustrate what Dubois wrote about oriented interpretation according to pre-defined categories and in Portugal, these were essentially organized to shape the individual's mind. Teachers encouraged reading habits in Portugal after 1974 within the framework of an historical approach with traces of the Republican propaganda which had influenced the Estado Novo's ideology: literary texts and writers were used as cultural symbols whose study envisaged the construction of national identity ('visão diacrónica do fenómeno literário português').[5]

---

3   Carlos Ceia, 'A Resistência ao Ensino da História Portuguesa' <http://www.fcsh.unl.pt/docentes/cceia/Educacao/ensino_hist_literaria.pdf> [Accessed in November 2007]. Author's italics.

4   SEEBS, 20th August 1979. Cited in Paulo Jaime Lampreia Costa, 'A Construção do Cânone Literário Escolar: Uma Análise de Textos Programáticos para o Ensino Secundário' (Unpublished Thesis, University of Évora, 1997), p. 107. Portuguese literature was taught in an historicist perspective, in which the teacher was 'um apresentador de notícias sobre factos literários passados' (Ceia, 'A Resistência ao Ensino da História Portuguesa'). The revised editions and reprints of António Saraiva's and Óscar Lopes's *História da Literatura Portuguesa* (Porto: Porto Editora) are indicative of the importance of literary history in the teaching of Portuguese literature between 1974 and 2000: between 1955 and 1973, it had seven revised editions; subsequent ones were: 8th (1975); 9th (1976); 10th (1978); 11th (1979); 12th (1982); and 13th (1985) in 1987; 14th (1987); by 2000, seventeen revised editions had been printed.

5   Lampreia Costa, p. 107. A comparison with the British secondary education is expressive of the oriented objectives of the Portuguese secondary education as the study of national language and literature are concerned. The IGCSE (International General Certificate of Secondary Education has been designed for 14 to 16-year-old students and is provided by the University of Cambridge International Examinations Board. It offers a broad programme

In 1991, students of secondary school level studied an array of classical and contemporary texts of the following literary forms: narrative ('narrativo'), poetry ('poesia lírica e satírica'), drama ('texto dramático') and argumentative text ('texto argumentativo'). This revision was carried out at the end of the Eleventh Constitutional Government (1987/1991). The new organization of the curriculum of Portuguese literature in secondary education divided the study of writers: the 10th Grade essentially focussed on fourteenth and fifteenth-century texts; the 11th Grade was primarily focussed on the writers who lived between the sixteenth and nineteenth centuries; and the 12th Grade approached nineteenth and twentieth-century writers, although it also included the study of part of Camões's *Os Lusíadas*. This curriculum was very extensive and reinstated texts that had been removed in 1978. It was particularly clear in the 11th Grade, especially in the study of Portuguese poetry. Like in 1978, contemporary writers were mostly studied in the 12th Grade.[6]

The writers studied at secondary education were Fernão Lopes, Bernardim Ribeiro, Fernão Mendes Pinto, Camões, António Ferreira, Alexandre Herculano, Almeida Garrett, Camilo Castelo Branco and Eça de Queirós. It is worthy of mention that Eça de Queirós's *Uma Campanha Alegre* was compulsory reading within the selection of argumentative texts in the 12th Grade in 1991 and in the 11th Grade in 1997.[7] In 1978 and in 1991, *Os Maias* and *A Ilus-*

---

of study including English Language and Literature whose aims were centered in the development of personal response to literary text: English Literature: 'You will be able to demonstrate an appreciation of texts and themes from a straightforward knowledge of content to an informed personal response'; First Language English: 'you will experience a wide variety of reading and writing opportunities to enhance your ability to understand and explain the meaning of texts and appreciate how writers achieve effects.' Quoted from <http://www.eisp.cz/upload/files/IGCSEs_ 1194599520. pdf> [Acessed in November 2007].

6   Canon revisions in 1954, 1979 and in the 1990s discussed in Carlos Ceia, 'A Questão do Cânone Literário: Da Teoria aos Programas Escolares', <http:// www.ciberkiosk.pt/arquivo/ciberkiosk2/debate/cannica.html> [accessed in October 2004].

7   *Uma Campanha Alegre*, included in *As Farpas*, is one of Queirós's texts on social criticism of principles which the State believed were unassailable before 1974: family, authority and Catholicism.

tre Casa de Ramires were two options for reading one work by Eça de Queirós's novel in the 12th Grade.[8] Between 1978 and 1997, contemporary Portuguese writers were introduced in the Ano Propedêutico/ 12th Grade: in 1978, Carlos de Oliveira and Soeiro Pereira Gomes as representatives of Portuguese Neo-Realism; in 1991, Agustina Bessa Luís (*A Sibila*), José Saramago (*Memorial do Convento*), Vitorino Nemésio (*Mau Tempo no Canal*) and Vergílio Ferreira (*Aparição*), were introduced to pupils as representatives of Portuguese contemporary narrative; no new contemporary novelist was introduced in 1997 and only Luís de Sttau Monteiro, Florbela Espanca, António Ramos Rosa and Eugénio de Andrade refreshed the study of Portuguese drama and poetry.

These changes show that literary consecration was a slow process; the study of these writers was addressed to those students who, in principle, wanted to complete their higher education. This approach also suggests that, despite their literary consecration, they were not to be considered the basis of literary education and, therefore, not to be studied in the early years of secondary education. Learning Portuguese literature during the 10th and 11th Grades was fundamentally based on texts produced until the nineteenth-century.

The study of Fernando Pessoa's works is of relevance to the understanding of Portuguese literary consecration between 1974 and the 1997. During the Estado Novo, *Mensagem* (Antero de Quental Prizewinner in 1934) was studied at secondary schools in the early 1950s, and its interpretation was oriented towards the affirmation of nationalist values. Apart from this work, Pessoa's literary production was ignored in public education until 1974, despite the fact that Luís de Montalvor and João Gaspar Simões started to publish Pessoa's works with Ática in 1943. His heteronyms as representatives of Portuguese Modernism were introduced in the 11th and 12th Grades in 1979. In the late 1970s and early 1980s, Fernando Pessoa was also used in the political debate as a cultural icon of the modern country. Making his various

---

8   This reference to *As Farpas* is included in António José Saraiva and Óscar Lopes, *História da Literatura Portuguesa*, 14th edn (Porto: Porto Editora, 1987), p. 927.

works compulsory reading at secondary school level after 1974 introduced a difference in the study of Pessoa between the approach during the Estado Novo and that after 1974.

Saramago and Fernando Pessoa were both included in the curricula of Portuguese literature in different periods of Portuguese history and share a common characteristic: both writers were compulsory reading in secondary education, despite not being particularly favoured by the Governments that decided on their consecration.[9] Nevertheless, the majority of the students who attended secondary schools, in the late 1970s and in the 1980s, studied Camões (*Os Lusíadas*), Bernardim Ribeiro (*Menina e Moça*), Alexandre Herculano (*Eurico, o Presbítero*), Almeida Garrett (*Frei Luís de Sousa*)and Camilo Castelo Branco (*Amor de Perdição*).Despite the fact that the texts were fundamentally the same, the approach to their reading differed drastically as pointed out by Carlos Ceia. He collaborated with the Ministry of Education in restructuring school texts for secondary education in 1995 and has stated:

> É preciso esperar por 1978, para que a reforma educativa então desencadeada prescreva claramente que o Estado não tem o direito de intervir nos conteúdos da educação e da cultura em nome de qualquer ideologia.[10]

Nevertheless, the political and social environment influenced teaching practices and literary consecration in many ways. In addition, the fact that, in the period immediately after 1974, the Provisional Governments promoted Marxist-based principles in cultural practices, which becomes relevant to discuss the failure to carry out a real cultural revolution in Portugal.

In 1974, when the Junta de Salvação Nacional was set up, its public commitment included promoting culture and education with the purpose of strengthening individual political awareness and participation:

> 8. Política educativa, cultural e de investigação
> Mobilização de esforços para a erradicação do analfabetismo e promoção da cultura, nomeadamente nos meios rurais.

---

9   I discuss Saramago's literary consecration in Portugal in Chapter 7.
10   'A Questão do Cânone Literário: Da Teoria aos Programas Escolares'

Desenvolvimento da reforma educativa, tendo em conta o papel da educação na criação de uma consciência nacional genuinamente democrática, e a
necessidade da inserção da escola na problemática da sociedade portuguesa.
[...]
h) Fomento das actividades culturais e artísticas, designadamente da literatura, teatro, cinema, música e artes plásticas, e ainda dos meios de comunicação social, como veículos indispensáveis ao desenvolvimento da cultura
do Povo.[11]

This programme laid down the foundation of a wide-ranging concept of the culture of the people ('cultura do povo') planned during the Third and Fourth Provisional Governments. During the
Third Provisional Government, General Costa Gomes set up the 5ª
Divisão whose structure was adapted from the North-American
Army's campaign during the Second World War. The major
purpose of 5ª Divisão was 'cumprir integralmente o programa do
MFA e colocar as Forças Armadas ao serviço de um projecto de
desenvolvimento do Povo Português" and was in charge of
'proceder a estudos e formulação de doutrina, organizar consultas,
colóquios e debates sobre assuntos de natureza sociomilitar'.[12]
These campaigns, known as Campanhas para a Dinamização Cultural, included sessions with the population, in particular those
living in rural areas, in order to explain the revolutionary process.
Short plays were staged and the local inhabitants could scrutinize
the military on their actions.

The commitment of Portuguese intellectuals with the ideals
emanating from the Revolution was encouraged by the Government and the President of the Republic immediately after the coup
d'état.[13] The 5ª Divisão aimed to discuss culture as 'uma revisão

---

11 *Diário do Governo*, No.113/74., I, 15 May 1974. Programme of the First
    Provisional Government: Decree-Law No.203/74 of 15 May.
12 See José Mattoso, ed., *História de Portugal*, 8 vols (Lisbon: Editorial Estampa,
    1994), VIII: Portugal em Transe (1974-1985), 'As Forças Armadas e o poder
    político', pp. 180-6 (p. 183).
13 The MFA programme approved of in 1974 declared: 'É dentro do âmbito de
    uma Revolução Cultural, pela aplicação das potencialidades militares e civis,
    nos campos técnico, humano e material que se mobilizará decisivamente o
    Povo para a Revolução. A prática começa a demonstrar este raciocínio, aliás

das obras executadas durante o fascismo'. The Campanhas should be oriented towards a 'mentalização política' and 'uma acção cívica de ajuda real à população'. In 1993, Eduarda Dionisio stated that those campaigns illustrated 'o conceito de cultura que se punha em causa, a actuação do centro para a periferia, de cima para baixo'.[14] In fact, those campaigns included cultural initiatives that ranged from sports, amateur drama, popular films during the Estado Novo (for example, 'A Canção de Lisboa') to concerts performed by the Gulbenkian orchestra. Books and magazines kept in municipal libraries were destroyed at the instructions of the Secretary of State for Education and Culture, Rui Grácio.[15]

There was, however, a conceptual difference between cultural revolution as understood by the MFA and the working class coordinated by Communist-oriented trade unions, and that supported by intellectuals who believed that cultural revolution implied a transformation of mentality beyond the organization of cultural events for the people.[16] José-Augusto França, essayist and editor of

---

óbvio'. Quoted from 'Projecto Povo-MFA', in *Conselhos Revolucionários Projecto Povo-MFA*. (Lisbon: Edições Revolução, [n.d.]), p. 30.

14   The Portuguese expressions and examples are cited in Eduarda Dionísio, *Títulos, Acções, Obrigações – A Cultura em Portugal, 1974-1994* (Lisbon: Edições Salamandra, 1993), pp. 184-5 and p. 202.

15   'Tendo sido informado de que nas bibliotecas dos estabelecimentos de Ensino existe quantidade apreciável de livros e revistas de índole fascista, determino que seja elaborada uma circular ordenando a destruição das publicações com esse carácter, depois de arquivados um exemplar, pelo menos, de cada revista, e alguns livros a seleccionar, que fiquem como documento ou testemunho de um regime' (17 October 1974), quoted in F.A Gonçalves Ferreira, ed., *15 Anos de História Recente de Portugal (1970-1984)* (Lisbon, 1985), p. 635. The Minister of Education and Culture disagreed with this decision and resigned. This is expressive of the lack of coordination of the cultural policy immediately after the Revolution.

16   The criticism of Portuguese Socialists in 1975 is also relevant of the lack of consensus of what a cultural revolution should be immediatly after the Revolution: 'Essa política [projecto democrático burguês] tem-se mantido numa ambiguidade que permite, do mesmo passo, visar os mais vastos projectos e reformar da forma mais inócua. Assim é que, por um lado, se lançou, com acentuada impreparação, campanhas maximilizantes (das 'campanhas de alfabetização' às campanhas de 'dinamização cultural' do MFA), se nomeia a própria 'revolução cultural' e por outro lado se

Colóquio-Artes, made that clear in 1975, when he defined that a cultural revolution was not to be based on popular initiatives led by the Government:

> A transformação da ordem social não pode deixar de ser também transformação na ordem cultural – e esta não reside, certamente, na ideia simples e simplista de levar a cultura ao povo, ou mesmo e mais dificilmente, o povo à cultura. A estes dois princípios tranquilizantes e paternalistas (que pensam a cultura em termos de elevador...) há que opor uma nova condição humanística da cultura, sempre de responsabilidade humanística.[17]

In balance, the Campanhas para a Dinamização Cultural lacked a structured project and were mostly used to promote the MFA and enhanced political legitimacy of the Provisional Governments. They were discontinued during the V Government (1975) As the MFA came under the increasing influence of the PCP (particularly with the III and IV Provisional Governments, 1974-1975), there were two initiatives of the Processo Revolucionário em Curso (PREC) that had an impact on national identity because they were based on the rejection of the social and economic structures implemented by Salazar: the Agrarian Reform and state control over the most important companies. The Agrarian Reform was implemented at the beginning of 1975 and mostly involved seizures of uncultivated land in the areas of the Alentejo and in the rural areas around Santarém and Setúbal. The Fourth Provisional Government (1975) encouraged this movement and cooperatives were set up under the centralized control and management of the Communist-dominated unions. After the 25 November 1975, seizures were repressed, although housing struggles and occupation of empty

---

introduzem, a nível legislativo, tímidos arranjos" [...] Lisbon vai à província ensinar, no pressuposto idealista que pouco tem de aprender e que a falada 'cultura do povo' é mais folclore que outra coisa. [...] O resultado foi o caos, ou projectos reformistas ou interclassistas, como as famosas campanhas, que ainda agora redundam em mascarada, a encobrir outros objectivos e tentativas de ditatorialismo culturista-partidário sem real projecto revolucionário'. Cited in Eduarda Dionísio, *Títulos, Acções, Obrigações – A Cultura em Portugal, 1974-1994* (Lisbon: Edições Salamandra, 1993), p. 185.

17   José-Augusto França, 'Sobre cultura e política cultural', in *Memórias da Academia das Ciências de Lisboa* (Classe de Letras, Vol.XVII, Lisbon, 1976), p. 345.

property broke out spontaneously in the poor neighbourhoods of Lisbon, Setúbal and Porto.[18] These events were enough to warrant the Government's accusations of serious infringements of the established order. Nevertheless, these were spontaneous and non-organized popular movements against what participants considered forms of capitalism.

The PCP was especially interested in controlling the political, economic and ideological fields, and in particular, getting control of public information. Between 1974 and 1976, *A Capital, República,* and *O Dia* were some of the few, when most other newspapers were under Communist control. The Provisional Governments (1974-1976), and the PCP in particular, were more interested in establishing positions of power and influence within the social order, than in actually leading the revolutionary process and this enraged some of the radical supporters of the Revolution. The fact that this party gained only 12.5 per cent in the election for the Constituent Assembly on 25 April 1975 indicated the population's lack of support and the people's disappointment with the PREC:

Diria mais tarde o tenente-coronel Arnão Metelo, um dos líderes máximos do 'Directório de Esquerda Militar': "O que se entende por área militar afecta ao PCP não era uma coisa claramente definida. Formávamos um grupo que, inclusivamente, era mais radical que o próprio PCP, partido disciplinado, que seguia as directivas elaboradas e estudadas pelo Comité Central; mas nós que éramos, em geral, bastante românticos, não tínhamos essa característica. O problema dos militares de esquerda com o PCP foi complicado porque todos éramos bastante diferentes nas ideias e objectivos e, inclusivamente diferenciávamo-nos por sermos da Armada, do Exército, etc. Algumas vezes reagíamos mal perante um determinado espírito de funcionalismo e de centralismo democrático que encontrávamos nalguns militares e isso não me agradava porque pressentia aí um certo controlo de máquina extramilitar.[19]

---

18   On 25th November 1975, a military coup (headed by Vasco Lourenço, Ramalho Eanes and Jaime Neves) defeated the radical left-wing military who had started the revolutionary process in 1974. Thus, some military members such as Otelo Saraiva de Carvalho resigned, although the Prime Minister of the VI Provisional Government continued in office.

19   Josep Sanchez Cervelló. ' O 25 de Novembro ', in *História de Portugal*, ed. by João Medina, 15 vols, (Lisbon: Ediclube, 1998), XIV, pp. 87-132 (p. 88).

Heterogeneous stances and over-enthusiasm following the Revolution were based on systematic questioning of the Estado Novo's values. Hayden White, in his study on national identity, pointed out that in times of sociocultural stress, when the need for positive self-definition asserts itself and there are no criteria of self-identification, it can emerge by negation.[20] Between 1974 and 1976 debates at the Assembly defined 'traditional values' as the basis of Portuguese cultural identity. In 1974, Mário Soares, as Prime Minister of the First Constitutional Government, resumed that expression used by Salazar but redefined it against the Estado Novo's ideology.[21] According to José Mattoso, redefining values in the years immediately after the Revolution was centred in the 'descolonização exemplar', in the 'mitificação da classe operária', and in the concept of 'internacionalismo proletário'.[22]

The debate on national identity was not only led by politicians: intellectuals, such as Eduardo Lourenço, José Fernandes Fafe, Agostinho da Silva and Manuel Antunes, participated in it actively, particularly in the first decade after 1974.[23] The absence of a consensual Portuguese post-Revolution cultural identity was suggested by Eduardo Lourenço in 1978:

---

20 See Hayden White, 'The Forms of Wildness', in *Tropics of Discourse – Essays in Cultural Criticism* (Baltimore and London: The Johns Hopkins University Press, 1985), pp. 150-182 (pp. 151-2).

21 'Há que reabilitar igualmente os valores nacionais e a cultura portuguesa. Não poderá ter um futuro democrático um país que não for capaz de honrar e dignificar os seus valores tradicionais, de respeitar as suas obras de arte e de cultura, de valorizar sem preconceitos ideológicos os seus centros de investigação científica. Ao tempo da propaganda obsediante e pseudocultural, ao serviço de um certo totalitarismo ideológico, tem de suceder a reintrodução crítica, serena, e livre dos valores caracteristicamente portugueses'. Cited in Dionísio, p. 282. Dionísio stated that 'A ideia de 'consenso nacional' vai substituindo a de 'unidade', o que parece acontecer com mais facilidade e mais rapidamente na Cultura'. See p. 306.

22 Mattoso, 'A Evolução da Sociedade Portuguesa', pp. 113-59 (p. 139).

23 See, among other works of these writers, Eduardo Lourenço, *Labirinto da Saudade; Psicanálise Mítica do Destino Português (1978)* (Lisbon: Dom Quixote, 1992); Manuel Antunes, *Repensar Portugal* (Lisbon: Multinova, [n.d.]); Agostinho da Silva, *Educação de Portugal* (Lisbon: Ulmeiro, 1989); José Fernandes Fafe, *Nação: fim ou metamorfose* (Lisbon: Imprensa Nacional Casa da Moeda, 1990).

Após essa fase, devíamos ter encontrado num projecto nacional de vocação socialista realmente popular pela sua consubstanciação com os interesses vitais da comunidade daquilo que se perdera jogando num extremismo ideológico sem raízes fundas na tradição portuguesa, em suma, um sentido à altura de uma Nação carregada de recordações grandiosas e cicatrizes cruéis. Faltou-nos imaginação.[24]

Lourenço pointed out that 25 April 1974 did not produce a debate of the Portuguese cultural identity that revised the conceptual definition of the Portuguese Nation as it had been established by the Estado Novo. In 1979, Manuel Antunes had a similar opinion and wrote that in the years that followed the Revolution, there had been too much idealism, and that national identity implied a serious and committed nationwide debate.[25] Fernandes Fafe discussed national identity relating it to the consequences of Portugal's joining the European Economic Community (EEC) and, in his works, Agostinho da Silva argued that Portugal should retain its spiritual mission, within the framework of its historical and cultural bonds with the Portuguese-speaking countries.[26] However, according to Nuno Monteiro and António Costa Pinto who discussed Portuguese identity in 2005, there was not a real crisis of Portuguese national identity after 1974 because joining the EC (1986), standing as a reference of social and economic development, emerged as a consequence of decolonization and the establishment of democracy.[27] The long process of joining it was presented by the Socialist and the right-wing parties, within the framework of the political

---

24   Lourenço, 'Psicanálise Mítica Do Destino Português', in *Labirinto da Saudade; Psicanálise Mítica do Destino Português*, pp. 23-66 (p. 63). Similar ideas were also expanded in his *O Fascismo Nunca Existiu* (Lisbon: Dom Quixote, 1976).
25   Antunes, p. 24.
26   In 1984, writers, including Sophia de Melo Breyner, Maria Teresa Horta and Vergílio Ferreira, surveyed on the long-term effects of the Revolution also expressed a cultural void and the collective inability to process revolutionary events into a nationwide effort to rethink Portuguese culture. See *Colóquio Letras, Dez Anos de Literatura Portuguesa 1974-1984*, 78 (March 1984); *Diário de Notícias*, 19 April 1984, pp. 14-5; *Diário de Notícias*, 24 April 1984, pp. 110-1; *Expresso Revista*, 23 April 1984.
27   Nuno G. Monteiro and António Costa Pinto, 'A Identidade Nacional Portuguesa', in *Portugal Contemporâneo*, ed. by António Costa Pinto (Lisbon: Dom Quixote, 2005), pp. 51-65 (pp. 62-63).

debate, as an essential step to consolidate domestic democracy and modernize the Portuguese economy.[28] As far as the literary field is concerned, and as shown in António Sousa Ribeiro's study in 1993, the 25 April did not bring Portuguese writers reassurances about their social role and, in the period 1974-1976, it made them focus on exacerbated national pride.[29]

The celebrations of the 10 June are also significant in discussions of national identity between 1974 and 2004. During the Estado Novo, the 10 June was called Dia da Raça but it was renamed Dia de Camões in 1974. Until 1976, this day was mostly celebrated by Portuguese intellectuals. The 25 April was made a public holiday and called Dia de Portugal but in 1978, it was renamed Dia da Liberdade and the 10 June was renamed Dia de Camões, Portugal e das Comunidades. These holidays became culturally and politically relevant because the arrangements conveyed how the political parties in power and opposition used them to mark their positions in the cultural debate, especially as far as literary consecration was concerned.[30] Jorge de Sena's speech in Guarda on the 10 June 1977 expressed the frustration of Portuguese writers (not openly speaking on their behalf, though). He used Camões as a symbol of the Portuguese writer as someone ahead of his time and deeply disappointed, physically and morally expatriated due to the lack of tolerance and national pride.[31] Fur-

---

28 See Aúrea Sampaio, 'Os três Governos de Cavaco Silva e a mudança de ciclo', in *História de Portugal*, ed. by João Medina, 15 vols (Lisbon: Ediclube, 1998), XIV, pp. 379-94.

29 'A relação entre o escrtor e a sociedade mantém-se, neste aspecto, marcada por descoincidências várias e pela correlativa dificuldade em encontrar a identidade dada por uma função social'. Quoted from António Sousa Ribeiro, 'Configurações do Campo Intelectual Português no Pós-25 de Abril: O Campo Literário', in *Portugal: Um Retrato Singular*, ed. by Boaventura de Sousa Santos (Lisbon: Edições Afrontamento, 1993), pp. 483-512, (498).

30 'Trata-se de demonstrar que a esquerda ama mais a Cultura e a Pátria do que a direita. Por esta via, Camões regressa ao 10 de Junho, Dia de Portugal'. Cited in Dionísio, p. 384.

31 'Ninguém como Camões nos representa a todos, repito, e em particular os emigrantes, um dos quais ele foi por muitos anos, e os exilados, outro dos quais ele foi a vida inteira, mesmo na própria Pátria, sonhando sempre com

thermore, General Ramalho Eanes's speech on that day also appealed to the consolidation of a nationwide cultural, political, and social project which could overcome long-standing problems which delayed the making of the Revolution.[32]

It was on the 10 June that the President of the Republic rewarded Portuguese personalities, including writers, and those honours were indicative of the relationships established between the political and the literary establishments. I will clarify those relations in Chapter 6.

The decisions taken by the Constitutional Governments between 1985 and 2000 influenced the transformations that occurred in the cultural field following the revolutionary years. When Cavaco Silva was sworn into office in 1985, he promised to raise the morale of the population in view of the fact that there were several economic ills that his Government had to tackle:

> Não têm fundamento sério as teses miserabilistas que ignoram as nossas realizações, subestimam as capacidades do nosso povo, que condenam à inferioridade o povo português.[33]

Decisions taken in this period show that the approach to culture was essentially directed towards the importance of Portuguese history, and the creation of cultural equipment. Governments supported cultural and artistic manifestations and preserved national heritage. Historical centres, such as Loulé, Nisa, Tomar and Vila Real, were restored, museums, libraries and cultural centres, such as the Centro Cultural de Belém, were set up and monuments were rebuilt. The Lisbon/94 celebrations and the work of the Commission for the Discoveries defined cultural identity in asso-

---

um mundo melhor, para si mesmo que para todos os outros.',Cited in Gilda Santos. *Jorge de Sena e Camões: um diálogo*. Inédito.

32 Marcelo Rebelo de Sousa, 'O Sebastianismo, a doença infantil do semipresente', *Expresso*, 18 June 1977, p. 2.

33 Cavaco Silva's speech at the swearing-in ceremony for the Eleventh Government. Cited in Aúrea Sampaio, "Os três Governos de Cavaco Silva e a mudança de ciclo", in *História de Portugal*, ed. by João Medina, 15 vols, (Lisbon: Ediclube, 1998), XIV ed. by João Medina, 15 vols (Lisbon: Ediclube, 1998), XIV, pp. 379-94, (p. 380).

ciation with tradition.[34] The Governmental aids to Portuguese culture were mainly subsidies and placing orders for cultural production. In 1986, the Lei do Mecenato offered tax benefits to those entrepreneurs who sponsored cultural production and the Secretary of State for Culture announced it within the framework of 'patrocínio particular e empresarial' as 'fonte de dinamismo cultural'. It is noteworthy that, in the Secretary of State's words, the State should economize its expenditure on culture in order to guarantee 'a formação da liberdade'. The objective was to transfer part of the responsibility of cultural promotion to private enterprises, which does not imply that the Government did not continue to control culture (understood as a representation of national values), as regards major events (for example, at Europália in 1991 and Seville Exhibition in 1992).[35] Therefore, the expression 'formação da liberdade' should not be taken in absolute terms.

Economic priorities prevailed over cultural activities at the end of the 1980s and early 1990s. Several professions associated to culture emerged, examples being cultural managers, travel agents specializing in cultural conferences, consultants.[36] After 1974, books became widely available to the public, and points of sale included supermarkets, hypermarkets and bookstores.[37] The number of publishing houses boomed immediately after the Revolution and, despite falling in the 1980s, they increased in the 1990s.[38]

---

34 Dramatization of historical events, such as the Bartolomeu Dias's reaching South Africa and D.Manuel's embassy to the Pope at 1992 Seville Exhibition, shows the priority given to Portuguese History; the Rede Nacional de Bibliotecas, set up in 1986, illustrates the priority given to the establishment of infra-structure. The Government defined the objectives of Lisbon/94 as 'promover a imagem de Lisboa como cidade cultural e posicioná-la no contexto europeu' and planned to show the Fado, working-class Lisboners and to celebrate the twentieth anniversary of democracy. Cited in *Público*, 12 May 1993, p. 5.
35 Dionísio, p. 358
36 Dionísio, p. 361.
37 See António Lobato Faria's interview in Appendix 2 on pp. 349.
38 In 1976, there were 1,276 publishing houses; in 1977 there was a slight rise to 1,308 only to fall to 1,219 in 1978 and again to 1,050 in 1979. The tendency was downward during the 1980s and only recovered in 1991, rising from 565, in 1990, to 673. Cited in Dionísio, p. 481.

The wide public access to books conveyed the idea of democratization of cultural production. At the same time, in the 1980s and, especially in the 1990s, publishing houses took advantage of the expansion of media and invested in the promotion of books. Book advertising on television benefited from considerable discounts in the 1980s. Nevertheless, in the 1990s, after the establishment of private television channels and the expansion of advertising, those discounts decreased and communication of book debuts was largely done through more direct forms of communication, such as book lists and mailings.[39] Nevertheless, and according to Jorge Martins's research on Portuguese publishing houses in 1999, marketing techniques assisted Portuguese publishers in book promotion but were almost non-existent as far as decision making was concerned. Many publishers disapproved of the importance of Marketing in the book trade because, they claimed that book purchasers would value details, such as binding and front covers, and neglect literary content.[40] Most Portuguese publishing houses were small and medium-sized between 1974 and 1999 (as they were during the Estado Novo); this fact is suggestive of a certain continuity of publishing business practices after 1974. In early 2000, publishing business showed some signs of change when the Spanish multinational Planeta took over Dom Quixote. This was the first of several takeovers in the Portuguese book business.[41]

When Mário Soares was elected President of the Republic in 1985, the Portuguese literary field was especially influenced by political instability arising from the opposition between the President and the Government. At this time and until 1995, the major political parties went through internal disputes and changes. The PCP's Committee was reshuffled when Carlos Carvalhas replaced Álvaro Cunhal as party leaders; the CDS (Centro Democrata Social) had a new leader, Manuel Monteiro, who supported the

---

39 See Zeferino's Coelho's interview in Appendix 1 on pp. 339.
40 For a study on business strategies and the importance of marketing in Portuguese publishing houses in the 1990s, see Jorge M. Martins, *Marketing do Livro: Materiais para uma sociologia do editor português* (Oeiras: Celta Editora, 1999), pp. 151-72.
41 DirectGroup Bertelsmann took over Círculo de Leitores in 2002 and Bertrand in 2006.

134

original values of Christian Democracy, causing the dismissal of the founder Freitas do Amaral and Lucas Pires who had diverted the party towards more liberal positions. The leadership of the PS was fragile after Mário Soares was elected President. Therefore, the President assumed the role of opposition and joined in protests against what he perceived to be the repressive authority of Cavaco Silva. Several writers such as Natália Correia, José Saramago and Pedro Tamen, backed the President and this made sense in view of their experience as adversaries of the Estado Novo. The political discourse of the left wing was rooted in the struggle against the Estado Novo and this was used as a common platform against the right-wing Government headed by Cavaco Silva.

The PSD Governments did not impose the trilogy God-Homeland-Family. Nevertheless, these values were claimed to be inherent to Portuguese cultural identity, especially at a time when Catholicism was losing ground to many religious sects that had begun to pervade Portuguese society. This had consequences for the consecration of some writers. A relevant example was the justification given by the Secretary of State for Culture for withdrawing *O Evangelho Segundo Jesus Cristo* from the Ariosto Prize on the basis of Portuguese Catholic values with effects on José Saramago's literary consecration, as discussed in Chapter 7. Canonicity of writers and fiction was influenced by their recognition by the Government and the President and by the stances taken by literary associations as far as this opposition was concerned.

Therefore, intellectuals, and writers in particular, who had opposed the Estado Novo, joined in protests against the Government's authority, in initiatives, such as the Frente Nacional para a Defesa da Cultura (FNDC) that opposed the Government's cultural policy, especially the Government's decision to charge a 5 per cent tax on the purchase of books and accused the Government of damaging Portuguese cultural identity by discontinuing Portuguese cultural institutions. The relationship between the President and the Government resumed part of the arguments that had opposed Salazar and adversaries in order to legitimate the power of both institutions in the 1990s. Some of the compromises made during the Estado Novo were not used in the 1990s and the fact that the President headed the opposition to the Government granted

135

some legitimacy to the opposition developed by intellectuals. Mário Soares attended lectures on Portuguese culture organized by intellectuals who had headed the struggle against the Estado Novo. This enhanced the sense of commitment led by brothers-in-arms.[42]

António Guterres was sworn in as Prime Minister in 1995 and headed the Socialist Governments that ruled until 2002 (XIII and XIV Constitutional Governments). In 1996, Jorge Sampaio was elected President of the country. The fact that the Government and the presidency were run by Socialist members was decisive in the dynamic of the literary field. In the official speeches delivered on 10 June, Sampaio urged the Portuguese, especially the youth, to value Portuguese history and cultural heritage without neglecting the fact that Portugal was a member of the European Union. Patriotism had to be reinvented within those terms.[43] The opposition between Mário Soares and Cavaco Silva had influenced the literary field as far as positions of the agents of consecration were concerned and was decisive in the relative consensus around the Government after 1995.

The constitution of the Governments elected after 1974 denoted that institutional autonomy was formally more visible during the PS Governments than during the PPD/PSD Governments. Up to the Ninth Constitutional Government (1983/1985), culture either was within the competence of the Minister of Education or subordinated to the Prime Minister directly. In the PPD/PSD Governments, Secretaries of State for Culture were appointed and

---

42   The 'Presidência Aberta'in Viana do Castelo in September 1992 included a cultural debate on Portuguese culture and Mário Soares also órganized the lectures 'Política e Cultura' at the Torre do Tombo (National Archives) in May 1992. Eugénio de Andrade, José Mattoso, Manuel da Fonseca, José Cardoso Pires were among those who participated in these events. Cited in Dionísio, pp. 410-5.

43   'Move-nos o desejo de valorização da história junto das gerações mais jovens. Sobretudo, acreditamos que a história é sempre susceptível de novos ângulos de abordagem, e que cada época acrescenta novos temas e perspectivas ao conhecimento que sobre o passado recebeu de épocas anteriores', Speech delivered on 10 June 1998. <http://jorgesampaio.arquivo. presidencia.pt/pt/noticias/noticias/discursos-42.html.> [Acessed in November 2006]

were under direct control of the Prime Minister, whereas in the PS Governments, they were subordinated to the Minister of Education.

Several State cultural and literary institutions were set up after 1974, replacing each other's competencies and suggesting an escalation of different perceptions regarding Culture. The Serviço Geral dos Assuntos Culturais was set up after the Revolution, discontinued in 1976 and replaced by the Instituto da Cultura Portuguesa (ICALP), under the supervision of the Ministry of Education and Scientific Research. Its aims include the promotion of the teaching of the Portuguese language abroad. Supervision was transferred to the Ministry of Culture in 1979. Only in 1980 was the Instituto Português do Livro (IPL) set up within a restructuring by the Secretary of State for Culture with the objectives of promoting Portuguese books and writers, under the assumption that some literary production was fundamental for Portuguese culture and that encouraging the reprints of works that represented part of the Portuguese literary heritage contributed to the cultural debate. In 1987, IPL was restructured and its competence included the coordination of a service of public reading. It was renamed the Instituto Português do Livro e da Leitura (IPLL) and was put under the supervision of the National Library. During this time, this Institute reorganized the public library service and created the National Bibliographical Database (PORBASE) that linked public libraries through a common system of bibliographical information accessed through electronic means. The IPLL supported the modernization and building of public libraries in several town halls; in some cases, IPLL aid amounted to 50 per cent of the initial investment.[44] At the beginning of the 1990s, the provision of public libraries was more focussed in the north and centre and along the coast. The inland and southern areas had fewer libraries belonging to this network system. The allocation of public libraries corresponded to the national distribution of the population. The most populated areas were those along the coast and, especially around Lisbon.

Having considered the evolution of the Portuguese educational system, and in particular, its role in literary consecration, it

---

44 <http://www.iplb.pt/pls/diplb/!main_page?levelid=190.> [accessed in March 2005].

is important to examine Portuguese readership during the last thirty years in order to evaluate the reception of Portuguese fiction. Several factors contributed to the profound and swift changes that have affected Portuguese society between 1974 and the early 2000s: the revolutionary process in 1974-1975; the end of the Colonial War, the integration of the country into the EC and the ageing of the population. This had significant repercussions, in the acceptance of fictional representation produced and in the constitution of the Portuguese literary canon.

Portuguese demography has changed significantly after 1974, although in many respects it has followed the average European demographic development. Emigration rates decreased significantly after 1974: in 1974, the total emigration was 70,273, whereas in 1984, it plummeted to 10,528. Decolonization had an effect on the Portuguese economy and altered the demographic picture of the country. More than 600,000 Portuguese were forced to leave the newly independent countries and return to Portugal. Between 1975 and 1976, the population increased by 7 per cent. Most returnees from the former colonies were highly qualified and only 7 per cent of them were illiterate. They contributed to changes in social patterns, such as the fall in illiteracy rates to around 20 per cent in the post-revolution years.[45] The social impact of the Colonial War and of the entire decolonization process was substantial insofar as it became a topic of some of the fiction consecrated after the Revolution.[46] In 1991, the Portuguese population reached 9,862,540 inhabitants and this corresponded to an increase of 11 per cent since the early 1970s.

Furthermore, Portugal evolved from a predominantly rural to an urban society: by 1990, the primary sector employed 17.9 per cent of the population; 34.5 per cent of the population worked in the secondary sector and 47.6 per cent of the workforce was em-

---

45   According to Instituto Nacional de Estatística, *Anuários Estatísticos e Estatísticas Demográficas*, in 1981, 19.8 per cent of the Portuguese was illiterate. Ten years later, it fell to 10.1 per cent.

46   António Lobo Antunes and Lídia Jorge are two important examples of contemporary writers whose oeuvres dealing with the Colonial War were appraised and consecrated in terms of fictional representation of individual perceptions and conflicts caused by the impact of the War.

ployed in the tertiary sector. In regard to literacy levels, in 1981, 26.4 per cent of the Portuguese could not read or write, and this rate fell to 15.3 per cent in 1991. In 1981, 47.6 per cent had primary education and 1.6 per cent had higher education; in 1991, 43.8 per cent of the Portuguese had completed primary school level and 4.9 per cent were graduates. Nevertheless, the number of university graduate soared in the 1980s and in the early 1990s. According to official statistics, 32,447 students completed their higher education in 1994.[47] Although illiteracy had fallen significantly, most Portuguese completed only their primary education.

Despite the expenditure on education being higher than that during the Estado Novo, its purpose was mainly to fight illiteracy and was ineffective with regard to encouraging the Portuguese to complete their secondary and higher education. Like the population of most European countries, the Portuguese were ageing. Whereas only 6 per cent of the population was older than 65 years old in 1960, this rate increased to 13.6 per cent in 1991. This rise was more pronounced during the 1990s.[48]

Pierre Bourdieu stated that cultural practices and preferences in literature were closely linked to educational level.[49] Two surveys carried out in Portugal at the end of the 1970s and early 1980s are worthy of mention in illustrating this point.

Thomas Bruneau conducted a survey amongst the Portuguese population in March 1978 in order to assess their views of the Revolution. Results showed that they were mostly concerned with their standard of living, though acknowledging the importance of the Revolution and the freedom of speech that came with it.[50] This

---

47 António Barreto, ed., *A Situação Social em Portugal, 1960-1995*, 3rd edn (Lisbon: Instituto de Ciências Sociais da Universidade de Lisboa, 1997) p. 103; p. 72; p. 93.

48 Barreto, p. 66.

49 Pierre Bourdieu, *Distinction – A Social Critique of The Judgement of Taste*, First published in French as La Distinction, *Critique sociale du jugement* by Les Editions de Minuit, Paris, 1979 (London: Routledge & Kegan Paul Ltd, 1986), p. 1.

50 Thomas Bruneau, 'Popular Support for Democracy in Postrevolutionary Portugal : Results from a Survey', in *In Search of Modern Portugal: The Revolution and its Consequences*, ed. by Lawrence Graham and Douglas L, Wheeler (Wisconsin: The University of Wisconsin Press, 1983), pp. 21-42.

survey also showed that the Regime as a political establishment was of less concern to the Portuguese than their own economic and social problems. This can be linked to the view of Bill Lomax that the Revolution was actually propelled by social and economic tension, a view which contrasted with the claims of the protagonists of the coup d'état.[51] Popular support was perceived to be driven more by expectations of better standards of living than by expectations of political changes. In 1983, Luís de França and Manuel Luís Marinho Antunes examined surveys among the Portuguese aged between 15 and 24 in order to characterize their religious and cultural practices.[52] As far as Catholic worship is concerned, belief was stronger in the north and along the coastal areas, whilst Lisboners and Portuguese southerners were among those who least claimed being Catholic believers. Female youngsters and young workers (as opposed to students) were stronger Catholic worshippers; graduates and the unemployed were among those whose beliefs were the least strong. As far as their spare time activities were concerned, sports, playing musical instruments, dancing and knitting were at the top of the list of activities. Reading was not considered a variable in this list. In view of the fact that 'others' was a possible answer, only a minority chose this variable. Up until the end of the 1990s and the early 2000s, surveys showed that the Portuguese did not develop solid book reading habits, although this was not a distinctive feature restricted to the Portuguese.[53]

---

51 'Thus I shall argue that, in the Portuguese case it was economic and social conflict within society, and not political or ideological intervention, that was responsible for the course of events that have paradoxically been described as constituting "The Portuguese Revolution"', in Bill Lomax, 'Ideology And Illusion In The Portuguese Revolution: The Role Of The Left', in *Search Of Modern Portugal: The Revolution And Its Consequences*, ed. by Lawrence Graham and Douglas L. Wheeler (Wisconsin: The University Of Wisconsin Press, 1983), pp. 105-129 (p. 106).

52 Luís de França, 'Os jovens portugueses perante a religião: caracterização global' and Manuel Luís Marinho Antunes, 'Representações sociais dos jovens e religião', in *Análise Social*, Revista do Instituto de Ciências Sociais da Universidade de Lisboa, 86, vol. 2 (1985), 247-311.

53 UNESCO statistics published in 2003: in 2002, a survey commissioned by the Orange Prize found that 40 per cent of the British did not have book reading

These results show that the Portuguese in the 1980s were not too different from the generations that went through the Estado Novo: religious practice was a feature that differentiated the urban from the rural and educated from the uneducated. Furthermore, it is also worthy of mention that knitting was chosen as an activity by a considerable percentage of Portuguese youngsters in view of the fact that this activity fitted the female role endorsed by the Estado Novo. This illustrates the importance of family background as a decisive variable in the constitution of readership, considering that the parents of youngsters in the 1980s were educated during the Estado Novo and that school education, in particular the teaching of reading as a skill, was not drastically different from that before 1974. Readership was also influenced by the growing number of Portuguese brought up and educated during that period, in view of the fact that families became smaller as years went by.

Portuguese culture was given institutional autonomy after 1974, through the establishment of Ministries and Secretaries of Culture. Nevertheless, educational reforms in the last three decades indicate that the revolutionary events in 1974-1975 were a turmoil that was particularly effective in sweeping away the Estado Novo ideology but ineffective in consolidating a sense of national unity. Cultural consensus was mainly reached in Parliament and, thus, unable to legitimize structural changes in the literary canon.

habits and Italy was also among the countries with low rates of reading habits. Statistics cited in < http://www.uis.unesco.org> [Accessed in February 2007].

CHAPTER 6
Consecration and Legitimacy in the Portuguese Literary Field between 1974 and 2004

This chapter sets out to show that the Revolution did not provide the cultural field with more autonomy. The Governments in office between 1974 and 2004 inherited the position of major agent of literary consecration conquered by Salazar's Government and did little to withdraw their influence on the literary field. The President of the Republic gained a significant importance in writers' consecration between 1978 and 2004 through the Honours awarded on the 10 June. Despite this information being publicized in the media every year, it has not been compiled in a single document. Therefore, for the purposes of this thesis three chronological tables were drawn with the Portuguese writers awarded by Presidents Ramalho Eanes (1978-1981), Mário Soares (1985-1994), and Jorge Sampaio (1996-2004). The purpose was to examine to what extent Honours illustrated criteria of literary consecration and exemplified the influence of the political environment in the literary field between 1978 and 2004. Three tables were also drawn with the prizewinners between 1978 and 2000, their prizewinning works, publishing houses and panels for the prizes of the Associação Portuguesa de Escritores, the Pen Club and Casa de Mateus, the Lisbon City Hall, the CP/AICL (literary critics' association), the Sociedade Portuguesa de Autores (SPA), the Government (Camões Prize) and Expresso/Unysis (Pessoa Prize).[1] The purpose was to establish to the extent to which: (1) the prestige and authority of those institutions as agents of literary consecration were constructed upon the involvement of their participants (panels and prizewinners) in their opposition to the Estado Novo; (2) there were repercussions on prizewinning narrative representation in

---

1 Due to their size and amount of information, they are included in Appendix 7, on pp. 383.

the debate on post-1974 cultural identity; (3) it was possible to define a profile of publishers of prizewinners; (4) it was possible to identify the publishers' prestige gained with those literary prizes.

Books most in demand in bookshops reflected Portuguese purchasers' interest in the political and social transformations after 1974 and also the effects of the campaigns promoted by the 5ª Divisão. Bestsellers between 1974 and 1976 were on political science, the Estado Novo, economy, education, and the Revolution. Spínola's *Portugal e o Futuro* and Mário Soares's *Portugal Amordaçado* were bestsellers after the Revolution, side by side with titles by Marx, Engels, Lenin, Fidel Castro and others on the independence of the colonies, the Colonial War, and Humberto Delgado. Social turmoil also encouraged the expansion of publishing houses. The titles that sold most between 1974 and 1976 were: Fernando Namora's *Estamos no Vento*; Baptistas Bastos's *Cão Velho Entre Flores*; Artur Portela's *A Funda IV*; Aquilino Ribeiro's *Quando os Lobos Uivam*; Luandino Vieira's *Luuanda*; José Gomes Ferreira's *Gaveta de Nuvens* and *Textos da Revolução*; Mário Ventura's *Morrer em Portugal*; José Rodrigues Miguéis's *O Milagre Segundo Salomé*; António Aleixo's *Este Livro que Vos Deixo*; and *Novas Cartas Portuguesas* by Maria Teresa Horta, Maria Velho da Costa and Isabel Barreno.[2] Whereas most titles mentioned above were published after the Revolution, Aquilino Ribeiro's and Luandino Vieira's novels were published in the mid-1960s and *Novas Cartas Portuguesas* was published in 1972. Their demand can be linked to the impact aroused at the time of their publication, involving lawsuits against their writers. The PIDE had censored those novels but the end of censorship awakened the purchasers' interest as they became available to the public.

Novelists, poets and critics, such as José Gomes Ferreira, Manuel Alegre, José-Augusto França and José Gaspar Simões, wrote about the Revolution between 1974 and 1976. That is worthy of note because it expressed the intellectuals' commitment. Bestsellers' lists showed that the titles in demand on politics and social sciences were essentially translations or authored by Portuguese

---

2   The sources are editions of *Expresso* and *Diário Popular*. See Dionísio, pp. 506-509.

politicians (for example, Garaudy, Duverger, Álvaro Cunhal, Che Guevara, Adriano Moreira). Equally illustrative of the writers' political and social commitment was the First Congress of the Associação Portuguesa de Escritores (APE) that took place on 10-11 May 1975, in which writers mostly discussed ideology, the Cultural Revolution and their social role as active participants.[3] This was the first major opportunity Portuguese writers had, after the Revolution, to discuss their role in society and also to ensure the terms of the autonomy of the literary field, as discussed in António Sousa Ribeiro's study in 1993.[4] The Congress showed the different stances about the legitimacy of writers' public image that ranged from those who believed that it was rooted in intellectual tradition and competence to those who defended that it was rooted in his communicating with and to the masses and his responsibility of participating in the revolution. The fact that the Prime Minister, Vasco Gonçalves, delivered the final speech illustrates the Government's support of the APE. This Congress was carried out when the Campanhas para a Dinamização Cultural were conducted by the 5ª Divisão and the Prime Minister appealed to the writers' participation in the revolutionary process. This shows that the degree of autonomy of the literary field changed very little after 1974. Between 1974 and

---

3   The Congress was organized in four panels (number of papers presented 'Ideologia, Revolução Cultural e o Papel do Escritor' (33); 'Comunicação e Pedagogia da Literatura' (13); 'Criação literária: a sua especificidade e/ou instrumentalização' (7); 'Crítica Literária' (4)). The second congress, in 1982, was also dominated by papers on the writer's social role presented in the panel 'O Escritor e a Sociedade' (35); nevertheless, the panel 'Questões Estético-Literárias' integrated 21 papers, showing that writers' interest on literary issues grew when compared to the 1970s. João Pedro George studied the First (1975) and Second (1982) APE Congresses in his *O Meio Literário Português (1960/1998)* (Lisbon: Difel, 2002), pp. 179-191. In this study, George stated that, in 1975, 'no interior da APE as questões políticas desempenhavam papel de relevo, influenciando as tomadas de posição pública da APE' (p. 186).

4   António Sousa Ribeiro, 'Configurações do Campo Intelectual Português no Pós-25 de Abril: O Campo Literário', in *Portugal: Um Retrato Singular*, ed. by Boaventura de Sousa Santos (Lisbon: Edições Afrontamento, 1993), pp. 483-512.

1976, several writers were employed in high positions in the media and in political institutions.[5] Those positions enhanced their prestige and legitimacy as agents of production and consumption and transferred this symbolical capital to the events in which they took part.

6.1 Honours given by the President of the Republic

One of the official acts of recognition of merit is the Orders given by the President of the Republic. Tables 8, 9 and 10 show the writers who were rewarded with the Orders between 1978 and 2004. Between 1974 and 1976, Orders were suspended and they were determined by decree to be given only exceptionally and were a decision of the President of the Republic. After 1976, Orders were especially handed out on the 10 June. The Portuguese Constitution of 1976 established that the President was the Grand Master of Portuguese Orders.

As shown in Table 8, in 1980, the First Constitutional Government set up the Ordem da Liberdade to distinguish 'serviços relevantes prestados em defesa dos valores da civilização, em prol da dignificação do Homem e à causa da liberdade'.[6] Up until the end of Ramalho Eanes's Presidency, only

---

5   David Mourão-Ferreira was editor of *A Capital*, deputy editor of *O Dia* and was appointed Secretary of State for Culture of the Sixth Provisional Government; José Cardoso Pires was deputy editor of *Diário de Lisboa* and chairman of the Cultural Commiteee of Lisbon City hall; Augusto Abelaira was editor of *Vida Mundial*; Ruben A. Leitão was Director General of Cultural Affairs and Eduardo Prado Coelho was Director General of Cultural Action during the Sixth Provisional Government.

6   See Table 8 on pp. 283. Quoted from <http://www.ordens.presidencia.pt/ ordem_nacional_liberdade_historia.htm>[accessed in June 2005]. The Ordem Militar de Sant'Iago da Espada rewarded 'o mérito literário, científico e artístico' <http://www.ordens.presidencia.pt/ordem_militar_santiago.htm>; the Ordem Infante D.Henrique rewarded 'os que houverem prestado serviços relevantes a Portugal, no país e no estrangeiro e serviços na expansão da cultura portuguesa, sua história e seus valores' <http://www.ordens.

one writer and journalist, Maria Lamas, was rewarded with the Ordem; Lamas's opposition to the Estado Novo had forced her into exile. The official celebrations of the 10 June took place in different cities, by turn, hosted by the President of the Republic. In 1978, they took place in Portalegre, a symbol of the impoverished country and of the need to draw attention to the under-developed inland regions and, in the following years, they took place in Leiria, Funchal, Figueira da Foz, Lisbon, Viseu and Évora as a way to decentralize the ceremonies away from Lisbon.[7] Vergílio Ferreira, Jorge de Sena, Fernando Namora, Vitorino Magalhães Godinho, David Mourão-Ferreira, Eduardo Lourenço, José Gomes Ferreira and Agustina Bessa Luís were the writers who participated in the celebrations of the 10 June until 1981 and spoke about the country's cultural identity.[8] The participation of these writers in the official ceremonies is an indicator of their political commitment to the democratic process. However, their speeches revealed that literary references were the same that had prevailed during the Estado Novo: Camões was the icon of Portuguese cultural identity during and after the Estado Novo and was used by intellectuals and, particularly, in the political field, to express the Portuguese dependence on this mythology to build its identity.[9] Honouring

---

presidencia.pt/ordem_nacional_infante.htm>; the Ordem do Mérito rewarded 'actos ou serviços meritórios praticados no exercício de quaisquer funções, públicas ou privadas, ou que revelem desinteresse e abnegação em favor da colectividade' <http://www.ordens.presidencia.pt/ordem_merito_ merito.htm>; and the Ordem da Instrução Pública rewarded 'altos serviços prestados à causa da educação e do ensino' <http://www.ordens.presi dencia.pt/ordem_merito_instrucao_publica.htm>. [accessed June 2006] There are several ranks for each Order, but those relevant for this dissertation are, from the highest to the lowest: Grã-Cruz, Grande Oficial, Comendador and Oficial.

7 Part of the speech by President Ramalho Eanes in Portalegre was reported in *Expresso*, 15 June 1978, p. 1.

8 Equally relevant was the attention given to emigrant communities; the Portuguese emigrant-oriented newspaper *Comunidade*, with a print run of 1,000 free copies, was published on that day. The first edition included texts by Álvaro Salema and Vitorino Nemésio. See *Expresso*, 10 June 1977, p. 1.

9 In 1972, Eduardo Lourenço wrote: 'Que essa mitificação contribuiu – e continua contribuindo – mais do que tudo o resto para nos descentrar em relação a nós mesmos e nos instalar numa perspectiva autista de configu-

both those who overtly opposed the Regime and those who did not turn down the Regime's literary prizes, such as Agustina Bessa Luís and David Mourão-Ferreira, shows that the ambiguous relations between politics and literature inherent to Portuguese consecration: David Mourão-Ferreira was an intellectual who had gained prestige within the PS, whereas Agustina Bessa Luís's literary prestige, expressed both in literary prizes and commercial success, could not be ignored.

The intellectuals, that is those persons who intervened in the Portuguese cultural field, honoured by Mário Soares outnumber those honoured by General Ramalho Eanes, as shown in Table 9.[10] Unlike what happened until 1985, they share the common feature of having been public opponents to the Estado Novo. None of them were committed with Salazar's policies or made appearances at public events organized by the Regime. Broadly speaking, political antagonism was strengthened by cultural (and literary) opposition which was constructed upon those who had struggled for legitimacy in the literary field before 1974, and those who emerged in the field after the Revolution with an untracked record of participation in the events that led to the crumbling of the Estado Novo. Cultural prestige acknowledged by the political field (focusing on the President) gave intellectuals, such as José Cardoso Pires, Natália Correia and Adolfo Casais Monteiro, the authority as accepted spokespeople of a certain historical/political/cultural period (based on their personal experience as opponents to the Estado Novo). They had earned a certain legitimacy (political, social and cultural) that the PSD Government did not have.

This contrast is shown in José Carlos Vasconcelos's comments, editor of *Jornal de Letras*, when he wrote:

---

ração esquizofrénica, também não parece pôr-se em dúvida. Camões conferiu-nos, colectivamente, uma existência epopeica e desta insolação sublime nunca mais nos curámos' in 'Camões no Presente', in *O Labirinto da Saudade – Psicanálise Mítica do Destino Português* (Lisbon: Dom Quixote, 1978, 1st edition rpt. Lisbon: Gradiva, 2000), pp. 148-157 (p. 152).

10   See Table 9 on pp. 284.

Perguntarão os 'actuais' adversários políticos do Presidente e desta iniciação, o que fica de concreto de tudo isto. A esta pergunta a primeira e óbvia resposta é que fica, antes de mais, o valor simbólico da importância e da atenção dada aos criadores e à cultura pela primeira figura de Estado; fica a exemplaridade do comportamento e dos actos; fica o sublinhar do debate e até da própria convivialidade como factores marcantes, que não se podem minimizar e muito menos esquecer.[11]

Writers were not only rewarded with the Ordem de Sant'Iago da Espada; they were also rewarded for their contribution to Portuguese democracy and expansion of Portuguese values (especially the Ordem do Infante D.Henrique, the Ordem da Liberdade and the Ordem de Mérito). The fact that Mário Soares's positions and those of Cavaco Silva's Governments diverged, especially during the President's second term, is relevant when it comes to analysing the honours given to intellectuals.[12] In his speech delivered on the 10 June 1985, Soares urged the Portuguese to rethink Portuguese culture and raise collective awareness of the nation.[13] Portuguese culture, scholars, poets and fiction writers were used by the President, through their participation at various events, to show that he, unlike the Government, was committed to a wide discussion on Portuguese cultural values.[14]

As far as fiction is concerned, the intellectuals honoured were also those who took more critical stances against the right-wing

---

11 *Jornal de Letras*, 16 February 1993.
12 According to *Expresso* editions in 1987, Mário Soares honoured eight persons on the whole, and in 1990, this number rose to eighty-eight. In 1994, the number of prizes topped 132, and in 1995, he honoured 126 persons on the 10 June. Mário Soares honoured the highest number of intellectuals, especially in 1988, 1991 and 1992. These years coincide with the elections of the Eleventh Constitutional Government (17 August 1987) and Twelveth Constitutional Government (31 October 1991).
13 *Expresso*, 10 June 1985.
14 'A cultura tornou-se uma peça fulcral no jogo entre poderes. Para isso a actuação do Presidente teve de ultrapassar largamente o tipo de actividades que tinham caracterizado as funções culturais dos presidentes anteriores'. Quoted from Dionísio, p. 411. For example, Soares participated at the conference 'Política e Cultura' at the Torre do Tombo (1992), discussions on Portuguese-Galician culture (1992) with Augusto Abelaira, Agustina Bessa Luís, Eugénio de Andrade and Rui Alarcão, among others.

Governments. Those who were assigned posts by those Government were not given any honours.[15]

The cultural discourse used by Mário Soares and by the Governments in the late 1980s and early 1990s was not so very different because both appealed to a 'portugalidade' based on traditional values, indicating that there was some sort of consensus in terms of discourse. The political apparatus (Government and Parliament) also instrumentalized the Portuguese literary canon to convey the nation's values. In 1986, Portugal joined the EEC and the Government's campaigns pointed out that Portuguese membership was a sign of Portuguese modernization. According to Nuno Monteiro and António Costa Pinto's study on Portuguese identity, acceptance of its benefits among the population was a slow process.[16] In 1985, it was the fiftieth anniversary of Fernando Pessoa's death. During the parliamentary debate on the IX Government's programme, Manuel Alegre suggested moving Fernando Pessoa's tomb to the Jerónimos Monastery and was applauded in Parliament. As regards the political establishment, Pessoa emerged in discussions and at cultural events (organized by the Government) to express the Government's commitment to national values and to Portuguese culture. The fiftieth anniversary coincided with the fact that Portugal joined the EEC and, thus the Government's celebration of this poet was within the framework of the modernization of the country. Eventually, Pessoa and Camões are used by the political apparatus as major cultural icons.[17] It is relevant for this discussion that the most important

---

15 For example, Mário Soares never rewarded Vasco Graça Moura and Agustina Bessa Luís, despite they had received several literary awards. Expresso reported that Cavaco Silva proposed Vasco Graça Moura to be included in the list of honoured authors but Mário Soares turned his name down. See *Expresso*, 11 June 1993, p. 6. Vasco Graça Moura was an overt supporter of the PSD Government, having been appointed Commissioner of the Discoveries and editor of Imprensa Nacional-Casa da Moeda.

16 Nuno G. Monteiro and António Costa Pinto, 'A Identidade Nacional Portuguesa', in *Portugal Contemporâneo*, pp. 51-65 (p. 64).

17 Dionísio, p. 384. This dichotomy was clear in the award of the prizes for essays. In 1981, the PEN prize for best essay was given to Jorge de Sena (posthumously) and to his *Trinta Anos de Camões*. In the following year, Joel Serrão received the same prize for his *Fernando Pessoa: cidadão do*

literary prize was named after Camões, and officially given on 10 June and that Pessoa was the name chosen for a prestigious prize sponsored by Unysis, a private company, and *Expresso*, a newspaper.[18]

Jacques Dubois mentioned in his work *L'Institution de la Littérature* that in order to overcome the contradictions inherent in the fact that the literary process is incompatible with the pressures exerted by the economic and political fields, writers very often participate in the system and, thus, ensure balance of fields.[19] During the Governments headed by Cavaco Silva, intellectuals, including Natália Correia, Pedro Tamen and José Saramago, protested at the fact that Culture was not a priority for the Government and that the Secretary of State for Culture confined it to patronage. The alliance between Mário Soares and the intellectuals, shown in the honours given on 10 June and in his support to those who organized the FNDC, was an indication of the feeble autonomy of the political and the cultural fields. Table 10 shows some differences in the way honours were distributed among intellectuals after 1995.

In his speeches on 10 June, Jorge Sampaio introduced a new emphasis into the official speeches and urged the Portuguese, especially the youth, to value Portuguese history and cultural heri-

---

imaginário.In 1986, the Portuguese Section of the International Association of Critics gave their "Jacinto do Prado Coelho Prize" ex-aequo to Yvette Centeno and Vasco Graça Moura for their *Fernando Pessoa, o Amor, a Morte, a Iniciação* and *Camões e a Divina Proporção*, respectively.

18   The name Pessoa was decided with the aim of rewarding any personality whose work had been outstanding in the previous year and was deliberately chosen to create an ambiguous relation with the poet Fernando Pessoa: <http://www.premiopessoa.pt/pessoa.html>.[accessed in June 2006]. Having been sponsored by Expresso and Unysis, it rewards the prizewinner with 50,000€. Camões-Pessoa dichotomy is also clear in street-naming because their names were both given to more than one street: Camões is the name of two streets and one square; and Lusíadas is also the name of another street in central Lisbon. Fernando Pessoa is the name of one street and of an avenue, both in newer parts of Lisbon.

19   Jacques Dubois, *L'Institution de la Littérature* (Brussels: Editions Labor/Ferdinand Nathan, 1986), p. 106 : 'L'écrivain qui choisit cette activité devient pleinement un agent du système, dans la mesure où il se place du coté d'un pouvoir et où il sera enclin à s'identifier aux forces qui assurent la conservation d'un ordre des choses.'

151

tage without neglecting the fact that Portugal was a member of the European Union.[20]

Table 10 offers an indication of the criteria that guided the President to honour intellectuals.[21] Jorge Sampaio honoured considerably fewer writers than Mário Soares. Both President and Government were PS and the tension that had surrounded the relationships between both powers before 1996 ceased. Mário Claúdio was the only writer honoured by Jorge Sampaio, who had emerged in the literary field after 1974, in view of the honours given since 1978. Mário Claúdio had been given the APE Literary Prize for Best Fiction in 1984 with *Amadeo*, (published by IN-CM), the PEN Literary Prize in 1997, and the Pessoa Prize in 2002. Despite the fact that many writers were awarded on merit for expanding Portuguese culture and values, it is interesting that Saramago. Moreover, it was also during Sampaio's Presidency that the highest honours were given to a great number of intellectuals.

As far as literary output is concerned, the writers honoured by the President between 1978 and 2004 were those who examined the country that had lived through the Estado Novo and examined its impact and the Revolution's in the construction of national identity.

6.2 Literary Prizes

Several literary prizes were set up in Portugal after 1974, especially in the 1980s, a fact that was not unique to Portugal. In the United Kingdom and in the Netherlands, for example, many literary prizes were also set up during the mid-1970s and early 1980s.[22]

---

20 See Jorge Sampaio's speech in 1997, 'Sessão Solene Comemorativa do Dia e Portugal, de Camões e das Comunidades Portuguesas' <http://jorgesampaio. arquivo.presidencia.pt/pt/main.html> [accessed in December 2006].
21 See Table 10 on pp. 285.
22 Some examples in the United Kingdom are the Thomas Cook (1980); the Arthur C.Clarke (1980); the Biography (1985); the Authors' Foundation (1984); the Jewish Quarterly (1977).

The expansion of marketing activities around literature in the 1980s, involving publicity and media exposure, enhanced the impact of prizes, the prestige of prizewinners and also the prestige and authority of panel members.[23] Television and radio audience increased considerably after 1974, and this boosted publicity techniques and encouraged purchasing. Although the Portuguese average print-run did not exceed 3,000 copies at this time, publicity surrounding literary prizes was decisive in the making of bestsellers and this is mainly relevant as far as purchasing is concerned. As the publisher of Bertrand stated in 1984:

> Não há mesmo outra maneira de fazer chegar o livro às pessoas, embora existam livros que fazem o seu caminho sem a ajuda dos mass media; fazem-no, contudo, muito mais lentamente. Não é um anúncio que faz vender um livro.[24]

Appendix 7 shows that literary prizes after 1978 were given mostly to novelists and that fiction prizewinning was the most financially rewarding to writers, as had happened during the Estado Novo. The tables included in this thesis also establish that the Revolution did not introduce a clear-cut distinction between the literary and the political fields as far as literary legitimacy is concerned. Although literary consecration was not controlled by the Government, as it was during the Estado Novo, most prizes set up by literary institutions were supported by the Government in

---

23   The results of my survey of Portuguese purchasers of fiction in 2001 show that motivations linked to publicity, advertising and bestselling lists were stronger at the time of purchase. Bestsellers' lists of 1977, published in *Expresso*'s editions, show that titles by Dinis Machado, Maria Velho da Costa, Artur Portela, Herberto Helder, Miguel Torga, José Cardoso Pires, Agustina Bessa Luís, and José Gomes Ferreira were among the best sold ones. In early 1980s prizewinning fiction featured top positions, a fact that confirms that social pressure determines purchase. See Appendix 5 on pp. 365.

24   Clara Ferreira Alves and Francisco Belard, 'Como é diferente o "best-seller" em Portugal', *Expresso-Revista*, 28 January 1984, p. 36-R. Bertrand published one of the first Portuguese bestsellers after the Revolution, *O que Diz Molero*. Dinis Machado's novel was one of the first examples of post-Revolution popular literature and its success was, according to the publisher, related to popular oral registers and direct references to the cinema, to well-known Lisbon streets and books.

two ways: financing and ceremony hosting leading to validation of the works. This was particularly clear as regards fiction.

As far as the APE prizes are concerned, those which reward poetry and essay were not supported by the State-controlled Instituto Português do Livro e das Bibliotecas and were jointly financed by the APE and commercial companies; PT (telecommunications) and CTT (post service) financed prizes for essay and poetry, respectively. The APE and the Ministry of Culture sponsored the literary prize for drama; Lisbon City Hall rewarded poetry, essay, fiction, drama and other types of art, such as sculpture, music, photography, architecture, radio and cartoons. Literary genres were equally financially rewarded. However this was considerably less when contrasted with prizes rewarded by other institutions, such as the APE, the PEN Club or Fundação Casa de Mateus. The PEN Club also rewarded poetry, fiction and essay with the same amount of money and the Fundação Casa de Mateus set up only one prize to reward poetry, essay and fiction. The PEN Club and the Fundação rewarded literary work with considerably less money than the APE alone and both institutions did not reward drama.

The APE, the Camões and the Pessoa Literary Prizes have been honoured with the presence of the President of the Republic, and the Secretary of State/Minister for Culture has attended the ceremony of the D.Dinis Prize and the PEN Club. The mayor hosted the ceremony for the Cidade de Lisboa Literary Prize. This means that the Critics', the SPA and the Lifetime's Literary Work have been the only ones whose ceremonies have not included the participation of members of the State.

The novel was and has been the privileged literary genre as far as prestige is concerned and the APE and the State have been the authorities that compete in terms of its consecration. The novels rewarded, in particular those during the years Mário Soares's tenure as President, represent the 1960s Portuguese generation, confronted with the Colonial War, the Revolution and the mayhem aroused by the rapid transformation of social, political and cultural institutions. Consecration was given to fiction that examined Portuguese history. Essays rewarded were basically on Portuguese literature and almost none reviewed these issues.

Tables included Appendix 7 confirm that very few new writers were given the most important prizes. In 1984, Eduardo Lourenço's comment illustrate that literary legitimacy was fundamentally constructed on an individually (socially, culturally and politically) engaged literary production:

> A verdadeira 'escrita' da época da Revolução não podia vir dos Namora, dos V. Ferreira, dos Abelaira, das Agustinas, nem mesmo dos Almeida Faria, de Maria Velho da Costa ou de Nuno Bragança, autores que nos deram *objectivamente* alguns dos mais vivos reflexos literários provocados ou intimamente relacionados com o fenómeno Revolução. Acontece que nenhum deles é *a geração literária da Revolução*, aquela que polariza o *élan* vital e imaginante do seu tempo próprio, aquela para quem esse tempo é história aberta, luz indecisa na rua, ocasião de descoberta ou reajustamento do seu ser, do seu viver, escolher, amar e morrer (pelo menos na ficção).[25]

The Cidade de Lisboa Literary Prize was the first literary prize set up after 1974, at the initiative of the APE and financially supported by Lisbon City Hall. According to the regulations, this prize for Portuguese fiction was awarded without contest: the panel selected the prizewinning title from among all published titles in the preceding year.[26] *Casas Pardas* (prizewinner in 1978) and *Finisterra* (prizewinner in 1979) deal with the individual's inner conflicts within the framework of social problems, raising differences between working class and bourgeoisie and the transformations that the country went through in the 1970s. These prizes gave literary

---

25 Eduardo Lourenço, 'Literatura e Revolução', *Colóquio Letras*, 78, March 1984, 7-16 (p. 13); Equally relevant are Vergílio Ferreira's and Augusto Abelaira's statements in 1984, claiming that in 1984 the crisis of cultural identity was not tackled properly and required more time and new cultural producers: *Diário de Notícias*, 'Vergílio Ferreira: A Arte exprime-se por uma certa orientação formal' (24 April 1984), p. 11; *Diário de Notícias*, 'Augusto Abelaira: Escreve-se hoje o que já se escrevia' (19 April 1984), p. 15. Appendix 7 on pp. 383.

26 According to 'Prémio Cidade de Lisbon: Regulamento' published by APE Doc.215/77 in 1977 (article 3, p. 5): the panel was composed of members of the APE board; the Cultural Department of the Lisbon City hall; the Classe de Letras da Academia das Ciências de Lisboa; the Department of Portuguese Literature of the Faculty of Letters of Lisbon University; Portuguese Division of the International Association of Literary Critics.

legitimacy to the literature produced outside the literary framework supported by the Estado Novo. As stated in Chapter 5, it was in 1979 that the revision of the educational system was implemented and novels by Carlos Oliveira and Soeiro Pereira Gomes were introduced into the Portuguese Literature curriculum in the 12th Grade. Consecration was also extended to literary producers who, in turn, consolidated their own position with their political involvement.

As far as writers whose literary production emerged after 1974, Lídia Jorge was rewarded with the D.Dinis Prize and the PEN Club Prize only a decade after having received the Município de Lisboa Prize. The few prizewinners who emerged after the Revolution also reviewed the impact of the late years of the Estado Novo and the Revolution such as that of emigration (João de Melo and Paulo Castilho) and of the Colonial War (Lídia Jorge and António Lobo Antunes) on the Portuguese way of thinking.

It is noteworthy that, as the impact of the Prémio Municipal Eça de Queirós dwindled due to the multiplication of literary prizes, which rewarded writers with substantially higher financial awards, it became an opportunity for debutants to acquire some literary prestige. Rodrigo Guedes de Carvalho, Seomara da Veiga Ferreira and Fernando Campos, for example, did not receive any other prizes but the Prémio Municipal gave them some visibility (and some commercial success). Major literary institutions (the APE, the PEN Club, Casa de Mateus) resisted to giving legitimacy to new literary production.

The multiplication of prizes also favoured some competition among consecrating authorities. The D.Dinis Prize rewarded poetry more often after the APE set up their prizes, indicating that legitimacy was essentially disputed between the APE and the PEN Club. Fictional representation was not significantly different between the APE and the PEN Club Prizes. The composition of panels for these prizes indicates that the D.Dinis Prize gradually stood farther from these struggles, in particular during Mário Soares's mandates and enabled new writers to be prizewinners in early 1990s (e.g. Joaquim Manuel Magalhães (1993), Luís Filipe Mendes (1994)).

The Ricardo Malheiros Prize was the only major literary prize that remained after the collapse of the Estado Novo, although until 1980. Table 11, listing the prizewinners between 1974 and 1980, shows that the valuing of fiction that rewarded writers, such as Orlando da Costa and Ruben A. in the 1960s continued after 1974: examples being fiction by Olga Gonçalves, Álvaro Manuel Machado and Lídia Jorge.[27]

Therefore, the fact that that prize was discontinued when several new literary prizes were set up, in particular the Pen Club and D.Dinis in 1980 and the APE Grande Prémio de Romance e Novela in 1982, suggests that literary consecration was repositioned in the Portuguese literary field. In view of the fact that the importance of the Ricardo Malheiros Prize diminished when the Estado Novo collapsed and competition increased as new literary prizes were established, literary consecration was transferred from an institution which was not primarily controlled by writers to others whose regulations and decision-making were determined by them. This indicates that literary production came to be largely legitimized among peers. Discontinuing the Ricardo Malheiros Prize illustrates that, after 1980, agents of consecration in the Portuguese literary field struggled for autonomization. As Bourdieu put it in his study:

> The autonomization of intellectual and artistic production is thus correlative with the constitution of a socially distinguishable category of professional artists or intellectuals who are less inclined to recognize rules other than the specifically intellectual or artistic traditions handed down by their predecessors, which serve as a point of departure or rupture.[28]

Since major literary prizes were sponsored by the Government and ceremonies hosted by governmental representatives, autonomization was not wholly achieved. This raises the question whether it can ever be achieved. In view of the organization of the Portuguese literary field, I am tempted to say it will not in its totality, in view of the fact that it has required the formality inherent to

---

27 See Table 11 on p. 286.
28 Bourdieu, *The Field of Cultural Production*, pp. 112-113.

public events, strengthened by the attendance of representatives of the political field. Portuguese history has shown that Portuguese writers played a fundamental role in the opposition to the Estado Novo and that after 1974; their participation in Portuguese politics strengthened their prestige. The Revolution introduced a redefinition of the concept of 'intellectual' and 'literary autonomy' whose scope was reoriented as discussed below.

6.3 The Symbolic Capital of Prizewinners and Publishing Houses

As in Chapters 3 and 4, I will examine who benefited from the literary prizes. Tables 12 and 13, based on the data shown in Appendix 7, indicates the incidence of prizewinning writers and their publishing houses at the time of the award. Publishing houses such as Tertúlia, Veja, Difel, Edições 70, and Texto Editora, with just one prizewinner, awarded once, were excluded.[29]

Tables 12 and 13 show that the writers receiving the highest number of awards were José Saramago, with eleven prizes; Vergílio Ferreira, with eight prizes; David Mourão Ferreira, with six prizes; and Agustina Bessa Luís, Augusto Abelaira and Maria Velho da Costa with five prizes each. They are followed by Lídia Jorge and José Cardoso Pires with four prizes each. A significant number of writers received three prizes each: Mário de Carvalho, Sophia de Mello Breyner, Eduardo Lourenço, Teolinda Gersão, Paulo Castilho, Mário Ventura, Fernanda Botelho, Eugénio de Andrade and António Lobo Antunes. Four writers received two prizes: Alçada Baptista, Luís Felipe Mendes, Nuno Júdice and Pedro Tamen.

---

29 See Table 12 (Frequency of Prizewinning Writers and Publishing Houses (1978-2000)) on p. 287; See Table 13 (Frequency of Juries at Literary Panels (1978-2004), Cont.) on pp. 291.

As far as publishing houses are concerned, those whose books received most prizes are Dom Quixote, with twenty-four prizes, followed by Editorial Caminho with twenty prizes. Presença has eighteen prizewinning books and Bertrand eleven. All the other publishing houses have published six or fewer prizewinning writers.

Eleven out of the fourteen publishing houses are small-sized. Saramago, David Mourão Ferreira, Alçada Baptista, Lídia Jorge, António Lobo Antunes and João de Melo have always had the same publisher. José Cardoso Pires, Augusto Abelaira, Maria Velho da Costa, Eduardo Lourenço, Sophia de Mello Breyner and Mário de Carvalho received prizes for books published by different publishers, which means that moving to a new publisher implied they carried prestige to become multiple prizewinning writers. Their first prize was given when they were using their works as training grounds, usually published by smaller publishers.[30] There are also the cases of Guimarães and Bertrand whose prizewinning novels were with their in-house authors Agustina Bessa Luís and Vergílio Ferreira, respectively. Publicity involving consecrated writers and was promoted by publishers, strengthened the literary prestige of those writers.[31]

The prestige and the struggles for legitimacy arc also shown in the activities promoted by *Jornal de Letras, Artes e Ideias*. It was set up within the framework of the cultural milieu that existed throughout the Revolution:

---

30 Frank de Glas also concluded this when he analysed the relations between Dutch publishers and debutant writers in his 'Authors' Oeuvres as the backbone of publishers' lists: Studying the literary publishing house after Bourdieu', *Poetics*, 25 (1998), 379-397 (p. 386). This is also clear when writers are published abroad for the first time, as the case with José Saramago.

31 In 1962, Vergílio Ferreira authored a preface to Almeida Faria's *Rumor Branco* and José Saramago wrote the preface to the anthology of poems by Armindo Rodrigues, published by Caminho in the late 1970s;In 1981, Fernando Namora attended Augusto Abelaira's book signing session at Sá da Costa bookshop; In 1984, João de Melo authored a preface to *(Sapa)teia Americana* by Onésimo Teotónio de Almeida. These two events were publicised by *Jornal de Letras* at the time.

Sem dúvida, O "JL" é uma aposta e um desafio. Contra muitas coisas, entre as quais se contam o obscurantismo, o sectarismo, a intolerância, as "guerras de alecrim e manjerona" de um certo subdesenvolvimento mental. E a favor de muitas outras, entre as quais avultam a mudança de mentalidades e as transformações culturais que se impõem e que o 25 de Abril – também nossa razão de ser e de existir – ainda não conseguiu realizar.[32]

This newspaper and the activities promoted by its editor are discussed in this dissertation because it was the only literary newspaper regularly published after the Revolution (unlike others, such as *Ideias e Letras*) up till the present-day. Furthermore, it has also been a project set up within the media framework and has shown how the approach to literary issues and their reception have evolved between 1981 and 2004. This newspaper had contributions by those who took the dominant positions in the literary field, including writers, university teachers and outstanding intellectuals: Agustina Bessa Luís, Alexandre Pinheiro Torres, David Mourão Ferreira, Eduardo Lourenço, Urbano Tavares Rodrigues, Eduardo Prado Coelho, Augusto Abelaira, Vergílio Ferreira, Fernando Assis Pacheco, Paula Morão, Maria Estrela Serrano, José Palla e Carmo, José Manuel Nunes, Maria João Brilhante, among others.[33] The association with these personalities enabled *Jornal de Letras* to be the cultural medium of those cultural producers (writers, critics) who accumulated more symbolic capital. It became fundamental in the process of consecration of authors and was related to the utopia of the transformation of mentalities through a cultural revolution.[34] Historically, for those who lived through the Estado

32 José Carlos Vasconcelos. 'JL', *Jornal de Letras, Artes e Ideias*, 3 March 1981, p. 2.
33 In November 1987, another newspaper, *Letras & Letras*, was launched and competed with *Jornal de Letras* for approximately six years, going through different strategies of formatting. It was based in Porto and the print-run was fewer than JL: 9,000 copies. It was discontinued in 1993, showing that the small market did not allow competition between cultural newspapers in this area. When it was published, a similar strategy to establish credibility in the field was used: the credits included a commission of support led by Agustina Bessa Luís, Mário Cláudio, Albano Martins, Paula Morão, António Reis and Alçada Baptista.
34 When *Jornal de Letras* was set up in March 1981, the initial print-run was 38,000. One month later, it fell to 33,750 and continued to fall to 27,000 in August 1981 to 25,550 in June 1982 and again to 15,290 in June 1986. The

Novo, the would-be revolution is connected with the disappointment and the search for the national identity that emerged from 1974-1976. In 1981, *JL* sponsored an initiative by the APEL and Brazilian Chamber of the Book to convene a meeting of Portuguese and Brazilian publishers, with the aim of promoting Portuguese books. The Portuguese commission included only publishers that did outstanding business during the Estado Novo: Publicações Dom Quixote, Presença, Livros do Brasil, Bertrand, Porto Editora, Lello & Irmão, Figueirinhas, Verbo, Livros Horizonte and Moraes. They published prestigious Portuguese contemporary authors and prizewinners: Sophia de Mello Breyner, Matilde Rosa Araújo, Vergílio Ferreira and Maria Velho da Costa, amongst others.[35] This initiative contributed to the *JL*'s positioning within the dominant literary field, promoting the Portuguese writers who received the highest honours and held senior ranks of cultural institutions. Furthermore, it enhanced the concept of literary prestige and authority based on the opposition to the Estado Novo, extended both to literary producers and to this newspaper.[36]

The developments of the late 1980s and the early 1990s led to the expansion of popular fiction and to a simultaneous decrease in number of publications and pages on the literary production of the

---

downward tendency continued throughout the 1990s and levelled off around 13,000 copies. The fragile readership supports the concept of restricted production oriented towards restricted consumption.

35   Equally relevant was the invitation to ten writers by the university teacher Cremilde Medina to participate in an event associated with Portuguese contemporary literature in Brazil in 1983: Saramago, Egito Gonçalves, Alçada Baptista, Pedro Tamen, Cardoso Pires, Alexandre O'Neill, Assis Pacheco, Almeida Faria, António Lobo Antunes and Lídia Jorge. Most had outstanding work published in the 1960s– except Lobo Antunes and Lídia Jorge – and all were prizewinning writers either after 1974 or by the SPE in the 1960s.

36   It is noteworthy that the promotion of the same consecrated writers has continued to the present and these writers feature on the first page of most of JL's editions as they did in the 1980s: Vergílio Ferreira, Miguel Torga, Carlos de Oliveira, Eduardo Lourenço, Urbano Tavares Rodrigues, José Cardoso Pires, and Eugénio de Andrade, among others. Others such as Mário de Carvalho, Lídia Jorge and Clara Pinto Correia feature on the first page in early 2000s, a long time after having received several literary prizes.

restricted field. National newspapers, such as *Expresso*, employed journalists to write reviews. According to Bourdieu, the critic's relationship in the literary field influences his work:

> In short, the most personal judgments it is possible to make of a work, even of one's work, are always collective judgments in the sense of position-takings referring to other position-takings through the intermediary of the objective relations between the positions of their authors within the field.[37]

Some writers resented the closure of the literary field to new production, because there were no literary reviews in Portugal. Literary writing expanded as literary reviewing dwindled and was underestimated by the press. There were fewer and fewer literary pages in major newspapers.[38]

Debutants, who started their career after 1974 and received their prizes in the 1990s, were mainly published by those publishers with the highest number of prizewinning writers: Seomara da Veiga Ferreira, Joaquim Manuel Magalhães, Pedro Rosa Mendes and Helena Marques. Moreover, the APE, the Camões and the Lifetime's Literary Work were given to writers published by the publishing houses with the highest number of prizewinning writers: Saramago, Sophia de Mello Breyner and Óscar Lopes are published by Editorial Caminho, José Cardoso Pires was published by D.Quixote, David Mourão Ferreira and Eduardo Lourenço are published by Presença and Vergílio Ferreira by Bertrand. Exceptions are Urbano Tavares Rodrigues and Eugénio de Andrade, who were not amongst those awarded more times. The Prémio Vida Literária (Lifetime's Literary Work) was never given to any writer who endorsed the policy of the PSD Governments publicly between 1985-1995. Moreover, the fact that the literary output is translated abroad and honoured by foreign peers precedes the most important honours awarded domestically.[39]

---

37 'The Field of Literary Production', p. 135.
38 One of the examples is in *Jornal de Letras*, 'Não há crítica literária em Portugal', 2 August 1995, p. 17.
39 In 1979, Natália Correia received La Fleur de Laure Prix and Fernando Namora received the French Golden Medal by the Societé d'Éncouragement. Sophia de Mello Breyner and Jacinto do Prado Coelho received the awards

If we compare these results with the President's honours, those writers who received literary prizes before being honoured were Saramago, Agustina Bessa Luís, Augusto Abelaira, Maria Velho da Costa, José Cardoso Pires and Pedro Tamen. Those who received honours first were Vergílio Ferreira, David Mourão Ferreira, Sophia de Mello Breyner and Eduardo Lourenço. This indicates that the literary prizes of the latter enhanced a symbolic capital already achieved through their role in the literary and cultural fields while the former authors consolidated a literary prestige acquired post-1974 with recognition given by the State.

Publishers benefit from these writers because prizes confer prestige and authority to the publisher and encourage new writers to send them their manuscripts.[40] Publishers, like Presença and D.Quixote, only started publishing popular literature in the late 1990s and early 2000s: Marta Gomes by Presença and Ana Bola by D.Quixote are two examples. Simultaneously, publishers like Oficina do Livro, Editorial Notícias and Difel increased their amount of highbrow literature in this period, too. This is a commercial strategy that challenges Bourdieu's clear-cut distinction between 'cultural business' and 'commercial business'.[41]

If we look into the bestsellers' lists of the 1980s and 1990s, there is evidence of development of the Portuguese book market: In the 1980s, lists of bestselling fiction were dominated by Agustina Bessa Luís, Alçada Baptista, Miguel Torga, Teolinda

---

of the French Legion of Honour and Miguel Torga's work was awarded the Montaigne Prix in 1981. This recognition was equally formalized by the Portuguese political and cultural agents after those honours. António Lobo Antunes was honoured by the President in 2004, long after his literary merits were recognized internationally and having been proposed as Candidate for the Nobel Prize.

40 In the early 1940s, Saramago first sent his manuscript of *Terra do Pecado* to Parceria António Maria Perreira, one of the most prestigious publishing houses. Beginners apparently believe that prestigious publishers can afford to have them and make them successful writers. There is evidence of this in the interviews with Zeferino Coelho and António Lobo Faria, where both state that they receive an impressive number of manuscripts every year. See Appendices 1 and 2 on pp. 339-54.

41 Bourdieu, p. 97.

Gersão, Vergílio Ferreira and Lídia Jorge.[42] In other words, literary prizes encouraged customers to buy novels. These novels also benefited from the fact that Portuguese popular literature was very scarce. The late 1990s book market changed with the expansion of popular literature. *JL's* inclusion of a 'bestsellers' list' in 1994 is evidence of this feature. This information about the Portuguese book market confirms what can be regarded as a market trend, echoing H. Verdaasdonk's conclusion that Dutch leading publishing houses were market-driven and involved competitor analysis.[43]

Table 14 was also built with information taken from Appendix 7.[44] It shows the panellists who were most often requested to adjudicate on literary prizes: Vasco Graça Moura, Maria Alzira Seixo, Pedro Tamen and Alçada Baptista appear more than ten times and are followed by Fernando Pinto do Amaral, Urbano Tavares Rodrigues, Carlos Reis and Júlio Conrado. Some novelists, such as Agustina Bessa Luís, David Mourão Ferreira and Almeida Faria, were panellists and there are also cases when prizewinners, such as Saramago, Lídia Jorge and Luísa Costa Gomes, sat on panels for poetry, short story and translation. The writers who sat most frequently on a panel are also published by the publishers with the highest number of prizewinners. A similar reading can be done on the chairpersons of the awarding institutions: Alçada Baptista, chairman of the IPL; Maria Alzira Seixo, chairwoman of the CP/AICL; Almeida Faria, Pedro Tamen and David Mourão Ferreira, chairmen of the PEN Club; Urbano Tavares Rodrigues and Óscar Lopes, chairmen of the APE.

According to de Nooy, prestige could be summed up in three major features: literary seniority, administrative experience and the continuous practice of literary criticism.[45] If we take for granted

---

42 Bestsellers lists taken from JL's editions.
43 H. Verdaasdonk, 'The Influence of Certain Socio-Economic Factors on the Composition of the Literary Programs of Large Dutch Publishing Houses', *Poetics*, 14 (1985), 575-608.
44 See Table 13 on pp. 291.
45 W. De Nooy, 'Gentlemen Of The Jury... – The Features Of The Experts Awarding Literary Prizes', 531-545. In his article, Nooy classified prizes with

that the prestigious literary prizes are those which have a higher financial reward and are attended by a member of the State at the ceremony, results for Portugal do not differ much from Nooy's research. Those members who adjudicated on the Camões Prize were Carlos Reis (five times), Idalina Regina Rodrigues (five times), Urbano Tavares Rodrigues (four times) and Alçada Baptista (three times); those who decided on the APE more often were Carlos Reis (four times), Óscar Lopes (four times), Maria da Glória Padrão (three times) and Maria Lúcia Lepecki (three times). Out of these, Óscar Lopes also sat on the panel for the Camões prize. In other words, novelists or poets sat on panels after having received a literary prize (for example, Teolinda Gersão), and also on less prestigious panels, such as Agustina Bessa Luís who was panel member for the Cidade de Lisboa Prize. Moreover, prizewinning writers also occasionally sat on panels for prizes given to other categories (for example, Saramago, Lídia Jorge and Luísa Costa Gomes, who sat on panels for poetry, short story and translation). Those members with the highest rates are those who had reached position of senior rank: Carlos Reis (Director at the National Library) and Alçada Baptista (chairman of the IPL) practiced literary criticism in national and weekly newspapers, such as Maria Lúcia Lepecki, Maria da Glória Padrão and Óscar Lopes. Moreover, a relevant number of persons who chaired the APE, the PEN Club, the CP/AICL and the IPL were members of the most prestigious prizes: Carlos Reis (IPL); Alçada Baptista (IPL and President Sampaio's cultural advisor); Urbano Tavares Rodrigues (APE); Fernando B. Martinho (CP); Óscar Lopes (APE); Maria Alzira Seixo (CP); José Manuel Mendes (APE); and David Mourão Ferreira (APE; PEN).

The principles that oriented instances of reproduction did not differ substantially from the ones that prevailed during the Estado Novo. As already mentioned in Chapter 4, publishers' aims had to do with educating the people and this was partly due to the re-

<hr>

a long and regular tradition or a large amount of money and a tradition or a large amount of money and a tradition of more than average length with Status 2 and state prizes awarding to complete works, combining a large amount of money with a long and regular tradition with Status 1.

straints imposed on their activity, for or against the Regime. Business strategies did not progress significantly after 1974 and this is still clear in more politically engaged publishing houses, such as Editorial Caminho.[46] Moreover, merging and conglomerating decisions that introduced decisive changes in foreign book markets, such as in Spain, in the United Kingdom and in the United States of America, did not involve Portuguese publishing houses until the late 1990s and early 2000s. Portuguese publishing continued to practise the same kind of management strategies until this period. This fact obstructed the inclusion of the Portuguese book market into the major channels of book distribution in key book markets, especially in the English-speaking countries. Appendix 6 shows that the same publishers in a restricted number of countries (United States, United Kingdom, Germany, France, Spain, Italy and Sweden) published the Nobel Prizewinners, indicating that some publishers operate as decisive agents of international literary visibility. Portuguese writers seldom had the opportunity of being published by major international publishers, although Portugal was not the same isolated country as it was before 1974. Nevertheless, its political and economic strategic importance remained far from propelling business expansion as far as the book market was concerned.

As Caminho publisher Zeferino Coelho, has pointed out, writing that centres on Portuguese affairs thwarts translation possibilities, despite the prestige of some writers. The fact that Portuguese fiction was engaged in a way that revised Portuguese cultural identity and, therefore, was less committed to represent the cosmopolitan and modern country affected the internationalisation of many consecrated writers. Frank Kermode stated that changes in the canon reflect the possibility of getting rid of embedded prejudices:

> At the simplest level, we know about the differences between our own understandings of old texts and the understandings of our predecessors, or even those of contemporaries in disagreement because of generational differences, or contrary political presumptions [...] yet it is just the assumption we are likely to say we feel an urgent need to question if we want to rid our-

---

46   See Appendix 1 on pp. 339.

selves of the historically embedded prejudices that are the main support of our conviction that we are historically privileged.[47]

By 'embedded prejudices', Frank Kermode refers to our own perception of reality which is shaped by education and culture. The fact that Portuguese consecrated fiction was committed to take a stance on the Portuguese political, social and cultural environment and was deeply rooted on individual and collective experience compromised the progress of fictional discourse to free itself from historical, political and social constraints.

---

47   Frank Kermode, *Pleasure and Change: The Aesthetics of Canon*, ed. by Robert Alter (Oxford: Oxford University Press, 2004), p. 36.

José Saramago and José Luís Peixoto: Two Case Studies of Literary Legitimacy and Consecration.

I will examine José Saramago's social trajectory between the 1960s and 1998, during which he reached an undisputed position in the Portuguese literary field, culminating with the 1998 Nobel Prize of Literature. I will endeavour to establish that there were four major decisive factors which influenced Saramago's canonicity: the Portuguese political, social and cultural environment; Saramago's social trajectory, that is, the making of his public persona; the timing of the publication of his novels; and the fact that he was published by Editorial Caminho. Furthermore, I examine the public recognition of José Luís Peixoto, who was first published in 2000 and benefited from the fact that José Saramago was a consecrated writer, when he was awarded the José Saramago Literary Prize in 2001. Saramago's authority became decisive in Peixoto's symbolic capital whereas Peixoto's position in the literary field also strengthened Saramago's authority and prestige.

7.1   JOSÉ SARAMAGO

7.1.1   Social Trajectory

In 1947, Saramago published his first novel, *Terra do Pecado*. Originally named *A Viúva*, he sent the manuscript to the publishing house Parceria António Maria Pereira but he did not receive any feedback from them. Later, unexpectedly, he received a phone call from the editor Manuel Rodrigues, of Minerva, asking to see him on account of the manuscript. Rodrigues agreed to publish it but suggested a change in the title to the more appealing *Terra do Peca-*

do. The young Saramago agreed. However, the novel was not promoted and sales were scarce. This book fell into oblivion for some decades and only after the consolidation of Saramago's literary career was it incorporated in the lists of Saramago's works.

Jornal de Letras's special edition on Saramago's fifty years of literary production had reviews of Editorial Caminho's reprint of that novel.[1] Editorial Caminho reproduced the facsimile of *Terra do Pecado's* front cover and publicised it as 'A Obra de Juventude de José Saramago'. That reprint's front cover broke with the front covers which characterise 'O Campo da Palavra' series (light yellow with the name of the author and title in black letters and no pictures). The preface and cover of that reprint are worthy of analysis because they show how Saramago's literary career was structured by the publisher and narrated by him.

In the preface, Saramago describes himself as a twenty-four-year-old in the third person and the circumstances involving the publication of that novel. He introduced a difference between the 'I' character and the 'I', omniscient mature narrator. The young 'I' illustrates Portuguese working-class reading patterns in the 1940s and his family background is narrated by a mature 'I' who developed social consciousness.[2] In his study on the Literary Field, Pierre Bourdieu differentiated biography from social trajectory:

It is within each state of the field, defined by a particular configuration of the structure of the possibles, that the dispositions linked to a certain social ori-

---

1   Fernando Venâncio, 'Moço promissor' and Carlos Reis, 'Terra do Pecado, 50 Anos Depois – Arqueologia de um romance', Jornal de Letras, 26 March 1997 pp. 14-15. Jornal de Letras asked these two academics to read the novel and review it within the context of Saramago's literary career. The section of these two articles is: 'José Saramago, 50 Anos De Escritor', pp. 11-17.

2   José Saramago, 'Aviso', in Terra do Pecado, 8th edn (Lisbon: Editorial Caminho, 2001), pp. 7-9. The first edition did not have any preface. His Cadernos de Lanzarote, Diário V (1998) also reproduced 'Aviso' (pp. 138-140), indicating that Saramago's preface is as significant as his political opinions to the making of his public persona. The relevante of his diaries will be analysed below.

gin orient practice towards one occupied and of the more or less clearly avowed feeling of success or failure associated to it.[3]

In an interview given to Beatriz Berrini in 1994, Saramago stated that he and Editorial Caminho had agreed not to publish this reprint.[4] The style and narration of *Terra do Pecado* are completely different from that of the rest of his literary production published by Editorial Caminho after 1980. Fifty years after its first edition, Saramago said that this book had been influenced by his reading of Eça de Queirós.[5] This link was accepted and developed by Fernando Venâncio and Carlos Reis in their reviews mentioned above. Nevertheless, linking Saramago's literary production in 1997 to Eça de Queirós does not mean the same as linking his novel to that writer in 1947. Had Editorial Caminho published Saramago's bibliography in the 1980s, this would have implied positioning a debutant's literary practice in relation to a literary authority (and in view of the fact that it was published during the Estado Novo, it would have positioned Saramago within the Regime's accepted literary practice). In 1997, having published regular literary production, that links becomes relevant to frame the writer within the Portuguese literary canon and strengthened his symbolic capital (in Saramago, it meant acknowledgement of literary value combined with commercial success). *Terra do Pecado* does not fit the bibliography of a writer who introduced himself to readers as the heir of the Neo-Realist literature and of the ideals of the Revolution. This was suggested in 1997 by Carlos Reis:

---

3   Pierre Bourdieu, *The Field of Cultural Production*. (Cambridge: Polity Press & Blackwell Publishers Ltd, 1993), p. 189.

4   'Se não incluo esse livro na minha bibliografia, é simplesmente porque ele foi escrito na minha bibliografia, é simplesmente porque ele foi escrito por outra pessoa, melhor ainda, por alguém que ainda estava a caminho de ser pessoa. Não o renego, apenas o deixo ficar lá onde está, quase na adolescência, no limiar da experiência e da vida.' Quoted from Beatriz Berrini, *Ler Saramago: O Romance* (Lisbon: Editorial Caminho, 1998), p. 228.

5   'O romancista sintetiza, aí, a acção do livro. 'É a história de uma senhora viúva, onde há uma criada que vem na linha directa da Juliana', diz, numa referência à conhecida e trágica figura de O Primo Basílio'. Quoted from Venâncio, p. 14.

José Saramago protagoniza e representa um projecto literário sólido e coe-
rente. Cinquenta anos depois de um romance que praticamente não teve vida própria, percebe-se bem que esse projecto foi lentamente sedimentado e
solidamente enraizado, para poder afirmar a sua pertinência e dar vida a
outros romances: aos que não lembram expressamente Terra do Pecado, mas
talvez não pudessem existir sem ele.[6]

This comment would not have been possible in 1947. However, in
1997, Saramago's first novel is validated as a document of the
writer's literary heritage and does not set him as a reproducer of
the Portuguese literary canon.[7]

This novel had several reprints after 1997, although they included less than the average print run of 3,000 copies.[8] It shows
that the decision to publish *Terra do Pecado* involved strengthening
Saramago's literary career and it was less a question of adding a
new title to his *oeuvre*. Moreover, the fact that it was not a bestseller (unlike most Saramago's novels when first published after
1980) also suggests that Portuguese readers did not clearly accept
that novel as part of Saramago's literary production.

The aspects of his life that concerned the period before 1974
were made available to the public after 1980, both by Saramago
and by his publisher, Zeferino Coelho, in such a way that they
expressed his views of social repression and discrimination against
the working class and Communists during the Estado Novo.[9]
Moreover, when he started giving interviews to the press in the
1980s, he never mentioned his professional life of the 1950s and
1960s. Interviews and short biographical profiles refer to his family

---

6   Carlos Reis, 'Terra do Pecado, 50 anos depois: Arqueologia de um romance',
    p. 15.
7   I am using the term 'reproduction' as Bourdieu used it: 'based on recogni-
    tion of the 'old' by the 'young' – homage, celebration, etc. – and recognition
    of the 'young' by the 'old' – prefaces, co-optation, consecration, etc.'. Quoted
    from Bourdieu, p. 57.
8   The 8th reprint was published in 2001. The print-run was composed of 2,000
    copies, as stated in *Terra do Pecado* (2001).
9   See Filipa Melo, 'A Vida Segundo José Saramago: Fotobiografia', Visão, 10
    December 1998, <http://www.instituto-camoes.pt/escritores/saramago/foto
    biografia.htm> [accessed in July 2003]. This report included statements by
    his publisher, Zeferino Coelho, who mentioned that Saramago invented the
    'comunismo hormonal' when he worked at a factory.

background, and to his professional life after 1974, with a few references to his activity as a translator and to his experience with the Estado Novo's censorship. This does not mean that the report about his life before the Revolution is non-existent but it is of restricted access. The National Library holds his literary papers and they refer only to the 1950s up till the 1970s. These files can be read from requesting authorization to the services.[10] Saramago's publicity involves his life experience after the 1970s. As far as the period preceding that decade, which was important for his formation of his class-consciousness was not included in public statements, interviews or any publicity material. The only exception is his childhood (working-class background).[11]

Bourdieu gave the term 'social trajectory' to a constructed biography.[12] Biographical profiles of Portuguese writers publicized on book flaps and in newspapers reviews, in particular those who belong to the 1950s and 1960s generation, legitimize their position in the literary field, substantiating literary achievement with personal experience (and thus authority) during the Estado Novo. For example, those of Miguel Torga and Vergílio Ferreira highlight part of the country's picture during that period: they lived part of their lives in the rural areas of the country and studied in urban

10 Readers have to go to the Library's reading service to request authorization to have access to Saramago's (or any other writers') literary papers. Authorization is decided in twenty-four hours and the reader has to explain why he wants to have access to papers (reasons that have to do with academic research are considered valid).

11 In 1973, he published a short story entitled 'O Embargo'. It describes a car driver's ordeal, fatally trapped in to death, being driven by a car that suddenly acquired a will of its own, thwarting the driver from letting him out. It is a politically conscious narrative, and was included in *Escrita e Combate – Textos de Escritores Comunistas*, published by Edições Avante in 1976. It included othershort stories by 46 writers, including Egito Gonçalves, Maria Alzira Seixo, Manuel da Fonseca, Maria Velho da Costa, Nelson de Matos, Urbano Tavares Rodrigues and Óscar Lopes.

12 'Social trajectory or constructed biography is defined as the set of successive movements of an agent in a structured (hierarchized) space, itself subject to displacements and distortions,or, more precisely, in the structure of the distribution of the different kinds of capital of consecration'. Quoted from *The Field of Literary Production*, p. 276.

centres; had very few opportunities to read books during child-hood and opposed the Estado Novo. As far as Saramago is concerned, a text on his biography published immediately after his Nobel Prize, legitimized his non-literary career through his acquaintances (writers, painters and publishers) in the 1950s.[13]

7.1.2 Reviewing and Prefacing

Saramago became engaged in professional writing in that decade when he started to translate French and German fiction for Publicações Europa-América and for Estúdios Cor and to review for *Vértice* and *Seara Nova*. At the beginning of the 1950s, he contributed to *Vértice*, authoring a short story and an essay on Gil Vicente.[14] In 1955, he started working in the production sector at Estúdios Cor but in 1959, Nataniel Costa embarked on a diplomatic career and invited Saramago to replace him at Estúdios Cor.[15] Saramago contributions to *Seara Nova* took place between May 1967 and November 1968.[16] He reviewed various authors for *Seara Nova*, such as Bernardo Santareno, Nelson de Matos, Urbano Tavares Rodrigues, Fausto Lopo de Carvalho, Augusto Abelaira,

13 See Filipa Melo, 'A Vida Segundo José Saramago: Fotobiografia'. According to this report, his friends and acquaintances (José Augusto França, Augusto Costa Dias, the publisher of Editora Portugália, Urbano Tavares Rodrigues, Manuel Dias Carvalho and Nataniel Costa introduced Saramago into the literary milieu. All of them (like Saramago) were subscribers to the MUD.
14 José Saramago, 'O Heroísmo quotidiano', *Vértice*: revista de cultura e arte, 13 (1953), 397-399 and 'A propósito duma "Cosmogonia" Vicentina', *Vértice*: revista de cultura e arte, 15 (1955), 321-329. A full list of Saramago's work translated between 1955 and 1981 is included in Horácio Costa, *José Saramago: O Período Formativo* (Lisbon: Editorial Caminho, 1997).
15 In a letter of 31 December 1959, Costa explained his reasons: 'Se o escolhi entre tantos outros possíveis candidatos, foi por julgar que V. reunia as condições intelectuais e morais necessárias'. The letters are included in José Saramago's literary papers held by the National Library [N. 45].
16 The circumstances of Saramago's assignment are described in his letter to José Rodrigues Miguéis on 8 May 1967. Saramago and José Rodrigues Miguéis exchanged letters between 1959 and 1971, when Miguéis was published by Estúdios Cor and these letters are also kept in Saramago's literary papers.

Agustina Bessa Luís, Manuel de Campos Pereira, Mário Ventura, Jorge de Sena, Álvaro Guerra, José Marmelo e Silva, Rúben A., José Cardoso Pires, Ferreira de Castro, and Rentes de Carvalho. In these reviews, Saramago focussed on aspects that had to do with literariness. In his reviews of Jorge de Sena's *Novas Andanças do Demónio*, he criticized the abuse of metaphors and of Ferreira de Castro's *O Instinto Supremo*, he criticized the narrative for being too elaborate.[17] His reviews indicate that he refused to accept this literary style and baroque language in the literary discourse and preferred Realist fiction to fiction encouraged by the SNI.[18] This criticism is exactly what characterized his writing after the 1980s, in particular after *Memorial do Convento* (1982). It showed that certain language or literary features signified differently depending on how the producer and consecrating agent position the writer and work in the literary field. In 1983, he suggested his reading of Latin-American literature had showed him that the baroque language could be reinvented in Realism.[19] His association with the Neo-Realist literature of García Marquez was what awakened foreign critics' interest in his novels, as will be shown in Chapter 8.

In 1966, Saramago prefaced Isabel da Nóbrega's *Já não há Salomão*, a special publication for 'the friends of Editorial Estúdios

---

17   José Saramago, 'Novas andanças do demónio', *Seara Nova*, 1460 (1967), 181; 'Sem Armas na floresta: sobre O Instituto (sic: "Instinto") supremo, de Ferreira de Castro', *Seara Nova*, 1474 (1968), 281.

18   Relevant examples of this preference are José Saramago, 'Um sorriso em Montedor: sobre o Montedor, de Rentes de Carvalho', Seara Nova 1471, (1968), 173; 'As relações mágicas: sobre Relações Humanas (Os Quatro Rios, A Dança das Espadas, Canção Diante de Uma Porta Fechada), de Agustina Bessa Luís', 1467, (1968), 29-30.

19   'Os escritores latino-americanos, por exemplo, estão a supreender-nos a toda a hora e a mostrar como o barroco pode ser realista e o realismo pode ser barroco'. Quoted from Fernando Dacosta, 'Escrever é fazer recuar a morte é dilatar o espaço da vida', *Jornal de Letras*, 18 January 1983, pp. 16-17 (p. 17). During the period Saramago was literary editor of Estúdios Cor (1955-1971), the publishing house's booklist suggested some favouring of Neo-Realism and left-wing orientation: Raúl Brandão and Alves Redol, José Rodrigues Miguéis, João Gaspar Simões, José Gomes Ferreira, Urbano Tavares Rodrigues, José Palma Ferreira, José Marmelo e Silva and António José Saraiva.

Cor' at Christmas.[20] His preface to Isabel da Nóbrega's small book is relevant because he prefaced a book by a SPE prize-winner. Prefacing is often used by consecrated writers to confer some prestige to another writer or a work, as indicated by Bourdieu.[21] That was not so in this case because Saramago was not a consecrated writer in 1966, although he had already published poetry (and *Terra do Pecado* in 1947).[22] *Já não há Salomão* was a short story of restricted circulation and his authority as literary editor was established in that preface. The fact that it was by a SPE prizewinner was prestigious to Estúdios Cor and to his literary editor. Only in 1979 did Saramago author another preface to Armindo Rodrigues's *O Poeta Perguntador*. It was a compilation of autobiographical poems edited by him and published by Editorial Caminho. This preface is relevant in Saramago's literary career because it enabled Saramago to take a position in the literary field, establishing a link with Neo-Realism before he produced regularly, in particular after *Levantado do Chão* (1980). Armindo Rodrigues was a prizewinner and an Editorial Caminho in-house writer. [23] Nevertheless, it should be pointed out that those prefaces were not publicized by Saramago's publishing house and their relevance emerges from research into his work and profile, thus enabling logical links to be made Saramago's decisions and activities during the 1950s.

---

20 Isabel da Nóbrega was not an in-house writer of Estúdios Cor. Her first novel, *Os Anjos e os Homens*, had been published by SIT in 1952 and *Viver com os Outros*'s first edition was published by Lux, although Portugália reprinted it in 1965.

21 Bourdieu, p. 42.

22 In 1966, Portugália published his *Os Poemas Possíveis*. This had only one edition and was reprinted again in 1982, by Editorial Caminho, after *Memorial do Convento*, and a third reprint was published in 1985.

23 Armindo Rodrigues received the Diário de Notícias Prize of Literature in 1972 and the António Patrício Prize of the Sociedade Portuguesa de Escritores Médicos in 1974. In 1971, he had turned down being shortlisted for the SEIT Prize for Poetry.

7.1.3 Political Awareness

Interviews and biographical reports show that his friends and acquaintances introduced him to the political environment. As far as his literary work was concerned, he had some poems and articles published in Diário de Lisboa between 1968 and 1972.[24] His political views encouraged him to participate in the third Congress of Democratic Opposition in Aveiro that took place between 4-8 April in 1973. Saramago sat on the 5th panel of this Congress, that discussed items related to Culture and Education.[25]

The fact that he came from a working-class environment, and his political ideology, made him develop class-consciousness, which was the cornerstone for the presentation of experience during the Estado Novo in the 1980s and in the 1990s.[26] Unlike many of his Communist friends, he was not tortured or arrested, as he stated in the 1990s:

> Como jornalista, ou simples colaborador, primeiro em A Capital e no Jornal do Fundão, e depois no Diário de Lisboa, onde em parte dos anos de 1972 e 1973 tive a responsabilidade da coluna 'Opinião' [...], isso sim, soube o que era a indignação de ver esfaqueadas palavras que escrevi e ideias que expressei [...] Também recordo o tempo em que trabalhei na editorial Estúdios

---

24 At Diário de Lisboa, he worked together with Urbano Tavares Rodrigues, Isabel da Nóbrega, Eugénio Melo e Castro, and José Carlos Vasconcelos, among other writers. See Melo, 'A Vida Segundo José Saramago: Fotobiografia'. In 1970, Livros Horizonte published his *Provavelmente Alegria*, also reprinted by Editorial Caminho in 1985. In 1985, Editorial Caminho also reprinted his *Deste Mundo E Do Outro*, a collection of essays originally published in *A Capital* in 1968 and 1969and Editora Arcádia published his book in 1971.Those reprints in the early 1980s legitimised Saramago's literary work, showing his mastery of literature through genre diversity and long-standing production.

25 José Saramago, 'Para um Estudo da Situação da Cultura e da Informação em Portugal'. The proceedings of the 5th panel were not recorded because the debates and conclusions were too extensive. According to the overall conclusions, the 5th panel accused censorship of keeping the Portuguese ignorant of the country's reality.

26 At *Diário de Lisboa*, he wrote articles claiming the reform of Education; he stood for fundamental human rights and freedom of press and against illiteracy.

Cor, quando uma vez ou outra recebemos a visita de agentes da PIDE que iam apreender livros.[27]

Joining the PCP in 1969 made him a clandestine due to his Communist activism. According to some of Saramago's brothers in arms, he was a very diligent activist, managing to distribute copies of *Avante!*.[28] He described his involvement in the Revolution to *Expresso*:

> Não esquecerei o 1º de Maio, nem o 28 de Setembro, nem o 11 de Março, nem a Assembleia do MFA em Tancos; nem os meses em que fui director adjunto do *Diário de Notícias*. Não esquecerei o Alentejo nem a cintura industrial. Não esquecerei o que então chamávamos Esperança.[29]

Saramago's political and cultural involvement in the Revolution and, in particular, in the MFA Project influenced the making of his persona. In 1974, he was appointed the coordinator of a commission working on cultural activities at the Fundo de Apoio aos Organismos Juvenis of the Ministry of Media. Between April and November 1975, he was deputy editor at *Diário de Notícias* and this post was relevant in the constitution of Saramago's public persona because of his involvement in a purge of journalists associated with the Regime. After the coup on 25 November, Saramago, together with Luís de Barros, the newspaper's editor and other Communist journalists, were dismissed. They were accused of taking too radical a stance against democratic values and were replaced by Víctor Cunha Rego and Mário Mesquita, editor and deputy editor respectively. The PCP did not support Saramago and he felt this as a betrayal. His resentment was documented in one of his diaries:

> O pior de tudo [...] foi aquele dia em que me defrontei com uma fria, gratuita e desapiedada indiferença, vinda precisamente de quem tinha o dever absoluto de oferecer-me a mão estendida. Sendo, porém, os casos e acasos da

---

27 Cândido Azevedo, *A Censura de Salazar e Marcelo Caetano* (Lisbon: Editorial Caminho, 1999), p. 32.
28 According to Urbano Tavares Rodrigues and Carlos Brito. See 'A Vida Segundo José Saramago: Fotobiografia'.
29 *Expresso*, 23 April 1994, p. 130.

vida férteis em contradições, sabe-se lá se a minha vida de escritor não terá começado justamente nessa hora?[30]

His involvement in the purge of journalists served the purpose of those of wanted to associate him to the 1974-1975 volatile events and to Communist rule. As far as his view of the events is concerned, they were documented in a text that prefaced *Os Apontamentos*:

> Desde o primeiro dia não faltaram incompreensões e ataques: eram facilmente previsíveis, mas não nos desviaram do caminho traçado e da obediência aos objectivos finais. Viria a ser precisa uma hábil e rápida manobra da direita militar para deter o curso da revolução – e levar o Diário de Notícias a (provavelmente) regressar a antigos e conhecidos trilhos, contra a vontade, enfim conhecida e outra vez recalcada, da maioria politicamente consciente dos seus trabalhadores.[31]

The author rationalised the events in terms of a serious setback to the ideals of the masses that included him. Saramago's disapproval of the course taken by the Portuguese government was clear on the days that preceded the 25 November:

> Este Governo não entende nada do que se passa no País que é suposto governar. Ou então entende tão pouco que vai acumulando os erros sem deles se dar conta.[32]

Cadernos de Lanzarote was published when he left for Lanzarote in 1994. Saramago compared this departure to an exile from Portugal.[33] The publication of diaries was not new in Saramago but,

---

30 José Saramago, *Cadernos de Lanzarote V* (Lisbon: Editorial Caminho, 1998), pp. 29-30.

31 José Saramago, 'Prefácio à 1ª edição', *Os Apontamentos – Crónicas Políticas* (Lisbon: Editorial Caminho, 1998), p. 192.

32 Saramago, 'Os saudosos do fascismo', *Os Apontamentos*, p. 359. This article was first published in *Diário de Notícias* on 7 November 1975.

33 'Eu não estaria a viver em Lanzarote se não tivesse vindo ao mundo um sujeito chamado Sousa Lara e não tivesse Portugal um governo, todo ele, capaz de dar cobertura cobarde ao seu vergonhoso acto de censura. Nunca havia pensado viver fora de Portugal.', Quoted from 'José Saramago: A escrita narcísiva por excelência', *Jornal de Letras*, 13 April 1994, pp. 4-5 (p. 5).

since he compared the incident with *O Evangelho Segundo Jesus Cristo* in 1992 with the censorship under the Estado Novo, his diaries were a walk down memory lane in relation to what happened to certain writers, who also published their own diaries when they were living abroad.[34] Some of the relevant examples are Miguel Torga's *Diário*, Vergílio Ferreira's volumes of *Conta-Corrente*, Eduardo Prado Coelho's *Tudo o que não escrevi* and José Gomes Ferreira's *A Memória das Palavras*. His *Cadernos de Lanzarote* was centred on showing the Portuguese his literary success outside Portugal, in particular in the United Kingdom, in Germany and in Spain. After 1997, his diaries also served the purpose of indicating his ideological stances and the confidence he had in the Revolution.

7.1.4 Novels

Saramago's fiction published between 1977 and 1978 was not bestseller. His political motivations were clear in narrative representation and, in particular, in his epigraphs.[35] In 1977, Moraes Editores published his *Manual de Pintura e Caligrafia*. This publishing house was oriented to Portuguese literature and published several writers and poets in the 1970s, such as Sophia de Mello Breyner, Jorge de Sena, Pedro Tamen, António Ramos Rosa, José Cardoso Pires, José Gomes Ferreira and Maria Velho da Costa. The publisher explained *Manual de Pintura e Caligrafia*'s subtitle 'Ensaio de Romance' on the back cover:

---

34 *Jornal de Letras* referred to the published diaries by Vergílio Ferreira, Mário Sacramento, Sebastião da Gama, José Régio, Eduardo Lourenço and José Gomes Ferreira to show that *Cadernos de Lanzarote* follow a certain tradition of Portuguese writers. (p. 4).
35 *Manual de Pintura e Caligrafia*'s epigraph was 'on revient de loin. La formation bourgeoise, l'orgueil intellectuel. La necessité de se réviser à tout moment. Les lieus qui subsistent. La sentimentalité. L'empoisonement de la culture orientée. Paul Vaillant. Couturier'; That of *Objecto Quase* was 'Se o homem é formado pelas circunstâncias, é necessário formar as circunstâncias humanamente. K. Marx and F. Engels. A Sagrada Família'.

(Em termos muito mais simples, explicaria o autor, e só a história de um pintor de retratos que decide escrever. E é ainda, por essa e outras razões ditas em seu tempo e lugar, um livro político). De facto, o homem não é um animal especializado nem especializável.[36]

This is an introspective novel, in which the 'I', a mediocre painter, aware of his limitations, seeks the reasons that compel him to paint, in the same way the writer is compelled to write. Painting and writing are represented as two ways of self-expression and of understanding the world during the Estado Novo.[37] As Luís de Sousa Rebelo observed in the preface to its reprint in 1983:

> No *Manual* examinam-se discretamente magnas questões de estética e esconjuram-se, no próprio exercício de escrita, as tentações que o neo-realismo oferece ao ficcionista do nosso tempo, empenhado em encontrar o seu próprio caminho para narrar a estória do contemporâneo em moldes adequados e diferentes dos que lhe oferece um prestigiado discurso do passado.[38]

In 1978, the publisher, this time Editorial Caminho, also publicised *Objecto Quase* on the back cover:

> *Objecto Quase* é um livro in-temporal, ninguém tem nele um bilhete de identidade: a des-situação é praticada desde a primeira página, embora a novela de abertura conte uma história que toda a gente conhece: "um dia Salazar caiu de uma cadeira...". Pensa o autor que, pela via de uma certa abstracção, se instalou, aqui, na dureza limpa do concreto.[39]

---

36 José Saramago, *Manual de Pintura e Caligrafia – Ensaio de Romance* (Lisbon: Moraes Editores, 1977), back cover.

37 José Saramago, *Manual de Pintura e Caligrafia – Romance* (Lisbon: Editorial Caminho, 1998) refers to the PIDE and to events that preceded the Revolution. Relevant examples are on pp. 271 and 293.

38 Luís de Sousa Rebelo. 'Os Rumos da Ficção de José Saramago', in José Saramago, *Manual de Pintura e Caligrafia*, p. 33.

39 José Saramago, *Objecto Quase* (Lisbon: Editorial Caminho, 1978), back cover. The back cover of this edition also publicised *Levantado do Chão* and *O Ano da Morte de Ricardo Reis*. Nelson de Matos, the publisher of Moraes Editores, explained to *Expresso* (27 November 2004, p. 29) that the publishing house's economic problems that led to its bankruptcy in the early 1980s were the major reasons for not having published *Levantado do Chão*. Saramago has stated several times that political pressures against him were the reason for the

At that time, Saramago was mainly known for his political activities and beliefs. His fiction sales were commercial flops, although reviews were favourable. The fact that they were published only in *Colóquio-Letras* might account for the books' lack of commercial visibility.[40] It is relevant that Editorial Caminho's reprints of *Manual de Pintura e Caligrafia* and *Objecto Quase* after *Memorial do Convento* did considerably better.[41] The timing was different and Saramago's prestige after the publication of *Levantado do Chão* and *Memorial do Convento* was also different from that in the late 1970s.

7.1.5 Editorial Caminho

Saramago moved to Editorial Caminho in 1979. This was set up in 1975. Its founders, Francisco Melo and Vítor Branco, as well as Zeferino Coelho who joined them some time later, were affiliated to the PCP. Editorial Caminho owned *O Diário* and still publishes *Vértice*. Francisco Melo also runs Edições Avante.[42] Editorial

---

publisher's turning down the novel. This incident marked the end of the relations between Saramago and Moraes.

40 António Ramos-Rosa, 'José Saramago: Provavelmente Alegria', *Colóquio Letras*, 59 (1970), 73; João Palma-Ferreira, 'José Saramago: Deste Mundo e do Outro', *Colóquio Letras*, 6 (1972), 83-84; Maria Alzira Seixo, 'José Saramago: Objecto Quase', *Colóquio Letras*, 49, (1979), 78.

41 Editorial Caminho reprinted *Manual de Caligrafia e Pintura* in 1983 and a third reprint in 1985; *Objecto Quase*'s second reprint was in 1984 and the third in 1986.

42 There were occasional rumours in the newspapers that the PCP invested some money in the company, although there is no clear evidence. Nevertheless, it is relevant that they referred to Jorge Araújo's consultancy at Editorial Caminho's publishers in the early 1990s; *Público*, 20 March 1990: 'Este dirigente "histórico" comunista é, dentro da direcção do partido, o responsável pela ideologia, e logo pela propaganda, e pela política editorial do PCP. Segundo um ex-funcionário do partido, deve-se a Araújo o "fechar das portas à divulgação de obras ideologicamente mais polémicas na Caminho'. However, times change. In 2000, Editorial Caminho turned down the publication of the Communist Carlos Brito's novel *A Páginas Tantas*, after this author had taken positions in favour of the modernisation of the Party's platform and hierarchies. The novel referred to the recent history of Communism and the PCP and was published by Campo das Letras, another puh-

Caminho started to publish books in 1977 and their first book was *Do fundo do Tempo* by Miguel Urbano Rodrigues. In 1979, their fiction series, O Campo da Palavra, consisted of seven authors: António Ramos Rosa, José Saramago, Faure da Rosa, Orlando da Costa, Miguel Urbano Rodrigues, Armindo Rodrigues and Urbano Tavares Rodrigues. Between 1977 and 2004, Editorial Caminho's interests covered fiction, essays, poetry, children's books, detective stories, painting, and photography, linguistics, science fiction, economics and management.[43]

Edições Avante is a publishing business directly associated to the PCP and *Avante* is also the name of the newspaper published by this Party. That publishing house prospered in the seventies but declined as national politics gave a turn to the right. Nowadays, Edições Avante is still active, but the catalogue chiefly offers books by Communist thinkers, such as Lenin, Marx and Engels and Álvaro Cunhal's literary *oeuvre*.

Editorial Caminho is not directly associated with the PCP. Their catalogue was expanded with books by writers who were either associated with the PS or played important roles in the opposition to the Estado Novo, such as Isabel Barreno, Sophia de Mello Breyner, Artur Portela, José Manuel Mendes and Maria Judite de Carvalho. In view of the profile of books published by Caminho, there is reasonable evidence that left-wing ideology has guided their editorial policy. Its aims were clear both in their initiatives and in their catalogues. Driven by Communist ideology, they wanted to have a participating role in society, to educate the Portuguese and, therefore, one of their market niches was and has been schools. They publish a magazine that has been distributed among students, and promoted children's books.[44] This is not far

---

lishing house set up in 1994 by Jorge Araújo who, after taking positions against dissidents, also left the Party's board. This affair was widely publicised, for example in *Público*, 26 October 2000.

43 One of the indications that this business prospered is the fact that they moved from a flat to a detached house in one of the main avenues in Lisbon in the late 1980s.

44 See interview with Zeferino Coelho, Appendix 1 on pp. 339. Their promotion of children's books was successful, since Alice Vieira, Editorial Caminho's in-house author, was awarded with the International Year of

from the purposes of most publishing houses set up during the Estado Novo. Editorial Caminho's purposes can be regarded as an attempt to pursue the Cultural Revolution promised by the MFA and their continuing activity reminds us of some of the publishers' opposition before 1974.

In 1979, Saramago wrote *A Noite*, a play published by Editorial Caminho. This was about the opposition between the board and editorial staff of a newspaper in Lisbon, working on the night between 24 and 25 of April 1974. It received the Portuguese Association of Critics Prize in 1979. The Revolution was one of the topics that prevailed in bestselling fiction between 1974 and 1979 and the fact that the play was staged added visibility to Saramago's work. Moreover, this happened at a time when new literary prizes were set up and became exposed to the media.

Publicity played an important role in the exposure of *Levantado do Chão*. Publishing in November is indicative of a business strategy to attract the readers' attention to the book and, thus, ensure sales. October-November is the beginning of the new publishing season, and just before Christmas, the period where book sales generally increase.[45] It is also a period in which critics are especially attentive. Before writing it, Saramago carried out fieldwork in the Alentejo, living in Lavre among the peasants for some months. He defined his stance thus:

> Um escritor é um homem como os outros: sonha. E o meu sonho foi o de poder dizer deste livro, quando o terminasse: "Isto é o Alentejo." Dos sonhos, porém, acordamos todos, e agora eis-me não diante do sonho realizado, mas da concreta e possível forma do sonho. Por isso me permitirei a escre-

---

Children Prize for Children's Fiction in 1979. She also received the Calouste Gulbenkian Prize for Children's Fiction published in 1983.

45 This has been a regular pattern in the publication of Saramago's books. *Memorial do Convento* was published in October 1982; *O Ano da Morte de Ricardo Reis* was published in November 1984; *A Jangada de Pedra* was published in November 1986; *O Evangelho Segundo Jesus Cristo* was published at the end of November 1991; *Ensaio sobre a Cegueira, Todos os Nomes, O Homem Duplicado, A Caverna* and some of his diaries *Cadernos de Lanzarote* were also published in these months; *História do Cerco de Lisboa* was the only exception in the period that preceded the Nobel Prize, having been published in April 1989, and *Ensaio sobre a Lucidez* was published in March 2004.

ver: "Isto é um livro sobre o Alentejo". Um livro, um simples romance, gente, conflitos, alguns amores, muitos sacrifícios e grandes fomes, as vitórias e os desastres, a aprendizagem da transformação, e mortes. [...][46]

The central story of *Levantado do Chão* involves three generations of a family between the end of the Portuguese monarchy and the Revolution of 1974, narrated in thirty-four chapters. The narrative endorses the points of view of the workers and focuses on their living conditions in the Alentejo. Chapter XVII describes the PIDE's torture and death of a peasant, Germano Vidigal. The writer paid tribute to him and to José Adelino dos Santos, also assassinated by the secret police, dedicating this novel to them. In the short text on the back cover, the writer endorsed the workers' claims and conveyed subtle disappointment for the fact that the Revolution did not go as he hoped.

Saramago's acceptance speech at the award ceremony for the Cidade de Lisboa Prize for this novel was the opportunity to draw the attention of the audience, journalists included, to the writer's role in the Portuguese society of the early 1980s:

Começarei por perguntar: é possível e desejável ser escritor em Portugal? [...] Aliás, o escritor português, se quiser viver à boa paz com o mundo das conveniências próprias e dos interesses alheios, há-de cultivar o sentimento de gratidão perpétua.[47]

He assumed the role of spokesperson of the Portuguese writers and his authority was rooted in his class-consciousness, in his fieldwork in the Alentejo, enhanced by his working-class back-

---

46 José Saramago, *Levantado do Chão* (Lisbon: Editorial Caminho, 1980), back cover.

47 José Saramago, 'Discurso por ocasião do recebimento do Prémio Cidade de Lisboa', *Folhas Políticas* (Lisbon: Editorial Caminho, 1999), pp. 109-110. The press reported that the prize was not consensual because Saramago was more politically than literarily well known. These facts enhanced Saramago and this novel's visibility as well as the topic, with some consequences for the publisher because the Agrarian Reform was a very sensitive issue and some writers did not want to be published by the publishing house that endorsed it. See Appendix 1 on pp. 339.

ground.[48] The book-signing session at the Casa do Alentejo, covered by the press, strengthened his claim that writers were men of the people and that, like blue-collar workers, their rights ought to be defended because they were assigned with the mission of drawing readers' attention to human misery. The role of Editorial Caminho in the promotion of Saramago's novels was and has been extremely helpful because every novel has been preceded by book-signing sessions.[49] This novel's exposure also benefited from the publication of *Jornal de Letras* in 1981. In November of that year, Maria Lúcia Lepecki, a well-known university teacher of Portuguese Literature and literary critic, associated *Levantado do Chão* with Garcia Marquez's, Nélida Piñon's and Guimarães Rosa's fiction, albeit deeply Portuguese-rooted and politically compromised.[50] The critic's positioning of Saramago in relation to Garcia Marquez's 'Magic Realism' was particularly helpful for his literary legitimacy, in particular in the United States and in the United Kingdom. The prize and the reviews positioned Saramago's literary work in relation to widely consecrated literature and enabled the publication of *Levantado do Chão* in Moscow and Brazil in 1982. This link was also accepted by Saramago, as mentioned above. As Bourdieu stated in his study on the Literary Field, a work of art exists only by virtue of the valuing community, which acknowledges it as a work of art and position-takings are constructed ac-

---

48 At the book-signing session, his mother was photographed with him, and as far as marketing strategy is concerned, this is evidence of the family background he referred to to prove his authority. It is equally relevant that up till the late 1980s, Saramago was often photographed, wearing long-sleeved shirt, no tie and a beret, similar to any blue-collar worker. During the 1990s, especially at the end of the decade, when his prestige was consolidated, he was photographed wearing a suit and tie.

49 *O Ano da Morte de Ricardo Reis*'s presentation took place at Cooperativa Árvore (cultural venue), Oporto; *Jangada de Pedra*'s was at Fórum Picoas (conference room), Lisbon; *História do Cerco de Lisboa*'s took place at Castelo de S.Jorge (historical site focussed on in the novel), Lisbon; and *Evangelho Segundo Jesus Cristo*'s took place at the Igreja de S.Domingos (where progressive Catholics organised a vigil of protest against the Regime, in particular against the Colonial War, on 1 January 1969).

50 Maria Lúcia Lepecki, 'Levantado do Chão: história e pedagogia', *Jornal de Letras*, 27 October 1981, p. 12.

cording to the disposition to take advantage of available possibilities:

> All agents, writers, artists or intellectuals construct their own creative project according, first of all, to their perception of the available possibilities afforded by the categories of perception and appreciation inscribed in their habitus through a certain trajectory and, secondly, to their predisposition to take advantage of or reject those possibilities in accordance with the interests associated with their position in the game.[51]

His epigraph taken from Almeida Garrett positioned the writer in relation to the Portuguese literary canon. On the one hand, this was an obvious reference to a consecrated writer, whose novel *Viagens na minha Terra* had been studied at secondary school level since the Estado Novo; on the other hand, the epigraph identified Garrett's political stances (including as deputee of the Assembly) on social differences. Saramago's epigraph legitimised his critical stance against class differences through the literary canon, although it also introduced some disturbance as far as the canon was concerned. Garrett as an icon of Portuguese Romanticism was underestimated and his words were reinvented in a novel of a clear Neo-Realist influence.[52] Saramago's authority was enhanced with commercial success, since in 1983, *Levantado do Chão* was fourth in bestselling fiction.[53]

The publication of *Memorial do Convento* in 1982 strengthened his stance as spokesperson of the working class.[54] In this historical novel, set at the time of the construction of the Covent of Mafra in

---

51   Bourdieu, p. 184.
52   In 1980, Saramago's *Viagem a Portugal*, commissioned and published by Círculo de Leitores also had an epigraph taken from Almeida Garrett's *Viagens na minha Terra* to legitimize, with the literary canon, his different trip. Without referring to it, Saramago's book reinvented Miguel Torga's *Portugal* (1950), taking a different point of view from that of Torga. Whereas Torga's *Portugal* examines the country's reality in the 1950s, showing the working class's hard work and difficulties (reflecting his stance against the Estado Novo's values), Saramago's *Viagem* endeavours to identify traces of genuine and traditional values in the country of 1980.
53   *Jornal de Letras*, November, 1983.
54   Equally relevant are his straightforward comparisons to peasants' life to comment on commercial and literary success. See Dacosta, p. 17.

the 1700s, workers are protagonists whereas the nobility is given a supporting role. This novel played a very important role in the public recognition of Saramago's work, because it was his first novel to be published in the English-speaking market and his first work to receive two literary prizes: PEN Club Prize (1982) and the Cidade de Lisboa Prize (1983). The fact that Saramago had received a literary prize for his first novel was important to draw the attention of the press and of critics; the publicity around the fact that it did not win the APE Literary Prize was particularly important for his prestige because press articles, particularly in *Jornal de Letras*, conveyed the idea at that time and up till 1992 that Saramago was neglected by the APE Prize panels.[55] This contrasted with the favourable reviews published following the publication of the novel.[56] The fact that important critics, who adjudicated on the most important literary prizes, signed these reviews was very important for Saramago's literary legitimacy. It is equally relevant that Lepecki identified that novel as being one of the most representative of the Portuguese fiction produced in 1982. This selection was made when Portuguese writers were becoming more productive after some years of slower output; therefore being among the most representative fiction was particularly significant in the increase of symbolic capital.[57] *Memorial do Convento* was reviewed in 1983 as a representation of the writer's social role.[58]

---

55 *Expresso*, 'Cinco votos de um grande prémio', 21 May 1983, pp. 38R-39R. It is interesting that, according to members of the jury, *Memorial do Convento* was not considered a potential winner, unlike the message in the articles published in *Jornal de Letras* (Jornal de Letras, '"Amadeo" e "Ricardo Reis" às portas da APE', 2 April, 1985; *Jornal de Letras*, 'O refém', 6 May, 1990, p. 30). Whether Editorial Caminho encouraged the rumours about Saramago's work being neglected is not clear, considering that publishers send copies of the novels to panels. Nevertheless, media pressure is one of the ways used by Editorial Caminho to have news about its writers published. See Appendix 1 on pp. 339.

56 Urbano Tavares Rodrigues, 'Um romance realistas e fabuloso', *Jornal de Letras*, 5 February, 1983, p. 26; Maria Lúcia Lepecki, 'Arquitectura e Música', *Expresso*, 14 May 1983, p. 35R; Dacosta, pp. 16-17.

57 Maria Lúcia Lepecki, 'Ficção 82: um percurso', *Expresso*, 15 January 1983, p. 28. Saramago's novel was among others surveyed, such as *A Balada da Praia*

The first interview Saramago gave to *Jornal de Letras* gave him the opportunity to expand on this role. He skilfully used his experience in journalism to describe the writer's role:

> Se a literatura nesta terra ainda serve para alguma coisa, isto é, se for mais do que alguns estarem ainda a escrever para alguns estarem ainda a ler, torna-se urgente recuperá-la já que a nossa sociedade corre o risco, devido aos audiovisuais, de emudecer, ou seja, de haver cada vez mais uma minoria com grande capacidade para falar e uma maioria crescente limitada a ouvir, não entendendo sequer muito bem o que escuta.[59]

Media exposure enabled Saramago to use his work, especially *Levantado do Chão*, *Memorial do Convento* and *O Ano da Morte de Ricardo Reis*, as a contribution to the ongoing cultural debate, making it timely. A clear example is his interview with Augusto Seabra, following the publication of *O Ano da Morte de Ricardo Reis* in 1984:

> Se este livro tivesse que levar um subtítulo poderia ser 'Contribuição para o diagnóstico da doença portuguesa'. Não sei muito bem que doença, uma vez que nem sequer estou a formular um diagnóstico, apenas me proponho contribuir para ele; mas há realmente, parece-me, uma doença portuguesa, que não é só lisboeta, mas que talvez assuma aqui as suas formas extremas.[60]

The fact that central issues discussed in Saramago's novels were also discussed in the political and cultural fields enhanced their visibility: *O Ano da Morte de Ricardo Reis* was published when the Portuguese State was preparing official ceremonies to celebrate the fiftieth anniversary of the death of Fernando Pessoa and used them to celebrate the country's modernity; *A Jangada de Pedra* was published when Portugal officially joined the EEC; and *História do Cerco de Lisboa* and *O Evangelho Segundo Jesus Cristo* were published

---

dos Cães, Rio Triste, Ora Esguardae, O Cais das Merendas and Paisagem com Mulher e Mar ao Fundo.
58 Lepecki highlighted that *Memorial do Convento* reflected the emotional and social instability of Portuguese society. See 'Arquitectura e Música', p. 28.
59 Dacosta, p. 17.
60 Augusto M. Seabra, 'José Saramago: o regresso de Ricardo Reis', *Expresso*, 24 November 1984 (pp. 32R-33-R) p. 32R

when the official cultural discourse appealed to the preservation of Portuguese historical heritage and beliefs.

Simultaneously, he expanded his diagnosis of Portuguese culture within the legitimacy rooted in his experience as Communist supporter and as a man concerned for welfare. These were non-literary qualities which contributed to determine his position in the Portuguese literary field.[61] In fact, other Portuguese novelists such as Maria Velho da Costa, Augusto Abelaira and José Cardoso Pires were also recognized as representatives of a certain generation of writers with particular political views and social concerns, as shown in Chapter 6. Saramago did not present himself to readers as a writer only; he was a man with experience in the field, who examined social and cultural problems and whose literary background was positioned in relation to Neo-Realism.[62]

At a time when the official discourse looked at Portuguese history for reassurance, Saramago's *oeuvre* introduced a disturbing stance that went against the Government's cultural policy. His stance was not new, being rooted in New Historicism:

> Quando digo corrigir, corrigir a História, não é no sentido de corrigir os factos da História, pois essa nunca poderia ser tarefa de romancista, mas sim de introduzir nela cartuchos que façam explodir o que até então parecia indiscutível: por outras palavras, substituir o que foi pelo que poderia ter sido.[63]

His 'if only' was particularly clear in his *História do Cerco de Lisboa*, but it was also behind the plot of *O Ano da Morte de Ricardo Reis*, *Jangada de Pedra* and *O Evangelho Segundo Jesus Cristo*: if the Crusades did not help the Portuguese to conquer Lisbon, then Portuguese history had been constructed to glorify Catholicism; if the

---

61 His detachment from the literary field is particularly clear in his interviews with Dacosta, p. 17 and Seabra, p. 33R. Equally relevant was his criticism against official presentations of literary prizes at his award of D.Dinis Prize in 1984, reported in *Jornal de Letras*, 4 August 1986, p. 19.

62 Urbano Tavares Rodrigues compared *Memorial do Convento*'s writing to Engels' Realism ('Um romance realistas e fabuloso', p. 26) and Saramago did not reject comparisons with the Portuguese Neo-Realist Literature (in Seabra, p. 33R).

63 José Saramago, 'História e Ficção', *Jornal de Letras*, 6 March 1990, p. 19. Saramago refers to George Duby's work in this article.

Iberian Peninsula became a raft, its floating in the Atlantic Ocean would show that Iberianism (the union among Portugal, Spain and South American countries) is deeply rooted in culture and history; if there are contradictions between the Gospels of Saint Mathew and of Saint Luke, then the life of Christ and his relationship with Mary Magdalene would have to be revised. The New Historicist approach was no longer new in 1990. Spanish historians, such as Ricardo de la Cierva and César Vidal, have re-evaluated the role of the Moors and the Jews in the History of Spain, left in oblivion after the Reconquista. Other contributions have re-evaluated the life of Jesus and of Mary Magdalene, shedding new light on Biblical Gospels.[64]

Iberianism emerged when the political debate confronted the pro-European PS and the right wing against the PCP which protested against Portuguese membership in 1992. It was not the first time that Iberianism had been discussed in the literary field. During the period of the Estado Novo, Miguel Torga also expressed his views on Iberianism in his *Diários* when he suggested that Portugal and Spain were closely linked by history and geography. Nevertheless, that topic takes a different meaning in Saramago's positioning in the literary field because, unlike other writers, Saramago's literary career was significantly substantiated by his political engagement.[65]

---

64   See, for example, Ricardo de la Cierva, *El Triangulo. Alumna de la Libertad* (1988).

65   In 1989, Saramago was a candidate in the CDU lists for the elections for the European Parliament. He was not elected but did become the Chairman of the Municipal Assembly of Lisbon. This was a short-lived position because Saramago endorsed the Instituto Nacional de Estudos Sociais, set up by CDU members who demanded a more flexible hierarchy in the CDU and open dialogue. The Party's Board did not accept these claims so Saramago resigned from the Municipal Assembly. The relations between Saramago and the Communist Party were controversial because his ideals collided with the Party's in the sense that he sought to revive the MFA ideals. In 1995, he said: 'num encontro do meu partido que houve em Lisboa, eu disse que se não desenvolvermos aquilo a que chamei cultura de participação, não sei onde iremos parar. Já se sabe que o cidadão deve participar na sociedade, onde está inserido. Mas é preciso que a participação seja uma forma cultural

When Saramago suggested in his work (for example, *História do Cerco de Lisboa*, 1989) that the official Portuguese history should be revised, he also implied that institutions and policies should be revised. As far as he was concerned, the country's modernity was wrong. Ironically or not, his stance was not too different from Salazar's in the sense that both resisted change. Whereas the Estado Novo sought to institutionalise the country as it had been in the 1930s, Saramago found it hard to accept that Portugal was not the country it was in the past, and that the Government did not identify Portuguese basic values in the working class.[66]

Endorsing Saramago's stance corresponded to going against the official establishment. *O Evangelho Segundo Jesus Cristo* was given the APE Grande Prémio de Romance e Novela in 1991 and Saramago was given the APE Vida Literária Prize in 1992, following the decision of excluding this novel from the shortlist for the Ariosto Literary Prize.[67] Moreover, despite the fact that Saramago had received several Portuguese and foreign prizes by 1991, he was not invited to participate at Europália.[68] By contrast, he was invited to deliver conferences in Brazil and in Spain by the local

---

de viver', in Maria Leonor Nunes, 'José Saramago – O escritor vidente', *Jornal de Letras*, 25 October 1995, p. 17.

66   In his *Viagem a Portugal*, Saramago suggested travelling through Portugal to find the genuine country in local villages and people. It is equally relevant of his resistance to time that he overtly turned down offers of adaptations of his novels for the cinema and accepted adaptations for the opera and drama. In the early 2000s, he spoke against the proliferation of shopping malls.

67   His play *In Nomine Dei*, staged by Teatro Aberto, received the APE/Secretary of State for Culture Prize for Drama in 1993. It was centred on the persecution of Protestants in the XVI century and, thus, did not question Catholic dogma.

68   Europália held in Brussels, showcases the major cultural achievements of the EEC countries. In 1991, it was Portugal's turn. When the Communist councillors of Mafra, supported by the PS members, suggested giving the municipality golden medal to Saramago in 1991, the PSD majority opposed it. The same happened when the local high school requested to change its name to Escola Secundária José Saramago. This change only happened after the Nobel Prize. One of the prominent PSD members of Parliament also criticised Sousa Lara's attitude and advised the government to apologise to the writer in public. This only happened in 2003, when the Prime Minister, Durão Barroso, did so.

institutions. Furthermore, the support he received from the President, Mário Soares, particularly in 1991, was significant and beneficial to Saramago.[69] When the incident with Sousa Lara came out, Saramago and the political and intellectual opposition inflated it, in particular in the foreign press, by raising comparisons with the Inquisition. The CDU also used the same comparison and the PS compared it to the Salman Rushdie case.[70] By using the comparison to the PIDE censorship, Mário Soares, who gave the APE Grande Prémio to the writer, used the writers' protest to strengthen the President's opposition to the Government.[71]

Writers who had lived through the Estado Novo and stood against the Government's cultural policy, such as Natália Correia, Sophia de Mello Breyner, and Pedro Tamen, set up, together with Saramago, the Frente Nacional para a Defesa da Cultura, to introduce their claims into the political debate. It was also at this time that Saramago's *Memorial do Convento* was introduced into the official curriculum of Portuguese Literature at secondary school level. It is relevant that the Government decided to include the novel that had received the highest number of Portuguese and foreign prizes and also one of those that least went against the official cultural identity. On the one hand, this was evidence for Saramago's literary value, widely appraised in Portugal and overseas; on the other hand, this indicated the Government's compromise between the accepted value and its own interests.

The fact that Saramago was in the media for political and literary reasons also enhanced the accumulation of his symbolic capi-

---

69 Equally appropriate is Saramago's comment to José Carlos Vasconcelos on standing for elections in 1989'. Tudo bem ponderado creio, sinceramente, que o partido convidou o escritor, que é conhecido, cuja imagem lhes pode trazer alguma vantagem eleitoral', in Vasconcelos, p. 11.
70 The fact that several Communist politicians attended the ceremony to present the APE Prize to Saramago was shown as a demonstration of the PCP to Saramago, strengthening the relevance of this incidence as a 'political' case. See '"Evangelho" no "index da SEC"', *Jornal de Letras*, 5 May 1992, p. 3; Saramago stated to the Italian press that 'Um romance não tem força para isso. Mas pode provocar um pequeno terramoto. Mas isto é a Inquisição'.
71 Mário Soares, 'A Liberdade contra qualquer tutela espúria', *Jornal de Letras*, 14 July 1992, p. 5.

tal, through commercial success. *Levantado do Chão* and *O Ano da Morte de Ricardo Reis* have sold more than 20,000 copies; *Memorial do Convento* has sold more than 100,000 copies; books were reprinted several times, including those that had not originally been published by Editorial Caminho. His consecration benefited from being widely publicised in the press, in particular from the controversies around his literary awards, from his political stances and from the fact that the political and cultural institutions took advantage of his stances.

The studies led by de W. de Nooy, Bourdieu's Literary Field and Dubois's Literary Institution show the importance of critics and panels in literary consecration.[72] Saramago's consecration also benefited from the fact that the panels that approved of his prizes were largely constituted by those critics, such as Urbano Tavares Rodrigues, Maria Lúcia Lepecki and Maria Alzira Seixo, who reviewed his work very favourably from the early 1980s.[73] The claims that Saramago was a potential Nobel Prizewinner emerged in the early 1990s, in reviews by foreign critics published in Portugal, and also through special supplements about him.[74]

---

72 See W. De Nooy, 'Gentlemen of the Jury... – The Features of the Experts Awarding Literary Prizes', Poetics, 17 (1988), 531-545; Jacques Dubois, *L'institution de la littérature* (Brussels: Editions Labor/Ferdinand Nathan, 1986), p. 100.

73 Baptista-Bastos, *José Saramago – Aproximação a Um Retrato*. Lisbon: Publicações D.Quixote, 1986; Maria Alzira Seixo, *O Essencial sobre José Saramago*. Lisbon: Imprensa Nacional – Casa da Moeda, 1987 reprinted as *Lugares da Ficção em José Saramago : O Essencial e outros ensaios*. Lisbon: Imprensa Nacional – Casa da Moeda, 1999; Teresa Cerdeira published her thesis as *José Saramago entre a História e a Ficção: uma Saga de Portugueses*, published by Editorial D.Quixote in 1989.

74 Rui Knopfli, '"O Novel e Nós", *Jornal de Letras*, 11 February 1992, p. 31; José Ferraz Diogo, 'O Nobel, o "Marketing" e os "Lobbys" culturais', *Letras & Letras*, 15 April 1992, p. 12 are some of the relevant examples; Benjamin Abdala Júnior (USP), 'O imaginário político em A Jangada de Pedra, de José Saramago', *Letras & Letras*, 1 December 1988, p. 3; Ana Luísa Andrade, 'O fantasma oculto de José Saramago', *Jornal de Letras*, 20 April 1987, p. 16. *Letras & Letras* published a dossier on José Saramago with several reviews by Isabel Pires de Lima, José Manuel Mendes, Conceição Madruga, François Baradez, Joaquim Matos, Laura Bulger and Anabela Dinis Branco de Oliveira. (19 June 1991, pp. 7-14).

Saramago's publishing house played a very important role in his consecration as novelist. *Levantado do Chão* was the only novel with a picture of Saramago on the back cover. The design of the cover was similar to that of Edições Avante with very strong pictures and lettering.[75] After 1980, the publishing house redefined the graphism of the whole series: light yellow, indicating only the name of the author and the title in black, with no photographs or images. This change gave more emphasis to the work and less to the author.[76] This was very important for Saramago because his literary legitimacy was enhanced by his literary output and it was also important for Editorial Caminho: the new design legitimised the publishing house's purposes of educating the people. Moreover, the reprints of the *oeuvre* of several writers such as Alves Redol, Sophia de Mello Breyner, Manuel da Fonseca, Bernardo Santareno, Soeiro Pereira Gomes, João José Cochofel, and Carlos Oliveira during the 1980s and 1990s, positioned Editorial Caminho in relation to the literary canon established after the Revolution. As far as Saramago is concerned, the publisher's decision to reprint older works in the mid-1980s strengthened the constitution of his public persona, in terms of pushing him towards the Neo-Realist literary tradition and of organising his literary production published in the right political and social context. His works were published in such a way as to consecrate him as novelist, whereas reprints of his political essays written in the early 1970s legitimized his political and social commitment.

---

75   In 1977, Moraes also published *Manual de Pintura e Caligrafia* with Saramago's picture on the back cover.

76   On 4th December 1984, *Jornal de Letras* advertised Saramago's novels: 'É indispensável ler José Saramago' and the advertisement pinpointed Saramago's literary prizes and his translations. It also included some blurbs signed by José M.Fernandes (*Expresso*), Óscar Lopes, Maria Lúcia Lepecki and Luís Sousa Rebelo (p. 9). *Expresso*, reported that *Memorial do Convento* had been translated into Italian: 'Memorial do Convento, de José Saramago, arribou aos difíceis portos da actividade editorial italiana (difíceis porque em geral neles atracam apenas navios onde se fala francês ou inglês e, por ordem decrescente, o espanhol das Américas e o alemão', in 'Memoriale del Convento', 1 September 1984, p. 6R.

Furthermore, and in particular by 1998, Editorial Caminho also encouraged the publication of critical work about Saramago's *oeuvre*, such as by Horácio Costa, Francisco José Viegas, Beatriz Berrini and Carlos Reis. This enhanced both Saramago as a 'classic' and the publisher's prestige. In 1989, Saramago's words were relevant as regards his success reached in a particular political and cultural environment:

> Se os meus livros se tornam conhecidos lá fora, isso não me torna menos ligado àquilo que faço e àquilo que sou **aqui**. Gosto do que este país fez de mim: talvez seja isto que, no fundo, está nos meus romances.[77]

And he should. Unlike Saramago, most Portuguese consecrated writers were not called upon to comment on politics, despite many of them having been politically engaged. Unlike others, Saramago became the government's major asset as far as promotion of contemporary Portuguese literature was concerned. The Nobel Prize made it impossible for the Portuguese government not to recognise his literary merit publicly.[78]After 1992, his novels no longer focussed on Portuguese history and this was relevant in terms of positioning the writer in international book markets and strengthening his literary prestige, enhanced by his departure from Portugal in 1993.[79]

---

77 Cited by Vasconcelos, p. 10.
78 After 1998, several municipalities decided to give the name José Saramago to their streets: Borba (Alentejo), Pinhal Novo (near Barreiro, on the south bank of the River Tagus), Ponta Delgada (S. Miguel – the Azores) and Samora Correia. Beja and Leiria gave his name to their municipal libraries, and a students' house in Leiria was also named after Saramago; in 1998, the President, Jorge Sampaio, rewarded him with the Grande Colar da Ordem de Sant'Iago da Espada and in 1999, the University of Évora was the first Portuguese university to give him an Honoris Causa Doctorate. In 1998, the Círculo de Leitores Foundation set up the José Saramago Literary Prize to encourage new novelists and the Círculo de Leitores publishing house reprinted Saramago's entire oeuvre. The José Saramago Prize, due to the financial reward (€25,000) and to being sponsored by a very important publisher, in association with the IPLB, has more impact than any other municipal literary prize.
79 The literary discussions and controversies that involved Saramago and Antonio Tabucchi, Autran Dourado and Vargas Llosa can be understood as

7.2 José Luís Peixoto

José Luís Peixoto (born in 1974) had his first novel, *Nenhum Olhar*, published by Temas e Debates, in 2000. In 2001, that novel was rewarded with the José Saramago literary prize by the Círculo de Leitores Foundation. His positioning as a debutant in the Portuguese literary field was essentially built through the promotion of his novels in relation to Saramago.

Peixoto belongs to the new generation of Portuguese writers who benefited from the proliferation of literary prizes (also given by private companies), from the expansion of the Portuguese media and the book market in the 1990s. In 1997 and in 1998, his poems were given the Prémio Jovens Criadores of the Instituto Português da Juventude, awarded by the Secretaria de Estado da Juventude. In 1998, this Institute invited him to represent Portugal at the First Biennial of Young Writers of the CPLP, in Cape Verde.

Nevertheless, and by analogy with many Portuguese writers of the 1950s and 1960s, he was born and spent part of his life in the rural part of the country. Galveias, his home town, is in the northern part of the Alentejo and offered few opportunities for reading and writing in the aftermath of the Revolution. In the 1980s, there was a mobile library that visited the district once a month and Peixoto had a reader's pass. While he was graduating in Lisbon, he was involved in the students' protests against paying tuition fees and coordinated the cultural supplement published by the Students' Union. He started writing poetry and had it published in *Jornal de Letras* and *DN Jovem* before writing novels. Part of his biography was described in the Press, in particular, that of mass circulation, such as *Expresso* and *Público* and also in *Jornal de Letras* and on the flaps of Peixoto's books. Some of his interviews also focussed on the writer's biography. His biography is constructed, in particular by the media of mass circulation, with details that were familiar to more than one generation of Portuguese readers.

Saramago's positioning as literary authority, enhanced by the fact that Autran Dourado and Vargas Llosa share the same publishers in the countries where the incidents occurred.

Temas e Debates's publicity in Peixoto's book and in literary periodicals chiefly focussed on his literary awards and experience in writing, indicating that his literary legitimacy was positioned in terms of recognition and literary prestige. Peixoto's legitimacy was not established in relation to his political stances (unknown so far).

The fact that he was awarded the José Saramago Literary Prize was decisive in the construction of Peixoto's prestige in writing and in social trajectory, developed by his publisher, the critics and himself. This construction was described in Bourdieu's theory:

> Structurally 'young' writers, i.e. those less advanced in the process of consecration (who may be biologically almost as old as the 'old' writers they seek to oust), will refuse everything their 'elders' (in terms of legitimacy) are and do, and in particular all the indices of *social ageing*, starting with the signs of consecration, internal (academies, etc.) or external (success), whereas the 'old' writers will regard the social non-existence (in terms of success and consecration) and also the 'obscurity' of their young rivals as evidence of the voluntaristic, forced character of some endeavours to overtake them.[80]

There are several aspects in Peixoto's constructed biography and in his points of view expressed at interviews that recall Saramago's biography: he was a regular reader at the local library; he read consecrated Portuguese writers; he began writing poetry and was involved in newspapers; his values are rooted in his rural background; he is, on the one hand, fascinated by cities as windows of opportunities and, on the other hand, he resents them as individual identity is lost there; he believes that Portugal and Galicia should be strengthen cultural links.[81]

---

80 Bourdieu, p. 59.
81 The frontpage of *Jornal de Letras*'s edition of 13 November 2002 is interesting for the present analysis. It is headed by a picture with Saramago and Peixoto standing side by side when Peixoto was awarded the 2001 Prize, with their names in bold. Despite the fact that the newspaper includes separate articles about both writers, it does not include any interview with both writers at the same time. Nevertheless, in an interview with Peixoto, the journalist asks two questions about Saramago. Also on 1 November 2003, Peixoto and Saramago were interviewed together for the television.programme Oriente (SIC Channel), in which both writers stood side by side.

Positioning in relation to Saramago was an association that the new writer did not assert himself but did not reject altogether:

> O José Saramago é o único Prémio Nobel que a nossa língua tem. Isso não será certamente por acaso. Eu compreendo porque isso aconteceu. Ele faz parte de um grupo de escritores que são importantes na minha formação, enquanto leitor. E aquilo que lemos acaba por ter importância naquilo que escrevemos.[82]

Following the publication of *Nenhum Olhar*, Eduardo Prado Coelho reviewed the novel as a 'surpresa absoluta' and recognized some Neo-Realist influence.[83] *Jornal de Letras* published a favourable review, which compared this novel to *Levantado do Chão*:

> *Nenhum Olhar* é, 20 anos depois do fracasso da família dos Mau-Tempo e da luta dos Germano Vidigal, a II Parte de *Levantado do Chão*, ou seja, depois do fracasso político-histórico da Reforma Agrária, é o perfeito retrato actual de um Alentejo que, tendo sonhado "levantar-se do chão", expulsando os ricos e concretizando o sonho triunfal do igualitarismo milenarista universal, acorda banhado numa imobilidade atemporal, em que as personagens, sob um um [sic] céu azul e uma planície castanha, ambos como imagens do deserto, só estabelecem um sentido para a vida dentro de uma contínua anormalidade.[84]

---

82 Manuel Halpern, 'As mutilações do amor', *Jornal de Letras*, 13 November 2002, p. 11. It is significant that in his first interviews, journalists did not suggest any comparisons with Saramago and Peixototo did not refer to him: See Círculo de Leitores online, 'José Luís Peixoto: "Não fechar portas"', <http://www.circulodeleitores.pt/ > [accessed in November 2004] ; Alexandra Lucas Coelho, 'Eu sou estas personagens', *Público Leituras*, 21 October 2000, pp. 1-3.

83 Eduardo Prado Coelho, 'Não há estrelas, mas o espaço negro que as separa', *Público*, 7 October 2000: 'Já José Luís Peixoto nos dá inesperadamente uma narrativa rural, feita de situações limite, onde evocamos algum Raúl Brandão, é certo, mas agora, como os tempos são outros, cada movimento do texto nos leva a subir "os últimos degraus da noite" até ao lugar onde os homens deixam de ser humanos"'.

84 Miguel Real, 'José Luís Peixoto: A 2ª Parte de Levantado do Chão', *Jornal de Letras*, 13 December 2000, p. 23.

There is very little in Peixoto's novel that directly refers to Saramago's and, since much of the narrative representation derives
from an ironical perspective of the Old Testament, with obvious
biblical references through names such as Moses, Eliajh, Gabriel,
Solomon and Joseph, and since the Alentejo only exists in terms of
representation of a deprived rural community, *Nenhum Olhar*
benefits from the discourse that is rooted in the literature produced by Saramago and António Lobo Antunes. As far as language is concerned, the deconstruction of sentence and the multiplication of voices and perspectives suggest an emotional and
ideological void. Moreover, and unlike Saramago, there is hardly
any political stance in that novel, nor in *Uma Casa na Escuridão*
(2002). Peixoto is not interested in introducing any political issue.
Nevertheless, critics positioned his literary writing as a contemporary development of Neo-Realism.

It is noteworthy that the novelist himself did not reject this influence; he acknowledged it critically though:

> O Alentejo é uma região já muito tratada pela literatura portuguesa, no en-
> tanto, modestamente, julgo que nunca foi vista da perspectiva dos indiví-
> duos. Porque foi sobretudo tratada pelos neo-realistas, que na maior parte
> dos casos tomaram o povo alentejano como povo. E eu tentei ir a cada alen-
> tejano. O facto de uma pessoa ser de uma determinada região não é por si só
> um elemento que a caracterize.[85]

He also did not deny being influenced by Magic Realism, and recognized that its style had contributed to his writing *Nenhum Olhar*.[86]

Miguel Real, in *Jornal de Letras*, also referred to Lobo Antunes's
influence but established Peixoto's success in relation to Saramago's career :

> Se *Levantado do Chão*, em 1980, anunciou o novo estilo de José Saramago que,
> dois anos depois publicaria *Memorial do Convento*, não é de duvidar que *Nen-*

---

85 Coelho, p. 3.
86 Coelho, p. 3:'Não me irrita esse tipo de comparações. Estou bastante seguro
    que não pretendi fazer um sucedâneo de Gabriel García Marquez. O que
    aconteceu foi que precisei de utilizar esses prodígios, que por acaso vêm do
    realismo mágico'.

hum Olhar possa constituir-se (caso haja alguma contenção no uso retórico e delirante na forma lírica de escrita de José Luís Peixoto) como o anúncio de um novo grande escritor à procura do seu *Memorial do Convento*.[87]

Bourdieu pointed out in his study that the best thing a critic can do for a book is to predict success; however, he associated this success to popular bestsellers.[88] This is also clear in Portuguese contemporary prizewinning highbrow literature and, particularly, in Peixoto's case. The favourable reviews and the literary prize boosted the sales of *Nenhum Olhar* and, by the beginning of 2003, it had been reprinted five times and was published abroad.

The José Saramago Prize was not the first attempt by Temas e Debates to have *Nenhum Olhar* honoured. In 2000, it was shortlisted for the APE Grande Prémio de Romance e Novela, together with novels by António Lobo Antunes, Helder Macedo, Luísa Dacosta, Mafalda Ivo Cruz, Maria Gabriela Llansol, Paulo Castilho and Maria Velho da Costa, who was awarded this prize. Very little is known about the decisions of the members of the panel, but the press often refers to them (informed by members of panels). This indicates the panels and the institutions' interest in attracting publicity to literary prizes. In 2000, Clara Rocha was reported as having voted for Peixoto's novel.[89] By that time, it was also publicised that his *Morreste-me* was shortlisted for the PEN Club Prize, (in the event, awarded to Ascêncio de Freitas), although less is known in terms of the decisions of the members of the panel.. Media emphasis was placed on the fact that the young writer was shortlisted to the most important literary prizes and this legitimised Peixoto's prestige, especially following the Saramago Prize. The panel that adjudicated on the latter prize in 2001 included Vasco Graça Moura, Pilar del Rio, Nélida Piñon, José Eduardo Agualusa and

---

87   Miguel Real, p. 23.
88   Pierre Bourdieu, p. 101. In 2000, José Mário Silva reviewed Peixoto's *Morreste-me* (published before *Nenhum Olhar* and in edição de autor) for the *DNa* and stated: 'a narrativa de José Luís Peixoto é também, sem exageros, um dos mais belos textos da literatura portuguesa contemporânea'.
89   Manuel Halpern, p. 10; Peixoto's *Uma Casa na Escuridão*, published in 2002, also includes this reference on the flap; *Portugal em Linha* is more detailed in terms of panel members and their decisions.

Guilhermina Gomes, editor of Círculo de Leitores. Saramago attended the prize-giving ceremony and pinpointed Peixoto's literary merit. A representative of the IPLB was also present at the ceremony, a fact that indicates the State as a tacit instance of consecration, despite the fact that the IPLB does not sponsor the José Saramago Prize officially.

Saramago is the only living Portuguese writer with a literary prize named after him that competes, in prestige, with the most important prizes sponsored by the State. Other writers, such as Vergílio Ferreira and Miguel Torga, also had prizes named after them while they were alive, but these were given by city halls and aimed to encourage local literary writing. Saramago's authority was enhanced with the emergence of a debutant who is associated with him, whereas the other literary prizes did not produce this effect of a particular literary trend (associated to one writer). It is the affirmation of Saramago as canon. As John Guillory wrote:

> An individual's judgement that a work is great does nothing in itself to preserve that work, unless that judgement is made in a certain institutional context, a setting in which it is possible to insure the reproduction of the work, its continual reintroduction to generations of readers.[90]

José Luís Peixoto's work does not directly address any particular aspect of Portuguese history. It primarily questions the institutional hierarchy of the Catholic Church as superior power but it does not question religious faith and the Bible; it primarily discusses civilization's ills, such as death, war, torture, slavery and physical and emotional suffering. Eduardo Prado Coelho, leading critic, reviewed Peixoto's second novel in relation to Saramago's first novel on the literary field.[91] This means that Peixoto's position was legitimized within the range of the autonomy of the literary field. This suggests a difference in how consecration works in the Portuguese literary field. Whereas between the Estado Novo and the late 1990s, literary consecration was evidence for the feeble

---

90 John Guillory, *Cultural Capital: The Problem of Literary Canon Formation* (Chicago and London: The University of Chicago Press, 1993), p. 28

91 Eduardo Prado Coelho, 'O problema geral das regras de atracção', *Público*, 2 March 2002.

autonomy of the Portuguese literary field, the expansion of the market, associated with the multiplication of prizes and the increase in literary output in the1990s favoured the extension of literary legitimacy to a new generation of writers which was not politically involved. Appendix 7 shows that after 1999, the APE, the PEN Club and the Casa de Mateus rewarded writers who did not belong to the 1950s and 1960s generation of writers, although the panels were constituted by the same persons. The fact that Peixoto published this novel in association with a Portuguese gothic music group, *Moonspell*, and that he was awarded a prize given by the SIC channel in association with the popular magazine *Caras* in 2004, is evidence for the change in Portuguese contemporary consecration. As Frank Kermode concluded: 'individuals [...] change the canon to match their modernity'.[92]

It goes without saying that Peixoto has been the only prize-winner of the Saramago Prize whose position in the literary field has been promoted and consecrated in relation to Saramago. Peixoto's social and cultural background and his tacit acceptance of this position in the literary field was a window of opportunity for him because it facilitated his promotion abroad, as will be shown in Chapter 8.

---

92 Frank Kermode, *Pleasure and Change: The Aesthetics of Canon*, with Geoffrey Hartman, John Guillory & Carey Perloff, Robert Alter (ed) (Oxford: Oxford University Press, 2004), p. 50.

CHAPTER 8
International Acceptance of José Saramago and José Luís Peixoto

This chapter will try to establish that acceptance of Saramago's *oeuvre* in Brazil, Spain, the United States and in the United Kingdom was determined by three essential factors: the choice of the right timing of publication of his works according to their political, social and cultural environments; Saramago's social trajectory in the literary field, in other words, the construction of his biography whose selection of aspects and events were presented differently by his publishing houses overseas, critics and by himself at interviews and other public appearances in those countries; and the importance of the publishing houses which published his oeuvre and were decisive for strengthening his international visibility. The combination of these three factors makes Saramago an unusual case of a successful literary career. Finally, this chapter will also endeavour to show that José Luís Peixoto's recent acceptance overseas benefited the expansion of Portuguese publishing industry in the 1990s; the improved visibility of Portuguese literature abroad; his literary awards; and also from Saramago's prestige.

The reasons to analyse Saramago's recognition in each of the countries mentioned above vary. In the United Kingdom, translations constitute a very small share of the book market, not exceeding 2.5 per cent, albeit prizes are given to foreign fiction.[1] It is not easy for a foreign author to overcome the obstacles imposed by the British publishing market. The United States of America share the same market share of translations. However, if a translation is successful in the United States, its chance of penetrating the British

---

1   G. Pontiero, 'Critical perceptions of Saramago's fiction in the English-speaking world', in *The Translator's Dialogue: Giovanni Pontiero*, ed. by Pilar Orero and J.C. Sage (Amsterdam/Philadephia: John Benjamin's Publishing Company, 1997), pp. 67-83 (p. 67).

market increases.[2] I will establish that this happened with José Saramago in 1987. Brazil and Portugal share an historical bond and the same language despite differences between the Portuguese and Brazilian registers. Spain is geographically close to Portugal, although it does not necessarily imply that the transactions of cultural goods between both countries have always been facilitated, as Zeferino Coelho mentioned in the interview conducted for this thesis.[3]

As far as foreign rights are concerned, there is a basis-contract in which Editorial Caminho retains worldwide rights and another that delegates those rights to Ray-Güde Mertin, German literary agent and translator of the Portuguese and Spanish languages. There is a specific literary agent for the French market and Editorial Caminho holds the rights for the Brazilian market.[4]

As far as publication in foreign markets is concerned, Saramago was first published in Brazil in 1982, then translated in Italy in 1984, in Spain in 1985 and in Germany in 1986. The first French and North-American editions of Saramago's novels were published in 1987 and the British in 1988. Saramago's drama and poetry were not translated into English but most of it was published in Spain, France, Italy and Brazil. Changing titles happened often in the United Kingdom and in the United States.[5]

According to Zeferino Coelho, editor of Editorial Caminho, Saramago's success in Europe was triggered by the Italian reception of the *Memorial do Convento*. It was enthusiastic and fascinated by the magic powers of the female character, the convent and the plot itself.[6] It is significant that Saramago was published by Feltrinelli, one of the major Italian publishing houses with a wide

---

2   Gregory Rabassa, 'The risks and rewards of literary translation', in Orero and Sager, pp. 17-32 (pp. 18-19).

3   See Appendix 1 on pp. 339.

4   According to Zeferino Coelho. See *Expresso*, 'Uma aposta recompensada' 17 October 1998.

5   *Baltasar and Blimunda* was also the title given to translations published in Denmark, the Czech Republic, Finland, Sweden, and Turkey. The French translation was completely different: *Le Dieu Manchot* (the 'One-Armed God', my translation).

6   See Appendix 1.

network of bookshops and a distributor. Feltrinelli published also Fernando Pessoa and Cardoso Pires. It has published major contemporary South-American writers, such as Jorge Luís Borges, Carlos Fuentes and Gabriel García Marquez. Giangiacomo Feltrinelli, founder of Giangiacomo Feltrinelli Editore who died in 1972, had much in common with the life of many Portuguese publishers during the Estado Novo. Feltrinelli's booklist reflected his ideological beliefs as member of the Italian Communist Party, publishing Che Guevara, Karl Marx and also the Nobel laureate Pasternak, Lampedusa, Duras, Yourcenar, Levi-Strauss and Henry Miller.

Since publishing houses publicize new books by sending copies and press clippings of new books, Portuguese critics' and Saramago's association of his early novels to those by García Marquez and Borges might have awakened the interest of those foreign critics who were not familiar with Saramago's work but knew South-American literature. My assumption is supported by the fact that many of the reviews published about Saramago's novels highlighted his use of Magic Realism, as shown below.

As regards to taking positions in the field of restricted production, Bourdieu posits that there is a gulf between those dependent on public success and those who depend on the recognition within the peer competing group and that constitutes an indicator of the autonomy of the restricted field.[7] Public success strengthens the process of recognition. As far as Saramago is concerned, this chapter will establish that publishing houses and critics identified and promoted him, with the author's consent within the framework of literary tradition. It encouraged the acceptance of Saramago's works as far as circulation channels, readership and publicity were concerned. Therefore, my analysis will follow the critical fortune of José Saramago through the Brazilian, Spanish, North-American and British press for the purpose of evaluating Saramago's acceptance in those countries between the 1980s and 1998.

---

7   Pierre Bourdieu, *The Field of Cultural Production*. (Cambridge: Polity Press & Blackwell Publishers Ltd, 1993), p. 116.

8.1 Brazil

DIFEL published *Levantado do Chão* in Brazil in 1982. DIFEL – Difusão Editorial, S.A. was the name taken by the publisher Bertrand Brasil in 1974 and its catalogue included authors, like Pablo Neruda, Autran Dourado, Jorge Luís Borges and Isabel Allende. Bertrand Brasil was set up in 1949 with the primary goal of importing French and Portuguese books. In 1986, DIFEL was taken over by the Portuguese Bertrand Editora and was renamed Editora Bertrand Brasil.[8] Immediately after this, Bertrand Brasil took over Editora Civilização Brasileira and enlarged its catalogue with Brazilian and foreign authors, such as José J. Veiga, Dias Gomes, Alberto Moravia, Noam Chomsky and Ernest Hemingway, among others. In 1988, DIFEL discontinued the publication of Saramago's works when Editorial Caminho negotiated a contract with Companhia das Letras which is his Brazilian publishing house.

Unlike what happened in the English-speaking countries, the Brazilian (and the Spanish publishing houses) have published Saramago's novels, essays, poetry and drama. Companhia das Letras published Saramago's travel book *Viagem a Portugal*, the plays *In Nomine Dei* and *Que farei com este livro?*, the diaries *Cadernos de Lanzarote*, the short story *Objecto Quase* and chronicles *A Bagagem do Viajante*.

The choice of the works by Saramago varied slightly from country to country. *Que farei com este livro?* was only published in Brazil, whereas *A Noite* and *O Ano de 1993* were only published in Spain. This is indicative of the fact that the contents of either of the works were not deemed equally interesting to both publics.

Levantado do Chão is set within the social changes undergone in Portugal since the end of the monarchy up till the 1974 revolution. The misfortunes and miseries of three generations of a family of landless peasants in the Alentejo who desperately eke out a living in times of repression was published when the movement of the

---

8   *Levantado do Chão* was published in 1982 by the imprints DIFEL and Bertrand Brasil and *Memorial do Convento* was published by DIFEL in 1983 and by Bertrand Brasil in 1987.

landless workers was emerging and finding support among several personalities working in the field of arts.[9]

Brazil was going through the last years of the military government. The first democratic elections took place in 1985, when Tancredo Neves, of the MDB Party, was elected President. He did not take office since he passed away suddenly during emergency surgery and was replaced by his Vice President José Sarney, who governed the country until 1990. MDB – Movimento Democrático Brasileiro – was supported by personalities that participated in the opposition to the military governments in Brazil. Therefore, at a time when movements in favour of workers' rights were flourishing, the subject dealt with in *Levantado do Chão* was potentially interesting to Brazilian readers. Moreover, it is noteworthy that it came from a country that, though historically close to Brazil, was hardly known to the Brazilian readers in terms of literature produced by contemporary authors.[10] History unites both countries but Saramago's novel showed also some aspects of the history of a recent past of Portugal that recalled much of what was happening in Brazil.

The choice of this novel also oriented the way how Saramago was introduced in Brazil – an author whose political views were openly discussed at interviews and someone who stood for the landless workers' rights. Exactly fifteen years after having published *Levantado do Chão* in Brazil, Saramago authored the preface to *Terra*, a book of photos of the Brazilian landless workers by Sebastião Salgado, published by Companhia das Letras, that draws the public's attention to Brazilian agrarian reforms.[11]

---

9   For example, in 1982, when *Levantado do Chão* was published in Brazil, Milton Nascimento sang Missa dos Quilombos, in which he stood for equality of opportunity for the long-oppressed landless black workers in Brazil. D. José Maria Pires, archbishop of João Pessoa and D.Helder Câmara, archbishop of Olinda and Recife, endorsed this work

10 'No Brasil, onde o conhecimento da literatura vinda do chamado "país irmão" muitas vezes não passa de Fernando Pessoa, Saramago é o mais popular autor português e tem os seus livros nas listas dos mais vendidos por várias semanas', in Bete Köninger. '"Atenção, este livro leva uma pessoa dentro" – Entrevista com José Saramago'. Quoted from <http://www.is-koeln.de/matices/16/16ksaram.htm> [accessed in April 2004].

11 This concern can be framed within the writer's promotion on the basis of working-class background and Communist views. This image was consis-

Therefore, the promotion of Saramago in Brazil was based on building his social trajectory (aspects of his life, experience and ideological beliefs) in relation to his legitimacy as socially committed writer. At an interview with *Folha de S. Paulo*, one of the outstanding quality newspapers in Brazil, Saramago underscored the unruffled coexistence between the writer he was and his Communist affiliation:

> Sou dentro e fora desse partido – fora quando não estou em relação direta com ele, dentro quando há o momento, quando estou em seu nome –, digamos assim, há uma perfeita lealdade, de perfeita responsabilidade e de perfeita liberdade. Quer dizer, eu escrevo exatamente o que quero, exatamente como quero, sem nenhuma prévia determinação, orientação, conselho, aviso, prevenção, arranjo todas as palavras que quiserem, vindas directa ou indiretamente do meu partido. E por uma razão imediata e simplicíssima, é que eu sendo convictamente aquilo que sou, também convictamente acho que o meu partido não é competente em matéria literária.[12]

According to Brazilian statistics in 2004, despite the Brazilian publishing market being the eight in the world ranking of production, illiteracy reached 38 per cent of the population in 2004 and 16 per cent bought around 73 per cent of books published.[13] Although

---

tently promoted between 1982 and 2004. Saramago was in Brazil for a series of interviews and other public appearances, together with Sebastião Salgado and Chico Buarque de Hollanda who composed a CD to be released together with the book. The publication was thoroughly covered by the Brazilian press in April 1997. Marili Ribeiro wrote in Jornal do Brasil: 'O presidente Fernando Henrique Cardoso poderia entrar para a história do Brasil como o homem que fez a reforma agrária no país. Dessa concepção comungam três monstros sagrados do universo artístico: o fotógrafo Sebastião Salgado, o escritor português José Saramago e o compositor e cantor Chico Buarque de Hollanda' (13 April 1997, p. 14) .

12 'Saramago conversa sobre o Ofício de Escritor', Folha de São Paulo, 6 May 1989.   <http://www1.folha.uol.com.br/folha/almanaque/entsaramago.htm> [accessed in September 2004]. In that interview Saramago was talked about himself as Saramago was reported to be a simple and down-to-earth man, who was attached to his old typewriter (on which he had written the book published in Brazil in that year), but was made to use computers because of modern times.

13 Statistics available on http://www.cbl.org.br/news.php?recid=1119&hl=oitavo [accessed March 2005].

there are no surveys supporting evidence on the purchase of Portuguese fiction in Brazil (including consumer segmentation), building Saramago's profile as a working-class man, socially committed and aware of Brazilian problems was likely to awaken the interest of Brazilian readers.

Saramago's views about religion were also topic discussed at interviews. They were published two years before the publication of the *Evangelho Segundo Jesus Cristo* and, with hindsight, can be read as ways to shape the minds of the Brazilian readers to his works that directly involved religion because up till 1989, only four novels were published, none to do with religion. *Evangelho Segundo Jesus Cristo* and *In Nomine Dei* were published in the early 1990s.[14]

When *In Nomine Dei* was published in Brazil, the fact that it was reprinted three times in Portugal in only three months was reported as evidence for the Saramago's literary value:

> De um ateu, podem-se esperar anátemas e blasfêmias contra os códigos religiosos. Mas de um ateu como o escritor português José Saramago, podem-se esperar investidas em temas religiosos como mais uma forma de redimensionar seu universo ficcional.[15]

Looking into the articles that dealt with Saramago up till 1998, Saramago's literary consecration was clearly defined in the early 1990s. Claims (by critics and readers) that he deserved the Camões and the Nobel Prizes were published as early as 1993.[16]

In 1994, the publication of *Objecto Quase* received very favourable reviews as well and Saramago's stature in Brazil was clear in Paulo Amador's review:

---

14   For example, see 'Saramago conversa sobre o ofício de Escritor'.

15   Macksen Luiz, 'Sangrento episódio da Reforma inspira nova peça de Saramago', *Jornal do Brasil*, 7 August 1993, p. 3.

16   *Jornal do Brasil* published in the section 'Opinião dos Leitores', a reader's letter arguing that Saramago deserved being awarded the Camões Prize in 1994 and also the Nobel Prize. (15 July 1993, [n.p]). Jorge Amado, consecrated author, suggested Saramago for the Nobel Prize in 1994, although the Portuguese author was not his first choice: Torga would be, in Amado's words, the Portuguese-speaking writer whose work deserved the Nobel Prize. See Otávio Dias, 'Llosa é um escritor clássico', *Folha de S.Paulo*, 27 November 1994, pp. 6-7.

Saramago dispensa apresentação, de tal modo tem sido abundante e merecidamente receptiva a crítica brasileira a esse desconcertante escritor português pós-moderno. Pós-moderno? Seja. Em livros anteriores.[...] Por tudo isso, é mesmo bom que se leia Saramago, neste seu Objecto quase. Até para se descobrir que, na linha da totemização da palavra, há no Brasil uma excelente produção de livros de contos.[17]

Unlike in other countries such as in the United States, in Brazil, there was virtually no direct allusion to Magic Realism. The Brazilian critics associated Saramago to Post-Modernist trends.[18] The Brazilian newspapers informed his readers of the success of the author in the United States, such as the positive reception of the *Gospel of Jesus Christ*[19] Harold Bloom's interview with *Folha de S. Paulo*, at the time of the publication of *The Western Canon* included the mention of the scholar's choice of Portuguese-speaking writers in his canon and Saramago was one of them.[20]

The Brazilian newspapers published some of Saramago's texts originally published in *El País*: *Folha de S. Paulo* published two in 1994, both about Lisbon, reflecting the author's interests about his country and his city:

Dir-se-ia que pouco interessam essas miudezas históricas. Estou de acordo, mas interessaria muito – a mim, pelo menos – não apenas saber, mas

---

17 Paulo Amador, 'Saramago se rende ao culto à palavra – Escritor opta pela experimentação sem abandonar a beleza do texto', *Jornal do Brasil*, 2 April 1994, p. 3. Equally relevant is Bob Fernandes's review published in *Folha de S.Paulo* (12 January 1994, p. 5-1), in which he compares some of the short stories to São Paulo's everyday life.

18 Unlike what was found in Saramago's critical fortune in the English-speaking press, the Brazilian press asked well-known Brazilian personalities to recommend a book to readers and very often referred to the Portuguese author: for example, Chico Alencar (writer), Carlos Zara (actor), and Ricardo Tacuchian (teacher) recommended Brazilians to read *O Evangelho Segundo Jesus Cristo*; and Pepita Rodrigues (actress and writer) suggested *A Jangada de Pedra*.. See 16 'O que eles estão lendo', *Jornal do Brasil*, 25 September 1993, p. 6; 'O que eles estão lendo', *Jornal do Brasil*, 13 May 1995, p. 6; 'O que eles estão lendo', *Jornal do Brasil*, 3 June 1995, p .6 ; 'O que eles estão lendo em Frankfurt', *Jornal do Brasil*, 24 September 1995, p. 6.

19 Luciana Villas-Boas, 'Informe/Idéias', *Jornal do Brasil*, 21 May 1994, p. 2.

20 Daniel Pisa, 'Erramos', *Folha de S.Paulo*, 25 August 1994, pp. 5-6.

também ver, no sentido mais exato da palavra, como Lisboa vem mudando daqueles tempos remotos até hoje.

Minha Lisboa foi sempre a dos bairros pobres, e quando, muito mais tarde, as circunstâncias e as mudanças da vida me levaram a viver em outros rios e ambientes, a memória que mais ciumentamente quis conservar, até hoje, foi a da Lisboa dos meus primeiros anos, [...[Basta que Lisboa seja o que simplesmente deve ser: feliz, culta, moderna, limpa, organizada, sem perder nada da sua alma antiga.[21]

Both articles were published under the headline: "O País de Saramago" (The country of Saramago) and it was placed in the section of "Tourism". This sounds contradictory, as the texts mentioned above do not recommend sightseeing in Lisbon as would a travel guide. It is a travel through a city that does not exist anymore and could have only existed in Saramago's mind because his memories, as published in those articles, were the result of his own experience as a person with humble origins. It is a text in many ways similar to *Viagem a Portugal*, published in Portugal in 1980. In the texts published in *Folha de S. Paulo*, he did not completely reject modern Lisbon; he appealed to the need to preserve tradition and the respect for the workers and peasants that have made Lisbon. These articles gave a more personal account of the author who stood for the workers' rights in Brazil.

The interviews with Saramago also covered Iberianism, focussing on bringing Portugal and Brazil together:

Há uma coisa que é o bem comum, a língua, que é a coisa mais importante que nós deixamos no Brasil. A língua, que foi o elemento de unidade neste país imenso. A questão é saber se os portugueses e os brasileiros têm consciência deste bem comum num mundo como este em que vivemos.[22]

---

21 José Saramago, 'Transformação de Lisboa daria um filme', *Folha de S.Paulo*, 22 September 1994, p. 6-17.; 'Capital abandona marasmo e indiferença', *Folha de S.Paulo*, 18 September 1994, pp. 6-17.
22 Bob Fernandes, 'Monstro da Intolerância voltou, diz Saramago', *Folha de S.Paulo*, 12 January 1994, pp. 5-6. Another clear example is the interview given to Köninger. 'Uma das questões que o Brasil teria de resolver na sua relação conosco é saber quando começa a literatura de língua portuguesa

The writer's opinions were reported as of some value within the framework of the discussions on the 'Pan-Iberian nation', which were encouraged by Saramago, adding to his interest in Brazilian issues.

As far as Saramago's participation in the purge in *Diário de Notícias* in 1975 was concerned, *Folha de S. Paulo* reported it in a different way from that in Portugal: it was added that he had been one of the few who had managed to escape the control of censorship and publish information about the Colonial War.[23] The more positive picture of that incident may be associated with the non-existence of a certain emotional involvement and experience of the Revolution which defined those who accused Saramago in Portugal. In Brazil, the experience of military government and political instability was recent and that incident was of some interest (familiarity) for Brazilian readers. This incident was not covered in the other countries as shown below.

Luiz Schwarcz, editor of Companhia das Letras, was interviewed in 2004 and stated that a publisher should play the role of 'interventor cultural, intervém com as suas escolhas".[24] This publishing house has published essays, poetry and fiction. The importance of history was clear in the way it presented itself and the work by Saramago. Its publicity texts which introduced Saramago's novels used the phrases 'recriar o passado e o presente', and 'a aventura ficcional da desconcertação das certezas das palavras [...] reencontram-se em signos velhos'. They underline the importance of New Historicism in Saramago. In that interview, Schwarcz also pointed out the importance of works about History for his publishing house:

> Por exemplo: que tal publicar uma historiografia que está produzindo obras bastante inovadoras, que traz a história para a vida cotidiana, traz para o Brasil uma nova história chamada história das sensibilidades, história das

---

para vocês.[...] Portanto, essa espécie de pan-Iberianismo, sem qualquer intenção imperial, evidentemente seria qualquer coisa a criar ou renovar.'

23   Hermes Rodrigues Nery, 'Luiz Schwarcz: O Bom leitor faz o bom livro', <http://www.companhiadasletras.br > [accessed October 2004].
24   'Luiz Schwarcz: O Bom leitor faz o bom livro'.

mentalidades, que ao mesmo tempo é nova no Brasil e tem interesse e importância para o público de historiadores, e atinge um público mais amplo.[25]

The importance of the publishing house in the making of a writer has been established in the research conducted by Frank de Glas, Wouter de N. Nooy and Verdaasdonk.[26] As far as Saramago's work is concerned and taking the publishing house's profile into consideration, his work fitted Companhia das Letras's publishing policy. Moreover, his public comments about society in general and workers' rights invested him with a peculiar authority to become one of the most popular Portuguese writers. Sharing a common language facilitated Saramago's public exposure. He was often asked to comment on Brazilian politics, and participated in various conferences and lectures. His opinions published in the press focussed on the need of the Brazilian people to participate in the political life.[27] He prefaced books by Brazilian authors, such as Sebastião Salgado and Horácio Costa.[28] His a dispute with Autran Dourado on the spelling agreement negotiated among the governments of the Portuguese-speaking countries granted some exposure to the press.[29] This kind of dispute increases press exposure and, as shown in my survey to Portuguese purchasers of Portuguese fiction (Appendix 5), publicity becomes essential to increase readership, which is also very important for the publishers.[30] In

---

25 'Luiz Schwarcz: O Bom leitor faz o bom livro'
26 In the course of a dispute between Saramago and Autran Dourado, the Brazilian writer said: 'José Saramago é grande escritor, mas ele só é lido aqui por ter sido editado por uma editora brasileira'. Quoted from Frases', *Folha de S.Paulo*, 23 February 1994, pp. 5-6.
27 Fernandes: 'Para falar com franqueza, ou o povo brasileiro intervém na sua própria vida – o povo, não os segmentos políticos que o representam – torna isto uma prática cotidiana, ou tudo continuará como sempre foi antes.'
28 Joyce Pascowitch, 'Entrelinhas', *Folha de S.Paulo*, 11 December 1994, p. 6-2. 'Com direito a prefácio mais que ilustre – de José Saramago –, Horácio Costa autografa quarta feira na livraria Cultura seu Menino e o Travesseiro'.
29 'Frases', *Folha de S.Paulo*, 23 February 1994, pp. 5-6. Dourado was published by Bertrand Brasil, He had one book, *Barca dos Homens* (Bertrand) published in Portugal in 2002
30 In Portugal, the uproar about José Cardoso Pires's *Dinaussauro Excelentíssimo* in 1972 led to massive purchases of this book. In Spain, the Spanish press covered the exchange of criticism between Vargas Llosa and Saramago in

Brazil, Saramago's books were in the bestsellers list. It is very difficult to measure the relevance of these disputes in the increase of
sales of well-known authors, but the fact is that they definitely
contribute to the publicity of the authors and, thus publishers also
profit from these situations.

The hue-and-cry enhanced Saramago's authority and official
consecration, in particular when he was included in the list of authors whose works were compulsory reading for the exams for
university in 1995. He was the only living Portuguese author to be
included in this list, with his novel *Memorial do Convento*. The other
Portuguese writers were Eça de Queirós, Bocage and Fernando
Pessoa.[31] Only two living authors were added to the list of compulsory reading: Saramago and Rubem Fonseca (both published
by Companhia das Letras). This also benefited the publisher because it implied a rise in sales.[32]

The 1998 Nobel Prize of Literature was reported – by journalists and by Saramago – as partly belonging to Brazil. The emphasis
was on the fact that the Portuguese language was awarded the
Prize and was, therefore, a reason for celebration in Brazil.[33]

1990, both published by Alfaguara, and these authors were also in the bestsellers' list.

31   'O que muda nos vestibulares', *Folha de S.Paulo*, 8 November 1994, p. 7.

32   Arthur Nestrovski, 'Os dez mais melancólicos", *Folha de S.Paulo*, 16 October
1994, pp. 6-7. The fact that *Memorial do Convento* and *A Grande Arte* by R.
Fonseca went suddenly to the ninth and tenth positions respectively is explained by the inclusion of these books in FUVEST's exams.

33   See 'Prémio para a Língua Portuguesa', *Estado de Minas*, 9 October 1998.
Saramago said 'A literatura brasileira não precisa que um escritor português
abra caminho para chegar a um Nobel. Até mesmo se deve dizer que os
brasileiros já deveriam ter ganhado antes o Nobel e então eles é que abririam
o caminho para a literatura portuguesa. Eles é que mereciam ganhar mais do
que eu. A verdade é que os escritores brasileiros, Cabral, Amado, Drum-
mond, teriam sido grandes escolhas', in Graça Magalhães-Ruethe, 'Amado e
Cabral mereciam o prémio mais do que eu', *O Globo*, 9 October, 1998

8.2 Spain

Seix Barral published Saramago's novels between 1985 and 1994; Ronsel published Saramago's chronicles *Deste Mundo e do Outro* and *Bagagem do Viajante* and his play *In Nomine Dei*. Círculo del Lector published *Viagem a Portugal*. Tres i Quatre published Saramago's plays *In Nomine Dei* and *A Noite*. Libros del Oeste published Saramago's poems *O Ano de 1993* and Alfaguara has published Saramago's novels since 1994, the short story *O Conto da Ilha Desconhecida* and his diaries. Moreover, there have been editions of Saramago's works in Catalan by Ediciones 62 and Proa and other Castilian re-editions of Saramago's novels by Círculo del Lectores, Planeta, Arquetipo and RBA.[34] Basilio Losada was the translator of Saramago's works until 1998, except for his short story, diaries, poetry and plays, and the editions in Catalan.[35]

A no less relevant aspect is the fact that Alfaguara became Saramago's main publishing house in Spain after the author's reputation was well consolidated in that country. Alfaguara belongs to the publishing group Santillana de Ediciones and is devoted to publishing "fundamental authors of Spain and Latin America. It was set up originally by the brothers Camilo José and Jorge Cela in 1960.[36]

---

34 Círculo del Lector published *O Ano da Morte de Ricardo Reis* in 1987, *Jangada de Pedra* in 1988 and *O Evangelho Segundo Jesus Cristo* in 1992. Planeta published *O Ano da Morte de Ricardo Reis* in 1995, and RBA published *O Evangelho segundo Jesus Cristo* in 1995. Arquetipo also published *Viagem a Portugal*, Saramago's travel book, in 1991. From 1995 on, there were a growing number of translated editions and reprints of Saramago's works in Castilian.

35 Eduardo Naval translated into Castilian *Objecto Quase*, published by Alfaguara in 1994; Albano Saraiva and Josep Lluis translated *In Nomine Dei* and *A Noite*, published by Tres I Quatre in 1994 and 1995, respectively. Ronsel also published *In Nomine Dei* in 1994 and the translator was Basilio Losada. Angel Campos Pámpano was the Castilian translator of *O Ano de 1993*, published by Libros del Oeste in 1996. The works translated into Catalan were *Memorial do Convento* published by Proa in 1988, *Jangada de Pedra* published by Ediciones 62 in 1989, which also published *História do Cerco de Lisboa* in 1990 and *O Ano da Morte de Ricardo Reis* in 1997.

36 <http://www.alfaguara.santillana.es> [accessed in September 2004].

When Seix Barral published *El Año de la Muerte de Ricardo Reis* in 1985, Portuguese contemporary fiction was little published and read in Spain. José Cardoso Pires, Virgílio Ferreira and Agustina Bessa Luís, among very few others, were the Portuguese authors translated and published in Spain. One year before the publication of the first novel by Saramago in this country, he, together with Lídia Jorge, Augusto Abelaira, Bessa Luís and Cardoso Pires, participated in several conferences on Portuguese contemporary fiction, with the main objective to present the major Portuguese novelists to the Spanish educated elite.[37] Moreover, Spanish academic studies on Portuguese literature were mainly confined to the University of Salamanca where there was a chair of Portuguese studies, committed to the study of Fernando Pessoa and also to the writers mentioned above who possessed the common characteristic of belonging to the 'Social-Neorealist literary trend that came out of the Estado Novo'.[38] Besides Salamanca, there were sections of Portuguese studies at the departments of Romance Languages at the Universities of Granada, Madrid, Barcelona, Cáceres and Santander. Therefore, the choice of *El Año de la Muerte de Ricardo Reis* was appropriate to present an unknown Portuguese writer to the Spanish public because the novel was centred on one of the few Portuguese writers known in Spain. In addition, it also had several references to Spanish politics in the 1930s. This strategy proved successful as it drew the attention of the Spanish media.[39] In 1986, Saramago attended a conference on Fernando Pessoa, organised by La Caixa, and mentioned his queries about Fernando Pessoa's work, framing them within those 'the average Portuguese' had about this writer. He also pointed out the success of

---

37 'representantes de una literatura ignorada en España y reconocida, sin embargo, en el resto de Europa'. Quoted from M.del Mar Rosell, 'Novelistas portugueses hablan de su obra en Salamanca', *El País*, 10 March 1984.

38 'Novelistas portugueses hablan de su obra en Salamanca'.

39 In 1997, during a conference that joined Portuguese and Spanish publishers, writers, translators and critics in Zamora, Professor Arnaldo Saraiva, of the University of Porto, pointed out that Pessoa had been the starting point in Spain to discover writers like Saramago and Eugénio de Andrade, among others. See José Lera, 'Las editorials intentan reforzar los lazos entre España y Portugal', *El País*, 2 December 1997.

Portuguese fiction in Portugal, attributing its success to a generation of writers aged around forty years old, whose fiction was original and had high quality. He concluded: 'Podemos ser optimistas en Portugal en cuanto a la próxima década en el campo de la ficción'.[40] Although he was one of the few Portuguese writers published in Spain, he spoke as an experienced writer on behalf of his generation.

At an interview with *El País*, after the publication of *Memorial del Convento*, Saramago emphasized that the output of the Portuguese writers had considerably increased since 1974 and that the world was at last interested in Portuguese literature.[41] This was an overstatement at that time in view of the fact that there had not been any increase in the number of Portuguese writers translated abroad; the United States and the United Kingdom (to mention just two of the most important book markets) had very few translations of Portuguese writers, not commercially successful and mainly circulated at Departments of Portuguese Studies. Nevertheless, the first translations of Saramago's novels into German, French and English were published in the following years and Saramago was one of the first contemporary Portuguese writers to be translated into those languages in a short period of time. His literary agent, Ray Güte-Mertin, taught at Frankfurt University and was specialized in Portuguese and Spanish literature.[42]

Saramago expressed some of his ideas that were expressed in the articles (by him and about him) published in the Spanish press: the need to get closer to Spain and his contempt for the European Union:

---

40   J.A.,'Saramago: Nadie puede tener una relación pacífica con Pessoa', *El País*, 18 November 1986.

41   Carlos G.Santa Cecilia, 'José Saramago recrea la construcción de un convento y de un aerostato en el Portugal del siglo XVIII', *El País*, 20 February 1986.

42   Mertin had promoted José Cardoso Pires in the late 1970s, who was published in Germany (Horst Erdmann Verlag and Rütten & Loening); Brazil (Bertrand Brasil),France (Gallimard), Italy (Editori Riuniti), Hungary (Íbisz), England (J.M. Dent & Sons), Finland (Gummerus Osakeyhtiö), the Netherlands (de Prom), Czechoslovakia, Romenia and Hungary. Most of his fiction was translated after 1974.

Lo que me parece importante es que hoy se está ampliando cada vez más y se está tomando conciencia de la necesidad vital de un conocimiento íntimo, realmente íntimo, de las culturas, o mejor, de la cultura portuguesa con las otras culturas de España.[43]

José Saramago's promotion in Spain was not very different from the one used in Brazil. Iberianism was the topic he developed in Spain while in Brazil, it was enlarged to Pan-Iberianism. Furthermore, Saramago occasionally published texts in the Spanish press about his views. The first was published in 1988 on the complexity of the work by Fernando Pessoa.[44] After the publication of *La Balsa de Piedra*, Saramago did not speak about Fernando Pessoa and he focused on Iberianism.

Publication of Saramago's novels in Spain required a kind of introduction to the scene. As happened with *El Año de La Muerte de Ricardo Reis*, Saramago had referred to *La Balsa de Piedra* one year before its publication in Spain. In 1986, at the conference on Fernando Pessoa, he talked about this novel that had just been published in Portugal: 'Es una gigantesca metáfora', explicó Saramago, que previno de que su nueva obra "es absolutamente una novela y no un ensayo sociológico'.[45] *La Balsa de Piedra* was published in Spain in 1987, one year after its publication in Portugal and, thus, was used in the discussions around the advantages and disadvantages of joining the European Union that occurred both in Portugal and Spain.

The concept of Iberianism played an important role in Saramago's promotion in Spain. He referred to *La Balsa de Piedra* as 'his most personal novel'. He insisted in bringing Portugal and Spain together to the point of presenting himself as an Iberian and not so much as a Portuguese: 'Mi patria chica es Portugal, pero mi patria mayor no es Europa, sino peninsula ibérica'.[46] His marriage to Pilar

---

43 'José Saramago recrea la construcción de un convento y de un aerostato en el Portugal del siglo XVIII'.
44 José Saramago, 'Sobre la impossibilidad de este retrato', *El País*, 5 November 1988.
45 J.A., 'Saramago: Nadie puede tener una relación pacífica con Pessoa'.
46 Pedro Sorela, 'La novella en que españoles y portuguese navegan juntos", *El País*, 14 October 1987.

del Río strengthened his closeness to Spain in the eyes of the Spanish press. It was reported in the press, including statements by the author giving an account of his joy in getting married to the young journalist of Seville.[47] *La Balsa de Piedra* naturally drew the attention of the Spaniards and the reviews were favourable to this novel:

Desde *la balsa de piedra* (1986) ya conocíamos el profundo Iberianismo de José Saramago, que combate como un nuevo Unamuno para estrechar los lazos culturales entre España y Portugal, tan próximas como separadas. […] *Alzado del Suelo, Memorial del convento, El año de la muerte de Ricardo Reis, La balsa de piedra* y *El cerco de Lisboa*, libros prodigiosos, realistas y fantásticos, barrocos y equilibrados, donde se alían lo épico y lo lírico, y el humor y la ternura lo controlan todo. Y siempre, como su concepción del mundo lo exige, todo lo preside la lucha por la libertad, la justicia, tan olvidada en Occidente estos últimos años.[48]

Rafael Conte summarized what can be understood as the main Spanish views on the work by Saramago and on the author; his proclaimed struggle for human rights and his interest in Spain.[49] Nevertheless, Conte used a comparison with Unamuno that became extremely important in the reviews and articles about Saramago up till 1998. Miguel de Unamuno participated in the opposition to Primo de Rivera and was forced to go to exile in Fuerteventura, in the Canary Islands. His ideas included the stance for the Iberian Peninsula as a cultural totality.

The acceptance of this novel was thoroughly favourable:

Saramago siente que su novela ha sido entendida en España, "incluso un político sin veleidades literárias acertó decir que el libro pretendía llevar a

47 'Enteramente vivo', *El País*, 14 October, 1987.
48 Rafael Conte, 'Imágenes de Saramago', El País, 16 December 1989.
49 His affiliation to the Communist Party was often referred to by the press, as for example Pedro Sorela. op. cit.;N.Guardiola, 'La crítica de Lisboa elogia la última novela de Saramago', *El País*, 21 April 1989. in this article there is a brief reference to Saramago being in the list of the Portuguese Communist Party to the European Parliament; Guillermo Altares, 'Saramago: No encuentro ningúm motivo para dejar de ser comunista', *El País*, 24 May 1993. However, these references do not serve as the basis to characterize him as a writer, in the same way he was presented in the English-speaking countries and in Brazil.

Europa hacia el Sur, cosa dificil", concluy, "en esta época, que se rige por la lógica de hierro de los negocios"[53]

Iberianism was an issue that became a topic in conferences, as at the meeting that brought together Portuguese and Spanish writers and was organised by both the Centro das Letras Españolas and the Instituto Português do Livro e da Leitura in June 1989. Saramago, Eugénio de Andrade, José Bento, Francisco José Viegas and Luísa Costa Gomes participated at this meeting. This discussion was encouraged by the organisers' outspoken urge to have more Portuguese authors published such as Eduardo Lourenço, in Spain so that the Spaniards could have a better understanding of contemporary Portugal. It is worthy of mention that *El País* emphasised that the new generation of Portuguese writers – like José Viegas and Costa Gomes – were not supporters of Iberianism in the sense of brotherhood and preferred to consider the Spanish friends of the Portuguese.[54] Furthermore, José Bento pointed out that the Iberian Community had to be well planned because each country's cultural differences had to be preserved. This shows that, although there was a young productive generation of writers in Portugal, in Saramago's words, their views were not altogether the same and that Saramago's Iberianism was not fully endorsed by his Portuguese colleagues. However, the Iberianism supported by Saramago resembled Unamuno's and gradually this stance helped the author to get from the Spanish press a feeling of membership: gradually, Saramago was understood more as an Iberian and almost as a Spanish writer. This was especially clear after the decision of Saramago to settle in Lanzarote, after the Portuguese

---

53 J.M., 'La balsa del Sur', *El País*, 7 June 1989.Saramago became known as one of the writers most concerned about the Iberian Peninsula for the Portuguese-Spanish relations: introduction to an article by Saramago entitled 'El concierto del unicornio', published in *El País*, 16 April 1989, few months before the Portuguese-Spanish conference.

54 José Méndez. 'Mejor amigos que hermanos', *El País*, 7 June 1989. El País also published a long article about the difficult relations between Spain and Portugal, starting with the question of what Portugal shared in common with Spain as far as culture is concerned. The conclusion was much was to be done and there were reasons for Spain to learn more about the Portuguese contemporary literature, in Manuel Rivas, 'El autismo ibérico', *El País*, 10 January 1989.

government's decision to bar Saramago's *Gospel According to Jesus Christ* from the Ariosto Prize competition:

> Esto, no pasa sólo en Espana, como es natural; pasa, por ejemplo en Portugal, que por otra parte es como decir España, que decía Miguel de Unamuno. De allí se vino a vivir a Lanzarote hace dos años José Saramago, el novelista de *La balsa de piedra* y de *la muerte de Ricardo Reis*; antes de marcharse de Lisboa vivió el cerco; [...] los argumentos literarios ingresaban en las descalificaciones propias de la intolerancia religiosa, que tantas veces, en nuestro ámbito es fundamento [...] de la intolerancia cultural.[55]

In 1997, when publishing his diaries in Spain, Saramago told *El País*: 'Soy un escritor ibérico antes que europeo y ahora me siento orgulloso de ser además un escritor de Lanzarote'.[56] In 1998, some months before the announcement of the Nobel Prize, there was a reference in *El País* that Saramago had been mistaken for a Spanish writer.[57] Spain's recognition of Saramago was strengthened when Alfaguara became his main publisher in Spain. This publishing house has primarily been committed to publishing Spanish-speaking writers and Saramago being an exception (in Portuguese contemporary literature) implied a full acceptance of his literary value.

When the 1998 Nobel Prize was announced, *El País* reported that Saramago insisted that the prize was not only for him; it basically rewarded Portugal, Spain and Iberian America.[58] Furthermore, it also reported that Portugal resented the fact that Saramago celebrated the Nobel Prize in Spain before coming to Portugal.[59] Saramago pointed out that he was a Portuguese at heart but he had always been treated kindly in Spain, in a way that he hoped Portugal would do to a Spanish writer one day. The

---

55 Juan Cruz, 'Todos somos unos pobres diablos', *El País*, 27 August 1994. In 1995, Juan Cruz writes: "no es casual que haya elegido Tías, la población citada por Miguel de Unamuno", *El País*, 11 November 1995.
56 *El País*, 19 July 1997. On El Mundo, Fernando Sanchez Drago also referred to Saramago as 'português de Lanzarote' (8 December 1998).
57 M.A.V, 'Portugués ibérico y europeo?', *El País*, 4 February 1998. It is not clear who made this mistake but Saramago referred to it to the journalist.
58 Juan Cruz, 'La alegría de Camoens', *El País*, 10 October 1998.
59 Javier García, 'Receio en Portugal por el protagonismo español en el Nobel de Saramago', *El País*, 14 October 1998.

statements reported in the Brazilian and Spanish press expressed different feelings about the writer in each country: Brazil celebrated the Nobel Prize given to an author who was very close to Brazil, having recognised that there were Brazilian writers who deserved the prize more than he; Spain celebrated the prize given to an adopted author who dedicated it to the country which cherished him throughout his career. Saramago's legitimacy as part of the Iberian canon was so clear that he was used as an example in a dispute between the Partido Socialista Operario Español and the Nationalists on the quality of the Spanish high schools.[60]

A few years after having been published for the first time in Spain, Saramago was said to be the Portuguese writer most read in Spain.[61] In a way, this author may have been responsible for the interest of the Spanish publishers in Portuguese contemporary writers and vice-versa. In 1990, there was news that the Portuguese publishers Editorial Caminho, Teorema and D.Quixote published contemporary Spanish writers such as Manuel Vázquez Montalbán, Eduardo Mendoza and Gonzalo Ballester. Seix Barral published some Portuguese authors in Spain, such as Cardoso Pires and Saramago. As a way of overcoming the cultural gap between Portugal and Spain, the Cervantes Institute was set up in Lisbon in 1990, promoting fundamental works by Spanish authors who were not sufficiently well known in Portugal. Meanwhile, the number of Portuguese contemporary writers published in Spain was increasing, though not quickly enough to include writer such as António Lobo Antunes and Maria Velho da Costa, prizewinners of Portuguese literary prizes.[62] In 1997, Spanish and Portuguese publishers, writers, translators and literary critics met in a conference to discuss ways to publish more in both countries and overcome the lack of publicity.[63]

---

60 'todos los niños saben hoy, cuando salen de la Secundaria, quién es Saramago'. Quoted from 'Rubalcaba cree que los alumnos salen uficientemente formados de Secundaria', El Mundo, 28 October 1997.
61 J.M., 'La balsa del Sur'.
62 N.Guardiola, 'El Instituto Cervantes comenzará la en septiembre sus actividades en Lisboa', El País, 9 August 1990.
63 Lera, 'Las editorials intentan reforzar los lazos entre España y Portugal'.

Saramago could not resent the lack of publicity; in 1988, José Donoso, a Spanish author, praised *El año de la muerte de Ricardo Reis*, as an example of a modern novel.[64] The first reference to Saramago as a potential candidate for the Nobel Prize came up in 1990. The critic Rafael Conte suggested the Portuguese author as a good example of a literary career whose success could be crowned with a Nobel Prize given for the first time to the Portuguese language.[65] His books were usually in the bestsellers' list. In 1992, his works were reported to have been in the top of the bestsellers during the Madrid Book Fair.[66] He was awarded with *Honoris causa* at several Spanish universities in the early 1990s and at the end of that decade, there were international conferences on Saramago's works organised in Spain.[67] It took less than ten years to make him a writer with an undisputed reputation in Spain.

The question whether Saramago opened the way for a better learning about Portugal is also relevant in terms of what aspects of his country were privileged by him. As in Brazil, Saramago also emphasized that he sought the 'old' Portugal. When his travel book about Portugal was published in Spain, he maintained to the Spanish press that it could be understood as a legacy of the old Portugal because everything changed too quickly. He added that he believed that in Portugal only the working class of the rural areas and cities found their way because the Government did not how to tackle problems.[68]

Being the best-known Portuguese writer in Spain, he published an article that was an elegy to Miguel Torga (also Alfaguara's author) in 1995, Saramago's publishing house since 1994. Sa-

---

64 José Donoso, 'Novelas sobre novellas', *El País*, 12 May 1988.
65 Rafael Conte, 'En busca del siglo perdido', El País, 4 January 1990. In 1994, on the eve of the announcement of the Nobel of Literature, Ricardo Moreno also informed that Lobo Antunes and Saramago were high regarded: 'La lengua portuguesa, favorita al Nobel de Literatura', *El País*, 13 October 1994.
66 Fernando Samaniego, 'La Feria del Libro llega al milión de visitantes', *El País*, 9 June 1992.
67 'Coloquio internacional sobre José Saramago', *El País*, 24 August 1996.
68 Andrés Fernandez Rubio, 'Saramago abre las puertas de Portugal', *El País*, 13 May 1995.

ramago authored the article, invested with a reputation that gave him legitimacy to write:

> Algunas veces, en estos últimos tiempos nuestros nombres aparecieron juntos, y siempre que esto sucedía no podía evitar la idea de que aquél no era mi lugar.[69]

This elegy establishes a nexus between Saramago and Torga, which transposes the fact that both were Portuguese authors published by the same publishing house. Saramago acknowledged his debt to Torga's literary heritage and this shows the coherence in the way Saramago promoted himself. Like Torga, Saramago supported Iberianism, although he reinvented it but promoted it at a time the topic was politically appropriate. In 1998, Miguel García-Posada, one of the literary critics who reviewed for *El País*, described Saramago in a way that sums up his position in Spain at the moment the Portuguese author received the Nobel Prize:

> Por lo demás, la obra de Saramago está perfectamente divulgada en España y el escritor, unido a nuestro país por vínculos diversos, incluido el terrritorial de su residencia en Lanzarote, ha hecho popular su figura entre nosotros, donde algunas de sus obras han alcanzado repercusión sobresaliente. La Academia no ha concedido esta vez su premio de literatura a un escritor extranjero. Pepe Saramago es, en cierto sentido, uno de los nuestros, aunque sea, sobre todo, portugués.[...] Hasta cierto punto cabría decir que Saramago es el último escritor comprometido[...], si son la historia, con todos aquellos que la sufren, pero comprometido en primer lugar con la literatura.[70]

As happened in Brazil, Saramago was involved in a literary argument with Vargas Llosa, published in Spain by Alfaguara as well. In 1990, Saramago, together with Professor Pablo del Barco of the University of Seville, accused Mario Vargas Llosa's *La Guerra del fin del mundo* of being a copycat novel of the historical study *Os Sertões* by the Brazilian Euclides da Cunha.[71] Llosa's counter accu-

---

69 José Saramago, 'Demasiado pronto, demasiado tarde', *El País*, 18 January 1995.
70 Miguel García-Posada, 'La ética como principio creativo', *El País*, 9 October 1998.
71 G.M./M.B, 'Saramago acusa Vargas Llosa de "mal imitador', *El País*, 22 August 1990.

sation came out in 1992, when the Peruvian author considered *The Gospel according to Jesus Christ* an anachronistic novel.[72] These disputes covered by the press because these authors were extremely popular in Spain.

To conclude, reactions in Brazil and Spain were similar. In both countries Saramago's legitimacy was strengthened by the fact that he oriented his statements to what could be more appealing to his public, ranging from working-class problems to Iberianism. His position in the literary field was consolidated through awards and recognition at secondary school level. His opinions were listened to and reported in the press with some emphasis.

Richard Zenith authored an article published in *The Times Literary Supplement* in which he used irony to portray the Portuguese cultural life as a complete contrast of what happened in London and Paris. In Portugal, he wrote, the writer imposed respect whereas in London and Spain writers could remain strangers and would be unlikely to achieve the status they could hold in Lisbon.[73] Looking into Saramago's reputation in Spain and Brazil, one cannot but agree that these countries share the same attitude towards the writers who tend to play an active participation in society and Saramago is definitely a clear example of this.

Therefore, it is only natural that the publishing strategies to promote Saramago in these three countries were very often agreed by local publishers. For example, in 1987, the Spanish Circulo del Lectores launched *El año de la Muerte de Ricardo Reis* in Spain and the Brazilian counterpart Círculo do Livro published *Memorial do Convento*. Simultaneously, Harcourt Brace published *Baltasar and Blimunda* in the United States. Círculo de Leitores, Circulo del Lectores and Círculo do Livro belong to the media giant Bertelsmann who also bought Random House in 1998. Furthermore, Editorial Caminho and Alfaguara agreed to publish *Viagem a Portugal* and *Viaje a Portugal* at the same time in Portugal and Spain in 1995.[74]

---

72 EFE, 'Vargas califica la novella de Saramago de "anacronismo', *El País*, 30 June 1992.

73 Richard Zenith, 'All in the Family', in *The Times Literary Supplement* (17 October 1997), 26.

74 At the ceremony that marked the publication of this travel book in Spain, Saramago recognised that this book owed much to Viaje a la Alcarria by

Since 1991, Companhia das Letras has flooded the Brazilian book market with works by Saramago, publishing two or more works by the Portuguese author in a year or publishing one every year. *Evangelho Segundo Jesus Cristo* and *Viagem a Portugal* were published in 1991, *Manual de Pintura e Caligrafia* and *Jangada de Pedra* were published in 1992 and in 1998, four works of different literary genres, ranging from the novel to chronicles and drama, were published.

Saramago's Spanish translator also benefited from his success. The main Spanish translator, Basilio Losada, received the National Prize of Translation in Spain in 1991 with his translation *Historia del cerco de Lisboa*. It is worthy of mention that only one translation of a work by a Portuguese author had received this prize besides Saramago's novel: in 1987, José Antonio Llardent and Juan E. Zúñiga received the prize for their translation of *Poesia e Prosa* by Antero de Quental. The Spanish National Prizes of Translation started in 1956 and had never focussed on any work by a Portuguese author till 1987.[75]

8.3 United States of America

When *Baltasar and Blimunda* was first published in the United States of America in 1987, the reaction of the literary critics conveyed a mixture of surprise and delight after reading a novel by an author little known in this market. Irving Howe, reviewing the novel for *The New York Times*, showed evidence in his introductory paragraph:

Camilio José Cela, who set up Alfaguara. In Carlos G. Santa Cecilia, '"Viaje a Portugal", o recorrido hacia el interior del viajero', *El País*, 15 May 1995. This statement sounds like a compliment to Saramago's publisher in Spain.

75   Losada received the Translation Prize Giovanni Pontiero (also Saramago's translator into English till 1997) in 2002, which is an interesting fact because it confirms Losada's popularity as Saramago's translator.

The most vigorous writing of recent years has come not from the great powers of the West but from small, impoverished and sometimes "backward" countries in Latin America, Eastern Europe and parts of Africa. As if to confirm this trend, there has now arrived from Portugal a brilliant novel by José Saramago, a writer who is highly regarded in Portuguese-speaking countries but little known elsewhere. This injustice should speedily be corrected with Giovanni Pontiero's translation, at once idiomatic and elegant, of "Baltasar and Blimunda". And apart from its strong intrinsic interest, this novel should help put to rest the notion recently expressed in these and other pages that living in the wake of the heroic period of literary modernism dooms us to a literature of timid voices and small consequence.[76]

The first two sentences are worthy of note as they introduce Portugal as the country of the unknown author. Portugal was definitely not the same impoverished country of Salazar and of the early years after the Revolution. However, this shows that externally, or at least to the United States, the country, and particularly the country's cultural production, was little known and that the old image of an impoverished, small country prevailed. As Giovanni Pontiero remarked, interest of the North-American academic circles was chiefly confined to works by Camões, Eça de Queirós and Fernando Pessoa. Fiction produced in the post-war years was scarcely recognized.[77]

Furthermore, the critics' words confirm what Giovanni Pontiero pointed out as one of the reasons for the American and British publishers' sudden interest in foreign fiction, especially in the wider European fiction: a 'general sense of sameness and even decline in American and British fiction'.[78]

As far as the reviewing of the novel is concerned, the critics compared it with Latin American novels, particularly with Garcia Marquez's novels. This was very subtly hinted in Howe's review:

---

76 Irving Howe, 'Fueling The Passarola', *New York Times*, 1 November 1987, p. 7.
77 Pontiero, p. 69. In 2001, fourteen years later, Erik T. Burns, a journalist in Lisbon, writing for *Newsday*, reviewed Saramago's Journey to Portugal under the headline is 'The Country That Is Not Spain'. Burns pointed out that Portugal 'is often erroneously thought to be a region of its bigger neighbour, Spain'. Equally expressive was Tom Dowling's review for the *San Francisco Examiner* published on 25 December 1987 and quoted in Pontiero, p. 70.
78 Pontiero, p. 69.

It is a work of harsh realism, picturing the abominations of absolute power and Inquisitorial fanaticism; but weaving around the realistic pages is a fable about a flight into the marvellous, a lyric fantasy about a company of free spirits escaping for a moment into freedom.[79]

The association between Saramago's and Garcia Marquez's styles was the basis of many of the North-American reviews of Saramago's works. Ilan Stavans referred to it in his review of *The Gospel According to Jesus Christ*, in *The Nation* and David Gilmour pointed it out as a fact in his review of *The Stone Raft*. Edmund White identified a resemblance in style to Borges in his review of *The History of the Siege of Lisbon* and David Streitfeld classified him as a 'magic realistic writer' in his article about Saramago the day after he won the Nobel Prize.[80] This fact becomes especially important when looking at the British reviews and blurbs for Saramago's British editions, which are dealt with below. The recurrent comparison to Latin American authors raises another relevant issue about the way Saramago is presented to North American readers. Harcourt Brace, present-day Harcourt Trade Publishers, is one of the few North-American publishing house committed to publishing translations in the United States of America, an effort that was publicly recognised, as shown in David Streitfeld's article published in *The Washington Post*:

> The award is a vote of confidence for Harcourt Brace, Saramago's American publisher, Harcourt is one of the very few major publishers with a strong commitment to translation – a devotion that has paid off with recent Nobels to Mexican poet Octavio Paz, Polish poet Wislawa Szymborska and now Saramago.[81]

---

79 Irving Howe, p. 7. Equally relevant was Walter Goodman's review 'In Mystic Realms' (*New York Times*, 5 December 1987, p. 12) in which his association to Magic Realism is very assertive.

80 Ilan Stavans, 'A Fisher of Men', *The Nation*, 16 May, 1994, 675-676; David Gilmour, 'Adrift in Iberia', *The New York Review of Books*, 42 (5 October, 1995); Edmund White, 'The Subversive Proofreader', *The New York Times*, 13 July, 1997; David Streitfeld, 'Magic Realized: Saramago wins Nobel', *The Washington Post*, 9 October, 1998.

81 Streitfeld.

In fact, this commitment started in the mid-1960s when Helen and Kurt Wolff, co-founders of Pantheon, joined Harcourt Brace, headquartered in New York, and brought with them Günter Grass, Hannah Arendt, Konrad Lorenz and Anne Morrow Lindbergh. It continued throughout the years and Harcourt is the North-American publisher of António Damásio, David Diaz, and Arturo Pérez-Reverte, among others. Harcourt Brace does not publish Garcia Marquez. He is published by Harper Collins, a subsidiary of News Corporation, also headquartered in New York. This was the parent company of Harvill until 1995. This means that Latin American authors were already familiar to the North-American readers. Therefore, presenting them a new author, coming from an unknown small country constituted a difficult task. The association with Gabriel García Marquez's Magic Realism was used to generate recognition. The fact that Marquez's woks were published and appraised in the United States encouraged acceptance.

The change of the title *Memorial do Convento* to *Baltasar and Blimunda* produced an emphasis on the love story and this was broadly taken as the centre of the novel. Contrasts between the monarchy and the labourers were not regarded as a central problem and, thus, Irving Howe wrote:

> Though Mr. Saramago often reveals a bracing contempt for the powerful of this world, he is not primarily concerned with the struggle between classes. What excites his imagination is the conflict between a stiff moralism of morals, manners of speech – those social and ecclesiastic rituals denoting the death of spirit – and a free play of feeling at a time when the idea of individuality has begun to stir European consciousness. [...] Meanwhile, Mr Saramago is constantly present as a voice of European skepticism, a connoisseur of ironies.[82]

In 1991, the critics received *The Year of the Death of Ricardo Reis* favourably. Herbert Mitgang, reviewing it for *The New York Times*, wrote:

> Mr. Saramago, author of an acclaimed historical fantasy, "Baltasar and Blimunda", tells an even richer story in "The Year of The Death of Ricardo

---

82 Howe.

Reis" about human relationships, class differences and dreams. It's a rare, old-fashioned novel – at once lyrical, symbolic and meditative – by one of Europe's major writers who deserves to be better known.[83]

Michael Wood reviewed it for *The New York Review of Books*:

> [...] and *The Year of the Death of Ricardo Reis* is also a patient, old-fashioned novel full of dialogue and detail, mist, streets, squares, statues, meals, rooms, neighbors, life in a particular hotel of modest pretensions. So much "reality", carefully documented, lovingly piled up. [...] Nineteen-thirty-six seems nearer, and certainly more solid, than 1991. Pessoa and his companions, one defunct and the others invented, have already lived for more than half a century, and even their ghosts are sturdier than we are.[84]

Two aspects are noteworthy. First, the use of the adjective 'old-fashioned' to qualify this novel and second the importance of Pessoa's work, especially mentioned in Michael Wood's article which also includes a very favourable review of *The Book of Disquiet* by Fernando Pessoa.

The adjective 'old-fashioned' is used in a positive meaning when framing it in the context of both reviews. Since the novel's central character is one of Fernando Pessoa's fictional heteronyms, the reviews set the author as an apprentice of Pessoa's mastery, in other words, stemming from the tradition of one of Portugal's few well-known Portuguese poets across frontiers. For the North-American scholars who were interested in learning more about Saramago, this association introduced new possibilities of interpretation, apart from the Magic Realism.[85]

Although the first two English translated editions were published at least five years after the original Portuguese editions, *The*

---

83 Herbert Mitgang, '2 Women, One Poet and the Ghost of Another', *The New York Times*, p. C17. The last sentence was quoted in the blurb of the British edition.

84 Michael Wood, 'The Sorcerer's Apprentice', *The New York Review of Books*, 17, 24 October 1991.

85 Irving Howe published several books, among them *The American Newness: Culture and Politics in the Age of Emerson*; Ilan Stavans is a Mexican novelist and critic, and teaches at Amherst College; Herbert Mitgang; Walter Goodman; Richard Eder; Michael Wood; Edmund White is a novelist, author of *The Farewell Symphony*, among other works.

Gospel According to Jesus Christ was published in the United States and in the United Kingdom considerably faster. It was first published in the United Kingdom in 1993, two years after the Portuguese edition and in 1994 in the United States. Unlike the previous novels, *The Gospel According to Jesus Christ* was not the novel that was written after *The Year of the Death of Ricardo Reis*. Before, in 1986, Editorial Caminho had published *A Jangada de Pedra* that was published in the United Kingdom in 1994 and in the United States in 1995. *The History of the Siege of Lisbon*, published in Portugal in 1989, was published both in the United Kingdom and in the United States in 1996.

In Portugal, the sales of *The Gospel According to Jesus Christ* rose and the publishing house and the author also benefited from the uproar by having the novel translated quicker. It is interesting that it was first published in the United Kingdom, unlike what happened to the previous novels. The fact that *The Year of the Death of Ricardo Reis* was chosen for the Independent Foreign Fiction Award in 1993 enhanced his position in the English-speaking world because his novels were translated and published considerably faster. Almost every year, a new translation came out on the bookstalls and from 1993 on, they were published in the United Kingdom before or at the same time they were published in the United States.

As far as the reviews of *The Gospel According to Jesus Christ* are concerned, some North American critics welcomed this novel, and demystified the reasons for the Portuguese protests. Richard Eder, reviewing for *Newsday*, remarked:

> Thus the tone that launches Saramago's New Testament reworking. It is a special blend of irony and innocence, of playfulness and melancholy; a disputatiousness that mocks not only received doctrine but its own mockery as well. It marks Saramago, Portugal's most distinguished living writer, as it marked his literary predecessors, Eça de Queiroz and Machado de Assis. It sounds a note as rooted in Portugal's character as Hemingway's clipped bark or Whitman's unclipped yawp were rooted in America's. [...]The notion is hardly new, Saramago spins his web around what is now a venerable paradox. The results are not always good – quite apart, of course, from the fact that he is playing exclusive left-field in a wider literary-philosophical

stadium where the devil has some of the best lines but not all of them. [...] is illuminated by ferocious wit, gentle passion and poetry.[86]

As far as the iconoclastic aspect of the novel was concerned, the North American views were not altogether unanimous. There was debate and disapproval of the novel as the readers can conclude after reading the articles by Stephen Schwarz in *The Wall Street Journal* and Tony Karon in *Time*, both published shortly after Saramago was awarded the Nobel Prize in 1998.[87] However, those who did not disapprove of this novel saw in Saramago's revising of the New Testament a barely new concept:

> It is the voice of a country whose long-departed imperial unboundedness left it bound in a misty veil that has kept it oddly out of modern history. No dialectical confrontations for Portugal [...] At most the oddly pleasant Revolution of Carnations in the early '70s that slipped away the remains of the Salazar dictatorship much as a sleeper half-awakes to shrug off an unneeded blanket.[88]

Although the critics did not see in it one of Saramago's best works, it is interesting that they considered that this. Therefore, this novel surprised the critics for being out of its time. Portugal was at last struggling to reach modernity, through a painful process of introspection.

A last noteworthy aspect is the affiliation of Saramago to Fernando Pessoa, which began with *The Year of The Death of Ricardo Reis* and continued with this novel. This is something that the author never refused, shown both in his participation in celebrations of Pessoa and in his statements to the press; but this, together with his influence of Borges and Marquez, became literary references used to legitimize the writer's work.

---

86   Richard Eder, 'Whose Life Is It Anyway?', *Newsday*, 23 January 1994, p. 37. Equally significant is Ilan Stavans' review 'A Fisher of Men', *The Nation*, 16 May 1994, 675-76 (676).
87   Stephen Schwarz, 'Another Nobel's Laureate's Stalinist Past', *The Wall Street Journal*, 14 October 1998 and Tony Karon, 'Another Left-Field Literature Award', *Time*, 8 October, 1998.
88   Eder, p. 37.

From the publication of the first novel by Saramago in the United States, Saramago's legitimacy in the literary field was strengthened with public recognition: 'Portugal's most distinguished living writer'; 'Portugal's most prominent man of letters'; and 'a perennial Nobel Prize contender, an award he richly deserves'.[89] This is relevant when considering that there was never any allusion to any other Portuguese writer in the reviews of Saramago. Although the *New York Review of Books* does not have a record of any reviews of another Portuguese writer, the *New York Times* and *Newsday* included other favourable reviews of António Lobo Antunes's works dated before the reviews of *Blimunda and Baltazar*.[90] Nevertheless, Saramago was represented as the voice that could best stand for Portugal. One of the reasons for this could be what Ilan Stavans wrote to summarise Saramago's work:

> Saramago has over the past few decades publicly re-evaluated Iberian history, offering insightful, at times uncomfortable reflections on Portugal's religiosity and daily behaviour.[91]

Richard Eder pointed out another reason in 1997:

> Saramago is one of Europe's most original and remarkable writers; among other reasons, because he is remarkable by being utterly and indelibly Portuguese, a quality that Europe – not to mention the United States – has little acquaintance with.[92]

He was present in many different places. Between 1987 and 1994, Saramago collected several international prizes in Italy and in Spain, the *Independent*'s prize, was a member of the International Parliament of Writers, the Universal Academy of Cultures and of the Argentinean Academy of Letters. Prizes accumulate prestige and demand for books. This becomes especially important when considering Portuguese fiction that only a handful of Portuguese

---

89 Richard Eder writes the first expression, p. 37 and the second and third expressions by Stavans, 675.
90 The oldest record is 1983 in *The New York Times*.
91 Stavans, 675.
92 Richard Eder, 'Love Lit by a 'Not'', *Newsday*, 25 May 1997, p. G10.

writers were translated and published outside Portugal and, consequently, very few international literary agents were engaged in promoting its literary production. As David Gilmour put it in *The New York Review of Books*:

> Saramago's ascent typifies that of a successful writer from a literature almost unknown outside its country of origin. After years in the wilderness, he is suddenly discovered and taken up by Western literary establishments amid much breast-beating about how Anglo/Francocentric we are to have ignored such a genius. Identified as the successor to García Marquez, he is then regularly touted as a future winner of the Nobel Prize – a possibility doubtless enhanced in this case by the fact that no Portuguese writer has ever won it. By the time he reaches Saramago's current position, his reputation is unassailable: each new novel is hailed as further evidence of his talent (and our blindness), and its author more or less acquires immunity from criticism. In this respect he is much more fortunate than major British novelists who are usually informed by reviewers that their latest work does not live up to the expectations aroused by the previous one.[93]

The Stone Raft also received the critics' attention and they were not unanimous. Richard Eder wrote:

> Saramago's balloons need time and patience, particularly at first. Bit by bit we do not simply get used to them; we find in them – skilfully translated by Giovanni Pontiero – the essence of his humane and magical art. [...] and soon we are moving giddily over a panorama of the world infinitely stretched out below.[94]

David Gilmour found the novel 'generally unsuccessful' when comparing it to his previously published novels, namely in terms of style and wit.[95] As for Saramago's stance, Gilmour questioned whether it actually reflected that of the Portuguese:

> I do not know Portugal and cannot say whether this is a common view. But it seems an exaggerated reaction to a fairly minor misdemeanour. After all, in the long list of Western crimes against the world, indifference toward Por-

---

93 David Gilmour, 'Adrift in Iberia', *The New York Review of Books*, 5 October 1995.
94 Richard Eder, 'The Island That Sailed Away', *Newsday*, 28 May 1995. p. 37.
95 Gilmour.

tugal hardly ranks in the first league. Perhaps the author's real grievance stems from history's diminishment of his country's international position.[96]

Gilmour found it strange that a Communist should maintain peninsular uniqueness, a stance that had much in common with General Franco's, for instance, and, at the same time, chose to leave Portugal and settle in the Canary Islands, complaining to a Spanish journalist that Portugal's culture was dead.

Gilmour's review goes against those who see in Saramago the voice of Portugal and questions the real motives for the grievances pointed out by the novelist. It is significant that Gilmour linked Portugal's lack of influence in the international arena to the novelist's resentment.[97]

One year before the Nobel Prize, *The History of the Siege of Lisbon* was published in the United States. Critics were very favourable to this novel. The main idea was that the novelist had established his reputation:

> Word has it that Saramago is overdue for a Nobel Prize; no candidate has a better claim to lasting recognition than this novelist who was born in 1922 but was in his mid 50's before he began to publish the fiction that has won him an international reputation.[98]

However, a question is overdue: as far as the United States is concerned, does it actually mean that Saramago was broadly well known? On the assumption of the validity of Ilan Stavans's words, he was not; when choosing *The History of The Siege of Lisbon* as one of his favourite books of 1997, he remarked:

---

96   Gilmour.
97   Carolyn See also reviewed this novel for *The Washington Post*: 'Drifting slowly, slowly', 2 June 1995, p. D2. See criticised this novel for being boring and pointless reading. There was also another review in the same newspaper by David Streitfeld, published on 14 May 1995, p. X15.
98   Edmund White, 'The Subversive Proofreader', *The New York Times*, 13 July 1997, p. 11.

Curiously, Saramago continues to elude American readership, so whenever I am fortunate enough to read something new by him, I feel like a member of some secret club.[99]

Stavans's words echoed in another short article published when Saramago won the Nobel Prize:

Don't feel ignorant if you haven't heard of 1998 Nobel Literature laureate José Saramago. You're not alone. "I've been reviewing books all my life and I've never heard of him", says *Time*'s literary critic Paul Gray.[100]

And that was true. *Time* never reviewed any of Saramago's books. On researching reviews of Saramago's work in the North American press, I found that most date from 1998 onwards. *USA Today* had one in 1988 and two in 1998; Richard Eder signed most reviews for *Los Angeles Times* and for *Newsday*. David Streitfeld signed several reviews of Saramago's work for *The Washington Post*. Harold Bloom included Saramago's *Baltasar and Blimunda* in his *The Western Canon*'s Appendix D 'The Chaotic Age: A Canonical Prophecy'.[101] Ilan Stavans's comment might have had the intention to break the 'secret club's' ties but, actually only after the Nobel Prize did Saramago was ninth in *Newsday*'s best-sellers' list with his *Blindness*.[102] Moreover, *The Philadelphia Inquirer* reported that this novel had jumped from a pre-award rank of 467 to Number 1 on the Amazon.Com bestseller chart, shortly after the award.[103]

It is impossible to segment purchasers of Saramago's novels in the United States. The Nobel Prize might have awakened some

---

99 Richard Eder, Dan Cryer, David Futrelle, Claire Messud, et al, 'A Literary Celebration/Our Favourite Books of 1997', *Newsday*, 28 December 1997, p. B09.
100 Tony K, 'Another Left-Field Literature Award', *Time*, 8 October 1998.
101 Besides Saramago, he also mentions works by Fernando Pessoa, Jorge de Sena, José Cardoso Pires, Sophia de Mello Breyner and Eugénio de Andrade.
102 This list was compiled from a survey of bookstores including Book Hampton, Book Revue, Coliseum Books, Corner Bookstore, B.Dalton Bookseller, Mostly Books, Rizzoli, Three Lives & Co. and Walden Books, all in New York. *Blindness* was included in Hardcover Fiction. This survey was published in *Newsday*, 13 December 1998,p. B10.
103 *The Philadelphia Inquirer*, 10 October 1998, p. D11.

interest among those who were not students of literature or professionals. The CNN covered the Nobel award ceremony. Nevertheless, the main target audience of Saramago's novels in the United States was apparently an elite: a few critics, who were mostly novelists and teachers, reviewed his novels and few were said to read them. Yet, many North-American reviews of Saramago's novels pointed out that the Nobel Prize was overdue. One month before he was awarded the Prize, Richard Eder wrote:

> Saramago, Portugal's greatest contemporary writer, is the author of such entrancing fictions as "Baltasar and Blimunda", "The Stone Raft" and "The History of The Siege of Lisbon". Each, in part, is the world and, in part, a counterworld. Saramago will win the Nobel Prize if his arteries hold out, though the Stockholm people are notably adroit at outwaiting arteries [...][104]

After the Nobel Prize, the same critic chose *Blindness* as one of his favourite books of 1998 and concluded:

> Saramago's Nobel Prize this year does not make him a better writer, but it improves the prize.[105]

The idea is that slowly but gradually, anticipation around the necessity to give Saramago a Nobel Prize rose, with a twofold purpose: on the one hand, to consolidate the mastery and international reputation of Saramago as Portuguese writer; and, on the other hand, to legitimate it as a prize which gave prestige to a certain kind of literature. At the news of the Prize, Stephen Schwarz accused the Swedish Academy of using it for the same purposes as the Norwegians were using the Peace Prize, awarding it to leftists:

> The message is clear: The snobs of the Scandinavian academies, secure in their wealth and power, remain doggedly faithful to their leftist fantasies.[106]

---

104 Richard Eder, 'IN A DARK TIME/José Saramago makes a mysterious epidemic of blindness a riveting descent into hell', *Newsday*, 6 September, 1998, p. B09.
105 Richard Eder, Dan Cryer, Laurie Muchnick, David L.Ulin, et al, *Newsday*, 'A Literary Celebration/Our Favourite Books of 1998', *Newsday*, 27 December, 1998, p. B09.

As for the way journalists introduced Saramago in the press at this time, it is interesting that there are some characteristics attributed to the laureate that had not all emerged before: the fact that he was a Communist, the scandal around his *The Gospel According to Jesus Christ* and the fact that he wrote about issues that could interest anyone, quoting him to this effect. When comparing the reception of his Communist beliefs in Brazil and in the United States, it differed in terms of how these beliefs were regarded in these countries. In Brazil, they were associated to a movement that emerged at the time of the publication of *Levantado do Chão*, and they were introduced as endorsing to it; in the United States, where this novel was not translated because the experience of the Agrarian Reform was unknown there, these were disregarded and only raised by more conservative sectors of society as another argument against his award. As far as *The Gospel According to Jesus Christ* was concerned, the uproar about it became more important than the novel itself. Those who read and reviewed his novels rarely rank it among their favourites.

8.4 United Kingdom

Giovanni Pontiero, who translated his novels between 1987 and 1996, when he passed away, played a fundamental role in his success in the English-speaking countries. His work as an academic and translator of Portuguese and South-American authors brought him recognition. Fourteen publishers employed him as literary consultant and/or manuscript reader. The introduction of Saramago's works into the English-speaking countries was largely due to his decision, according to a tribute written by José Saramago.[107]

In the United Kingdom, Saramago's novels are published by Harvill with a hardback cover. However, in 1987, *Baltasar and Bli-*

---

106 Stephen Schwarz, Op. Cit.
107 José Saramago, 'To write is to translate', in Pilar Orero, Juan C.Sager (ed), pp. 85-86.

munda was published by Jonathan Cape, Ltd., a smaller publishing house. It was Saramago's only novel to be published by Jonathan Cape because in that year this publishing house was acquired by the North-American Random House Inc., together with Chatto, Virago and Bodley Head. Moreover, the Random House Group was strengthened with the acquisition of Century Hutchinson Ltd. in 1989 and the Trade Division of Books in 1997. Although the Random House Group shares the same name and owner as Random House Inc. in the United States, they have not always published the same books. They are independent companies that come together on many projects and have their own catalogues. Saramago's *The Year of The Death of Ricardo Reis* and other translated novels were published by Harvill, a publishing house founded in 1946 with a clear editorial purpose: to offer foreign literature to British readers.[108]

Baltasar and Blimunda was published in hardcover, with blurbs taken from *New York Times Book Review*, *World Literature Today* and *La Repubblica*. Although Saramago's novel was published in other countries, these blurbs indicate some of the foremost countries as far as the world circulation of books is concerned. The flap summarized the writer's biography, emphasizing his experience in the book business, and also his literary prizes and appraisal.[109] It is very difficult to find reviews in the British press about this novel that gained so many favourable reviews in other countries. However, Christopher Wordsworth signed a very favourable one for *The Guardian*:

---

108 Harvill published the bestselling *Doctor Zhivago* and *The Leopard*. This company was bought by Harper Collins and between 1995 and 2002, Christopher MacLehose, former literary editor of *The Scotsman*, run the imprint. In 2002, Random House Group bought it.

109 ' José Saramago was born in 1922, in Portugal. Before becoming a full-time writer, he worked as a translator, editor and journalist', in José Saramago, *Baltasar and Blimunda* (London: Jonathan Cape, 1987). It is interesting that Harvill's editions introduced relevant changes in Saramago's biography: a brief reference to his various professions (including mechanic and technical designer), his embracing of different genres and attention of the wide English-speaking public, extensive to his translator.

A richly caparisoned novel from Portugal, "Baltasar and Blimunda", set in the early eighteenth century at the point of balance between Enlightenment and superstition, has inevitably inspired comparison with Gabriel García Marquez's "One Hundred Years of History" for its fresh view of black human comedy, its finger-wagging at the transgression of men and duty and its use of pure magic to shake the old world out its coma. [...] and José Saramago affirms the simple truths as only a writer of rare stature can.[110]

Portugal was not strange to the British eyes, the United Kingdom being one of the countries whose inhabitants fly most to Portugal for tourism purposes. However, the country and its literary production are two completely separate realities. The country was familiar but its contemporary literature was not. On looking at Random House Group's booklists, they feature only two Portuguese writers: José Saramago and Lídia Jorge. Saramago's novels are all included in the booklists and Lídia Jorge is only represented by the *Migrant Painter of Birds*, a Harvill hardcover edition. As with Saramago, Jorge's novel was translated by Margaret Jull Costa and was first published by Harcourt Trade Publishers in March 2001 and by Harvill in October of the same year.[111] It is worthy of note that the front cover of the British edition included the following praise of José Saramago: "A remarkable book". Taking into account that Saramago was successful in breaking through the British book market, the first edition of another Portuguese writer, unknown in the United Kingdom, carries the praise of the well-known writer, a publicity resource to attract the British readers.

As in the North-American reviews, the comparison to García Marquez's Magic Realism was used to explain the literary worth of Saramago, and his good reputation in the literary scene is confirmed in Wordsworth's review. In 1988, Saramago was already translated in the United States, not to mention other European countries and Brazil and had, therefore, gathered a solid corpus of favourable reviews of his work.

Up till 1992, there was no review of any of Saramago's work. After 1992, *The Independent*'s critics were attentive to what was

---

110 Christopher Wordsworth, 'Wagging a Finger at God', *The Guardian*, 4 March 1988, p. 23.
111 Margaret Jull Costa has been Saramago's English translator since 1996.

242

published by Saramago in the United Kingdom. The United Kingdom did not share the good reception of *Baltasar and Blimunda* in Italy, Spain, the United States and Brazil. In the United States, Saramago was published by a major publisher but the British publisher did not have a significant share of the book market, although it was behind some important commercial successes such as Salmon Rushdie, Margaret Atwood and Isaac Bashevis Singer. Publishing a translated novel and being successful at doing that in the United Kingdom require much more than publishing a good novel. Since the British public resist to translations, an added investment in publicity and pressure on the media are necessary to make a translation a potential commercial success. Apparently, and in comparison with *The Year of The Death of Ricardo Reis*, that was lacking with Jonathan Cape's edition. Saramago was not successful in attracting media attention the same way he did in Spain and in Brazil. The language probably constituted an obstacle but the kind of attention given to important writers in the English-speaking countries was different to that given in those countries, especially when they are foreign. Writers are not so often called to the fore to comment on political or social issues and, thus, their public exposure is restrained to cultural issues.

In the same year that *Baltasar and Blimunda* was published, Saramago published an article entitled 'A Country Adrift' in *The Times Literary Supplement*, the first time that an article by or about Jose Saramago was published in this journal.[112] In this article, he exposed his distrust for Eurocentrism and the need to contextualise Portugal with South-America and the Iberian nation. This was the topic of his *The Stone Raft* and this article indicated an attempt to arouse the critics' interest in his work. In 1990, Basilio Losada also signed an article in *The Times Literary Supplement*, entitled 'An Iberian voice'. It is an extensive review of Saramago's work, with emphasis on *The Stone Raft*, and detailed references to *Levantado do Chão*, *Baltasar and Blimunda*, *The Year of The Death of Ricardo Reis*, his poems and articles published in volume, and *The Manual of Painting and Calligraphy*. The one-page article, with picture, draws the

---

112 Jose Saramago, 'A Country Adrift', *The Times Literary Supplement*, December 1988.

British reader's attention to the then unknown writer, portraying him:

> José Saramago dislikes being considered Europe's or the world's most representative modern Portuguese novelist. [...] books that are immediately translated into the main Western languages and which, for the first time in the recent history of the Portuguese novel, are guaranteed to attract a wide European readership. Saramago is writing for the whole continent from its westernmost corner [...][113]

As far as the impact created by Euroscepticism in the United Kingdom is concerned, the emphasis on Saramago's stance as a Eurosceptic showed that the writer and the agent saw in it an opportunity to raise interest among British publishers, reviewers and readers. In his article, Losada explained the difference between Saramago's point of view and the Portuguese and Spanish authorities' on a possible Iberian union, and his legitimacy as 'the most representative figure of contemporary Portuguese fiction' accounted for his judgment.[114] The novelist's literary skills were reviewed in terms of his reinvention of the language through the recovery of the vocalized reading and his baroque style represented as 'a subtle play of conceits combined with a meticulous structure that obliges the reader to participate in the play of the text'.[115]

In the same year, the *PN Review* included an interview conducted by Giovanni Pontiero with Saramago.[116] Saramago summarized his career as a novelist and his past as a humble man; he was asked about his open distrust for Eurocentrism, his success across the world, and his ideas about literature, especially the importance of literary predecessors in literary writing and a comparison between his ideas and Borges's and Marquez's. His comments and

---

113   Basilio Losada, 'An Iberian Voice', John Butt (transl.) *Times Literary Supplement*, 1 (1990), Liber 3.
114   Losada, Liber 3.
115   Losada, Liber 3.
116   Giovanni Pontiero. 'Interview with Jose Saramago', *PN Review*, 16.4 (1990), 38-42.

his public appearances confirmed his first introduction on the 1987 Jonathan Cape's edition.

The Year of The Death of Ricardo Reis was the second novel by Saramago to be published in the United Kingdom and not *The Stone Raft*. This raises the question of what might have swayed the publishers to publish one novel instead of another. Taking into account the words of Saramago's editor, Zeferino Coelho, the interest in the publication of foreign authors is aroused by something other than the publisher's good words about the author and the work. It is not enough to claim that the book has quality. It is in the publisher's best interest to sell his author because both parts win prestige and money. Therefore, a publisher will always praise his own author. International publishers need guarantees and that includes public recognition of that quality: volume of sales and prizes are guarantees that a book might be a promise of commercial success.[117] By 1992, *The Year of The Death of Ricardo Reis* was the novel which had most received widespread praise: the Portuguese Pen Club prize and the Reviewers' Prize by the Portuguese Association of Reviewers in 1984, the D. Dinis Prize by Casa de Mateus in 1986, the Italian Grinzane-Cavour prize in 1987, besides having the Italian Bracati prize and International Literary prize for the complete works by Saramago in 1992. *The Stone Raft* had not received any specific prize.

By the time *The Year of The Death of Ricardo Reis* was published by Harvill in the United Kingdom, *The Gospel According to Jesus Christ* was withdrawn from the shortlist for the Ariosto Literary Award. Pontiero tried to draw the attention of the British publishers, agents and critics to this affair.[118] According to Robert Winder, Literary Editor of *The Independent*, the translator was not successful because Saramago was a faraway name of which the British knew very little at the time. Nevertheless, the publication of this novel

---

117 'Não basta dizer que um livro é muito bom porque um editor preocupa-se em saber se o livro vendeu bem em Portugal, se as pessoas reconheceram essa qualidade'. Quoted from Appendix 1 on pp. 339.

118 Robert Winder, 'Death in Lisbon: a poet disintegrates: The Year of The Death of Ricardo Reis – Jose Saramago; Tr. Giovanni Pontiero:Harvill: 7.99 pounds', *The Independent*, 7 August 1992, p. 17.

was a turning point for the author's booming reputation in the United Kingdom.

The binding of *The Year of The Death of Ricardo* was considerably more eye-catching. The front and back covers included snippets of reviews of this novel, published in *Philadelphia Inquirer*, *Wall Street Journal* and *New York Times* signed by Richard Locke and Herbert Mitgang. The novel was preceded by a long preface entitled 'The Portuguese Heritage: José Saramago's The Year of The Death of Ricardo Reis', authored by Giovanni Pontiero. According to him, Saramago was right in saying that this novel demanded considerable knowledge about Portuguese history and culture of the period of the Estado Novo. The translator wrote an overview of this period and of Fernando Pessoa's work and, more specifically, of Ricardo Reis's poems. According to him, this novel provided 'factual documentation with idiosyncratic commentaries' seen through the eyes of Reis and Pessoa and, simultaneously, the author Saramago questions the values that prevailed in this period.[119] Pontiero pointed out that this Portuguese author's vision of the world as a theatrical arena resembled Borges, especially in his *Ficciones*. He also pinpointed Saramago's accurate and specialised use of the Portuguese language. The final sentence of this preface subtly encouraged readers to take Saramago into a universal context and not leave him confined to a position in Portuguese literature:

> In the end, we care passionately about 'the timid voice of Portugal' and endorse its plea to be heard in a universal context.[120]

The capacity of an author to transcend the specificity of his culture is extremely important when it comes to being published abroad and is the basic criterion taken by the publisher when he decides to try to get his author published in foreign book markets.[121] *The*

---

119 Giovanni Pontiero, 'The Portuguese Heritage: José Saramago's *The Year of The Death of Ricardo Reis*.', Preface to José Saramago, *The Year of The Death of Ricardo Reis* (London: Harvill: 1992), p. ix.

120 Pontiero, p. xv.

121 At the interview Zeferino Coelho said: "É suposto que um português escreva sobre coisas portuguesas e isso é normal, mas a capacidade de

Year of The Death of Ricardo Reis showed this capacity. As far as Portuguese literature is concerned, international promotion was insufficient. The *"Portuguese heritage"*, as shown by Pontiero, was to take the legacy left by Fernando Pessoa, one of the few Portuguese writers well known across frontiers, and eventually place Portuguese literature in a universal context. The comparison with Borges, a consecrated writer, was important, as mentioned above, in order to determine Saramago's literary position in the field.

Reviews were not unanimous in their appraisal of *The Year of The Death of Ricardo Reis*. Robert Winder, *The Independent*'s Literary Editor, acknowledged the stature of Saramago as an author as well as the talent of his British translator:

> Ostensibly, then, the novel would seem to require both a basic knowledge of Portuguese history and a working acquaintance with the work of Fernando Pessoa. That this is not the case is a tribute to Saramago's exceptional craftiness as a dramatist, and also to Pontiero's heroic inventiveness in finding a vigorous English version.[122]

Gabriel Josipovici agreed that this novel was 'not the masterpiece the puffs on the dust-jacket insist it is', but it was 'nevertheless the work of a fine and interesting writer'.[123] He was the first critic to affiliate this novel to Borges's and to Pessoa's work and reject a simple connection between it and the Magic Realism.

The impact of this novel was undoubtedly more significant than that of *Baltasar and Blimunda*. On the one hand, this can be measured by reviews, considering that the first novel was almost

---

transcender essas particularidades é mais raro e, naturalmente, limita porque se confina a um sector do público que conhece as coisas de Portugal'. See Appendix 1 on pp. 339.

122 Robert Winder. Equally relevant are Martin Cropper's article 'Book: A dead person, the ideal confidant – Fiction: a labyrinthine lover; the unreadability of all published texts; a stiff dose of hormonal poison', *The Daily Telegraph*, 22 August 1992, expressing a less favourable opinion about Saramago's language; and Kate Chisholm, 'A Portuguese Odyssey – Kate Chisholm on a medidative novel set in Lisbon'. *The Sunday Telegraph*, 23 August 1992, confirming the writer's talent despite using difficult language.

123 Gabriel Josipovici, 'Poet and revenant', *The Times Literary Supplement*, 11 September 1992.

left to oblivion.[124] On the other hand, in 1993, it was given *The Independent*'s Foreign Fiction Prize. This prize is administered and financially supported by Arts Council England and assesses fiction issued by the British publishers within one calendar year. The prize seeks to encourage publishers to invest more effort and resources in translation and draw the readers' attention to the potential wealth of foreign fiction and its importance for British culture.[125] The panel of judges that gave the prize to *The Year of The Death of Ricardo Reis* was composed of Penelope Fitzgerald, the Booker Prizewinner in 1979, Jonathan Keates, writer and critic, Gabriel Josipovici, Anthony Lane, the newspaper's Deputy Literary Editor, Doris Lessing, Trevor McDonald, the well-known newscaster, Jill Neville, Blake Morrison, Natasha Walter, all writers, Tim Waterstone, founder of the well-known chain of bookshops, Robert Winder and Michael Wood, academic and critic who reviewed the novel for the North-American *New York Review of Books* in 1991. This fact is interesting because some critics reviewed Saramago's novels for North-American and British newspapers and journals and, thus, gave a contribution to the consolidating of Saramago's reputation in both countries. Moreover, the inclusion of one of them in the panel strengthened his consecration in the English-speaking countries. His legitimacy was also enhanced, in particular in Portugal, with references to other well-known writers who contended for this prize in the same shortlist: Günter Grass, Juan Goytisolo, Ismail Kadare and Ivan Klima. The prize also crowned the efforts of Giovanni Pontiero in the promotion of Saramago's work. Robert Winder wrote an editorial on Pontiero as the translator of Saramago, highlighting his career as an academic

---

124 At the end of 1993, George Steiner considered *The Year of The Death of Ricardo Reis* one of the best international books of the year and compared Saramago's style to Musil's. The repercussion of these appraisals is relevant for the consecration in the respective circles, in *Times Literary Supplement*, 3 December 1993, p. 10. Almost one year later, *the Sunday Times* included this novels in the books' shortlist for Christmas: Ian Critchley. 'Shortlist; Books for Christmas', *Sunday Times*, 27 November 1994, p. 7.

125 Robert Winder, 'Foreign Fiction/ A far cry from Kensington: Robert Winder reflects on the first annual shortlist for the 10,000 pounds Independent Award', *The Independent*, 1 June 1991, p. 30.

and translator of Saramago and Clarice Lispector.[126] The fact is that this was not the only translation of a novel by Saramago which gave a prize to Pontiero. In the following year, he won the Outstanding Translation Award of the American Literary Translators' Association for his version of Saramago's *The Gospel According to Jesus Christ*. This means that in four years, three novels by Saramago gave prizes to their translators, Basilio Losada and Giovanni Pontiero. Occasionally there were articles in the British press campaigning for the recognition of the translator's work. *The Independent* led this campaign in the press, with its prize. In 1994, after rumours that Harvill could be facing its demise, *The Scotsman* published an article enhancing the role of Harvill in seeking new European talents. Moreover, in 1998, when Saramago won the Nobel Prize, this newspaper published another article in which the journalist, Catherine Lockerbie, hoped that the prize could nourish the appetite of British readers for translated fiction and highlighted the role of Harvill in this respect.[127] This strengthened both the reputation of the translators and the work of the novelist. As Winder wrote, a poor translation of a great book is penalised but a great translation of a poor book is very awkward. Therefore, this constituted the best opportunity to promote the author in the United Kingdom, similarly to the way he was promoted in Brazil and Spain, that is, with public appearances. In 1993, under the sponsorship of the Camões Institute, Saramago attended ceremonies at Manchester and Edinburgh Universities, where Pontiero worked, and at the Portuguese Embassy in London. At the same time, there were some broadcasts for the BBC and interviews in which he also talked about the scandal over the publication of *The*

---

126 Robert Winder, 'Independent Foreign Fiction Award: Adventures in humility: Robert Winder talks to Giovanni Pontiero, who translated *The Year of The Death of Ricardo Reis* by Jose Saramago', *The Independent*, 17 July 1993, p. 28.

127 *The Scotsman*, 29 May 1994. No headline available; Catherine Lockerbie, 'Volume Control', *The Scotsman*, 10 October 1998. As stated in this article, the director of Harvill until 1995 was Christopher Maclehose who was the former literary editor of *The Scotsman*. Both articles serve the purpose of publicity to Harvill Press as a publishing house of "serious literature" and, in a way, also to the newspaper because of the connections established.

Gospel According to Jesus Christ in Portugal.[128] His speech was published in a special volume of the *Bulletin of Hispanic Studies*, entitled 'Do Canto ao Romance, do Romance ao Canto'.[129] In his speech, Saramago stated the importance of great writers of literature in the constitution of literary dispositions, conventions and rules that contribute to the making of a novel, such as his, and its vocation to express knowledge of the world, a cosmovision in Saramago's words:

> Mas este mesmo romance, que assim pareço estar condenando, contém acaso em si, e já nos seus diferentes e actuais avatares, a aberta possibilidade de se transformar no lugar literário (propositadamente digo *lugar*, e não género) capaz de receber como um grande convulso e sonoro mar, os afluentes torrenciais da poesia, do drama, do ensaio, e também da ciência e da filosofia, tornando-se expressão de um conhecimento, de uma sabedoria, de uma cosmovisão, como o foram, para o seu tempo, os poemas da antiguidade clássica.[130]

This speech is especially relevant because it shows that the writer also contributed to his positioning in the literary field. It confirmed Saramago's determination to be accepted by his readers, accepting conventions and rules, which are what Bourdieu defined as the 'habitus'.

The Gospel According to Jesus Christ was published by Harvill in 1993, shortly after *The Independent*'s Foreign Fiction Award and, along with the publicity obtained with the scandal over the publication of the novel in Portugal, Saramago benefited from the critics' attention. This does not mean that the scandal itself had sig-

---

128 In a long article published in *The Daily Telegraph* (28 August 1993), James Woodall writes about this scandal and this is perhaps one of the most emotional articles written in the British press on this affair and also one that shows the benefits of Saramago's public appearances in the U.K. Woodall criticised the Portuguese government for taking a decision that resembled those taken in Islamic theocracies, he is quoted several times on the occasion of his visit to the U.K. In his statements, Saramago expressed his shock and compared the Portuguese Government to the Inquisition. His humble origins and his career are also referred to.

129 José Saramago, 'Do Canto ao Romance, do Romance ao Canto', *Bulletin of Hispanic Studies*, 71 (1994), 119-123.

130 Saramago, p. 122.

nificant repercussions in the United Kingdom. Above all, and bearing in mind the short period between the Prize and the publication of the following novel, it served the purpose of commenting on the episode and attracting more attention to the author's work, strengthening what was achieved with the Prize.[131] Critics could not see any firm reasons for the uproar in Portugal, confirming the North-American reviews. Lack of unanimity was solely due to the novel's literary merits. Ruth Pavey recalled interpretations of Christ's life that preceded this novel and stated that Saramago was nearer to Shusaku Endo, a Japanese Catholic novelist, when he celebrated human affection and questioned the horrors of Christian martyrdom.[132] Although Gabriel Josipovici admired Saramago's talent, he could not see any radical stance in this novel that belonged to 'a common Western genre':

> As with *The Year of The Death of Ricardo Reis* we are aware that the writer has been deeply affected by Pessoa and Borges, but has found a way of marrying their scepticism to his own novelistic concerns. [...] For much of this novel it is in fact quite difficult to assess his tone – and this is a major source of the novel's success.[133]

Jamie McKendrick also expressed some admiration for Saramago's gifts as a storyteller and his literary style.[134] The fact that *The Independent* included a picture of Saramago next to the review signed by Josipovici is also noteworthy because it contributed to the enhancement of the author's visibility, along with the fact that this newspaper published reviews of Saramago's work very frequently, two of them on successive days. John Butt emphasized

---

131 It is also relevant that, for the first time, the paperback edition of a Saramago's novel included a blurb from *Jornal de Letras* ('A narrative of extraordinary harmony and luminosity'). This can be regarded as the publisher's way to underplay the Portuguese hue-and-cry about *The Gospel According to Jesus Christ*.

132 Ruth Pavey, 'Jealous God', *New Statesman & Society*, 27 August 1993, p. 40.

133 Gabriel Josipovici, 'Son of God tries to outwit his mad father', *The Independent*, 11 September 1993, p. 31.

134 Jamie McKendrick, 'Father, Son and much free spirit', *The Independent* on Sunday, 12 September 1993, p. 31.

the novel's originality and absence of any content capable of producing reactions against its representation of Christianity:

> But even more paradoxical is the fact that he should write such an original, wild and beautiful book that will surely soften the heart of the most obdurate infidels in favour of the figure of Christ.[135]

Emily Robinson in *The Guardian* was less favourable because of the novel's excessive "bitterness".[136] Despite *The Gospel According to Jesus Christ* not being as appreciated as *The Year of The Death of Ricardo Reis*, it was in the shortlist of seven titles selected by libraries in 108 cities around the world for the IMPAC Dublin Literary Award in 1996. The others were works by John Banville, Naipaul, Cees Noote Boom, Connie Palmen, Urquart and David Malouf, who received the prize.[137] This fact shows that Saramago managed to find a place in the British book market and that the attempts to achieve visibility were successful.

After *The Year of The Death of Ricardo Reis*, there was a change in the periods of publication of Saramago's novels in the United Kingdom. The intervals between publications were considerably less in this country and, furthermore, some of the author's work was published in the United Kingdom and not in the United States; one of the novels was *Manual of Painting and Calligraphy*, published in 1994 by Carcanet, a poetry-oriented publishing house. Publishing one of his least-known novels was a risk for a smaller publishing house that also invested some efforts in translation. Nonetheless, being a relatively well-known and prizewinning author could mean the chance of enlarging the number of buyers and, thus, the profits usually obtained in these investments. Pontiero's efforts in having Saramago's work translated and published in the United Kingdom were also behind the publication of this novel.

---

135 John Butt, 'The crimes of God', *The Times Literary Supplement*, 22 October 1993, 22. Equally relevant, endorsing a similar opinion was the Karen Armstrong, 'God the villain', *Daily Telegraph*, 2 October 1993, p. xxvi.
136 Emily Robinson, 'The Gospel According to Jesus Christ', *The Guardian*, 7 December 1993, p. 8.
137 *The Times*, 'IMPAC Dublin Literary Award', 15 June 1996, p. 11.

The Carcanet edition presented Saramago as an 'award-winning author' and 'the most celebrated of contemporary Portuguese novelists' and the foreword, authored by Pontiero, reviews the author's literary career. The *Manual of Painting and Calligraphy* is presented as the 'matrix of the more capacious books that were to bring Saramago fame' and the translator compares some passages with Yourcenar's *Hadrian*.[138] There is an aspect worthy of note: the title is slightly changed from its original as it includes the explicit reference to 'Novel', as if to clarify any confusing thoughts when considering the novel by its title only. After all, the title that aroused erroneous reading was pointed out by some Portuguese critics as one of the reasons why this novel was so unsuccessful. As far as the reception of this novel is concerned, the reviews were quite favourable, although there was a unanimous position that this novel was clearly a minor one when compared with those already published.[139]

The publication of *The Stone Raft* did not constitute any surprise to the publishers or critics. Saramago's stature in the United Kingdom at this time was, broadly speaking, consensual. When referring to the author, expressions like "writer of European status', 'Portugal's leading novelist' or 'Europe's most original writer' were common. His prizes from various European institutions consolidated his reputation. Rebeca Gowers pointed out the relations established between the writer and reader, in which 'at times Saramago almost pits the reader against the novel'.[140] In *The European*, Paul Hyland wrote that it is 'a parable of cultural potency with a deliciously written account of the characters' geographical, philosophical and sexual pilgrimage to an unknown

---

138 José Saramago, *Manual of Painting and Calligraphy: A Novel* (Manchester: Carcanet, 1994), p. ix.
139 Adrian Tahourdin wrote that this was 'interesting mainly as groundwork for Saramago's subsequent writing' and Suzi Feay considered it 'a quiet triumph' and an easier read. See Adrian Tahourdin, 'Preliminary Sketches', *The Times Literary Supplement*, 15 April 1994; Suzi Feay. 'Books in Brief', *The Independent on Sunday*, 3 July 1994, p. 34.
140 Rebecca Gowers, 'Starlings on a moving island', *The Independent*, 19 November 1994, p. 27

destination.'[141] James Woodall was less favourable, albeit he recognised this writer's worthiness to receive a Nobel Prize:

> If this book does not quite have the stamp of greatness (unmistakable in *Ricardo Reis* and *Jesus Christ*), it is further evidence that talk of his likely Nobel laureateship is not premature.[142]

After 1993, the number of reviews of Saramago's works increased, a fact that accounts for Saramago's growing visibility among literary critics. Two significant examples are *The London Review of Books* and *The European* the reviews of which included an overall enthusiastic view of the works published by Saramago in the United Kingdom. Michael Wood introduced refined ironic remarks about the British resistance to translated fiction, challenging readers to learn more about what was published in European countries. He was involved in the recognition of translated fiction in the United Kingdom with reviews of translated novels published both in North-American and British journals and involved in the jury of *The Independent*'s Foreign Fiction Prize. *The Times* is also another clear example. Reviews and references to Saramago appear only consistently from 1994. However, this does not mean that all journals and literary supplements continued to give the same attention to every Saramago novel. The impact of publicity on the press did not have a homogeneous effect. *The Times*, for example, published reviews of Saramago's work, considerably later after the date of their publication in the U.K.; sometimes one year after, while others, such as *The Daily Telegraph*, often reviewed the novels some weeks before their publication in translation.[143] Until 1998, for example, *The London Review of Books* did not feature any other review on any of Saramago's works or by any other Portuguese novelist, a fact that accounts for the difficulty of penetration of Portuguese fiction in the United Kingdom.

---

141 Paul Hyland, 'Floating pilgrimage to an unknown destination', *The European*, 25 November 1994, p. 13.
142 James Woodall, 'A daring literary prankster', *The Daily Telegraph*, 14 January 1995, p. 9.
143 James Woodall's review published in 1993 is one of the examples mentioned above.

1996 was marked by the death of Saramago's translator, Giovanni Pontiero, which was reported in the media with sorrow for the loss of an important contributor to the publication of Portuguese and South-American fiction in the U.K.[144] The loss was especially emphasised in the media that campaigned for the increase of readership and publication of foreign fiction in the U.K. In the same year, *The History of The Siege of Lisbon* was published, shortly after Pontiero's death and it was received with very favourable reviews.[145]

One year before the Nobel Prize, *Blindness* was published in the U.K. and this was the last novel translated by Pontiero, a fact that was pointed out by critics who paid tribute to him for his translation skills. 1992-1997 is a long period of conquest and consolidation of a reputation and that is very clear after the publication of *Blindness*. Saramago's European stature had definitely found a place in the British book market, as shown in Michael Kerrigan's review:

> Comedy for a world of atheists, Saramago has at least succeeded in articulating our inarticulacies, producing in the process one of the most remarkable bodies of work of any living novelist. In this, at any rate, we can all believe.[146]

The allusions to the fact that Saramago deserved a Nobel Prize were not so frequent in the British reviews as they were in the North-American, Brazilian or Spanish ones. The emphasis of the British reviewers was placed on his stature as one of the most original, talented and leading novelists of Europe. This shows that the British concerns were different in so far as Saramago's reputation served some critics' aim to campaign for translated fiction, rather than promoting the author and work for themselves. The

---

144 Nigel Griffin, 'Obituary: Giovanni Pontiero', *The Independent*, 11 March 1996, p. 16.

145 Jonathan Keates, 'Making History', *The Times Literary Supplement*, 28 June 1996, p. 24; Lisa Jardine. 'In clear sight; Books', *The Times*, 20 November 1997, p. 40; Sarah Anderson. 'Rich terrain for bookworms; Summer holiday reading; Travel', *The Times*, 13 July 1996, p. 19.

146 Michael Kerrigan, 'The I of Saramago', *The Times Literary Supplement*, 19 December 1997, p. 20.

debate on the importance of translation arising among critics and journalists after the announcement of the Novel Prize for Literature in 1998 is relevant for this respect. The Nobel Prize was reported in brief, whereas longer articles started with the Prize and discussed the benefits that it might have on the increase of circulation of translated fiction in the United Kingdom. *The Independent* regretted that the name of Saramago was not popular among British readers and blamed publishers and booksellers for recoiling at the idea of translation while Saramago received worldwide honours and his books sold out quickly in other countries. *The Scotsman* focussed on the importance of Harvill publishers in the promotion of foreign fiction, an effort that gave them the possibility of having three Nobel-prize winning authors in their booklists. *The Times* emphasised the book translators' struggle for public recognition and quoted some translators who blamed the British publishers for 'conceit and insularity'.[147]

Saramago was not the only Portuguese prizewinning author referred to by the British press. Mário de Carvalho, also an author published by Editorial Caminho, received the Mobil Pegasus Prize for Literature in 1994. This is a North-American prize established to promote fiction from countries whose literature is rarely published in English. The impact was not very significant because the winning novel, *A God Strolling in the Cool of the Evening*, was only published in the United States in October 1997 and in the United Kingdom on 10 November 1997. The publication was reported in the British media.[148] However, it was not much emphasised. It is not very difficult to understand why Mário de Carvalho's literary stature in Portugal is unquestioned and he has received some prizes in Portugal. However, unlike Saramago, besides the Pegasus Prize, he did not receive any other foreign prizes; therefore, the range of his reputation is confined geographically. The fact that he was published by relatively smaller publishing houses both in the

---

147 Robert Winder, 'Notes on what's gained in translation', *The Independent on Sunday*. 11 October 1998; Lockerbie; Dalya Alberge, ' A talent lost in translation', *The Times*, 2 December 1998, p. 12.

148 Stephanie Merritt, 'Good Year for Portugal, not much fun in France: Stephanie Merritt picks 1997's best: Foreign Fiction', *The Daily Telegraph*, 20 December 1997.

United States and in the United Kingdom, Louisiana Press and Weidenfeld & Nicholson, respectively, could be a reason for the different repercussion of his popularity. The pressure exerted by small and big publishing houses or conglomerates varies according to size. Furthermore, the impact of Mário de Carvalho's prize in Portugal was also considerably less than Saramago's British prize. In 1994, Saramago was identified as the most representative Portuguese novelist and his frequent public statements enhanced his symbolic capital. The prize also strengthened the reputation of Editorial Caminho's booklist as further evidence of the international recognition of its authors.

8.5 José Luis Peixoto

The analysis of the promotion of José Luís Peixoto's novels will establish that he benefited from an environment which was different from that when Saramago's translations were published. This analysis will be based upon the interview with Maria do Rosário Pedreira, editor of Temas e Debates, the flaps of his two novels and the information on his literary career available in Peixoto's web site. In view of the fact that it comprises a very short period, the purpose of this analysis is to examine the basis of his literary legitimacy which was quickly achieved.

Peixoto's public exposure was developed after Saramago's Nobel Prize in 1998, which raised international awareness of Portuguese literature. Several Portuguese fiction writers such as António Lobo Antunes, Lídia Jorge and Mário de Carvalho were translated writers in the European and Anglo-American book markets in the 1990s. José Luís Peixoto's early consecration did not make him a writer published in the United States at the beginning but granted him the opportunity of being the first Portuguese young writer to stay at Leding House, New York, in 2002. From the time Peixoto was awarded the José Saramago Literary Prize, his international promotion was conducted by Güte Mertin until 2003. In 1993, he moved to Curtis Brown, a literary agency.

Between 2001 and 2003, his *Nenhum Olhar* was published in Spain (Hiru, 2001) Italy (La Nuova Frontiera, 2002), France (Grasset, 2003), and the Netherlands (Tyhja Taivas, 2003); in 2004, his *Uma Casa na Escuridão* was published in Italy (La Nuova Frontiera). [146] According to the publisher, Maria do Rosário Pedreira, the promotion of José Luís Peixoto abroad, especially in the Netherlands, was essentially based on an association with Saramago.[147]

Promotion of his literary quality of his books and evidence for this can be shown in the diversity of appraisal of his work and In *Nenhum Olhar*, blurbs were signed by In *Uma Casa na Escuridão*, blurbs are authored by Portuguese intellectuals and also include those taken from *L'Unitá* and *Vogue Italia*.[148] Furthermore, Peixoto's profile was also improved in the Portuguese editions from one novel to another: in *Nenhum Olhar*, his biographical and academic background was complemented by indications of the prizes he won in 1997 and 1998 for young writers, his contributions to several magazines and an indication of his production in fiction and poetry, in *Uma Casa na Escuridão*, the profile is constructed in so far as to strengthen his literary maturity. His prizes as a debutant disappear and are replaced by the information that he was shortlisted for the APE and the PEN Club prizes; his José Saramago Prize; his participation at several international literary events; and the fact that he is widely translated. In other words, his international recognition strengthens the domestic promotion of his profile.[149]

---

146 José Luís Peixoto's *Nenhum Olhar* [The Implacable Order of Things] was published by Nan A.Talese, a subsidiary of Random House in the United States in April 2007 and by Bloomsbury in the United Kingdom [Blank Gaze]in December 2007. The release of these translations will not be analysed in this thesis, because the terminus quem of this analysis is 2004.

147 See Appendix 3 on pp. 357.

148 José Luís Peixoto, *Nenhum Olhar*, 4th edn (Lisbon: Temas e Debates, 2002, 1st edn, 2000); José Luís Peixot, *Uma Casa na Escuridão* (Lisbon: Temas e Debates, 2002).

149 In 2007, the José Luís Peixoto Literary Prize was set up by Ponte de Sor City Hall with the purpose of rewarding debutants.

8.6 Conclusion

Bourdieu stated that the true producer of the value of the work is the publisher:

> The ideology of creation, which makes the author the first and last source of the value of his work, conceals the fact that the cultural businessman (art dealer, publisher, etc.) is at one and the same time the person who exploits the labour of the 'creator' by trading in the 'sacred' and the person who, by putting it into the market, by exhibiting, publishing or staging it, consecrates a product he has 'discovered' and which would otherwise remain a mere natural resource; and the more consecrated he is, the more strongly he consecrates the work.[150]

Choosing the right publisher is decisive for the writer to reach his position in the literary field. Despite contending against Bourdieu's premise that the publisher is basically a 'talent-spotter', publishers, as well as critics, determine the recognition of the value of the work of art and its positioning in the literary field. Being published by a small publishing house is not the same as being published by a large one and publishers are aware of that, in particular when it comes to promote their own writers abroad.[151] Nevertheless, the acceptance of the aesthetic and literary value is stronger if the work is published in the right timing. The decision to publish in the right timing makes publishers and other instances of reproduction, such as critics, gatekeepers of ideas. In other words, publishers decide who and when will be published, opening gates of ideas that determine the position of the writer in the literary field.[152]

---

150 Bourdieu, p. 76.
151 The fact that Peixoto was included in the curriculum of Portuguese Literature at Santiago de Compostela University in 2003 is noteworthy of the raising of awareness of Portuguese contemporary literature from the 1980s.
152 The concept of gatekeeping associated to publishing is also discussed, for example, in Lewis A. Coser, Charles Kadushin and Walter W.Powell, *Books – The Culture and Commerce of Publishing* (Chicago and London: The University of Chicago Press, 1982) and Frank de Glas, 'Authors' Oeuvres as the back-

The publishers' decision to introduce different novels as Saramago's first works in different markets was motivated by the countries' political and cultural environment: the subject discussed in *Levantado do Chão* fitted the Brazilian market when the landless workers' movement aroused considerable exposure; *El Año de La Muerte de Ricardo Reis* followed the academic conference on Fernando Pessoa and aroused the critics' and scholars' interest; *Baltasar and Blimunda* benefited from the associations to the South American Magic Realism and from Giovanni Pontiero's professional prestige in the United States and in the United Kingdom. Had any other novel by Saramago been published in either of these countries, the impact would not have been the same and evidence of this is shown in the fact that different works were published in different countries, by different publishing houses, in different years.

These book markets also offered different degrees of exposure of the writer: the Brazilian political timing, together with the publication of *Levantado do Chão*, provided Saramago with the opportunity to speak about his work and comment on Brazilian internal affairs, and his public stances enhanced his literary legitimacy; in the United States and, particularly in the United Kingdom, his exposure was limited to the academic debate and this constrained the nature of his public appearances in countries where writers hardly assume the status achieved in South-America or in southern Europe.

Therefore, Saramago's social trajectory was constructed differently as the social value attached to them was a construct, quoting Bourdieu again, 'in terms of the socially constituted categories of perception and appreciation they [the different classes of agents] applied to them'.[153] Saramago's endorsement to the Communism was more emphasized in Brazil than in the English-speaking countries because his stances were more relevant in a country where the cultural debate has essentially been headed by left-wing parties; his aversion to technology, emphasized in Brazil, would have

---

bone of publishers' lists: Studying the literary publishing house after Bourdieu', *Poetics*, 25 (1998), 379-397.
153 Bourdieu, p. 65.

been a pointless subject of discussion in the United States; in the countries where the writers' exposure is chiefly centered on literary issues, his biography was constructed to give him more legitimacy to his position in the literary field.

Finally, a last note on the publishing houses, which were responsible for promoting Saramago abroad. The importance of determinate countries in the promotion of writers was already mentioned above. Appendix 6 shows that the Nobel Prizewinners were translated and published by a not too vast number of publishing houses. Some are responsible for publishing Nobel Prizewinners as their in-house authors, such as Seix Barral, others are responsible for publishing translations of foreign authors before they receive the award, such as Éditions du Seuil, Harcourt Brace, Harvill, Random House, Feltrinelli and Jonathan Cape. These publishing houses distribute symbolic capital, being able to get the attention of critics due to their importance in the market, and their own prestige is also enhanced by the fact that they are recognized for publishing writers that receive the highest literary reward and also encourage the production of literary criticism on these writers. The fact that Saramago was published by these publishing houses and not any others was decisive for his consecration process because the prestige of these publishers aroused interest and enabled the production of literary criticism on his oeuvre, enhancing his literary prestige. Smaller publishing houses also profited from this prestige when they published works of different genres, such as poetry, with less impact in the construction of the writer Saramago because it was essentially centered on his promotion as novelist. Nevertheless, these smaller publishing houses also contributed to the dissemination of his work and, thus, enhanced his literary prestige. It also benefited those who worked with him, such as his translators, because, translating a well-known writer contributed to the recognition of their literary expertise.

Conclusion

This thesis has endeavoured to show that: during the Estado Novo (1933-1974), the Government oriented education and literary practice with the purpose of legitimizing its rule; between 25 April 1974 and 2004, the Government and the President inherited the power of literary consecration established during Salazar's rule and did little to withdraw their influence, suggesting that Portuguese culture and, particularly literary practice, did not develop a fully-fledged autonomy as far as relations of legitimacy and consecration are concerned.

This analysis was supported by the theoretical models developed by Pierre Bourdieu (Theory of the Literary Field), Jacques Dubois (Theory of Literary Institution), and Itamar Even-Zohar (Polysystem Theory), within the framework of systems theories which suggest examining literature as an autonomous system where dynamic relations of their agents establish particular positions of literary legitimacy and consecration.

Grounded on certain values that were linked to Roman-Catholic worship, anti-liberal traditionalist and right-wing ideology, the Regime of Salazar took advantage of social problems, especially illiteracy, to implement its policies under the banner of national regeneration. The Ministry of Education carried out educational reforms which included campaigns against illiteracy in the 1950s. They also involved shortening the length of time of compulsory education and revising primary and secondary school literary texts of the subjects of Portuguese language and literature. Reading skills were developed through texts which were meant to illustrate national values, ranging from Roman-Catholic worship, respect and admiration for the Portuguese nation (rooted in Colonialism and in Portuguese history valuing), obedience to hierarchical organizations, preservation of family structure and paternal authority and the importance given of work. Despite the Government working for the modernization of national infrastructure, particularly in the 1950s and 1960s, Portuguese cultural values were associated with a eulogy of social structures which reflected the country, predominantly rural, in the 1920s and in the 1930s.

The analysis of the syllabi at secondary school level established that the Government showed little interest in teaching contemporary Portuguese literature. Legitimacy of the Estado Novo was built upon the valuing of Portuguese history organized around three basic historical landmarks: the establishment of the nation; the Discoveries and Restoration of Independence. These landmarks were shown as to provide the Portuguese with evidence for the nation's mission in the world, and thus earn the population's acceptance of the Government's policies.

Therefore, literature teaching was organized with the purpose of showing Portuguese belligerent and heroic tradition, popular value (related to rurality and peasantry) and national pride. Portuguese consecrated fiction was taught as literary heritage and was rooted in nineteenth-century literary output (Eça de Queirós, Camilo Castelo Branco and Júlio Dinis). Studying *Mensagem* at school, the only contemporary text of compulsory reading during the Estado Novo, was also oriented to expound the concept of the Portuguese nation and glorify the Discoveries. The value of literary heritage also encouraged the establishment the literary prizes sponsored by the Government's Secretariado between 1933 and 1974.

The analysis of the Tables of the SPN/SNI/SEIT literary prizes between 1934 and 1973 showed that the Government rewarded texts which endorsed official values, especially fiction and works on Portuguese history, (better financially rewarded). Financial rewards were used as valid indicators of literary prestige.

Receiving a literary prize meant taking a position in the literary field, and strengthening symbolic capital through recognition of readers and of the SPN/SNI/SEIT (and thus the Government's). Likewise, turning it down was a way to demonstrate opposition to the Regime and it was often done by intellectuals who were politically committed against the Estado Novo.

Even-Zohar's Polysystem Theory has proved helpful for my analysis insofar as the heterogeneity of the Portuguese literary field during the Estado Novo manifests two separable systems that operate in the same community (despite using the same language), struggling permanently for autonomy and public recognition. As far as fiction was concerned, it was the Regime's unwillingness (shown in various ways, ranging from literary awards to control under censorship) to accept the emerging literary trends, such as Neo-Realism (1940s), and Existentialism (1960s) that contributed to the non-existence of a consistent corpus of literary output that represented the Estado Novo's literature. Government's control of literature, and particularly fiction, was based on its need to consolidate political validity through the maintenance of certain social, economic and cultural (and literary) structures. The emerging literary trends disturbed representations of the country which were meant to be reassuring of the Estado Novo's legitimacy. Moreover, the new literary practices disapproved of by the Government were developed side by side with the commitment to political and social opposition to official policies.

Therefore, the establishment of the Ricardo Malheiros Prize and the SPE literary prizes were discussed in this dissertation as ways to challenge the Government's role as sole consecrating agent. It is worthy of note that the Ricardo Malheiros Prize was set up one year before the SPN literary prizes; in this context, the SPN prizes were discussed in this thesis as a way to legitimize the Government's authority over the literary field. Nevertheless, as the Estado Novo showed signs of collapsing (especially during the Colonial Wars which hit national cultural identity based on the concepts of unity and empire), the Ricardo Malheiros Prize rewarded novels which challenged the Government's approved literary practice (topics approached and literary style), whereas the SNI/SEIT literary prizes did not (and could not for the sake of preservation of the Regime) show similar signs of literary recognition.

The relative political isolation of the Portuguese Government from international politics, favoured by geographical periphery, added to Portuguese publishers' difficulty in legitimizing their position in the world book markets, which was already constrained by the fact that output was concentrated on domestic values and issues. This had an effect on the development of Portuguese publishing companies which found it hard to expand their business, also tightly controlled by the Regime. The economic environment was not particularly favourable to Portuguese publishing business. The Government's policies deterred Portuguese publishers from setting up larger companies; literary agents were almost non-existent in the Portuguese book market. This was relevant to the lack of overseas visibility of Portuguese literature, and particularly fiction. Cultural and literary promotion endorsed by the Portuguese Government was predominantly directed to the Portuguese-speaking countries and occasionally to Spain, France and the Portuguese community living in the United States. The Regime and the large majority of Portuguese publishers overlooked fundamental world literary events such as the Frankfurt Book Fair.

This thesis also looked at Nobel prizewinners between 1945 and 2004 with the purpose of identifying certain publishing houses that tend to publish them and relate this analysis to the translation of Portuguese fiction during the Estado Novo and after 1974. The list shows laureates are recurrently published by the same publishing houses (at the time of the award) such as Farrar, Straus & Giroux, Gallimard, Harcourt Brace, Harvill, Norstedt, Rowohlt, Jonathan Cape and Seix Barral, and in the same countries. The Anglo-American book market is of importance for the promotion of literature, including Sweden, Norway and Denmark. Since that market, in particular the United Kingdom, is not receptive to translations and constitutes a large book market, being translated there means an improvement in the writer's literary career. It tends to increase the potential of visibility of the writer's works, measured in commercial sales, publication of substantial literary critique, and awards. Changes in business structures, usual in most industries and involving takeovers and mergers, also tend to facilitate writers' promotion: catalogues are reorganized and business contacts among publishers may evolve from relationships between small and medium-sized companies to large international corporations. The complex structures of the world publishing industry involving a large number of specialized professionals, ranging from publishers, editors, literary agents, scouts to translators (particularly when compared with the Portuguese publishing business) facilitate comprehensive promotion in a large number of countries: France, Germany, Italy and Spain are key book markets. Their importance dates back before the Second World War, whereas the United States's weight in the world book market was strengthened after 1945.

Only a few Portuguese SNI prizewinners reached foreign markets. Assuming that the statements of the Portuguese publishers interviewed for this dissertation are also valid for the period before 1974, translation of their books was stimulated by literary awards but they did not ensure commercial success abroad; for example, Joaquim Paço d'Arcos was a bestseller in Portugal but his translations were not reprinted in the countries where they were published. The fact that he was published by small publishing houses might have contributed to his lack of external visibility.[1] Police repression, Government control and writers' political affiliation contributed to the fact that translations of works by those writers who opposed the Regime were mainly published in Eastern European countries and by small publishing houses with little influence in the world book market to promote Portuguese literature. Portuguese readers were educated to buy and read works similar to those studied at school during the Estado Novo. Although universities were under relative control of the Government, higher education was more independent of the established literary canon. Nevertheless, motivation and learning of new literary production affected no more than a minority. The fact that agents of production and legitimacy were mostly concentrated in Lisbon and few major urban centres along the coastland was of relevance to the deficient circulation of the book trade in the rest of the country. Those were also the regions where illiteracy prevailed. Readership was also influenced by the economic ills and

---

1   As mentioned in Chapter 3 and in my interviews with the publishers of Editorial Caminho, Oficina do Livro and Temas e Debates, cosmopolitanism is a central feature when it comes to deciding whether to translate fiction. This decision does not exclude another fundamental: literary quality. Nevertheless, as defended in this dissertation, despite the fact that literary quality is an essential requirement for any work of art to be published and receive awards, it is also a fact that its public legitimacy is also dependent on factors, such as timing of acceptance and position of the publishing house in the literary field, that have little to do with literary issues.

the Colonial War because they encouraged emigration and the depopulation of many rural areas.

This dissertation also analysed the relations of legitimacy and consecration after 1974 and established that, despite changes, these were not drastic as far as consecration was concerned. 25 April 1974 opened up the discussion of cultural identity seeking to redefine national values as distinctive of the Estado Novo. Literary production, in particular novel production, took over that discussion and their producers found opportunities in the visibility they achieved during the revolutionary years to strengthen legitimacy in representation. Their visibility was encouraged by the Provisional Governments which encouraged the participation of Portuguese intellectuals in the making of cultural revolution. This thesis has established that cultural revolution was not successful because cultural practice was oriented towards the establishment of Governments' legitimacy and, in that regard, the relations between the political apparatus and cultural producers did not undergo drastic changes since 1933. The appointment of a Minister of Culture in the PS Government and of the Secretary of State for Culture in the PSD Governments did not introduce significant changes as far as autonomy in cultural policies are concerned. The analysis of the establishment of literary prizes has established that those awards were sponsored by Government's institutions such as the IPLB and official ceremonies were hosted by the Minister of Culture or the Secretary of State for Culture. This was discussed as indicative of the fragile autonomy of the Portuguese literary field. Further evidence was also established through the analysis of the Honours given by the President of the Republic between 1978 and 2004.

As regards teaching literature, curricula revision was carried out in 1979 and motivated by the new Governments' concern to remove the Estado Novo's ideology. The canon was practically unchanged in the early years of secondary education. Neo-Realism and Existentialism which had influenced part of Portuguese fiction since the 1940s (that had acquired legitimacy through the SPE literary prizes) was introduced into the syllabus of Portuguese literature studied on the 12th Grade in 1978 and removed in the 1990s. The percentage of literacy and school attendance increased significantly after 1974 but factors such as ageing and lack of reading habits have apparently dissuaded a significant expansion of Portuguese readership until the late 1990s.

The interviews conducted for the purposes of this dissertation have also established that most Portuguese editors' ways of regarding the Portuguese market did not change significantly. Their aims involved tracking quality and highbrow writers whose consecration would inevitably bring some prestige, among literary producers and agents of consecration, to them. Only in the late 1990s, due to economic expansion that involved also the proliferation of book points of sales (not only bookshops but also supermarkets, book clubs, etc., as shown in the survey submitted to Portuguese purchasers of Portuguese fiction) and new publishing houses were set up by a new generation which had not lived through the Estado Novo, did business evolve. One of the results, not expanded in this thesis since it was not part of its focus, was the expansion of popular fiction. In addition, takeovers of Portuguese publishing houses led by foreign publishing groups intensified competition and also opened up further opportunities to promotion of writers overseas.

All things considered, my research on the Portuguese literary field has shown that, unlike what has been proposed by Bourdieu and Dubois, its dynamics has been affected by the low degree of autonomy in relation to the political and social field. Despite the progress of Portuguese fiction being clear in production and sales, consecration has been bounded by political and social commitment and by the hegemonic influence of Governments.

This dissertation has also established that José Saramago's consecration was achieved in different terms and that, despite being a non-typical case, it confirmed the analysis of the relations of the Portuguese literary field. The analysis of Saramago's literary career has shown that his legitimacy was successfully determined by the Portuguese political, social and cultural environment; the making of his public persona; the timing of the publication of his novels; and the fact that he was published by Editorial Caminho. Saramago's past connected him with the turbulent years that followed the Revolution and that introduced some difficulty to achieving consecration in Portugal. His social and family background were decisive in constructing his trajectory as legitimating for his *oeuvre* and his publishing house competed in taking a position in the literary field. His revision of history, more than literary genius, was fundamental for his exposure in the political debate because they responded to the nation's inner crisis.

Since his works were carefully promoted in different countries, taking advantage of their political, social and cultural context was decisive in his quick international consecration, enhancing his recognition in Portugal. The thesis has also shown that, within the framework of the literary institution, Saramago's consecration also benefited those who translated him, such as Basilio Losada and Margaret Jull da Costa, because, translating a well-known writer contributed to the recognition of their literary expertise through important prizes.

The analysis of the process of consecration of José Luís Peixoto has established him as a typical case of legitimacy in the post-Revolution literary field. Having received the José Saramago Literary Prize in 2001, his legitimacy was positioned by critics, within the framework of promotion strategies led by the press, in relation to José Saramago. This has oriented the critique to establish him as a follower of the Nobel writer and of Magic Realism. The fact that Peixoto started being published in 2000 has been relevant for the impact of publicity around his works. They have gained visibility with the expansion of the book trade in Portugal, technology, such as the Internet, and the influence of media. Despite consecration of Portuguese writers being restricted mostly to those who had had a role in the establishment of democracy in Portugal, it was also legitimized by popular success associated to sales and media exposure in the 1990s.

The impact of Portuguese fiction outside Portugal can only be analysed thoroughly when the habits of purchase and reading of the Portuguese communities, in particular those of the children of Portuguese emigrants, are known. These results require further research, which could be of relevance to study the effectiveness of present-day cultural activities led by Portuguese Governments abroad.

Tables

List of Tables

Table 1A: SPN Literary Prizes (1934-1939)

Prizes	Camões Work on Portugal Published Abroad, 20,000$ Biennial	Eça de Queirós Novel, 10,000$ Biennial	Alexandre Herculano History, 10,000$ Annual	António Enes Political Principles, Annual
1934			Caetano Beirão, *D. Maria I*, Emp. Nac. De Publicidade	Augusto da Costa, *Portugal Vasto Império*, Imprensa Nacional
1935		Conde de Aurora, *O Pinto*, Liv. Tavares Martins	Queirós Veloso, *D. Sebastião*, Emp. Nac. Publicidade	Fernando Campos, *No Sagüão do Liberalismo*, s/n
1936		Joaquim Paço d'Arcos, *Diário de Um Emigrante*, Comp. Edit. Minho	J. Leite de Vasconcelos, *Etnografia Portuguesa* (Vol.II), Impr. Nacional	Samuel de M.Oliveira, *A Nova Ordem Económica*, Empr.Nac. Publicidade
1937	Earl Gonzague de Reynold, *Portugal*, Éditions Ipes		Alfredo Pimenta, *Subsídios para a História de Portugal*, Europa	Luís de Pina, *Em Verdade Vos Digo*, Imp. Portuguesa
1938			Pe Serafim Leite, *História da Companhia de Jesus no Brasil*, Portugália	Abranches Martins, *O Estado e a Pessoa Humana*
1939	John Gibbons, *I Gathered No Moss*, Robert Hale		Pe.Francisco Rodrigues, *Hist. da Comp. de Jesus na Assist. de Portugal*, Apost.da Impr.	Augusto da Costa, *O Pecado Mortal do Teatro*

Table1B: SPN Literary Prizes (1934-1939)

Prizes	Antero de Quental Poetry, 5,000$00	Fialho de Almeida, Shortstory, 5,000$	Ramalho Ortigão, Essay, 5,000$	Gil Vicente, Drama, 5,000$	MªAmália V.Carvalho Children's Fiction, 4,000$
1934	Pe.Vasco Reis, Romaria,Coimbra; F.Pessoa, Mensagem, A.M. Pereira		João Ameal, No Limiar da Idade Nova, Imp. da Universidade		
1935	Carlos Queirós, Desaparecido, Empr.Anuário Comercial		Alfredo Pimenta, Novos Estudos Filosóficos E Críticos, Impr.Nacional	Vasco Mendonça Alves, O Meu Amor é Traiçoeiro, A.M.Pereira	
1936	Azinhal Abelho, Confidências de Um Rapaz Provinciano, Imp. Baroeth	Luís Trigueiro, Caminho Sem Luz, Europa	Luís Vieira de Castro, Limbo, Império	Alfredo Cortez Tá Mar, Imp. Lucas	
1937	R.Guedes Campos, Portugal, Edit.Império			Carlos Selvagem, Telmo, O Aventu-reiro, Europa	Adolfo Simões Müller, Caixinha de Brinquedos, Império
1938	Miguel Trigueiros, Resgate, Tip. Americana	Raquel Bastos, Um Fio de Música, Europa	Luís Teixeira, Perfil de Salazar, L.Teixeira	Virgínia Vitorino, Camaradas, A.M. Pereira	Mª Archer, Viagem à Roda de Africa, O Século

1939	P. Homem de Mello, *Segredo*, Imp. Portuguesa			Vasco Mendonça Alves, *Pátria*		Olavo d'Eça Leal, *História Extraord. de Iratan e Iracema*, Jorn. do Com. e das Colónias

Table 2A: SPN/SNI Literary Prizes (1940-1945)

Prizes	Camões	Eça de Queirós	Alexandre Herculano	António Enes	Pero Vaz de Caminha **Coordinated with DIP (Brazil)**	Anselmo de Andrade, Political or Economic Essays – 6,000$
1940			Pe.Miguel de Oliveira, *História Eclesiástica de Portugal*, União Gráfica			
1941	Jesus Pabón, *La Revolucion Portuguesa*, Espasa Calpe		João Ameal, *História de Portugal*, Liv.Tavares Martins	Pe.João Mendes, *Os Três Verbos da Vida*, Portugália		
1942			Costa Brochado, *Inf.D.Henrique*, Império			

1943	Elaine Sanceau, Portugal in Quest of Prester John, Hutchison		Eduardo do Couto Lupi, A Empresa Port.no Oriente, Ag.Geral das Colónias	José S.Silva Dias, Escândalo da Verdade, Edições Juventude	José Sebastião da Silva, O Problema da Europa, Coimbra
1944	Francisco Costa, A Garça e A Serpente, AM.Pereira		Costa Veiga, Estudo da História Militar (Vol.III)	Dias M.Almeida, Articles publ. in Diário da Manhã	
1945	Perez Embid, Arquit Port. de la Epoca Manuelina, Ed. Católica Espaenola	Amadeu Cunha, Sertões e Fronteiras do Brasil		Hernâni Cidade, A Literat.Port. e a Expansão Ultramarina, Ag.Geral das Colónias	

Table 2B: SPN/SNI Literary Prizes (1940-1945)

Prizes	Antero de Quental	Fialho de Almeida	Ramalho Ortigão	Gil Vicente	MªAmália V.Carvalho
1940		Loureiro Botas, Litoral a Oeste, Portugália	Manuel Múrias, Portugal:Império 1939,A.M Teixeira	Olga Alves Guerra, Tempos Modernos	
1941	Américo C.Pinto, A Alma e O Deserto, Portugália			Carlos Selvagem, A Encruzilhada, Sá da Costa	

1942	Campos de Figueiredo, *Navio na Montanha*, Tip. Atlântida	Joaquim P. D'Arcos, *Neve* sobre *o Mar*, A.M.Pereira	Pe.Moreira das Neves, *Guerra Junqueiro*, Domingos Barreira	Armando V. Pinto, *Coristas*, Tip. Sequeira	Adolfo S. Müller, *O Feiticeiro da Cabana*
1943	Cabral do Nascimento, *Cancioneiro*, Ed.Gama				Olavo d'Eça Leal, *História de Portugal para Meninos Preguiçosos*, Liv.Tavares Martins
1944	Folgado da Silveira, *O Vinho é Sangue*, Ed.Gama		F.A.Oliveira Martins, *O Socialismo na Monarquia*, A.M.Pereira	Joaquim P. d'Arcos, *O Ausente*, A.M.Pereira	José de Lemos, *O Sábio que Sabia Tudo e Outras Hist.*, Gama
1945	Amândio César, *Batuque na Guerra*, Tip. Ed.do Povo			Eduardo Schwalbach, *As Duas Máscaras*, Emp. Nac. Publicidade	Salomé de Almeida, *Falam os Animais*, Imp. Nac.Universal

Table 3A: SNI Literary Prizes (1946-1961)

Prizes	1946	1947	1948	1961
Camões		Harold Livermore *History of Portugal*, Cambridge University Press		
Eça de Queirós			Tomás de Figueiredo, *A Toca do Lobo*, Ática	Ester de Lemos, *Companheiros*, Ática

	1946	1947	1948	1961
Alexandre Herculano	Queirós Veloso *O Reinado do Cardeal D.Henrique*, Empresa Nac. Publicidade		Pedro Batalha Reis *Numária d'El Rei Dom António*, Acad. Port. História	Américo C. Pinto *Da Famosa Arte da Imprimissão*, Ed. Ulisseia Limitada
Anselmo de Andrade	José Nascimento Ferreira *Linhas de Rumo* (Vol.I), Clássica Editora			

Table 3B: SNI Literary Prizes (1946-1951)

Prizes	1946	1947	1948	1961
Antero de Quental	Maria Teresa A.Santos *Manta de Retalhos*	Natércia Freire *Rio Infindável*, Of.Gráfica	Ribeiro Dias *A Seiva do Mistério*, Coimbra Ed	Fernando Guedes, *A Viagem de Ícaro*, Verbo
Fialho de Almeida	Heloísa Cid *Vidas Cercadas*, Império		Olavo d'Eça Leal *O Processo Arquivado e Outras Novelas*, Ibérica	
Ramalho Ortigão	Father Diamantino Martins *Bergson*, Liv. Tavares Martins		José B.Carreiro *Antero de Quental*, Instituto Cultural Moraes	Carlos Eduardo de Soveral, *A Nostalgia de Hesíodo*, Verbo
Mª Amália V.Carvalho	Isaura Correia Santos *O Senhor Sabe Tudo Conta*	José de Lemos *Histórias e Bonecos*, Ática	Aurora Constança *História do Coelho Kalulu*, Liv. Portugal	

Table 4: SNI/SEIT Literary Prizes (1966/1970)

Prize/ Years	Grande Prémio Nacional de Literatura	Prémio Nacional de Poesia	Prémio Nacional de Novelística	Prémio Nacional de Ensaio
1966	Vitorino Nemésio	Ant.M. Couto Viana, *Poesias (1948-1963)*, Verbo	Domingos Monteiro, *O Crime de Simão Bolandas*, Sociedade Expansão Cultural	
1967		Tomás Kim, *Exercícios Temporais*, Guimarães	Tomaz de Figueiredo, *Tiros de Espingarda*, Verbo	Túlio R.Ferro, *Tradição e Modernidade em Camilo*, A.M. Pereira
1968	Augusto de Castro	Rui Cinatti, *Sete Septetos*, Guimarães	Agustina Bessa Luís, *Homens e Mulheres*, Guimarães	
1969		Fernando Guedes, *Poesias Escolhidas 1948-1968*, Verbo	João de Araújo Correia, *Horas Mortas*, Imprensa Douro	Manuel de O.Pulquério, *Problemática da Tragédia Sofocliana*, Instituto da Alta Cultura
1970		Fernanda de Castro, *Poesia 1919 a 1969*, F.Castro	Graça Pina Morais, *Jerónimo e Eulália*, Sociedade Expansão Cultural	

Table 5: SEIT Literary Prizes (1971/1973)

Prizes/ Years	Prémio Nacional de Poesia	Prémio Nacional de Novelística	Prémio Nacional de Ensaio
1971	José Régio, *Música Ligeira*, Portugália	Maria da Graça Freire, *O Inferno está mais perto*,Liv. Tavares Martins	Orlando Ribeiro, *Ensaios de Geografia Humana e Regional*, Sá da Costa
1972	Natércia Freire, *Os Intrusos*, Soc. Expansão Cultural; David Mourão Ferreira, *Cancioneiro de Natal*, Verbo	Fernanda Botelho, *Lourenço é Nome de Jogral*, Bertrand	
1973	Pedro Homem de Mello, *Eu Desci aos Infernos*, Asa	Domingos Monteiro, *Letícia e o Lobo Júpiter*, Sociedade Expansão Cultural	Gustavo de Fraga, *Fenomenologia e Dialéctica*, Universidade de Coimbra

Table 6: Academia de Ciências, Classe de Letras: Ricardo Malheiros Prizes (1933/1971)

Years	Prizewinners	Genre
1933	Aquilino Ribeiro, *As três Mulheres de Sansão*, Bertrand	Fiction
1934	Ferreira de Castro, *Terra Fria*, Editorial Século	Fiction
1935	Antero de Figueiredo, *Miradouro*, Bertrand	Fiction
1936	Samuel Maia, *Dona sem Dono*, Bertrand	Fiction
1938	Joaquim Paço d'Arcos, *Ana Paula: Perfil de Uma Lisboeta*, Parceria António Maria Pereira	Fiction
1939	António Guedes de Amorim, *Aldeia das Águias*, Minerva	Fiction
1940	Mário Beirão, *Novas Estrelas*, Portugália	Poetry
1941	Augusto da Costa, *As Inocentes*, Parc. Ant. Maria Pereira	Fiction
1942	Vergílio Godinho, *Calcanhar do Mundo*, Gama	Fiction
1944	Vitorino Nemésio, *Mau Tempo no Canal*, Bertrand	Fiction

Years	Prizewinners	Genre
1945	Fernanda de Castro, *Maria da Lua*, Tavares Martins	Poetry
1946	Assis Esperança, *Servidão*, Imp. Lucas	Fiction
1947	Manuel Teles de Carvalho (Noel Teles), *Terra Campa*, Emp. Nacional de Publicidade	Fiction
1948	Urbano Rodrigues, *O Castigo de D.João*, Emp. Nac. de Publicidade	Fiction
1950	Alves Redol, *Horizonte Cerrado*, Gráfica Lisbonense	Fiction
1951	Sousa Costa, *Entre Duas Labaredas*, Guimarães	Fiction
1952	Maria da Graça Azambuja, *A Primeira Viagem*, Par. Ant. Maria Pereira	Fiction
1953	Fernando Namora, *As Minas de San Francisco*, Inquérito	Fiction
1954	Cármen Figueiredo, *Criminosas*, Editorial Século	Fiction
1955	Natércia Freire, *Infância que nasci*	Fiction
1957	Campos de Figueiredo, *Obed*, Coimbra Editora	Poetry
1958	Urbano Tavares Rodrigues, *Uma pedrada no charco*, Bertrand	Fiction
1959	David Mourão-Ferreira, *Gaivotas em Terra*, Ulisseia	Fiction
1960	Mário Braga, *O Livro das Sombras*, Arcádia	Fiction
1961	Orlando da Costa, *O Signo da Ira*, Arcádia	Fiction
1962	Manuel Ferreira, *A Hora di Bai*, Portugália	Fiction
1963	Augusto Abelaira, *As Boas Intenções*, Bertrand	Fiction
1964	Ruben A., *A Torre de Barbela*, Livraria Portugal	Fiction
1965	António Quadros, *Histórias do Tempo de Deus*, Morais	Fiction
1966	Agustina Bessa Luís, *Canção diante de uma porta fechada*, Guimarães	Fiction
1967	Adelino António Peres Rodrigues, *O rio que vem do Lugo*, Sociedade de Expansão Cultural	Fiction
1968	José Rodrigues Júnior, *Era o terceiro dia de vento sul*, Agência Geral das Colónias	Fiction
1969	Graça Pina Morais, *Jerónimo e Eulália*, Soc. Exp. Cult.	Fiction

Years	Prizewinners	Genre
1970	Maria Ondina Braga, *Amor e Morte*, Soc. Exp. Cult.	Fiction
1971	Luís Cajão, *Um Castelo na Escócia*, Soc. Exp. Cult.	Fiction

Tabela 7A: SPE Literary Prizes (1961/1965)

Prize	Camilo Castelo Branco	Panel	Grande Prémio de Poesia	Panel
1961	Vergílio Ferreira, *Aparição*, Portugália	Mário Dionísio, João Gaspar Simões, David Mourão-Ferreira, Óscar Lopes, Jacinto do Prado Coelho		
1962	Fernanda Botelho, *A Gata e a Fábula*, Presença	Mário Dionísio, João Gaspar Simões, David Mourão-Ferreira, Óscar Lopes, Jacinto do Prado Coelho	José Gomes Ferreira, *Poesia III*, Portugália	Maria de Lourdes Belchior, Álvaro Salema, Vitorino Nemésio, Eugénio de Andrade, Manuel da Fonseca
1963	Jorge Reis, *Matai-vos Uns aos Outros!*, Prelo	António Coimbra Martins, João Gaspar Simões, Óscar Lopes, Mário Sacramento, Jacinto do Prado Coelho		
1964	José Cardoso Pires, *O Hóspede de Job*, Arcádia	Mário Dionísio, João Gaspar Simões, David Mourão-Ferreira, Óscar Lopes, Jacinto do Prado Coelho	Sophia de Mello Breyner, *Livro Sexto*, Edições Salamandra	Alexandre Pinheiro Torres, Álvaro Salema, Eugénio de Andrade, Manuel Antunes, Manuel da Fonseca

| 1965 | Isabel da Nóbrega, *Viver com os Outros*, Portugália | José Régio, Óscar Lopes, Mário Dionísio, José Palla e Carmo, António Coimbra Martins |

Tabela 7B: SPE Literary Prizes (1964/1965)

Prizes	1963	1965
Grande Prémio de Novelística	José Régio, *Há Mais Mundos*, Portugália	José Luandino Vieira, *Luuanda*, ABC
Panel	Maria de Lourdes Belchior, Marmelo e Silva, Alexandre Pinheiro Torres, Augusto Abelaira, Manuel da Fonseca	João Gaspar Simões, Alexandre Pinheiro Torres, Manuel da Fonseca, Fernanda Botelho, Augusto Abelaira
Grande Prémio de Ensaio	Mário Dionísio, *A Paleta e o Mundo*, Europa-América	Armando de Castro, *A Evolução Económica de Portugal dos Séculos XII a XV*, Portugália
Panel	Adriano Gusmão, Augusto Saraiva, Luís Albuquerque, Paulo Quintela, Vergílio Ferreira	Augusto Saraiva, Castelo Branco Chaves, José Cardoso Pires, Mário Sacramento, Teixeira Mota
Prémio de Revelação: Prosa	Almeida Faria, *Rumor Branco*, Portugália	Ângela Caires, *As Pedras Envelhecem*
Panel	Maria Judite Carvalho, Aleixo Ribeiro	Fernando Namora, Esther de Lemos, Orlando Costa
Prémio de Revelação: Poesia	César Pratas, *Post Scriptum*, Portugália	Armando Silva Carvalho, *Lírica Consumível*, s/n
Panel	Sallete Tavares, Alexandre O'Neill, João José Cochofel	José Gomes Ferreira, Ruy Belo, João José Cochofel

Table 8: Honours given during General Ramalho Eanes's Presidency (1978-1981)[10]

Year	Author	Militar Sant'Iago da Espada	Ordem da Liberdade
1978	Jorge de Sena*	Grã Cruz	
1978	Vitorino Nemésio	Grã Cruz	
1979	Bento de Jesus Caraça*	Grã Cruz	
1979	Vergílio Ferreira	Grande Oficial	
1979	Fernando Namora	Grande Oficial	
1979	José R. Miguéis	Grande Oficial	
1980	Maria Lamas		Grande Oficial
1980	José G. Ferreira	Grande Oficial	
1980	Sophia M.Breyner	Grande Oficial	
1981	David Mourão-Ferreira	Grande Oficial	
1981	Agustina B. Luís	Grande Oficial	
1981	Eduardo Lourenço	Grande Oficial	
1981	João G. Simões	Grande Oficial	
1981	Natália Correia	Grande Oficial	
1981	Branquinho da Fonseca*	Grande Oficial	
1981	Bernardo Santareno*	Grande Oficial	

10 Tables 8, 9 and 10 are short lists of the Honours Lists given by the Chancellery of Honours at the Presidency of the Republic in April 2005 and refer only to intellectuals. Asterisks mean that intellectuals were honoured posthumously.

Table 9: Honours given during Mario Soares's Presidency (1985-1994)

Year	Author	Militar Sant'Iago da Espada	Ordem do Infante D.Henrique	Ordem de Mérito	Ordem da Liberdade	Ordem da Instrução Pública
1985	José Cardoso Pires	Comendador				
1985	José Saramago	Comendador				
1987	Jaime Cortesão					
1988	José Cardoso Pires			Grã Cruz		
1988	Fernando Namora		Grã Cruz			
1988	José Marmelo e Silva			Comendador		
1988	Óscar Lopes					Grã Cruz
1988	Eugénio de Andrade			Grã Cruz		
1989	Manuel Godinho			Oficial		
1989	António Rodrigues		Comendador			
1990	Alexandre O'Neill	Grande Oficial				
1990	Carlos de Oliveira	Grande Oficial				
1990	João José Cochofel		Grande Oficial			
1991	Alexandre Cabral		Grande Oficial			
1991	Natália Correia				Grande Oficial	
1991	António Valdemar	Comendador				
1991	José dos Santos Cabral		Grande Oficial			
1991	José Augusto França		Grande Oficial			
1992	Rui Cinatti		Grã Cruz			
1992	Nuno Júdice	Oficial				

Year	Author	Militar Sant'Iago da Espada	Ordem do Infante D.Henrique	Ordem de Mérito	Ordem da Liberdade	Ordem da Instrução Pública
1992	Al Berto	Oficial				
1992	António Ramos Rosa	Grande Oficial				
1992	Eduardo Lourenço		Grã Cruz			
1992	Adolfo Casais Monteiro				Grã Cruz	
1993	Pedro Tamen		Grã Cruz			
1993	Alice Jorge	Oficial				
1993	Luís Amaro		Comendador			
1993	Sebastião da Gama		Grã Cruz			
1993	Maria Alice Jorge	Oficial				
1994	Francisco Cachapuz				Grande Oficial	
1994	Luís Sttau Monteiro	Grande Oficial				
1994	Egito Gonçalves		Grande Oficial			

Table 10: Honours given to Intellectuals during Jorge Sampaio's Presidency (1996-2004)

Year	Author	Militar Sant'Iago da Espada	Ordem do Infante D. Henrique	Ordem de Mérito	Ordem da Liberdade
1996	António Gedeão	Grã Cruz			
1996	David Mourão Ferreira	Grã Cruz			
1997	António Ramos Rosa		Grã Cruz		
1997	Augusto Abelaira	Comendador		Comendadora	
1997	Mª Adelaide Amaral			Comendadora	

1998	Sophia de Mello Breyner	Grã Cruz	Grã Cruz		
1998	António Quadros		Grã Cruz		
1998	José Saramago	Grande Colar			
1999	Maria Aliete Galhoz		Grande Oficial		
2000	António Valdemar				Grande Oficial
2000	Mário Claúdio	Comendador			
2000	Isabel da Nóbrega			Grande Oficial	
2003	Maria Velho da Costa		Grande Oficial		
2004	Maria Isabel Barreno		Grande Oficial		
2004	Maria Teresa Horta		Grande Oficial		

Table 11: Academias das Ciências, Classe das Letras: Ricardo Malheiros Prize (1974–1980)[26]

Years	Prizewinners
1974	Fausto Lopo de Carvalho, *Ouvem-se vozes ao longe*, Parceria António Maria Pereira
1975	Olga Gonçalves, *A Floresta em Bremerhaven*, Seara Nova
1976	Romeu Correia, *Um Passo em Frente*, RPA
1977	Agustina Bessa Luís, *As Fúrias*, Guimarães
1978	Álvaro Manuel Machado, *Exílio*, Moraes
1979	Cristovão Aguiar, *Raíz Comovida*, Centelha
1980	Lídia Jorge, *Dias dos Prodígios*, Dom Quixote

26 See Prémio Ricardo Malheiros: Regulamento. [accessed September 2007].
<http://www.acadciencias.pt/html/menuacademiadigital/premioricardomalheiros/premio.pdf >

Table 12: Frequency of Prizewinning writers and Publishing Houses (1978-2000)

D.Dinis	P.E.N.	APE	Crítica	Município	Cidade	Vida Literária	Consag. SPA	Camões	Pessoa	Total
Guimarães										
Agustina Bessa Luís	Agustina Bessa Luís	Agustina Bessa Luís	Agustina Bessa Luís, Alexandre O'Neill	Agustina Bessa Luís						6
Moraes										
Pedro Tamen					Maria Velho da Costa					2
Bertrand										
Vergílio Ferreira, Fernando Namora	Teolinda Gersão, Vergílio Ferreira (x2)	Vergílio Ferreira (x2)	Vergílio Ferreira	Vergílio Ferreira	Augusto Abelaira			Vergílio Ferreira		11
O Jornal										
Maria Velho da Costa	Baptista Bastos	José Cardoso Pires		Baptista Bastos						4

D.Dinis	P.E.N.	APE	Crítica	Município	Cidade	Vida Literária	Consag. SPA	Camões	Pessoa	Total
Caminho										
Saramago	Saramago (x2), Mário Ventura, Mª Isabel Barreno	Saramago, Mário de Carvalho	Saramago (x2), Manuel Alegre	Saramago, Maria Ondina Braga	Saramago	Saramago, Sophia de Mello Breyner, Óscar Lopes	Saramago	Saramago, Sophia de Mello Breyner	Manuel Alegre	20
Rolim										
Mª Gabriela Llansol, Mário de Carvalho		Mª Gabriela Llansol								3
In-CM										
Fernando Guimarães		Mário Claúdio								2
Presença										
David Mourão Ferreira, Joaquim Manuel Magalhães, Eduardo Lourenço	Alçada Baptista, David Mourão Ferreira, Fernanda Botelho, Augusto Abelaira	David Mourão Ferreira, Augusto Abelaira, Fernanda Botelho	David Mourão Ferreira	Alçada Baptista, David Mourão Ferreira, Augusto Abelaira, Seomara da Veiga Ferreira	Augusto Abelaira		David Mourão Ferreira	Eduardo Lourenço		18

D.Dinis	P.E.N.	APE	Crítica	Município	Cidade	Vida Literária	Consag. SPA	Camões	Pessoa	Total
Limiar										
Eugénio de Andrade			Eugénio de Andrade			Eugénio de Andrade				3
Quetzal										
Luísa Costa Gomes, Nuno Júdice, Luís Felipe Mendes	Júlio Moreira, Nuno Júdice, Luís Felipe Castro Mendes									6
Relógio d'Água										
José Bento, Fiama Hasse P. Brandão		Rui Nunes								3

D.Dinis	P.E.N.	APE	Crítica	Município	Cidade	Vida Literária	Consag. SPA	Camões	Pessoa	Total
D.Quixote										
José Cardoso Pires, Lídia Jorge, António Lobo Antunes	Mário Ventura, Mª Velho da Costa, Teolinda Gersão, Lídia Jorge, Pedro Rosa Mendes, Mário Cláudio	António Lobo Antunes(x 2), João de Melo, Helena Marques, Teolinda Gersão, Maria Velho da Costa	José Cardoso Pires, Mª Velho da Costa	Lídia Jorge(x2), João de Melo, Mário Ventura, Mário Cláudio		José Cardoso Pires			José Cardoso Pires	24
Europa-América										
	Teresa Salema, Mª Judite Carvalho		Urbano Tavares Rodrigues				Urbano Tavares Rodrigues			4
Contexto										
	Paulo Castilho	Paulo Castilho	Fernanda Botelho	Paulo Castilho, Rodrigo Guedes de Carvalho						5

Table 13: Frequency of Juries at Literary Panels (1978-2004)

Jury	No.Panels
Agustina Bessa Luís	2
Alçada Baptista	11
Almeida Faria	1
Álvaro Salema	6
Ana Hatherly	3
Carlos Reis	8
Casimiro de Brito	5
Clara Rocha	7
Vasco Graça Moura	14
Mª Glória Padrão	4
Manuel Frias Martins	6
Manuel Gusmão	6
Maria Alzira Seixo	13
Maria Lúcia Lepecki	9
Óscar Lopes	5
Teolinda Gersão	4
Urbano Tavares Rodrigues	9

Jury	No.Panels
Eduardo Prado Coelho	4
Fernando J.B. Martinho	4
Fernando Pinto do Amaral	9
Jacinto Prado Coelho	4
Júlio Conrado	8
Liberto Cruz	4
David Mourão Ferreira	4
Pedro Tamen	11

Bibliography

Theory

Baizun, Jacques and Arthur Krystal, ed., *The Culture We Deserve* (Middleton, Connecticut: Westleyan University Press, 1989)

Bloom, Clive, *Cult Fiction, Popular Reading and Pulp Theory* (Houndmills: Macmillan Press, 1996)

—, *Bestsellers: Popular Fiction since 1900* (Houndmills: Palgrave Macmillan, 2002)

Bloom, Harold, *The Western Canon – The Books and The School of The Ages* (New York: Harcourt Brace & Company, 1994)

Bourdieu, Pierre, *The Field of Cultural Production – Essays on Art and Literature*, ed. and intr. by Randal Johnson (Cambridge: Polity Press & Blackwell Publishers, Ltd, 1993)

—, *Distinction – A Social Critique of The Judgement of Taste*, first published in French as *La Distinction, critique sociale du jugement* by Les Editions de Minuit, Paris, 1979 (London: Routledge & Kegan Paul Ltd, 1986)

—, 'Le marché des biens symboliques', *L'année sociologique*, 2 (1971), 49-126

—, 'Champ du pouvoir, champ intellectuel et habitus de classes', *Scolies*, Cahiers de recherches de l'École normale supérieure, 1 (1971), 7-26

—, 'La production de la croyance : contribution à une économie des biens symboliques', in *Actes de la recherche en sciences sociales*, 13 (February 1977), 3-43

—, La distinction, Critique sociale du jugement (Paris, Minuit, 1979)

Chaney, David, *The Cultural Turn – Scene-Setting: Essays on Contemporary Cultural History* (London: Routledge, 1994)

Ceia, Carlos, 'A Questão do Cânone Literário: Da Teoria aos Programas Escolares', <http://www,ciberkiosk,pt/arquivo/ci

293

berkiosk2/debate/cannica,html,com> [accessed on 1 October 2004]

Cox, Jeffrey N. and Larry J. Reynolds, eds., *New Historical Literary Study, Essays on Reproducing Texts, Representing History* (Princeton, New Jersey: Princeton University Press, 1993)

Coser, Lewis A., Ch. Kadushin and W. Powell, *Books – The Culture and Commerce of Publishing* (New York: Basic Books, 1982)

Crane, Diane, 'High Culture versus Popular Culture Revisited: A Reconceptualization of Recorded Cultures', in *Cultivating Differences; Cultivating Symbolic Boundaries; Differences and the Making of Inequality* ed. by Michèle Lament and Marcel Founier (Chicago and London: The University of Chicago Press, 1992), pp. 58-74

De Glas, Frank, 'Authors' oeuvres as the backbone of publishers' lists: Studying the literary publishing house after Bourdieu', *Poetics*, 25 (1998), 379-397

De Glas, Frank, 'Literature, "In-House" Writers, and Processes of Success in Publishing' *CLCWeb: Comparative Literature and Culture* 1.4 (1999): http://docs.lib.purdue.edu/clcweb/vol1/iss4/3'[accessed November 2009]

De Nooy, W. 'Gentlemen of the Jury... The Features of Experts Awarding Literary Prizes', *Poetics*, 17 (1988), 531-545

Dubois, Jacques, *L'institution de la littérature* (Brussels: Editions Labor/Ferdinand Nathan, 1986)

Estivals, R. J. Meyrat, and F. Richaudeau, eds., *Les Sciences de l'écrit, Encyclopédie internationale de bibliologie* (Paris : Retz, 1993)

Even-Zohar, Itamar, 'Polysystem Theory', in *Poetics*, 11:1, (1990), 9-26 (First version published under the title 'Polysystem Theory', *Poetics Today* (1991), 287-310)

Frow, John, *Cultural Studies and Cultural Value* (Oxford: Clarendon Press, 1995)

Furtado, José Afonso, *Os Livros e as Leituras – Novas Ecologias da Informação* (Lisbon: Livros e Leituras, 2000)

Goldman, Lucien, *Method in The Sociology of Literature*, trans. and ed. by William Q. Boelhower (Oxford: Basil Blackwell, 1981)

Guillory, John, *Cultural Capital – The Problem of Literary Canon Formation* (Chicago & London: The University of Chicago Press, 1993)

Hall, John, *The Sociology of Literature* (New York: Longman, 1979)

Hobsbawm, Eric and Terence Ranger, eds., *The Invention of Tradition* (Cambridge: CUP, 1992)

Hyland, Paul & Neil Sammels, eds., *Writing and Censorship in Britain* (London: Routledge, 1992)

Holub, Robert C., *Reception Theory – A Critical Introduction* (London & New York: Methuen, 1984)

Johnson, Lesley, The Cultural Crisis – From Matthew Arnold to Raymond Williams (London: Routledge & Kegan Paul, 1979)

Kermode, Frank, History and Value – The Clarendon Lectures and The Northcliffe Lectures 1987 (Oxford: Clarendon Press, 1988)

Kermode, Frank, *Pleasure and Change – The Aesthetics of Canon*, ed. and intr. by Robert Alter (Oxford: Oxford University Press, 2004)

Kolbas, E.D., *Critical Theory And The Literary Canon* (Oxford: Westview Press, 2001)

Leavis, Q. D., *Fiction and The Reading Public* (London: Chatto & Windus, 1932)

Luhmann, Niklas, *Social Systems*, trans. by John Bednarz, Jr and Dirk Baecker (Stanford, California: Stanford University Press, 1984)

Luhmann, Niklas, *Art As A Social System*, trans. by Eva M, Knodt (Stanford, California: Stanford University Press, 2000)

Macherey, Pierre, *A Theory of Literary Production*, trans. by Geoffrey Wall (London, Henley and Boston: Routledge & Kegan Paul, 1978)

Machor, J. and P. Goldstein, eds., *Reception Theory – From Literary Theory to Cultural Studies* (New York & London: Routledge, 2001)

Mann, Peter H., *Books: Buyers and Borrowers* (London: Andre Deutsch Ltd. 1971)

Mann, Peter H., 'Book Reading and Public Libraries in the United Kingdom', *Poetics*, 16 (1987), 213-226

Martins, A., *História e Ficção: Um Diálogo* (Lisbon: Fim de Século, 1994)

Martins, Jorge M., *Marketing do Livro – materiais para uma sociologia do editor português: De Camilo à Internet – O Prazer de Editar* (Oeiras: Celta 1999)

MacCracken, S., *Pulp – Reading Popular Fiction* (Manchester and New York: Manchester University Press, 1998)

McGuigan, Jim, *Culture and The Public Sphere* (London: Routledge, 1996)

Michon, Jacques, 'Fondements d'une histoire institutionelle de l'édition littéraire', in *La Recherche Littéraire*, ed. and rev. by C. Duchet and S. Vachon (Montréal: XYZ éditeur, 1998), pp. 65-75

Milner, Andrew, *Literature, Culture & Society* (London: University College London, 1996)

Newton, K.M., ed., *Twentieth-Century Literary theory: A Reader* (Houndmills: Macmillan Press Ltd, 1997)

Peterson, R.A., 'Six Constraints on the Production of Literary Works', *Poetics*, 14 (1985), 45-67

Peterson, R.A., 'Understanding Audience Segmentation: From Elite and Mass to Omnivore and Univore', *Poetics*, 21 (1992), 243-258

Pratt, Annis et al., *Archetypal Patterns in Women's Fiction* (Bloomington: Indiana University Press, 1981)

Ryan, Kiernan, New Historicism and Cultural Materialism – A Reader (London: Arnold, 1996)

Rusch, G., 'The status of authors within literary systems: Challenging the canon, An explorative investigation of Alfred Döblin's status within the German literary system in 1997', *Poetics*, 26 (1999), 367-384

Sapiro, G., 'The literary field between the state and the market', *Poetics*, 31 (2003), 441-464

Schmidt, Sigfried J, Foundations For The Empirical Study of Literature: The Components of A Basic Theory, trans. by R.de Beaugrande (Hamburg:Helmut Buske, 1982)

Storey, John, ed., *Cultural Theory and Popular Culture – A Reader* (Essex: Pearson Education, 1994)

Van Campenhoudt, L., *Introdução à Análise dos Fenómenos Sociais*, trans. by Eduardo de Freitas (Lisbon: Gradiva, 2001)

Veeser, H.Aram, ed., *The New Historicism – Reader* (New York and London: Routledge, 1994)

Verbod, M., 'Classification of authors by literary prestige', *Poetics*, 31 (2003), 259-281

Verdaasdonk, H., 'Effects of Acquired Readership and Reviewers' Attention on the Sales of New Literary Works', *Poetics*, 16 (1987), 237-253

Verdaasdonk, H., 'The Influence of Certain Socio-Economic Factors on the Composition of the Literary Programs of Large Dutch Publishing Houses', *Poetics*, 14 (1985), 575-608

West, J., *The Reading Public* (New York: Harcourt Brace, 1952)

White, Hayden, *Tropics of Discourse, Essays in Cultural Criticism* (Baltimore and London: The Johns Hopkins University Press, 1978)

Williams, Jeffrey J., ed., *The Institution of Literature* (Albany: State University of New York Press, 2002)

Williams, Raymond, *The Long Revolution* (Harmondsworth: Penguin Books, 1965 and Rpts, 1st edn, 1961)

Williams, Raymond, *Marxism and Literature* (Oxford: Oxford University Press, 1977)

Zepetnek, S. Tötösy, *Comparative Literature – Theory, Method, Application*, (Amsterdam: Atlanta, GA, 1998)

Zima, Peter V., *The Philosophy of Modern Literary Theory* (London and New Brunswick NJ: The Athlone Press, 1999)

Politics, Economy, Social Facts and Culture

'Results of the Plebiscite in 1933', Diário de Notícias, 27 March 1933, in Rosas, Fernando, *As Primeiras Eleições Legislativas do Estado Novo*, Cadernos O Jornal, Lisbon (1985), p. 81

Almeida, D., *Ascensão, Apogeu e Queda Do M.F.A.* (Lisbon: Edições Sociais, [n.d.])

Andringa, Diana and Alfredo Caldeira, *Em Defesa De Aquilino Ribeiro* (Lisbon: Terramar, 1994)

Antunes, José Freire, *Salazar e Caetano – Cartas Secretas 1932-1968* (Lisbon: Difusão Cultural, 1994)

Associação Portuguesa De Escritores, Levantamento da Situação Sócio-Económica do Escritor Português em 1980 (Lisbon: APE, [n.d.])

Azevedo, Cândido, *A Censura De Salazar e Marcelo Caetano* (Lisbon: Editorial Caminho, 1999)

Azevedo, Cândido, Mutiladas e Proibidas, Para a História da Censura Literária em Portugal nos tempos do Estado Novo (Lisbon: Editorial Caminho, 1997)

Baganha, Maria Ioannis B., 'Portuguese Emigration After World War II', (pp. 1-19) <http://www,cphrc,org,uk/sources/so-stat/stat2,htm> [accessed in April 2000]

Baptista, César Moreira, Informação, Cultura Popular, Turismo – Discursos Pronunciados (Lisbon: SNI, 1965)

Baptista, Jacinto, 'À Procura do Espírito na 'Política do Espírito' do Estado Novo', in *História de Portugal*, ed. by João Medina, 15 vols (Lisbon: Ediclube, 1998), XIII, pp. 63-113

Barreto, António, ed., *A Situação Social em Portugal, 1960-1995* 3rd edn (Lisbon: Instituto de Ciências Sociais da Universidade de Lisboa, 1997)

Braga, Mário, ''Letras'e Números', *Vértice*, XIII, 123 (1953), 350-356

Bruneau, Thomas C., 'Popular Support for Democracy in Postrevolutionary Portugal : Results from a Survey', in *In Search of Modern Portugal: The Revolution and its Consequences*, ed. by Lawrence Graham and Douglas L, Wheeler (Wisconsin: The University of Wisconsin Press, 1983), pp. 21-42

Bruneau, Thomas C., *Politics and Nationhood, Post-Revolutionary Portugal* (New York: Praeger Publishers, 1984)

Cádima, Francisco Rui, *Salazar, Caetano e A Televisão Portuguesa* (Lisbon: Editorial Presença, 1996)

Caetano, Marcello, *Minhas Memórias De Salazar* (Lisbon: Editorial Verbo, 1977)

Carvalho, Alberto Duarte, 'Comentário sociológico das publicações literárias', *Balanço da Actividade Literária Portuguesa (1983/1984)*, CP/AICL (1985)

—, 'Comentário Sociológico', *Balanço da Actividade Literária Portuguesa (1985)*, CP/AICL (1985)

Carvalho, Joaquim Barradas de, *O Obscurantismo Salazarista* (Lisbon: Seara Nova, 1974)

Carvalho, Joaquim de Montezuma de, O que pensa um Português da candidatura do Poeta Miguel Torga ao Prémio Nobel de 1960 (Figueira da Foz: [n.pub.], 1959)

Ceia, Carlos, 'A Resistência ao Ensino da História Literária' < http://193.136.113.38:8080/FCSH/docentes/cceia/educacao/ensi no_hist_literaria.pdf > [Accessed in November 2009]

Cervelló, Josep Sanchez, ' O 25 de Novembro ', in *História de Portugal*, ed. by João Medina, 15 vols (Lisbon: Ediclube, 1998), XIV, pp. 87-132

Conselhos Revolucionários Projecto Povo-MFA. (Lisbon: Edições Revolução, s/d)

Costa, Paulo Jorge Lampreia, 'A Construção do Cânone Literário Escolar – Uma Análise de Textos Programáticos para o Ensino Secundário' (unpublished thesis, Évora University, 1997)

Curto, Diogo Ramada, ed., *Estudos de Sociologia da Leitura em Portugal no Século XX* (Lisbon: Fundação Calouste Gulbenkian and Ministério da Ciência e do Ensino Superior, 2006)

Dicionário Cronológico de Autores Portugueses, 6 vols (Lisbon: Europa-América, 2005)

Dionísio, Eduarda, Almeida Faria and Luís Salgado de Matos, eds., *Situação Da Arte* (Lisbon: Europa-América, 1968)

Dionísio, Eduarda, *Títulos, Acções, Obrigações – A Cultura em Portugal, 1974-1994* (Lisbon: Edições Salamandra, 1993)

Feltrinelli, Carlo, *Senior Service*, trans. by Simonetta Neto (Lisbon: Âmbar, 2002)

Ferreira, F.A., G., ed., 15 Anos de História Recente de Portugal (1970-1984) (Lisbon: [n.pub.], 1985)

Ferreira, Hugo G. and Michael W, Marshall, *Portugal's Revolution: Ten Years On* (Cambridge: Cambridge University Press, 1986)

Ferreira, Serafim, *Olhar de Editor* (Lisbon: Editorial Escritor, 1999)

Ferro, António, *Salazar: O Homem e A Sua Obra*, pref. by Oliveira Salazar (Lisbon: Empresa Nacional de Publicidade, 1933)

Ferro, António, *Prémios Literários (1934-1947)* (Lisbon: SNI, 1950)

Fialho, Irene Maria Leandro, 'Popular e Popularizante nos Manuais Escolares do Estado Novo' (unpublished thesis, Universidade Nova de Lisboa, 1993)

França, José-Augusto, 'Sobre cultura e política cultural', in *Memórias da Academia das Ciências de Lisboa*, Classe de Letras, XVII, (Lisbon: Academia das Ciências de Lisboa, 1976), 337-345

Gallagher, Tom, 'From Hegemony to Opposition: The Ultra Right before and after 1974', in *Search of Modern Portugal: The Revolution and its Consequences*, ed, by Graham, Lawrence and Douglas L, Wheeler (Wisconsin: The University of Wisconsin Press, 1983), pp. 81-98

Gallagher, Tom, *Portugal – A Twentieth-Century Interpretation* (Manchester: Manchester University Press, 1983)

Garcia, José Martins, 'Introdução', in Vitorino Nemésio, *Obras Completas*. 12 vols. (Lisbon: Imprensa Nacional-Casa da Moeda, 2002), VIII: *Mau Tempo no Canal*, pp. 14-15.

George, João Pedro, O Meio Literário Português (1960-1998), Prémios Literários, Escritores e Acontecimentos (Lisbon: Difel, 1998)

Grémio Nacional de Editores e Livreiros, *Relatório de Contas – Gerência de 1950* (Lisbon: Grémio Nacional de Editores e Livreiros, 1951)

—, *Relatório de Contas (Exercício de 1947 e 1948)* (Lisbon: Grémio Nacional de Editores e Livreiros, 1948)

—, *Relatório de Contas do ano de 1944* (Lisbon: Grémio Nacional de Editores e Livreiros, 1944)

—, *Relatório de Contas do ano de 1946* (Lisbon: Grémio Nacional de Editores e Livreiros, 1946)

—, *Relatório de Contas do ano de 1949* (Lisbon: Grémio Nacional de Editores e Livreiros, 1950)

—, *Relatório de Contas do ano de 1951* (Lisbon: Grémio Nacional de Editores e Livreiros, 1951)

—, *Relatório de Contas do ano de 1952* (Lisbon: Grémio Nacional de Editores e Livreiros, 1952)

—, *Relatório de Contas do ano de 1953* (Lisbon: Grémio Nacional de Editores e Livreiros, 1953)

—, *Relatório de Contas do ano de 1970* (Lisbon: Grémio Nacional de Editores e Livreiros, 1970)

—, *Relatório de Contas do ano de 1971* (Lisbon: Grémio Nacional de Editores e Livreiros, 1971)

—, *Relatório de Contas do ano de 1972* (Lisbon: Grémio Nacional de Editores e Livreiros, 1972)

Guedes, Fernando, *Os Livreiros em Portugal E As Suas Associações Desde O Século XV Até Aos Nossos Dias* (Lisbon: Editorial Verbo, 2005)

<http://www.iplb.pt/pls/diplb/!main_ page?levelid=190> [accessed in March 2005]

<http://www.angelfire.com/pq/unica/francisco-rolao-preto.htm> [accessed in May 2006]

<http://www.premiopessoa.pt/pessoa.html>.[accessed in November 2009]

'Inquérito sobre O Congresso Luso Brasileiro de Escritores', *Vértice*, XIII, 123 (1953), 641-648

Kay, Hugh, *Salazar and the Modern Portugal* (London: Eyre and Spottiswoode, 1970)

Kayman, Martin, *Revolution and Counter Revolution in Portugal* (London: The Merlin Press, 1987)

Leite, Pedro Jorge de Oliveira P., 'Mercadores de Letras – Rumos e Estratégias dos Editores e Livreiros na Divulgação Cultural durante o Estado Novo (1933-1974)' (unpublished thesis, Faculty of Letters, University of Lisbon, 1998)

Lepecki, Maria Lúcia, 'Ficção', *Balanço da Actividade Literária Portuguesa (ano de 1982)*, CP/AICL (1983), pp. 13-17

Lisboa, Irene, *Inquérito ao Livro I – Editores e Livreiros* (Lisbon: Seara Nova, 1944)

Lisboa, Irene, *Inquérito ao Livro II – A Arte do Livro* (Lisbon: Seara Nova, 1946)

Lomax, Bill, 'Ideology And Illusion In The Portuguese Revolution: The Role Of The Left', in *Search Of Modern Portugal: The Revolution And Its Consequences*, ed. by Lawrence Graham and Douglas L. Wheeler (Wisconsin: The University Of Wisconsin Press, 1983), pp. 105-129

Lourenço, Eduardo, *Cultura e Política na Época Marcelista – Entrevista de Mário Mesquita* (Lisbon: Edições Cosmos, 1996)

Lourenço, Eduardo, *O Fascismo nunca existiu* (Lisbon: Publicações Dom Quixote, 1976)

Lourenço, Eduardo, *O Labirinto da Saudade – Psicanálise Mítica do Destino Português* (Lisbon: Gradiva, 2000, 1st edn, Lisbon: Dom Quixote, 1978)

Lourenço, Eduardo, 'O imaginário português neste fim de século', *Jornal de Letras*, 29 December 1999, pp. 20-23

Lucena, Manuel de, *O Regime Salazarista e a sua Evolução: Matosinho Conferences* (Matosinhos: Câmara Municipal de Matosinhos, 1995)

Macedo, Hélder and G.M. de Melo e Castro, eds., *Contemporary Portuguese Poetry* (Manchester: Carcanet, 1978)

Madeira, João, *Os Engenheiros de Almas – O Partido Comunista e os Intelectuais (dos anos trinta a inícios de sessenta* (Lisbon: Editorial Estampa, 1996)

Malheiros, Jorge, 'Portugal Seeks Balance of Emigration, Imigration', *Migration Information Source*. Washington, DC: Migration Policy Institute, December 1, 2002, <http://www.migrationinformation.org/feature/display.cfm?ID=77> [accessed November 2009]

Martins, A., *História e Ficção: Um Diálogo* (Lisbon: Fim de Século, 1994)

Mascarenhas, João, ed., *Relação das obras, cuja circulação esteve proibida em Portugal durante o Regime de Salazar/Marcello Caetano* (Lisbon: Câmara Municipal de Lisboa/Biblioteca República e Resistência, 1996)

Matos, Norton de, 'Manifesto', printed in Lisbon and distributed on 9th July 1948 < http://www.arqnet.pt/portal/discursos/julho05.html> [accessed November 2009]

Mattoso, José, ed., *História de Portugal*, 8 vols (Lisbon: Editorial Estampa, 1994), VII: *O Estado Novo (1926-1974)*

Mattoso, José, ed., *História de Portugal*, 8 vols (Lisbon: Editorial Estampa, 1994), VIII: *Portugal em Transe (1974-1985)*

Mccolvin, L, And J.Rene, *British Libraries* (London: Longman Green, 1946)

Melo, Daniel, *A Leitura Pública No Portugal Contemporâneo 1926-1987* (Lisbon: Imprensa De Ciências Sociais, Instituto De Ciências Sociais, 2004)

Mineiro, Adélia Carvalho, Valores e Ensino no Estado Novo: Análise dos Livros Únicos (Lisbon: Edições Sílabo, 2007)

Mónica, Filomena, Educação e Sociedade no Portugal de Salazar (A Escola Primária Salazarista 1926-1939) (Lisbon: Colecção Análise Social, Editorial Presença/Gabinete de Investigações Sociais, 1979)

Mónica, Maria Filomena, Mónica, 'A Evolução dos Costumes em Portugal, 1960-1995', in Barreto, António, ed., A Situação Social em Portugal, 1960-1995 3rd edn (Lisbon: Instituto de Ciências Sociais da Universidade de Lisboa, 1997), pp. 215-231

Nogueira, Albano, 'Uma iniciativa cultural', Presença, 40 (1940), 15

Nogueira, Fernando, O Estado Novo (1933-1974), pref. by Marcelo Rebelo de Sousa (Lisbon: Civilização Editora, 2000)

Norrie, Ian, Mumby's Publishing And Booselling In The Twentieth Century, London: Bell and Hyman, 6th edn, 1982 (Mumby, Frank, Publishing And Bookselling, London: Jonathan Cape Ltd, 1930),

Nunes, Henrique Barreto, Da Biblioteca Ao Leitor – Estudos Sobre A Leitura Pública Em Portugal (Braga: Autores De Braga, 1996)

Ó, Jorge Ramos do, 'O Dispositivo Cultural nos Anos da Política de Espírito (1933-1949)', (unpublished thesis, Faculty of Letters, University of Coimbra, 1993)

Ó, Jorge Ramos do, 'Salazarismo e Cultura', in Nova História de Portugal, ed. by Joel Serrão and A.H. de Oliveira Marques, 12 vols (Lisbon: Presença, 1992), XII, pp. 391-454

Owen, Hilary, Portuguese Women's Writing – 1972 to 1986, Reincarnations of a Revolution (Lampeter: The Edwin Mellen Press Ltd, 2000)

Palma, Ernesto, A Orientação da Leitura (Lisbon: Sociedade de Expansão Cultural, [n.d.])

Paulo, Heloísa, Estado Novo e Propaganda em Portugal e no Brasil – O SPN/SNI e o DIP (Coimbra: Livraria Minerva, 1994)

Pedroso, Alberto, 'A Polícia Política', História de Portugal, ed. by João Medina, 15 vols (Lisbon: Ediclube, 1998), XIII, pp. 11-38

Pereira, António Maria, Parceria António Maria Pereira, Crónica de Uma Dinastia Livreira (Lisbon: Pandora Edições, 1998)

Pimlott, B., and J. Seaton, 'Political Power and the Portuguese Media', in *Search of Modern Portugal: The Revolution and its Consequences*, ed. by Lawrence Graham and Douglas L, Wheeler (Wisconsin: The University of Wisconsin Press, 1983), pp. 43-57

Pina, Álvaro, 'Intellectual spaces of practice and hope: power and culture in Portugal from the 1940s to the present', *Cultural Studies*, 17:6 (2003), 751-766

Pinto, António Costa, ed., *Portugal Contemporâneo* (Lisbon: Dom Quixote, 2005)

Portela, Artur, *Salazarismo E Artes Plásticas* (Lisbon: Instituto De Cultura E Língua Portuguesa, Colecção Breve, 1982)

Quintas, José Manuel Alves, 'Integralismo Lusitano – uma síntese', <http//www.angelfire.com/pq/única/il_jmq_integralismo_lusit ano_sintese.htm> [accessed in May 2006]

Príncipe, César, *Os Segredos Da Censura* (Lisbon: Editorial Caminho, 1979)

Ramos, Rui, 'Os Intelectuais e o Estado Novo', article based on 'The Intellectual Origins of Democracy and Dictatorship: Portugal, 1926-1974', typed text handed in to participants at the workshop *Assessing the Portuguese Experience of Regime Transformation* (University of Reading, Great Britain, 18 February 1994)

Ramos, Victor, 'Breve Análise da Repressão à Vida Intelectual em Portugal', ed. by *A Situação da Cultura em Portugal sob o Regime de Salazar*, pp. 7-25

Prémio Ricardo Malheiros: Regulamento. <http://www.acad-cien cias.pt/html/menuacademiadigital/premioricardomalheiros/pre mio.pdf> [accessed September 2007]

Reis, Carlos, 'A produção cultural entre a norma e a ruptura', in *Portugal Contemporâneo (1928-1958)*, ed. by António Reis, 5 vols (Lisbon: Alfa, 1990), V, pp. 201-270

Ribeiro, António Sousa, 'O Povo e O Público, Refexões Sobre A Cultura Em Portugal No Pós-25 de Abril', in *Revista Crítica de Ciências Sociais*, no.18/19/20 (1986), 11-26

Robinson, R.A. H., *Contemporary Portugal – A History* (London: George Allen and Unwin, 1979)

Rodrigues, Graça Almeida, *Breve História Da Censura Literária Em Portugal* (Lisbon: Instituto De Cultura E Língua Portuguesa, Colecção Breve, 1980)

Rosas, Fernando, O Estado Novo Nos Anos Trinta: Elementos Para O Estudo Da Natureza Económica E Social Do Salazarismo (1928-1938) (Lisbon: Editorial Estampa, 1986)

Rosas, Fernando and J.M. Brandão de Brito, eds., *Dicionário de História do Estado Novo*, 2 vols. (Lisbon, Bertrand Editora, 1996)

Rose, J. and P. Anderson, eds., *Dictionary Of Literary Biography, A Bruccoli Clark Layman Book* (Detroit, London: Gale Research, 1991)

Salazar, António de Oliveira, Antologia – Discursos, Notas, Relatórios, Teses, Artigos e Revistas (Lisbon: Editorial Vanguarda, 1954)

Sampaio, Aúrea, 'Os três Governos de Cavaco Silva e a mudança de ciclo', in *História de Portugal*, ed. by João Medina, 15 vols (Lisbon: Ediclube, 1998), XIV, pp. 379-394

Santos, Boaventura dos, ed., Portugal: Um Retrato Singular – O Estado, as Relações Salariais e o Bem-Estar Social na Periferia: O Caso Português (Lisbon: Edições Afrontamento, 1993)

Santos, Maria de Lurdes Lima, ed., *Dinâmicas da Aplicação da Lei do Preço Fixo do Livro* (Lisbon: Observatório das Actividades Culturais, Colecção OBS – Pesquisas 7, 2000)

Saraiva, José and Lopes, Óscar, *História da Literatura Portuguesa*, 14th edn, rev. (Porto: Porto Editora, 1955; repr.1987)

Schmitter, Philippe C., 'The 'Regime d'Exception' that Became the Rule: Forty-EightYears of Authoritarian Domination in Portugal', in *Contemporary Portugal – The Revolution and its Antecedents*, ed. by Lawrence Graham and Harry Mackler (Austin and London: University of Texas Press, 1979), pp. 3-41

Seara Nova, 3º Congresso de Oposição Democrática: Conclusões (Lisbon: Seara Nova, 1973)

Seabra, Augusto M., 'A crise da intelectualidade nacional', *Expresso*, 21 April 1984, pp. 28-R-30-R

Secretariado Nacional de Informação, Catorze Anos de Política de Espírito – Apontamentos para uma exposição apresentados no Secretariado Nacional de Informação (Palácio Foz) em Janeiro de 1948 (Lisbon: SNI, 1948)

—, *Decálogo do Estado Novo* (Lisbon: Edições SPN, 1934)
—, Roteiro da Exposição 30 Anos de Cultura Portuguesa (1926-1956) (Lisbon: SNI, 1956)
—, *Um Instrumento do Governo: 25 Anos de Acção (1933-1958)* (Lisbon: SNI, 1958)
Sérgio, António, *Democracia* (Lisbon: Sá da Costa, 1974)
Sociedade Portuguesa de Escritores, *Relatório de Contas – 1956-1961* (Lisbon: SPE, [n.d.])
Spínola, António de, *Portugal e O Futuro* (Lisbon: Arcádia, 1974)
Tavares, Marília de Assis, 'Os Congressos Republicanos de Aveiro' (unpublished thesis, Faculty of Letters, University of Coimbra, Coimbra, 1994)
Torres, António Maria M. Pinheiro, *Igreja e Estado: História de Uma Relação* (Lisbon: Edual, 2006)
Ventura, António, 'Oposição Ao Estado Novo', *História de Portugal*, ed. by João Medina, 15 vols (Lisbon: Ediclube, 1998), XIII, pp. 149-205

Literary Criticism

Arias, Juan, *Saramago: O Amor Possível* (Lisbon: Publicações D,Quixote, 1998)
Bastos, Baptista, *José Saramago – Aproximação A Um Retrato* (Lisbon: Dom Quixote, 1996)
Blanco, José, 'A Verdade sobre *A Mensagem*' <www.portalpessoa. org> [accessed September 2007]
Berrini, Beatriz, *Ler Saramago: O Romance* (Lisbon: Editorial Caminho, 1998)
Bulletin of Hispanic Studies, LXXI (1994)
Carvalho, A. D., 'Comentário Sociológico Das Publicações Literárias', in CP/AICL, *Balanço Da Actividade Literária Portuguesa* (Lisbon: CP/AICL, 1982), pp. 29-36
Cerdeira, Teresa Cristina, *O Avesso do Bordado: Ensaios de Literatura* (Lisbon: Editorial Caminho, 2000)
Coelho, Eduardo Prado, 'Ensaio', in *Colóquio Letras*, 78 (1984), 43-54

Costa, Horácio, *José Saramago: O Período Formativo* (Lisbon: Editorial Caminho, 1997)

Hispanofila, 36.1 (1992)

Lourenço, Eduardo, 'Literatura e Revolução', in *Colóquio Letras*, 78 (1984), 7-16

Orero, Pilar and J.C. Sager, *The Translator's Dialogue: Giovanni Pontiero* (Amsterdam/Philadephia: John Benjamin's Publishing Company, 1997)

P. N. Review, 16.4 (1990)

Reis, Carlos, *Diálogos Com José Saramago*, Lisbon: Editorial Caminho, 1998

Reis, Manuel, *A Falsa Questão Ateísmo-Teísmo. Crítica Necessária a José Saramago* (Aveiro: Estante Editora, 1992)

Saraiva, António José and Lopes, Óscar, *História da Literatura Portuguesa*, 14th edn rev. (Porto: Porto Editora, 1987)

Seixo, Maria Alzira, 'Ficção', in *Colóquio Letras*, 78 (1984), 30-42

Seixo, Maria Alzira, Lugares Da Ficção Em José Saramago – O Essencial E Outros Ensaios (Lisbon: Imprensa Nacional Casa Da Moeda, Temas Portugueses, 1999)

Teixeira, Ramiro, Ficção Portuguesa Pós-Abril – Percursos, Caminhantes e Bandeirantes (Lisbon: Escritor, 2000)

Trigueiros, Luiz Forjaz, 'Ficção', In CP/AICL, *Balanço Da Actividade Literária Portuguesa (1983/1984)* (Lisbon: CP/AICL, 1985), pp. 19-20

Viegas, Francisco José, ed., *José Saramago: Uma Voz Contra O Silêncio* (Lisbon: Editorial Caminho, 1998)

Zékian, S., 'Prosateurs Portugais: José Saramago' <*http://www.instituto-camoes.pt/escritores/saramago/prosatrsarmg.htm*> [accessed in November 2002]

Portuguese Fiction

Barreno, Maria Isabel, Maria Teresa Horta, Maria Velho da Costa, *Novas Cartas Portuguesas*, 3rd edn (Lisbon: Moraes Editores, 1980)

Faria, Almeida, *Rumor Branco*, 4th edn (Lisbon: Editorial Caminho, 1992)

Ferreira, Vergílio, *Conta-Corrente I* (Lisbon: Bertrand, 1982)

Fonseca, Manuel da, *Cerromaior* (Lisbon: Editorial Caminho, 1977)

Gonçalves, Olga, *A Floresta em Bremerhaven*, 4th edn (Lisbon: Editorial Caminho, 1992; 1st edn, Lisbon: Seara Nova, 1975)

Oliveira, Carlos, *O Aprendiz De Feiticeiro*, 3rd edn (Lisbon: Sá Da Costa, 1979)

Peixoto, José Luís, *Nenhum Olhar* (Lisbon: Temas & Debates, 2000)

—, *Uma Casa Na Escuridão* (Lisbon: Temas & Debates, 2002)

Pires, José Cardoso, *E Agora José?* (Lisbon: Edições D, Quixote, 1997)

Redol, Alves, *Gaibéus* (Lisbon: Publicações Europa-América, 1971)

Saramago, José, *Levantado Do Chão* (Lisbon: Editorial Caminho, O Campo Da Palavra, 1980)

—, *Memorial Do Convento* (Lisbon: Editorial Caminho, O Campo Da Palavra, 1982)

—, *Manual De Pintura E Caligrafia* (Lisbon: Editorial Caminho, O Campo Da Palavra, 1983)

—, *O Ano Da Morte De Ricardo Reis* (Lisbon: Editorial Caminho, O Campo Da Palavra, 1984)

—, *A Jangada De Pedra* (Lisbon: Editorial Caminho, O Campo Da Palavra, 1986)

—, *História Do Cerco De Lisboa*, 6th edn (Lisbon: Editorial Caminho, O Campo Da Palavra, 1989)

—, *O Evangelho Segundo Jesus Cristo* (Lisbon: Editorial Caminho, O Campo Da Palavra, 1991)

—, *Cadernos de Lanzarote: Diário-I* (Lisbon, Editorial Caminho, O Campo da Palavra, 1994)

—, *Ensaio Sobre A Cegueira* (Lisbon: Editorial Caminho, O Campo Da Palavra, 1995)

—, *Todos Os Nomes* (Lisbon: Editorial Caminho, O Campo Da Palavra, 1997)

—, *Cadernos de Lanzarote: Diário IV*, 3rd edn (Lisbon: Editorial Caminho, O Campo da Palavra, 1998)

—, *Cadernos de Lanzarote: Diário-V*, 2nd edn (Lisbon, Editorial Caminho, O Campo da Palavra, 1998)

—, *Os Apontamentos: Crónicas Políticas*, 3rd edn (Lisbon: Editorial Caminho, O Campo da Palavra, 1998)

—, *Folhas Políticas: 1976-1998*, 2nd edn (Lisbon: Editoral Caminho, O Campo da Palavra, 1999)

—, *Deste Mundo e do Outro: Crónicas*, 6th edn (Lisbon: Editorial Caminho, O Campo da Palavra, 1999)

—, *A Caverna* (Lisbon: Editorial Caminho, O Campo Da Palavra, 2000)

—, *Terra Do Pecado*, 8th edn (Lisbon: Editorial Caminho, O Campo Da Palavra, 2001)

—, *O Homem* (Lisbon: Editorial Caminho, O Campo Da Palavra, 2002)

—, *Ensaio Sobre A Lucidez* (Lisbon: Editorial Caminho, O Campo Da Palavra, 2004)

Newspapers and Magazines

United Kingdom

The Independent

Craig, Jamie, 'Father, Son and much free spirit', *The Independent*, 12 September 1993, p. 31

Feay, Suzi, 'Manual of Painting and Calligraphy by Jose Saramago, trs Giovanni Pontiero, Carcanet £14,95,', *The Independent*, 3 July 1994, p. 34

Griffin, Nigel, 'Obituary: Giovanni Pontiero', *The Independent*, 11 March 1996, Gazette, p. 16

Gowers, Rebecca, 'Starlings on a moving Island', *The Independent*, 19 November 1993, p. 27

Hilton, Isabel, 'A writer of immense talent and no ambition', *The Independent*, 31 July 1993, p. 27

Josipovici, Gabriel, 'Son of God tries to outwit his mad father', *The Independent*, 11 September 1993, p. 31

Saramago, Jose, 'Culture: The Tale of the Unknown Island', trans, by Christine Robinson, *The Independent*, 27 December 1998

Winder, Robert, 'Foreign Fiction: A far cry from Kensington: Robert Winder reflects on the first annual shortlist for the pounds 10,000 Independent Award', *The Independent*, 1 June 1991, p. 30

Winder, Robert, 'Books: Independent Foreign Fiction Award: Adventures in humility: Robert Winder talks to Giovanni Pontiero, who translated The Year of the Death of Ricardo Reis by Jose Saramago (Harvill 14,99)', *The Independent*, 17 July 1993, p. 28

Winder, Robert, 'Death in Lisbon: a poet disintegrates: The Year of the Death of Ricardo Reis – Jose Saramago; Tr, Giovanni Pontiero: Harvill: 7,99 pounds', *The Independent*, 7 August 1992, p. 17

Winder, Robert, 'Remaining faithful to the translation', *The Independent*, 30 July 1993, p. 20

Winder, Robert, 'Notes on what's gained in translation', *The Independent*, 11 October 1998

Yuste, Miguel, 'Culture: Paying the Nobel price: When Jose Saramago won the Nobel Prize for Literature last week, it didn't change his views on the emptiness of fame', *The Independent*, 11 October 1998

'A romantic pseudonym on the loose in Lisbon', *The Independent*, 5 September 1992, p. 26

The Times / The Sunday Times

Alberge, Dalya, 'A talent lost in translation', *The Times*, 2 December 1998, p. 12

Anderson, Sarah, 'Rich terrain for bookworms; Summer holiday reading; Travel', *The Times*, 13 July 1996, p. 19

Armstrong, Karen, 'He knows not what he does', *The Times*, 4 September 1997, p. 34

Baker, Phil, Balfe, Ned, Barrett, Pam, Critchley, Ian and Hill, Ivan, *The Times*, No headline available, 29 August 1993, p. 6/14

Critchley, Ian, 'Shortlist; Books for Christmas', *The Sunday Times*, 27 November 1994, p. 7/15

Critchley, Ian, No headline available, *The Sunday Times*, 27 November 1994, p. 7/15

Jardine, Lisa, 'In clear sight', *The Times*, 20 November 1997, p. 40

The Daily Telegraph

Armstrong, Karen, 'God the Villain', *The Daily Telegraph*, 2 October 1993, p. xxvi

Chisholm, Kate, 'A Portuguese Odyssey – Kate Chosholm on a meditative novel set in Lisbon', *The Daily Telegraph*, 23 August 1992

Cropper, Martin, 'A dead person, the ideal confidant – Fiction: a labyrinthine over; the unreadability of all published texts; a stiff dose of hormonal poison', *The Daily Telegraph*, 22 August 1992

Lessing, Doris, 'The last book I bought', *The Daily Telegraph*, 14 October 2000, p. 2

Merrit, Stephanie, 'Good year for Portugal, not much fun in France: Stephanie Merritt picks 1997's best: Foreign Fiction', *The Daily Telegraph*, 20 December 1997

Woodall, James, 'Banned: a vision of Jesus Christ – Flyleaf/ James Woodall on Jose Saramago, whose alternative version of Jesus's life has divided Portugal and troubled her government', *The Daily Telegraph*, 28 August 1993

Woodall, James, 'A daring little prankster', *The Daily Telegraph*, 14 January 1995, p. 9

'Author, 75, wins Nobel', *The Daily Telegraph*, 9 October 1998, p. 34

The Guardian

Kerr, Sarah, 'The Leonard Cohen of the World Lit', *The Guardian*, 18 October 1998

Robinson, Emily, 'The Gospel according to Jesus Christ', *The Guardian*, 7 December 1993, p. 8

Wordsworth, Christopher, 'Wagging a Finger at God', *The Guardian*, 4 March 1988, p. 23

The Scotsman

No headline available, *The Scotsman*, 29 May 1994

Lockerbie, Catherine, 'Volume Control', *The Scotsman*, 10 October 1998

Times Literary Supplement

Butt, John, 'The crimes of God', *Times Literary Supplement*, 22 October 1993, p. 22

Duguid, Paul, 'Nameless virtues', *Times Literary Supplement*, 15 October 1999, p. 26

Josipovici, Gabriel, 'Poet and revenant', *Times Literary Supplement*, 11 September 1992

Keates, Jonathan, 'Making History', *Times Literary Supplement*, 28 June 1996, p. 24

Kerrigan, Michael, 'The I of Saramago', *Times Literary Supplement*, 19 December 1997, p. 20

Losada, Basilio, 'An Iberian Voice', *Times Literary Supplement*, 23 February 1990, p. 208,3 Liber

Steiner, George, 'International Books of the Year', *Times Literary Supplement*, 3 December 1993, p. 10

Tahourdin, Adrian, 'Preliminary Sketches', *Times Literary Supplement*, 15 April 1994

Zenith, Richard, 'All in the family', *Times Literary Supplement*, 17 October 1997, p. 26

New Statesman & Society

Pavey, Ruth, 'Jealous God', *New Statesman & Society*, 27 August 1993, p. 40

The European

Hyland, Paul, 'Floating pilgrimage to an unknown destination', *The European*, 25 November-1 December 1994, p. 13

London Review of Books

Wood, Michael, 'Secession', *London Review of Books*, 23 March 1995

The Salisbury Review

Lança, Patricia, 'An Ignoble Nobel or the strange story of a literary humanist', *The Salisbury Review*, Summer 1999

The Observer

'Profile – Dr,Salazar', *The Observer*, August 29, 1954
Heawood, Jonathan, 'Baltasar and Blimunda', *The Observer*, October 7, 2001

Portugal

Revista Ler, 34 (Lisbon: Círculo de Leitores, 1994)
'Literatura e Artes plásticas no pós-25 de Abril', *Diário de Notícias*, 19 April 1984,pp. 15-17
'José Saramago 'levantou a voz', *Jornal de Letras*, 8 June 1982, p. 18
'240 Escritores em "Le Nouvel Observateur" Tabucchi responde a Saramago', *Jornal de Letras*, 21 December 1994, p. 14
'José Saramago: Viagens através do tempo', *Jornal de Letras*, 6 March 1990,pp. 19-20
'Evangelho no 'index' da SEC', *Jornal de Letras*, 5 May 1992, p. 3
'José Saramago, 50 anos de escrita', *Jornal de Letras* 26 March 1997, pp. 11-17
'José Saramago, Doutor Honoris Causa: O Tempo e a História', *Jornal de Letras* 27 January 1999, p. 5
'José Saramago: A escrita narcísica por excelência', *Jornal de Letras* 13 April 1994, p. 4
'José Saramago', *Jornal de Letras* 30 December 1999, pp. 14-18
'José Saramago': Blimunda, nome com música', *Jornal de Letras*, 15 May 1990, p. 29
'Saramago: Viagem a Portugal', *Jornal de Letras*, 14 April 1981, p. 26
'Saramago aceita prémio mas dinheiro vai para os PALOP', *Jornal de Letras*, 23 June 1992, pp. 8-9
'Inquérito à edição em Portugal', *Jornal de Letras*, 29 September 1981, pp. 14-15
'Crise do livro: as propostas dos editores', *Jornal de Letras*, 5 November 1991, pp. 11-15
'O programa de Lucas Pires para o Ministério da Cultura', *Jornal de Letras*, 15 September 1981, pp. 19-20
A.M.F./I.P., "Amadeo' e 'Ricardo Reis' às portas da APE', *Jornal de Letras*, 2 April 1985, pp. 18-19

Andrade, Ana Luísa, 'O fantasma oculto de José Saramago', *Jornal de Letras*, 20 April 1987, p. 16

Bernardes, Jaime, 'José Saramago no Brasil', *Jornal de Letras*, 31 May 1988, p. 2

Carvalho, Mário Vieira de, '*Blimunda* ou a Paixão de Baltazar, segundo Scarlatti', *Jornal de Letras*, 29 May 1990, pp. 22-23

Conrado, Júlio, 'o refém', *Jornal de Letras*, 8 May 1990, p. 31

Costa, Linda Santos, 'Trocar de rosa', *Jornal de Letras*, 23 May 1989, pp. 16-17

Dacosta, Fernando, 'José Saramago: 'Escrever é fazer recuar a morte é dilatar o espaço da vida', *Jornal de Letras*, 18 January 1983, pp. 16-17

Filipe, Manuel, 'O Intelectual e a consciência colectiva', *O Diabo*, 21 February, 1939

Fragoso, Isabel, 'Caminho' sem atalhos', *Jornal de Letras*, 7 July 1986, p. 16

Fragoso, Isabel, 'Publicar em Portugal: uma aventura quixotesca', *Jornal de Letras*, 14 July 1986, p. 21

Fragoso, Isabel, 'Ricardo Reis teria escrito assim o último ano da sua vida', *Jornal de Letras*, 4 October 1986, p. 19

França, José Augusto, 'Meu caro Saramago', *Jornal de Letras*, 2 June 1992, p. 10

Guennes, Duda, 'Saramago é o "xodó" dos leitores brasileiros', *Jornal de Letras*, 14 September 1987, p. 5

Gomes, António Martins, 'A última tentação de Saramago', *Jornal de Letras*, 28 January 1992, p. 13

Guennes, Duda, 'Saramago é o 'xodó' dos leitores brasileiros', *Jornal de Letras*, 14 September 1987, p. 5

Halpern, Manuel, 'As mutilações do amor', *Jornal de Letras*, 13 November 2002, p. 11

Knopfli, Rui, 'O Nobel e nós', *Jornal de Letras*, 1 December 1992, p. 31

Lepecki, Maria Lúcia, '"Levantado do Chão": história e pedagogia', *Jornal de Letras*, 27 October 1981, pp. 12-13

Lopes, Óscar, 'Um Nobel levantado do chão, *Jornal de Letras*, 21 December 1994, p. 47

Lourenço, António Apolinário, 'José Saramago: A falácia do romance histórico', *Jornal de Letras*, 26 February 1990, p. 9

Lourenço, Eduardo, 'Memorial, terrestre e divino', *Jornal de Letras*, 29 May 1990, p. 24

Luís, Sara Belo, 'Memorial do Convento em Teatro: As figuras de Saramago', *Jornal de Letras*, 19 May 1999, p. 5

Luís, Sara Belo, 'A vez dos livreiros', *Jornal de Letras*, 5 May 1999, pp. 15-21

Martins, Luís Almeida, 'A Jangada de Pedra: finalmente, a condição ibérica', Y *Jornal de Letras*, 10 November 1986, p. 26

Martins, Luís Almeida, 'Epístola aos troianos', *Jornal de Letras* 14 July 1992, pp. 4-5

Matos, Nelson de, 'O que vai mal, piora', *Jornal de Letras*, 5 November 1991, p. 11

Moura, Vasco Graça, 'O ano do prémio de Saramago', *Jornal de Letras*, 28 July 1986, p. 8

Nunes, Maria Leonor, 'José Saramago: O escritor vidente', *Jornal de Letras* 25 October 1995, pp. 15-17

Pedrosa, Inês, 'José Saramago: "A Península Ibérica nunca esteve ligada à Europa"', *Jornal de Letras*, 10 November 1986, pp. 24-26

Praça, Afonso, 'O Evangelho de Saramago na capela do Rato', *Jornal de Letras*, 3 December 1991, p. 5

Real, Miguel, 'José Luís Peixoto: A 2ª Parte de *Levantado do Chão*', *Jornal de Letras*, 13 December 2000, p. 23

Rocha, Clara, 'Saramago e a ficção sobre a ficção', *Jornal de Letras*, 13 November 1984, p. 9

Rocha, Clara, 'Revistas literárias em Portugal a partir dos anos 70', *Jornal de Letras*, 1 May 1988, p. 21

Rodrigues, Urbano Tavares, 'Um romance realista e fabuloso', *Jornal de Letras*, 15 February 1983, p. 26

Saramago, José, 'O poder deve deixar-se molhar...', *Jornal de Letras*, 28 July 1986, p. 8

Saramago, José, 'A necessária reinvenção da língua portuguesa', *Jornal de Letras*, 3 October 1987, pp. 7-8

Saramago, José, 'História e ficção', *Jornal de Letras*, 6 March 1990, pp. 17-19

Saramago, José, 'O (meu) iberismo', *Jornal de Letras*, 31 October 1988, p. 32

Seixo, Maria Alzira, 'José Saramago: O caso da mulher desconhecida', *Jornal de Letras* 22 October 1997, pp. 25-26

Silva, Rodrigues, 'José Saramago, balanço do Ano Nobel: O que vivi foi mais importante que escrever', *Jornal de Letras* 1 December 1999, pp. 6-10

Soares, Mário, 'A Liberdade contra qualquer tutela espúria', *Jornal de Letras*, 14 July 1992, p. 5

Vale, Francisco, '"Neste livro nada é verdade e nada é mentira"', *Jornal de Letras*, 30 October 1984, pp. 2-3

Vasconcelos, José Carlos, 'José Saramago: "Gosto do que este país fez por mim"', *Jornal de Letras*, 18 April 1989, pp. 8-12

Vasconcelos, José Carlos, 'Deus é o mau da fita', *Jornal de Letras*, 5 November 1991, pp. 8-10

Avelar, Idelber, 'O ano 1993: Sobre as Ruínas da Anti-Utopia', *Letras & Letras*, 21 July 1993, pp. 39-42

Cortes, Cristino, 'A Coragem de afirmar em José Saramago', *Letras & Letras*, 4 March 1992, p. 12

Dossier José Saramago, *Letras & Letras*, 19 June 1991, pp. 7-14

Filho, Leodegário A, De Azevedo, ' Saramago ou a ficção que reinventa a história', *Letras & Letras*, 3 April 1991, p. 11

Júnior, Benjamin Abdala, 'O imaginário político em A Jangada de Pedra, de José Saramago', *Letras & Letras*, 1 December 1988, p. 3

Lisboa, Eugénio, 'A Outra face de Saramago', *Letras & Letras*, [n.d.], 1994, pp. 5-6

Martins, Francisco, 'O inverosímil segundo Saramago', *Letras & Letras*, 4 March 1992, p. 13

Oliveira, Rosa Maria, 'A Nova Literatura no contexto do Portugal contemporâneo', *Letras & Letras*, 16 December 1992, p. 10

Sá, Daniel de, 'A exegese segundo Saramago', *Letras & Letras*, 15 April 1992, p. 5

Saramago, José, 'A Propósito de 'Presságios do Sul', *Letras & Letras*, December 1993, p. 24

Almeida, São José, 'História de uma demissão', *Público*, 20 March 1990, p. 6

Coelho, Alexandra Lucas, 'Eu sou estas personagens', *Público Leituras*, 21 October 2000, pp. 1-3

Coelho, Eduardo Prado, 'Não há estrelas, mas o espaço negro que as separa', *Público*, 7 October 2000

Coelho, Eduardo Prado, 'O problema geral das regras de atracção', *Público*, 2 March 2002

Leme, Carlos Câmara, 'Diálogos de Lanzarote', *Público*, 3 February 1997, pp. 22-23

José Luís Peixoto: "Não fechar portas"', <http://www.circulodelei tores.pt/> [accessed in November 2004]

Alves, Clara Ferreira and Francisco Belard, 'Como é diferente o 'best-seller' em Portugal', *Expresso*, 28 January 1984, pp. 35-R-39-R

Alves, Clara Ferreira and Francisco Belard and Augusto M. Seabra, 'A facilidade de ser ibérico', *Expresso*, 8 November 1986, pp. 36-R-38-R

Bethencourt, Francisco, 'Um mercado em mudança', *Expresso*, 28 November 1992, pp. 109-110

Bom, João Carreira, 'A maioria dos portugueses nem lê', Expresso, 12 June 1982, pp. 20-R-21-R

Bom, João Carreira, 'Livro: cada vez mais electrodomesticado', *Expresso*, 12 June 1982, pp. 22-R-23-R

Carneiro, António, 'Quantos analfabetos ainda somos?, *Expresso*, 4 September 1982, pp. 16-R-17-R

Castanheira, José Pedro, "Os jovens matam e comem os velhos", *Expresso Revista*, 27 November 2004, pp. 28-30

Coelho, Eduardo Prado, 'A política dos rios', *Expresso*, 24 April 1982, p. 19-R

Fernandes, José Manuel, 'Guias e roteiros', *Expresso*, 4 August 1984, p. 12

Ferreira, António Mega, 'Saramago e a caldeira da cultura', *Expresso*, 9 May 1992, pp. 83-R-83-R

Guerreiro, António, 'Livros & livros limitados, *Expresso Revista*, 13 April 2001, pp. 74-81

Lepecki, Maria Lúcia, 'Arquitectura e música', *Expresso*, 14 May 1983, p. 35-R

Lepecki, Maria Lúcia, '"Balada da Praia dos Cães":o caso das apropriações indébitas', *Expresso*, 21 May 1983, pp. 38-R-39-R

Lourenço, Eduardo, 'Da Ficção do Império ao Império da Ficção', *Expresso*, 24 April 1984, pp. 26-R-27-R

Louro, Regina, 'Grande prémio para um escritor: quem será, será...', *Expresso*, 1 April 1983, p. 18-R

Seabra, Augusto M., 'José Saramago: o regresso de Ricardo Reis', *Expresso*, 24 November 1984, pp. 31-R-34-R

Soares, Rodrigo, 'A Missão dos novos escritores', *O Diabo*, 21 October, 1939

Soromenho, Ana, 'Um rapaz comum', *Expresso Única*, 25 January 2003, p. 24

'Aumenta procura de livros', *Expresso*, 18 January 1980, p. 4-S

Luís, Sara Belo, 'José Saramago: "Centro comercial é a nova universidade"', *Visão*, 26 October 2000, pp. 19-22

Vasconcelos, José Carlos, 'O mundo de Saramago', *Visão*, 16 January 2003, pp. 92-101

Vitória, Ana, 'Não posso deixar de ser comunista', *Jornal de Notícias*, 17 November 2000, pp. 39-40

Diário de Lisboa, 29 November 1933, p. 16

Spain

A. J., 'Saramago: Nadie puede tener una relación pacífica con Pessoa', *El País*, 18 November 1986

Altares, Guillermo, 'Saramago: 'No encuentro ningún motivo para dejar de ser comunista'', *El País*, 24 May 1993

Cecilia, Carlos G, Santa, 'José Saramago recrea la construcción de un convento y de un aerostato en el Portugal del siglo XVIII', *El País*, 20 February 1986

Cecília, Carlos G, Santa, ''Viaje a Portugal', o recorrido hacia el interior del viajero', *El País*, 5 May 1995

Conte, Rafael, 'En busca del siglo perdido', *El País*, 4 January 1990

Conte, Rafael, 'Imágenes de Saramago', *El País*, 16 December 1989

Cruz, Juan, 'La alegría de Camoens', *El País*, 10 October 1998

Cruz, Juan, 'Los editores portugueses empiezan a publicar a los autores españoles actuales', *El País*, 19 November 1990

Cruz, Juan, 'Pepe y Camoens', *El País*, 11 November 1995

Cruz, Juan, 'Todos somos unos pobres diablos', *El País*, 27 August 1994

Donoso, José, 'Novelas sobre Novelas', *El País*, 12 May 1988

EFE, 'Vargas califica la novela de Saramago de 'anacronismo', *El País*, 30 June 1992

'Coloquio internacional sobre José Saramago', *El País*, 24 August 1996

'Comienzan los debates sobre la literature portuguesa actual', *El País*, 6 June 1989

'Enteramente vivo', *El País*,14 October 1987

'José Saramago', *El País*, 25 November 1991

'La Feria del Libro de Madrid vende 40,000 libros más que en 1994', *El País*, 13 June 1995

'Ser comunista: un estado de espíritu', *El País*, 9 October 1998

García, Javier, 'Receio en Portugal por el protagonismo español en el Nobel de Saramago', *El País*, 14 October 1998

Guardiola, Nicole, 'La crítica de Lisboa elogia la última novela de Saramago', *El País*, 21 April 1989

Guardiola, Nicole, 'El Instituto Cervantes comenzará la en septiembre sus actividades en Lisboa', *El País*, 9 August 1990

Lera, José, 'Las editorials intentan reforzar los lazos entre España y Portugal', *El País*, 2 December 1997

M., G.,/ B., M., 'Saramago acusa a Vargas Llosa de 'mal imitador'', *El País*, 22 August 1990

M., J., 'La balsa del Sur', *El País*, 7 June 1989

Méndez, José, 'Mejor amigos que hermanos', *El País*, 7 June 1989

Moreno, Ricardo, 'Le lengua portuguesa, favorita al Nobel de Literatura', *El País*, 13 October 1994

Posada, Miguel Garcia, 'La ética como princípio creativo', *El País*, 9 October 1998

Rico, Maite, 'Alfaguara reitera su vocación hispanista al celebrar su 30º aniversario', *El País*, 4 June 1994

Rivas, Manuel, 'El autismo ibérico', *El País*, 10 January 1989

Rosell, M, del Mar, 'Novelistas portugueses hablan de su obra en Salamanca', *El País*, 10 March 1984

Rubio, Andrés Fernández, 'Saramago abre las puertas de Portugal', *El País*, 13 May 1995

Samaniego, Fernando, 'Le Feria del Libro llega al million de visitants', *El País*, 9 June 1992

Saramago, José,'Sobre la imposibilidad de este retrato', *El País*, 5 November 1988

Saramago, José, 'Demasiado pronto, demasiado tarde', *El País*, 18 January 1995

Saramago, José, 'El concierto del unicornio', *El País*, 16 April 1989

Saramago, José, 'La herencia cultural del país', *El País*, 27 October 1998

Saramago, José, 'No estamos en manos de Dios', *El País*, 8 February 1992

Sorela, Pedro, 'La alegoría llega cuando describir la realidad ya no sirve', *El País*, 22 May 1996

Sorela, Pedro, 'La novella en que españoles y portugueses navegan juntos', *El País*, 14 October 1987

V., M.Á., 'Portugués ibérico y europeo?', *El País*, 4 February 1998

'Rubalcaba cre que los alumnus salen suficientemente formados de Secundaria', *El Mundo*, 28 October 1997

Rodríguez, Emma, 'Lo efímero de la vida en 'Ensayo sobre la ceguera', *El Mundo*, 16 June 1996

United States of America

Burns, Erik T, 'The Country That is not Spain', *Newsday*, 11 March 2001, p. B13

Eder, Richard, 'A Literary Celebration/ Our Favourite Books of 1997', *Newsday*, 28 December 1997, p. B09

Eder, Richard, 'A Literary Celebration/Our Favourite Books of 1998', *Newsday*, 27 December 1998, p. B09

Eder, Richard, 'In a Dark Time/ José Saramago makes a mysterious epidemic of blindness a riveting descent into hell', *Newsday*, 6 September 1998, p. B09

Eder, Richard, 'Love Lit by a 'Not'', *Newsday*, 25 May 1997, p. G10

Eder, Richard, 'The Island That Sailed Away', *Newsday*, 28 May 1995, p. 37

Eder, Richard, 'Whose Life is It Anyway?', *Newsday*, 23 January 1994, p. 37

Gordon, Emily, 'Flash! The Latest Entertainment news and more', *Newsday*, 9 October 1998, p. A12

'Bestsellers', *Newsday*, 13 December 1998, p. B10

Gilmour, David, 'Adrift in Iberia', *New York Review of Books*, 42, No,15, October 5,1995

Parks, Tim, 'Sightgeist', *New York Review of Books*, 46, No, 3, February 18, 1999

Wood, Michael, 'The Sorcerer's Apprentice', *New York Review of Books*,38, No, 17, October 24, 1991

Goodman, Walter, 'In Mystical Realms', *New York Times*, 5 December 1987, p. 12

Howe, Irving, 'Fueling The Passarola', *New York Times*, 1 November 1987, p. 7

Miller, Andrew, 'Zero Visibility', *New York Times*, 4 October 1998

Mitgang, Herbert, '2 Women, One Poet and the Ghost of Another', *New York Times*, 30 April 1991, p. C17

White, Edmund, 'The Subversive Proofreader', *New York Times*, 13 July 1997, p. 11

Nova, Craig, 'Now You See, Now You Don't', *The Washington Post*, 9 October 1998, p.,D2

See, Carolyn, 'Drifting Slowly, Slowly', *The Washington Post*, 2 June 1995, p. D2

Streitfeld, David, 'Magic Realized: Saramago wins Nobel', *The Washington Post*, 9 October 1998, p. D1

Locke, Richard, 'Novel from the Portuguese', *The Wall Street Journal*, February 5, 1991, p. 20

Schwarz, Stephen, 'Another Nobel Laureate's Stalinist Past', *The Wall Street Journal*, October 14, 1998

Stavans, Ilan, 'A Fisher of Men', *The Nation*, May 16, 1994, pp. 675-676

Brazil

Amador, Paulo, 'Saramago se rende ao culto à palavra – Escritor opta pela experimentação sem abandonar a beleza do texto', *Jornal de Brasil*, 2 April 1994, p. 3

Ribeiro, Marili, 'Autores de "Terra" acreditam que FH pode fazer reforma', *Jornal de Brasil*, 13 April 1997, p. 14

Lluíz, 'Sangrento episódio da Reforma inspira nova peça de Saramago', *Jornal de Brasil*, 7 August 1993, p. 3

Villas-Boas, Luciana, 'Informe/Idéias', *Jornal de Brasil*, 21 May 1994, p. 2

'O que eles estão lendo', *Jornal de Brasil*, 25 September 1993, p. 6

'O que eles estão lendo', *Jornal de Brasil*, 13 May 1995, p. 6

'O que eles estão lendo', *Jornal de Brasil*, 3 June 1995, p. 6

'O que eles estão lendo em Frankfurt', *Jornal de Brasil*, 24 September 1995, p. 6

'Saramago conversa sobre o Ofício de Escritor', *Folha de S,Paulo*, 6 May 1989, <http://www1,folha,uol,com,br/folha/almanaque/entsaramago,htm> [accessed 22 September 2004]

'Frases', *Folha de S,Paulo*, 23 February 1994, p. 5-3

'O que muda nos vestibulares', *Folha de S,Paulo*, 8 November 1994, p. 7

Chicareti, Marco,'Acordo ortográfico cria nova polémica', *Folha de S,Paulo*, 23 February 1993, p. 5-3

Dias, Otávio, 'Llosa é um escritor clássico', *Folha de S,Paulo*, 27 November 1994, pp. 6-7

Fernandes, Bob, 'Monstro da Intolerância voltou, diz Saramago', *Folha de S,Paulo*, 12 January 1994, p. 5-1

Nestrovski, Arthur, 'Os dez mais melancólicos', *Folha de S,Paulo*, 16 October 1994, pp. 6-7

Pisa, Daniel, 'Erramos', *Folha de S,Paulo*, 25 August 1994, p. 5-1

Pascowitch, Joyce, 'Entrelinhas', *Folha de S,Paulo*, 11 December 1994, p. 6-2

Saramago, José, 'Transformação de Lisboa daria um filme', *Folha de S,Paulo*, 22 September 1994, p. 6-17,

Saramago, José, 'Capital abandona marasmo e indiferença', *Folha de S,Paulo*, 18 September 1994, p. 6-17

'Prémio para a Língua Portuguesa', *Estado de Minas*, 9 October 1998

Magalhães-Ruether, Graça, 'Amado e Cabral mereciam o prémio mais do que eu', *Estado de Minas*, 9 October 1998

Köninger, Bete, 'Atenção, este livro leva uma pessoa dentro', <http://www,is-koeln,de/matices/16/16ksaram,htm> [accessed 29 April 2004]

Interviews

Oral Interview with Zeferino Coelho, editor of Editorial Caminho at Caminho on 8 November 2004
Oral Interview with António Lobato Faria, editor of Oficina do Livro at Oficina do Livro on 17 November 2004
Oral Interview with Paul Langridge, director at A,& C, Black, on 20 December 2004

Written Interview with Maria do Rosário Pedreira, publisher of Temas e Debates by e-mail on 23 November 2004
Written Interview with Margaret Jull da Costa, translator of José Saramago's novels into English, by e-mail on 13 March 2005
Written statement by Ilídio Matos, literary agent, by e-mail on 3 May 2005
Written Interview with Carola Hermelin, of the Swedish Academy of the Nobel Prizes, by e-mail on 18 and 22 November 2004

Documents

List of the Writers who received honours by the President sent by the Chancellery of the Honours of the Presidency of the Portuguese Republic in April 2005
List of the Writers rewarded with the *Cidade de Lisboa*, the *Município de Lisboa* Prize and *Eça de Queiroz* Literary Prizes given by Dra, Maria Teresa Santos, Assessor at the Lisbon City Hall in March 2005
Constituição Política da República Portuguesa de 1933
Decree-Law No.25 495, on 13 June 1935
Decree-Law no.27603 of 29th March 1937
Decree-Law no.36969 of 27th October 1952

Archives

'Gabinete de Leitura', PIDE/DGS File CI (1), no.14, Pt.5, ANTT (Torre do Tombo, Lisbon)
'Livrarias', PIDE/DGS, File no.D, Inf. 11, Pasta 15, 41.A (Torre do Tombo, Lisbon)
'1º Congresso dos Editores Pedagógicos Socialistas', PIDE/DGS, no.690/-SC-CI (2), Pasta 136 (Torre do Tombo, Lisbon)
'Associação Mundial de Escritores', PIDE/DGS, no.1812 – SR/58 (Torre do Tombo, Lisbon)
'Associação Portuguesa de Escritores', PIDE/DGS, no.69/73 – CI (2) (Torre do Tombo, Lisbon)
José Saramago's Papers, BN Esp. No.45 (National Library, Lisbon)
José Rodrigues Miguéis's Literary Estate, BN F.R. 132 1-30 (National Library, Lisbon)

Surveys

Analfabetismo em diferentes países (Lisbon: Instituto Nacional de Estatística, 1915)
Anuário Estatístico (Lisbon: Instituto Nacional de Estatística, 1941)
Anuário Estatístico (Lisbon: Instituto Nacional de Estatística, 1960)
Deane, Marjorie, *United Kingdom Publishing Statistics*, Rpt, The Journal of the Royal Statistical Society, CXIV, Part iv (1951)
Estatística de Educação 1951-1952 (Lisbon: Instituto Nacional de Estatística, 1952)
Giles, R, ed., *Social Statistics of Great Britain* (Birmingham: Clearway Publishing Company 1969)
Instituto Nacional de Estatística, *Census*, vol 1, 1940
Instituto Nacional de Estatística, *Census*, vol 3, I, 1950
Instituto Nacional de Estatística, *Census*, vol 5, II, 1960

Rendeiro, Maria Margarida, *Survey to the Portuguese Habits of the Purchase of Portuguese Novels,* October-December 2001 [unpublished]

UK Printing and Publishing Industry Statistics (Surrey: Pira International, 1993)

UNESCO, *Public Expenditure on Education Statistical Report prepared by the Department of Social Sciences, Statistical Divisions in 1953,* Available on http://unesdoc.unesco.org/images/0012/001278/ 127876eb.pdf [Accessed in March 2007]

Translations of Portuguese Quotations

Chapter 2

p. 35, n. 1: 'But the State's fortune, a necessary requirement to rescue Nation from total ruin and disorder, is not enough to sustain material and moral renovation and it does not ensure stability, the future of accomplished work. That must be based on the reform of education'.

p. 37, n. 8: '[…] we have respected the believer's conscience and have consolidated religious peace – We do not question God […] We have resolutely placed nationalism at the indestructible basis of the New State […] we do not question the Mother Country. We do not question authority […] it is a fact and a need […]we do not question family. Man is raised in it, and generations are brought up in it […] we do neither question Work, both as a right nor as an obligation'.

p. 37, n. 9: 'The Education to be implemented, at a time of national rebirth, has to start from an act of faith in the Portuguese nation and be inspired by healthy nationalism. You have to love and get to know Portugal – its past heroic greatness, its present of material and moral possibilities and foresee it in its future of progress, beauty and harmony'

p. 38, n. 11: 'I consider more urgent the creation of vast elites than the necessity to teach the people how to read. Because major domestic problems must be solved by elites and not by masses. Because major domestic problems must be solved by elites that comprehend the masses'

p. 39, n. 16: [Virgínia de Castro Almeida] 'The most beautiful, the strongest and healthiest part of Portuguese soul resides in those 75 per cent of illiterates'; [João Ameal] Portugal does not need schools […] Teaching how to read is to adulterate origins'; [J. Pereira Coutinho] 'Happy are those who do not know how to read!'

p. 45: 'However, the comment on the relative success of this attempt is that it was not modest. It soon resulted in systematic and expensive fabrication of an exemplary 'lusitanidade', covering the present and the past chosen according to its archaic and reactionary mythology that little by little substituted the image that was to a greater or lesse extent appropriate to the actual country at the beginning of the New State by an ideological, sociological and cultural fiction unrealistic than that proposed by the Republican ideology. It was the official fiction, an uncontrolled image and incontrovertible image that of a country without problems, a peaceful oasis, model of nations and of the ideal solution that reconciled capital and labour, order and authority with a harmonious development of society.

p. 52: 'an impressive number of villagers made mass emigration a symbol and the ultimate expression to complete this process The organic nationalism of the old regime favoured the clear denationalization of thousands of Portuguese'.

p. 53: 'We have to close in, on this side and beyond the sea, and move on together prudently but surely. Division may be fatal to us all. Splitting will irremediaby weaken us'

Chapter 3

p. 57, n. 3: 'It should correct the idea that each one involuntarily creates of national reality, arguing on the doorstep, about what everybody should know about the same facts of the whole of the Nation's way of living. And, externally, providing those who speak and write about Portugal, with enough material in order not to distort truth unconsciously and not make our kind welcoming be broadcast as evidence of moral inferiority'

p. 59: 'But let us make the Spiritual Policy, intelligent and constant, consolidating the discovery of Portugal by the Portuguese, giving it stature, significance and eternity [...] the Spirit, after all, is also matter, a precious substance, the raw material of the soul of men and the soul of people [..].'

p. 60: 'It is impossible in this conception of life, and society, and indifference for the writer's or artist's mental and moral formation, and for the character of its work; it is impossible to socially value in the same way what he builds and what he destroys, what he educates and what he demoralizes, the creators of civic or moral energies and the nostalgic dreamers of discouragement and decay'.

p. 61: 'As writers we can read and admire certain unconformist literary compositions, which we consider dangerously debilitating. As leaders of an organism of the New State, we cannot accept or reward certain works'.

p. 62: 'We have been making a Revolution for 36 years; we have a doctrine, we stand up for moral values and rules of law that we have institutionalized [...] We are going through a period when ideological conflicts embrace practically all the forms of thought [...] it seems right that the Regime ought to stand up vigorously for what is correct because we are living an abnormal period, war, that is affecting us from outside and that inside, some, even if they may be a few, support'.

p. 64: 'Portuguese provincialism – which does not need, for its definition, abundant examples or strong accusations – is limited, internally, to the unconditional obedience to a canon. The canon is imposed, divulged, multiplied, becomes ordinary. The 'canonical' reader appreciates stereotypes. And the cultural producer, if he does not want to be an outsider, produces a consumable stereotype'

p. 67, n. 27: 'despite acknowledging remarkable quality in some of the works submitted', considered that 'in none of them did they find all the requirements laid down for that competition and its high demands and aims to which their decision should correspond'

p. 75: 'But some books appear in each section, chosen among many published, to be permanent, representative, and with its graphic aspect taken into account. Of each author only one work is included in each section nor books published before 1926 except for some important reprints.'

p. 82: 'The small size of Portuguese companies is not able, now and in the future, to allow the approach to international markets to develop as a healthy stimulus, in so far as not to prejudicing the results they desire'

p. 85, n. 67: 'a writer widely appraised by readers with poor spiritual resources', 'looks for suggestive motives, privileging disbelief, aversion to a leader or a wealthy person, and fomenting social disrespect'.

Chapter 4

p. 94, n. 13: [António Maria Pereira, Parceria António Maria Pereira], 'The choice of manuscripts is often based on hunches, a nose for what is in demand; [Manuel Rodrigues, Editorial Minerva], 'There is a nose, a perspicacity I make good use of'; [António de Sousa Pinto], 'The Portuguese publisher is usually poor, and its range of action is always limited [...] everybody moans – authors, publishers – it is so confusing! Everybody reproaches but no one is right'.

p. 96, n. 19: 'To be quite honest, Dr Vilela exclaims, [Lobo Viella, Editorial Gleba], we are all writers in our spare time, and not professional ones. Novels may suffer from a lack of constant work, from a certain literary professionalism! The Portuguese have more or less been poor writers of fiction'.

p. 104, n. 32: 'Therefore, a programme for several achievements was defined in favour of the writers' standing and interests, of creating conditions and opportunities for wider communication and solidarity among them.'

p. 109, n. 44: 'freedom was stifled, the greatest motivation to creative intelligence was removed, the people lacked enlightenment about their own problems, which should be the intellectuals' primary mission, and intellectuals lacked the due sovereignty which can only be conferred by the people'.

p. 110, n. 45: 'fear guards the vineyard [...] fear has mostly dominated the present-day *status quo*. Fear may also be its best guardian. Not only in Portugal but also in any country where a regime took over power by force and governs by force, that powerful enemy of the soul grew to the point of erasing all expectations'

p. 110: 'It is urgent that we realize that new writers, integrated in a new historical chain and illuminated by a new conception of the life, are not to be detached from the major struggle involving all fronts of opposing interests that express the irreducible contradiction of present-day society [...] novelists, essayists, critics, poets, polemicists and translators – everyone must understand the mission they have been assigned'

p. 111: 'I published chronicles and stories on the Ribatejo, taking refinement for style, in an amalgam of Romantic poetry and Fialho [de Almeida], baroque style and a certain melodramatic tone that corresponded, on the one hand, to the false idea that "to write difficult" would be the supreme objective of a real writer, and, on the other hand, to the exaltation which I felt about the problems of the characters I cherished due to family background and a premeditated consciousness'.

p. 111: 'Censorship compelled the writer to make his pen a subtle weapon, of harsh subtlety. On the other hand, from the reader's the point of view, it compelled him to read in between the lines, in the half words, to strive to apprehend what the writer wanted but he was not allowed to say at ease'

p. 113: 'The Foundation set up a Board of Reading, composed of people who have long been outstanding, not only because of their culture, but also for the balance of their ideals. It is fitting, however, that they represent various trends in contemporary thought in order to eliminate any risk of literary, philosophical, social or political proselytising'.

Chapter 5

p. 124: 'Only in 1978, does the educational reform state clearly that the State does not have the right to intervene in the contents of education and culture on behalf of any ideology'

p. 124: '8. Cultural and Educational Policy and Research

Mobilization of efforts for the eradication of illiteracy and promotion of culture, particularly in rural areas.

Development of the educational reform, including the role of education in establishing a genuinely democratic national awareness, and the need to frame school in the discussion of Portuguese society

[...]

h) Promotion of cultural and artistic activities, especially literature, theatre, cinema, plastic arts and music, and also media as indispensable vehicles to the development of people's culture.'

p. 125 n. 13 'It is within the framework of Cultural Revolution, through the application of military and civilian potential in technical, human and material fields, that people will be mobilised to the Revolution. Practice is evidence of this obvious thought'.

p. 126, n.15: 'Having been informed that there is a significant number of books and magazines on fascist issues at some school libraries, I demand that a memo is circulated, determining the destruction of any such publication and that a copy of each is kept to document the Regime.'

p. 126, n. 16: 'That policy [bourgeoisie democratic Project] has been kept ambiguous, enabling harmless wide-ranging projects and reform. Therefore, on the one hand, unplanned maximum-ranging campaigns (from literacy campaigns to the MFA's campaigns of cultural dynamization) were set out and, on the other hand, few legislative amendments were introduced. [...] Lisbon goes to rural areas to teach, on the idealised assumption that has not much to learn and that popular culture is folklore. [...] Result is either chaos or reforming and inter-classes projects, such as the well-known campaigns that only conceal certain objectives and attempts of cultural and partisan dictatorship with no real revolutionary purpose'

p. 127: 'Transformation of social order has to imply cultural transformation – and that is not a simple and simplistic idea of serving culture to people or, even more difficult, take people to culture. These two paternalist and tranquillising principles (those who regard culture as a lift) have to be fought against by a new humanist condition of culture, it must be of humanist responsibility'.

p. 128: 'Lieutenant-Colonel Arnão Metelo, one of the senior ranks of the Board of Left Wing Military said later: "The military section of the PCP can not be clearly identified. We formed a group that, inclusively, was more radical than the PCP itself, a disciplined party that followed the principles elaborated and planned by the Central Committee; but we were, broadly speaking, sufficiently romantic and did not possess such characteristic. The problem of the left wing military with the PCP was complicated because all of us had quite different ideas and aims and we also were different because some of us belonged to the Navy, others to the Army, etc. Sometimes we reacted badly due to a certain spirit of bureaucracy and of democratic centralism that we found in some military and this did not please me because I foresaw a certain control of extra-military machinery.'''

p. 129, n. 21: 'We have to revive national values and Portuguese culture. There will not be any democratic future in a country which does not do justice to its traditional values, respect its works of art and culture, value its scientific research centres without any ideological prejudice. Genuine Portuguese values must replace a certain pseudocultural propaganda at the service of a certain ideological totalitarianism'.

p. 130: 'After that phase, we should have found a national project of a truly popular socialist vocation merging the vital interests of the community, partly lost because of ideological extremism, not deeply rooted in Portuguese tradition; in short, a perception of the Nation's dimension, loaded of great remembrances and cruel wounds. We lacked imagination.'

p. 132: 'Commiserating stances ignoring our achievements and underestimating our people's capacities, sentencing the Portuguese to inferiority, are pointless'

p. 136, n. 43: 'We are moved by our wish of promoting history valuing amongst the young generations. We especially believe that it is possible to approach history in various points of view and that each era adds new topics and points of view to knowledge about the past heritage'.

Chapter 6

p. 149: 'Present-day political opponents of the President wonder what is really left. The most obvious answer is the symbolic value of importance and attention given to the first figure of State by producers and culture; exemplary behaviour and acts; highlighting debate and companionship as determining factors that cannot be underestimated or forgotten.'

p. 153: 'There is not any other way to take books to people, although there are books which do not need media to find their way; nevertheless they find it slowly. A commercial does not sell a book'.

p. 155: 'The real writing of the Revolution cannot be by by Namoras, V.Ferreiras, Abelairas, Agustinas, Almeida Farias, Maria Velho da Costa and Nuno Bragança; these are writers who have clearly given us some of the most evident literary reflections emerged from or related to the Revolution. However, none are the Revolution's literary generation, expressing the vital and imaginative feeling of its own time, to whom time is an open story, discovery and readjustment to being, living, choosing, loving and dying (at least in fiction).

p. 160: 'JL is undoubtedly a challenge. Against many things, amongst them are obscurantism, intolerance, pointless fighting out of a certain mental underdevelopment. And in favour of others and, amongst them, a change of minds and cultural transformations that the 25 April did not accomplish.'

Chapter 7

p. 171, n.4: 'If I do not include that book in my bibliography, that is because it was written by another person, someone who was on his way to become a person. I do not refuse it, I just leave it where it is, almost in my adolescence, on the brink of experience and life'.

p. 172: 'José Saramago represents a solid and coherent literary project. Fifty years after a novel which practically did not exist, we can see that that project was slowly built and rooted to be able to give a life to further novels: those which are not related to Terra do Pecado (Land of Sin), but probably would not have existed without it.'

p. 177: 'Censors never approached me because of my literary production until 25 April. As journalist and contributor, first at A Capital and at Jornal do Fundão and then at Diário de Lisboa, where I wrote for the 'Editorial' section [...] I learned rage when I saw words I had written and ideas being stabbed. [...] I also remember the time I worked at Editorial Estúdios Cor, when we were approached by the PIDE agents who came to arrest books'

p. 178: 'I will never forget 1 May, 28 September, 11 March the MFA general meeting in Tancos, the months I was deputy director at Diário de Notícias. I will never forget the Alentejo and the industrial areas. I will never forget what we called Hope'

p. 178: 'The worst of all [...] was the day I faced cold, free and merciless indifference, coming from those who had the duty to give me a hand. Life is full of cases, randoms and contradictions and maybe the life of a writer started then.

p. 179: 'From the first day there were attacks and unkindness: they were predictable but did not divert us from the plans and from compliance with ultimate purposes. A skilful and quick manoeuvre of the right wing military thwarted Revolution and took Diário de Notícias (probably) to go back to well-known tracks, against the will of the politically aware majority of its workers.

p. 179: 'This Government does not understand the country it is supposed to rule. Or maybe its understanding is so little that errors are gradually accumulated.'

p. 181: '(To use simple terms, the writer would explain, it is only the story of a painter who decides to write. And it is also, for this and other reasons, which have to be stated in their time and space, a political book). Actually, man is not a specialized and specializing animal.'

p. 181: 'Major topics on aesthetics are scrutinized in *Manual*, and temptations that Neo Realism offers to the novelist of our time are exorcized. The novelist is committed to finding his own way to narrate contemporary stories in suitable terms and different from those of the prestigious discourse of the past.'

p. 181: 'Objecto Quase is a timeless book, nobody holds an identity card : the reverse of the situation is practised from the first page, although the opening short story tells one familiar to us all: "one day, Salazar fell off a chair..." The writer believes that by using a certain abstraction clear reality emerged.'

p. 184: 'A writer is a man like others: he dreams. And my dream was to say when I finished this book: "that is the Alentejo". We wake up from all dreams and now I am not before a fulfilled dream but of dreaming a possible way. That is why I will write: "that is a book on the Alentejo". A book, a simple novel, people, conflicts, some love affairs, much sacrifice and hunger, victories and disasters, learning change and death.'

p. 185: 'I will ask: is it possible and desirable to be a writer in Portugal? Well, Portuguese writers who want to live in peace in a world of convenience and interests, have to retain the feeling of perpetual gratitude'.

p. 189: 'If literature is still of some use here, that is if it is more than just for some to write what others will read, it has to be regained because our society is in peril of becoming mute because of the audio visual. There is the risk of a shrinking minority being able to speak and a growing majority only being able to listen and not being able to understand what is being spoken.'

p. 189: 'If this book was to have a sub-title, that might be 'Contribution to the diagnosis of the Portuguese disease'. I do not know exactly which disease, because I am not even identifying which diagnosis; I am just contributing to establishing one; but I believe there is a Portuguese disease, not only in Lisbon – despite it being more acute there.'

p. 190: 'When I say correcting History, I do not mean correcting historical facts because those are not the novelist's responsibility. He is assigned introducing some disturbance into what seemed unquestionable; in other words, replacing for what might have happened.'

p. 196: 'If my books become well-known abroad, that fact does not make me less attached to what I do and what I am here. I like what this country has done for me: maybe that is what is, after all, in my novels.'

p. 199: 'He is part of a group of writers who are important to my reading background. And what we read is important for what we write.'

p. 199: 'Nenhum Olhar is, 20 years after the failure of Mau-Tempo family and the struggle of Germano Vidigal, the second part of Levantado do Chão, that is, after the political-historical disaster of the Agrarian Reform, it is the perfect picture of an Alentejo which, after having dreamed 'rising from the ground', expelling the wealthy and fulfilling the ultimate dream of universal ancient egalitarianism, wakes up in timeless immobility, in which its characters under a blue sky and on a brown plain, both as desert pictures, are meaningful to life in continuous abnormality'.

p. 200: 'The Alentejo is a land much discussed in Portuguese literature [...] above all it was discussed by the Neo-Realist writers who took the people of the Alentejo as all the people. And I tried to reach every person from the Alentejo. Just because a person is from a certain area does not mean that that area will characterize him or her.

p. 200: If *Levantado do Chão*, in 1980, showed the new style of José Saramago, who two years later published *Memorial do Convento*, *Nenhum Olhar* will surely be (as long as José Luís Peixoto's rhetoric and delirious poetic writing are controlled) a promise of a great new writer looking for his *Memorial do Convento*

Chapter 8

p. 209, n. 10: 'In Brazil, where knowledge of the literature coming from an country akin is usually confined to Fernando Pessoa, Saramago is the most popular Portuguese writer and he has had his books in bestsellers' lists for weeks'

p. 210: 'I am inside and outside the Party – outside when I am not in direct relation and inside when there is the moment, when I am on its behalf –, let us say there is perfect loyalty, perfect responsibility and perfect freedom. I mean, I write exactly what I want, exactly how I want and there is no prior determination, guidance, warning or advice, I use all the words whether coming or not from my Party; and there is a very simple explanation; I am genuinely what I am and I also genuinely believe that my party is not competent in literature'

p. 211: 'You can only expect anathema and blasphemy against religious codes from an atheist. However, from the atheist José Saramago, we can expect na attack to religious topics as ways to redimension his fictional space.'

p. 212: 'Some would say that those historical details are of little interest. I agree but it would be very interesting – at least to me – not only to know but also to see how Lisbon has been changing since remote ages.

p. .213: 'My Lisbon has always been that of poor neighbourhoods and later when circumstances and changes in life moved me to other rivers and environments, the remembrance I most wanted to keep was the Lisbon of my early days [...] It is enough for me that Lisbon is what it should be: joyful, educated, modern, clean, organized, retaining its ancient soul.'

p. 213: 'There is one common good, language, and that is the most important we left in Brazil. Language was the unifying link in this immense country. The question is whether the Portuguese and the Brazilian are aware of this common good in this world we live.

p. 214: For example: what about publishing the innovative works on history being written and that focus on everyday life and raises the so called history of mentality, which is new in Brazil and is important and interesting to historians and reaches a wider public.

Appendix 1:
Interview with Zeferino Coelho at Editorial Caminho's Head Office on 8th November 2004

1. How does Editorial Caminho get manuscripts? Is it through literary agents or do writers themselves send them to you?

We mostly publish Portuguese speaking writers; In this field, writers do not employ literary agents and approach publishers directly.

2. And how do you decide on manuscripts? Do you try to track the writer's personal style?

Most come by mail. Probably around six hundred offerings every year. And then, there are people we know and they approach us personally; but the large majority comes by mail. We read them. If we think the manuscript is good, we publish it. If we believe that it does not bring anything new, we turn it down. This is basically how it works.

3. There are publishing houses oriented towards the publication of debutants; there are others which publish writers who have achieved a certain literary stature. Does Editorial Caminho follow this second orientation?

I beleive we try to reach a balance. Having the writers we publish already, we pursue the publication of new texts worth being published. For example, Ondjaki, a new and talented writer, and Gonçalo M. Tavares. We try to be balanced. And we publish just a few new ones a year. This is basically because we cannot afford it. But we are not desperately trying to find new writers.

4. How do you take care of your writers and their careers throught the year? Are there different procedures depending on the writers or whould you say that there is a pattern?

We believe we approach all writers alike. But they are different; we try to follow the same procedures. But the most important thing is his writing; it is not what the publisher does. If his writing is good, so the publisher should do what he is supposed to do to get results. Of course, if I am dealing with the launch of a new Saramago's book, I can assume that there will be 1,500 people in a room but I am not going to assume the same about Ondjaki. We do not take less care of a lesser known writer than another better known.

5. Has your publishing policy defined a certain reader's profile?
No, there are certain people who are interested in certain books and others prefer other books, particularly as far as essays are concerned. There is a book on the Medieval Portuguese-Galician literature which appeals only to people who are interested in that topic. As far as literature is concerned, writers do not address a particular reader. As far as publishers are concerned, if a certain book is interesting to some people, there are promotional tools to reach them. However, I do not believe that our books are classifiable. As regards popular writers, we are not very impressed by them. That happens a lot in France and in Spain: publishers approach a media personality and ask her to write something... but we are not interested in that.

6. How do you try to encourage your readers and develop your marketing activities?
Well, marketing activities are expensive, everything we want to do to create impact is very expensive. Commercials are expensive and the price is disproportionate in relation to the book's budget. I can spend on dealing with sales instead of spending on that. Even with no losses and that would mean we are spending more than what we receive. There will come a day when we will have no more money and cannot afford to publishing books. It is not easy because print advertisements are very expensive, TV commercials are even more expensive In the old days, books had a special status, but not anymore. This happened in the 1990s, with the establishment of private TV channels. There was an official decree imposing a discount of 90 per cent in commercials advertising books – and that was very good and it was widely praised; then, the discount fell to 50 per cent and that made a big change. Furthermore, in the old days, we could choose the broadcasting schedule. When the discount fell to 50 per cent, we could choose the schedule but did not have the right to the discount, or vice versa. Or we could ask for the slot after the news, but they would say it was taken and put us on at 2 or 3 a.m.. In addition, there

were more and more channels (with private televisions including cable television) and zapping made it hard for commercials on books to be effective.Nobody watches them. But commercials used to have substantial impact in the old days, though. So, as far as (paid) marketing is concerned, we advertise in two ro three monthly publications (and Jornal de Letras is one of them) publicizing releases.We also send mail leaflets to people, put things on the web, but impact varies We organize book-signing sessions and do some PR in the press because we want the press to review our books and interview our writers.So that's it, we can't afford more money for releases because if we did, we could not afford to publish the actual book.

Surveys show that reading habits are poor; how do you assess purchase?
They have improved consistently in recent years as far as I am concerned. And this is not something we can compare; it has to be shown in the long run. We have to see what it was like twenty, thirty, let's say forty years ago. We buy more than we read and that is quite natural. There are many more books worth being read than those we actually have time to read. And those I bought were good purchases. Reading rates worry publishers because they assume that the higher it is, the more we read. There are several problems and the country's tradition [of reading habits]is one of them. But the major problem is affordability. We can compare reading rates with those in Spain, France, England but we have to add affordability. If we do not add it, we do not have the real picture. If a book is cheaper in Germany and a German earns twice or three times more than a Portuguese or if a Portuguese spends in one book the amount of money a Spaniard would spend on two books, thus affordability in Portugal is lower and that makes me conclude that Portuguese readings habits are poor but not catastrophic.And there is also the problem of population: there are forty million people in Spain, and 60 million in England, whereas we are just ten million. So, here it is not catastrophic and hasgradualy risen to the European average. On the other day, I was speaking to an English publisher and she told me that she saw many expensive cars in Portugal. So I asked her if there were not expensive cars in England too and she replied there were and argued that [Portu-

guese] people could buy more books instead of cars. So I told her that we have a different problem. Imagine, I told her, that you publish books to a population the size of Greater London and she was surprised and said that they would not be able to make it. And that is London where purchasing power is higher… but if we underestimate that, print-runs would fall because we are talking about ten million people. That is the basic issue and nobody talks about it. I am sure that if the English purchasing power fell to Portuguese levels, so would book buying.

How do you try to increase the number of readers?
Developing a good relationship with libraries, doing book launches, we organize dozens, if not hundreds of them every year. We publish a magazine addressed to youngsters which is quite successful. We have a nucleum there (at schools) and reading is extremely important; that is where we can work effectively. Readers are out there but how do you get through to them? Well, that is difficult but schools and teachers have done a great job in promoting reading.

9. Leaving commercial issues aside, does your publishing house try to shape society? Caminho publishes many essays, discussing the past and present-day issues, and novels too. Do you see yourself as doing a service for society? Moreover, you work with schools.
We do not give up that role.If I am offered something consistent such as publishing Portuguese Philosophical Thought in five volumes, I find it hard to turn it down. Even thoug I know that will require a lot of work and will not sell much… if we do not make a loss, that is fine.Maybe it will but still we find it hard to turn that offer down.

10. How do you arrange interviews and events with your writers?
Well, we arrange book launches because they are in our remit: you just have to find a room and send invitations to people. Then, we have to make the part that has to have some impact: get newspapers to advertise the book in their literary sections. That is very important. Sometimes we are not successful, but still it is utterly important. We have to be very attentive and that has an effect on book sales. It is easier to get coverage for a book by Saramago than

342

to a lesser-known writer. Quality is the most important feature because if it is a quality book sooner or later it will work. But thereare not many literary sections and are not very relevant in newspapers. We wish every newspaper had a literary section. Newspapers report yesterday's news but, broadly speaking, with books things do not work that way. Some days ago, *Expresso* published a very favourable review on a book we had published nine or ten months ago. This happens a lot. But books have a short life at bookshops, around two or three months, and when news come out, the book has gone. The book life cycle is very short, no more than three months and of the book works, when it is a bestseller, otherwise, it is returned to publishers.

11. Are there writers more suitable to overseas markets? What are the differences?
Yes. Portugal is a small country, little known abroad, even less so in the past, but anyway, when people think about Portugal, they think about beaches. Then there is a minority who really knows but that is a tiny minority. Most people do not know what happens here. A good part of literature published here focuses on what we are, our problems, and that is very limiting because it does not appeal foreigners. The Portuguese are supposed to write about Portuguese issues but the capacity to transpose that limit is rare to find and thus that writing interests only the Portuguese. Saramago has evolved to issues that have nothing to do with Portuguese issues, with the Alentejo, to his *Ensaio sobre a Cegueira* – realing with more universal topics and more appealing to other readers. As regards fiction, we have plenty books translated, Mário Carvalho, Almeida Faria (he has now stopped writing), Gonçalo Tavares. Poetry is more difficult but it is being translated slowly. The Nobel helped, though there was some translated already.

12. Which is the easiest market to get through to?
Spain not always. Mainly France, Italy and sometimes Germany. England and the United States are very difficult. The Anglo-Saxon world is very closed to translations, a world apart. There is always an Englishman everywhere who might give the impression that they are very open-minded, but they are not. They are very closed.

And it is difficult to persuade an English publisher that something interesting was published here. And English readers are also difficult to persuade; if they see a non-English name on the cover of a book, they will not buy it. Even those who publish [foreign/Portuguese] books claim it is very difficult and sooner or later a senior person decides to discontinue the series because it will not sell.

13. How do you get a book of yours to be translated? At what particular phase of a writer's career?
When an author is a debutant, it is not easy. It is easier if he is well knwon because his press fortune is bigger. And just because a writer did well here, it does not mean that he will do well somewhere else. However, saying that he did well here helps a lot. It is not enough to say that a certain book is very good because the publisher wants to know whether sales were good and if readers found him or her good. But there is more of an opening than about thirty years ago. Gonçalo Tavares has a French-Swiss edition and has negotiated contracts with Italy and Germany. We also have the difficulty of the language, they [foreigners] do not speak Portuguese and those who speak or know about Portugal are usually small publishing houses. They entrust the manuscript to people who can read Portuguese and have to trust their decision whether to publish it or not. As regards Saramago, the first success was *Memorial do Convento*, the first translation was Italian and then it was promoted in France, Germany, Spain, Scandinavia. Now publishers want to publish Saramago and his career is more cosolidated. The United States are very important because books are promoted from there to everywhere and Saramago's critical fortune is excellent, especially after *Ensaio sobre a Cegueira*, which was very favourably reviewed. Two months ago, John Updike reviewed Saramago's work and tha had impact.

14. As regards Saramago, were he younger would he have had the same acceptance and the same publicity?
I cannot identify a big difference. Saramago used to write books that nobody read. Then he wrote *Levantado do Chão* and things changed and continued with *Memorial do Convento*, a key in his evolvement. Saramago was little known, he was more known as a

344

journalist and less as a writer. *Memorial do Convento* produced some kind of enchantment; the monastery, the sorceress, that elaborate prose helped to draw foreigners' attention to him. I do not think age made a difference.

15. Was he marketed as a Portuguese writer?
He was marketed as a writer who had written a good book. Our goal is to have it published overseas, and if possible by a big publishing house. For example, publishing with Carcanet is good if you cannot to do so with a larger one; it is excellent because it is better to have Carcanet than nothing but the book remains in a ghetto and is published with a subsidy and circulates in a very restricted field – only among those who are interested in Portuguese issues and not the wide public. If the book is good it does not matter whether it comes from here or there. In Italy, the first edition was printed by Feltrinelli, a publishing house which publishes to the wide public and then it was promoted to other parts. In England, I do not know in detail, but Jonathan Cape published it first and subsequently Harvill on account of takeovers that happen all the time.

16. How was Caminho set up?
The first books were published in 1977 but the publishing house was set up in 1975. We all knew each other; I had worked at a publishing house, Vítor Branco (who is no longer alive) had also worked at another. I was already here when the first books came out, though I cannot say I was here from the first day. The founder was Francisco Melo, who had been my colleague at university and had also worked in the book industry before 25 April . I had worked before then at Inova, publishing house and we decided to do what we knew, work with books. I cannot say we were the first publishing house setting up after 25 April since a lot happened at the same time, but we were among the first ones. As for the name, it simply popped up then; since there was nothing better, it was accepted.

17. Was ideology what got you together?
That too. First, we like books. Then, Francisco Melo and I knew each other from school, Vítor Branco was an undergraduate in

Economics and I was an undergraduate in Philosophy, we all lived in the same 'República' [student residence] and we set up a book society (it still exists), Unicer, and that was a way to do politics because we merely had to go to the notary. Setting up a publishing house required getting authorization from the Government which obviously would not do. So, all you had to do was go to the notary and start working and see how it went. And then there were ideological issues, because we were colleagues and political comrades. That's natural, because my social friends are the ones I share political views with.

18. What is Caminho's share in the book market?
I do not know exactly. If you pick five publishing houses like ours, Caminho will be there. Of course, you will have to exclude publishing houses specializing in school books and Círculo de Leitores [book club] which is completely different. Probably you will find Europa-América, Presença and Dom Quixote. Only recently has Bertrand become more active after quite a long lull.

19. As far as interviews are concerned, do you advise or orient writers?
No, there is a kind og guidance as regards the type of events the author attends but as far as interviews are concerned, the publishing house does not interfere. When Saramago's latest book was launched, [Ensaio sobre a Lucidez] I was scared because I had read it and knew on the spot what people would see. Saramago has many enemies, political, literary, there is envy of his succcess but he is not afraid of them and he says what he wants. I was afraid that only a very small news item about his book would come out given the content. So I had the idea of arranaging a debate; involving different people – the press covered it, radio broadcasted it live and things worked.

20. And as regards events overseas?
Saramago has a completely different approach in Brazil and in Spain (even taking into account the period before his departure) from that in the United States and in the United Kingdom. As far as book launches are concerned, we cooperate, depending on the type of event and on how easily Saramago functions in those countries and on the language and contacts.

[During our conversation, I ran out of recording tape and had to take notes of Zeferino Coelho' answer. Therefore, his last statements are reported according to my notes.]

Zeferino Coelho stated that *Levantado do Chão* was Saramago's first novel sto stir the conscience of readers and that Memorial do Convento captivated more readers. *Levantado do Chão* focussed on the Agrarian Reform and because it came to represent a historical landmark which deeply affected the Portuguese, there was a female author (not identified by Coelho) who refused to be published by Caminho, arguing that she had lost land in the Ribatejo because of the Agrarian Reform. Quoting Eduardo Prado Coelho, Zeferino Coelho said that *Memorial do Convento* extended the social basis of support for Saramago because he moved away from that topic.

Appendix 2:
Interview with Marcelo Teixeira (Editorial Coordinator) e António Lobato Faria (Editor) at Oficina do Livro on 17 November 2004

1. Oficina do Livro is a recent publishing house, who has set it up?
[António Lobato Faria] Gonçalo Bulhosa and me. Gonçalo had worked at a bookshop with his brothers for many years and then moved to Difel. I worked also at Difel as advisor to the board. We drew up a project that we believed filled in the market's needs uncovered by other publishers. We offered that project to Difel and they turned it down. We decided to resign and set up another publishing house in 1999. By 2000 we were being supported by a major company, Lusomundo and later by PT. We have always preserved publishing and management autonomy, though.

2. What is the mission of Oficina ?
[António Lobato Faria] Money is the mission. [Laughs]. Working with books is not financially rewarding. It is rewarding only when you like to work with books. We had the project of setting up a publishing house to promote books, make them popular and of mass consumption, leisure and we wanted to make books that made history because that is added value. People do not understand this. In the short run, if we do not have quality books, we will be punished for that. I am not interested in selling many books by authors like Margarida [Rebelo Pinto] because I know that they will only last a year, maybe two. [...]

There is one thing I have learned as a publisher: in order to become a author you have to enjoy writing. There is also another important detail: Gonçalo and I have always been self-conscious about our products. We do not see each other as publishers of books; we are managers of books and print-runs. Traditionally, the Portuguese publisher has acted as the people's teacher; 'I have to carefully choose my books because they will teach people'; Caminho is clearly an example and every [Portuguese] publisher believes he is assigned people's education. I am not looking forward to that; I distribute my books to various targets and every

book of Oficina has quality of its own. I do not believe in quality when we talk about literature, there is no such thing; there is the quality of a certain product, of that particular book, of that particular product which has to be redefined. There are different needs when we consider literature and we must understand that. We have to admit that there are people who do not feel the need to understand Saramago and enjoy reading Saramago. What did we have in Portugal in the old days? Either you were a Saramago or you would not be published in Portugal;
I have to detach myself as an appreciator of literature or of specific books. There are good books I do not like and would not buy and there are authors I prefer. Nevertheless I enjoy publishing them. I am not a publisher too concerned about what people will read, whether they wil enjoy such and such book. Sometimes, we do not have books which are well-written; however, they make some sense in the book market because they approach interesting topics which will be developed by subsequent authors.

3. *Does your publishing policy target a reader's profile?*
[António Lobato Faria] We take that into account but we do not have one target only; we want them all. If there are people interested in a certain topic, maybe it is interesting to create a nice and interesting product about that. However, I believe that hás to do with trends.

4. *How do appeal to your readers and try to increase their number?*
[António Lobato Faria] Before I answer that question, let me just make a point here. We have a basic criterion: if the book is fabulous, we will never turn it down and it may be about anything. I usually say, there aare a few very good books, there are plenty of good books everywhere and there is not a sufficient number of publishers to publish all the good books. From the moment you believe this, you have to choose the right time to launch the book, otherwise it will not sell. Will you believe in reviewing? Forget it, I can give you examples of reviews and outstanding critics who say wonders about poor books; and I am not referring to Margarida's because everybody reviews her badly and that is funny. We know Portugal is a small country and there are a few good authors and fewer critics but they will not recognize that fact. So, we have to

350

address readers and claim the quality of a certain book. They believe they are gurus and often they do not read those books; it only because they are by a friend or an acquaintance and they review those books favourably. There is not a credible set of critics/evaluators who can, for a fact, claim that this book is good and that is bad. Therefore, we have to move on and refine our criteria; we learn too. Readers are more and more demanding. [...]

As for manuscripts, we have published plenty Portuguese literature and that has had some impact on the media and, consequently, people have offered their manuscripts, sent by mail, personally, but most of them are bad. Most books of our catalogue are chosen according to the market's evolution and we approach those peple we believe they can write well (and have written elsewhere including for newspapers and magazines, academics and, broadly speaking. People who write a lot.Eventually, we establish a sort of network because a good author can bring another and there are those who are not pleased with their publishers. Most times, thrdr publish prominent authors and the debutants are left behind as far as promotion is concerned. They prefer to be a more important author in a small publishing house than a less important in a bigger one. That is how it works.That is how the market works. The importance of publishers and companies is high and everybody has to learn the signs of the market.

5. Do you accept or reject the system of approaching people and request production?
[António Lobato Faria] We maintain that approach because we are the ones who know the market, its unfulfilled needs. There are people who do not even dream that their material may be interesting for a book and we propose them that. These are the cases we prefer because we are not just waiting for people to come to us.

6. How do you manage the risk of having a significant percentage of debutants?
[António Lobato Faria] Oficina has 59 per cent of authors whose first work was published by us.
Tehn, there is a segment with writing potential that we explore, although not very commercially successful.We have several literary guidances albeit people know us for our popular literature

351

(he rejects the terms 'light' and 'mass' literature). I believe there is a huge publishing fault and I am answering as an economist; I believe managing a publishing house has risks and those have to be managed carefully. Every book implies a risk in resources (financial and design since we explore a lot in covers and in communication). We have to balance risky launches with less risky ones. It is not justa matter of launching the book into the market, you have to have a clear idea about the right timing. Otherwise, it will be a disaster. Without sounding pretentious, Portuguese publishers have survived on translation for quite some time and do nothing for literature, they just choose or publish those books recommended by their international literary agents.Then, they speak bad about Portuguese publishers who publish Portuguese authors.

7. How do you take care of your authors' career?
[António Lobato Faria] It varies but I would say that most publishers do the same. They try to look after authors, look after debutants, advise them, talk to them about what they have in mind, see what he needs and if he needs some help. We talk to them about the market, how it works nowadays. There must be a balance between what is publishing and what is the professional life of an author (most of them work). You must manage that and that encourages friendship. It is very difficult not to see that; writing implies sacrifice and we know our authors' personal lives. We hope to work as a start up for new authors and spot new talents.

8. Does the large majority of authors stay with you or is there any percentage of those who come and go?
[joint answer] Most of them continue. Only rarely do they go because it is part of the job to invest a little bit in the author's career. With his/ her second work, we give him/her that opportunity. If we feel there is interest and comittment to writing, with the market, and art, we support as we can. Nevertheless, we cannot launch as many authors as we would like. If we are waiting for a masterpiece we will never publish anything. We have just two or three authors, one of whom I am in great terms with but whose manuscripts we did not accept because you have to feel you want to evolve..
[...]

I believe Margarida [Rebelo Pinto] is part of a literary tradition common to Portugal and to the rest of the world. It has to do with talent and with the moment. If we read Manuel Arouca's Os Filhos do Sol, it is funny and historically identifiable because it depicts society [in the 1980s]. And Margarida, like Rita [Ferro] had done, is traditionally rooted in society documenting .Eça had done that too. At the end of the 1980s, Rita Ferro and Paulo Castilho (*Fora de Horas*) emerged in the market; in the 1990s, was Margarida [Rebelo Pinto] and she was the first author to write about the advertising and the Press environments. No one knew about these environments some years ago. Nowadays they are public figures. But Margarida's success did not only depend on her; she came up in the right time, when Portugal was developing and certain people were more open to cultural products, as spare time. In the 1990s, hypermarkets multiplied and they marketed household appliances, CDs, and books – everything for mass consumption. This introduced a difference as far as points of sale are concerned because books were no longer bought in bookshops only. [...] the public expanded and developed books purchasing habits, despite some booksellers predicting the failure of book retail. Purchasing habits are directly associated with shopping malls: even if you have a small bookshop on the street, people will clearly prefer the one in a shopping mall unless the small bookshop is in a convenient spot where people pass by – But this hit primarily street retail because this is a question of change of purchasing habits.Bertrand was aware of that and set up a store in a shopping mall, next to a hypermarket that sells books too and both sell. Some people did not go to bookshops and became in contact with books at the alternative points of sale. That was not just the question of getting to books because books had to get to people too.
[...] I believe we were among the first publishing houses to realize that. I spend in good communication, image and cover but I do not force people to buy books. Not every book is for everyone.
[...]
Margarida's first book cover with Difel was awful, so we came up with a more hard selling type of approach. Nowadays, others follow us [...] I believe we became specialized in book cover production for certain market niches].

9. How do manuscripts get through to you?
[Marcelo Teixeira] We are clearly among those publishers. We receive an unbelievable number of manuscripts by mail and, unfortunately, we are currently taking three up to four months to reply. We have a mind to reply within a month or a fortnight soon.
[António Lobo Faria] We have concluded that the number of good texts is virtually the same; therefore, we will not spend more in human resources to read the increasing number of manuscripts that get through to us. However, our strategy is oriented towards selection and not reaction. Our small editorial board examines all manuscripts and those we shortlist are read more thoroughly, with a report. [Marcelo Teixeira adds] there is not one publishing house that has not turned down a bestseller and excellent authors, too.

10. In which phase of the author's career do you manage to get a translation?
[António Lobato Faria]It is very difficult and I assume it is also the case with other publishing houses; exceptions are Saramago, Lobo Antunes and Lídia Jorge. When our catalogue is made up of public figures, such as Judite Sousa [outstanding journalist] the potential of interest is mainly local. But we also have some young authors whose potential is maturing, such as Margarida published in Brazil, the Netherland, Spain and Germany, Miguel Sousa Tavares, in Castillian and Catalan, England, and Brazil, e *O Meu Pipi* in France and Brazil, and a book by Cristina Águas in France. As regards the British book market, Miguel {Sousa Tavares] book [Equator] involves the English,and thus their interest.

11. The easiest markets are....
[António Lobato Faria] Depending on what we are talking about. Spain, due to geographical proximity, in some areas. We have not much experience in the foreign market because of the target of our publishing house. Margarida was translated because none should be indifferent to her commercial success

12. What is Oficina's market share?
[António Lobato Faria] It is not very relevant but we are among the top ten major publishers; together with Editorial Notícias, we are even bigger [Editorial Notícias is part of the same group].

There are also Porto Editora, Asa, Texto, Presença, Bertrand and Dom Quixote.

13. Are there any groups imposing difficulty in (your) authors' consecration?

[António Lobato Faria] It is a very closed system and the fact that we are different and emerged when the market was changed encouraged some negative reaction; but that is normal.

14. The lack of reviewing can be extremely painful....

[António Lobato Faria] There are two aspects: they rejected us although that did not concern us since we were not very interested Moreover, our target is not concerned about reviews. No one reads the JL and Expresso's reviews.

15. How do you develop your marketing activities, do they depend on the book?

[António Lobato Faria] As far as I am concerned, Marketing is very natural and has alwats existed; those who are not in Marketing assume that it is something special. Publishers assumed that communicating was selling.Marketing, communication and sales are appealing to internal and external aspects (a good book cover is extremely important because it is good money for value.

16. Was Margarida Rebelo Pinto marketed as a Portuguese author, an example of contemporary women's writing when she was translated?

[António Lobato Faria] She was marketed as a phenomenon of bestselling fiction and with indications of certain places in Portugal. Her books market a European and sufficiently developed country; women's writing, urban, a bit like Bridget Jones, *Sex and the City*, modern writing. Both Margarida [Rebelo Pinto] and Miguel [Sousa Tavares] were accepted in the Netherlands, an open country.

Appendix 3:
Interview with Maria do Rosário Pedreira, Publisher of Temas e Debates, sent by E-Mail on 23rd November 2004.

1. How do you choose manuscripts? Do you try to identify a writing style? What are the criteria which enable you to determine 'quality' standards for Temas e Debates?

There are several ways of choosing a manuscript for publication; however, as far as our Portuguese fiction series is concerned, our criteria have been based upon quality and not so much on the potential to be market-appeal (let's say we are more interested in an author who is determined to continue writing and may be included in future histories of Portuguese Literature than in an author who is a bestseller because of a timely issue put before the public but who does not evolve. This 'quality' standard includes the writing style, since a good story without a 'writing style' may be poor. What we feel about most manuscripts that we turn down is that lack of 'style'. That style is often the result of reading multiple styles (it is very easy to track an author who has not read anything). Broadly speaking, when the writing style is clearly marked (either because it is completely different from other authors' – originality – or because of allusions, associations and reference to styles of consecrated authors), we are half-way there; afterwards we just need to check whether there are any contradictions, errors, mistakes, incoherences, etc.) in the narration (when there is one, though there is almost always) and if the author has a good command of language in terms of grammar and vocabulary. There is also another aspect, this one more subjective and almost unexplicable, which has to do with the 'nose', inuition. In any case, we never decide on the publication of any book without it having been read by more than one person at the publishing house (and sometimes by an external reader).

2. How do you take care of your authors and their careers?

We do not have many resources because there are just a few of us at the publishing house. Nevertheless, we pursue their promotion with booksellers, the media, domestic readers, official institutions which might invite them to participate at events abroad, etc. We write press-releases about their books and send them to a whole range of interested parties, we photocopy proofs and send them to a few critics and journalists, we organize a launch and public book-signing sessions in major bookshops and libraries throughout the country. We are usually supported by a literary agent abroad who pursues possibilities of translation into other languages. We do not achieve the same impact with every author, since it is also influenced by the author's availability and personality; he may be good at meeting readers but he may also write well but may have no talent for personal appearances.

3. Does your publishing policy include a reader's profile?
The profile is not well defined, but there is one; we may turn down the publication of a too difficult book because we consider that it will not have many readers and it may not cover its initial investment. However, when we publish a new Portuguese author, we usually bear in mind that he or she will not be read by the same people who read light and popular literature. Therefore, the profile of our potential reader is that of one who clearly has reading habits but he or she does not have to be an intellectual.

4. How do you try to motivate your readers? And increase the number of readers?
Since we do not contact readers directly (and we do not know there are readers up till the author's first public events), we can only motivate them through the media. Of course there is also word of mouth and we talk about a new author to everybody but we are just a drop in the ocean. Motivating readers is also carried out by the author in public events.

5. How do you receive manuscripts? Through literary agents, authors? Is there any percentage about each source?
In Portugal, literary agents are almost non-existent. Authors usually send their own manuscripts, and receive 10 per cent of sales; usually they are paid an advance, corresponding to around 30 per cent of copyright of the first print-run (between 1,500 and 3,000 copies for a debutant). Anyway, most interesting manuscripts are

sent by a published author or by someone who cooperates with the publishing house. There is only a very small percentage of manuscripts that arrive anonymously by mail and get published. But there are some.

6. How do you organize interviews and events in which your authors participate?
As mentioned under point 2, we send press-releases and proofs to people we believe might contribute to the author's and book's publicity. Then, the request for interviews may come or not. If we are publishing a second book and the first one was a clear succeess, thereare more requests for interviews and we organize onterviews and events with the author's input. His or her ideas are very important for promoting the book in question. It is easy to organize these kind of events for a second book because the success of the first book is always a mystery.

7. Are there authors more suitable to overseas markets? How would you qualify such difference?
There are authors we can call international, whose language or topics are more universal. We also have the case of an author who is too 'local', who uses medieval and picaresque Portuguese terms. This author will find it hard to be translated. Apart from this situation, I believe everybody has the same possibilities because overseas publishers are also very different and it is always possible to direct a specific work to a potential publisher in another country.

8. How do you manage to have a particular book translated? In which phase of the author's career?
We are usually supported, as mentioned above, by an agent abroad who knows the international book market potentially interested in Portuguese authors. But the book we want to translate has to have had some kind of consecration in Portugal (prizes, reviews, etc.). Supported by this material (copies of reviews, etc.), we manage to awaken the interest of overseas publishers.We organize a file for each author, translate extracts of the work and visit international book fairs to meet publishers who might be interested in new authors.

9. How did Temas e Debates came up; year, founders? Have you always belonged to Bertelsmann group and what was your mission?
Temas e Debates belongs to Bertelsmann group, the major communication group in Europe and third in the world. Círculo de Leitores is the major stockholder and Temas e Debates was set up at the end of 1995 with the purpose of selling reference books published by Círculo de Leitores, such as *História da Arte* and *História da Expansão*, books composed of several volumes, with the contribution of major Portuguese specialists. In early 2000, Temas e Debates explored new areas which rewarded this publishing house with public and media recognition: fiction (foreign and Portuguese). Its commitment to new Portuguese fiction was widely recognised by the critics, with the launch of José Luís Peixoto and Filipa Melo, promising novelists who have their work translated in several countries such as Spain, Italy, the Netherlands, the Czech Republic, Bulgaria, Turkey and Finland. This is Temas e Debates's strongest area at present.

10. Is José Luís Peixoto fundamentally marketed as a Portuguese author in those countries where his works are translated?
No, just like when we publish a Hungarian or an American author and we market him or her purely as a good author, the same happens with José Luís Peixoto abroad. In some countries, (the Netherlands, for example), his image was associated with Saramago (a Portuguese Nobel prizewinner advises a young Portuguese author) because the series was organized that way (the same was done with authors of different languages).

11. How does Temas e Debates understands itself in the literary system?
Temas e Debates is above all committed to creating Portuguese literature which will in the future replace major authors, many of whom are over 50 years old, and which will last (unlike some Portuguese literature published nowadays, owing much to fashion, and hence, ephemeral). Therefore, if you will excuse our lack of modesty, we see ourselves as a publishing house which encourages new Portuguese literature and, indeed we are approached by many young authors, aiming to become part of a group writing quality literature.

12. How would you qualify the relationship between an author and your publishing house?

I would not call this dependence but complicity. Of course, if a author is well looked after, he will not leave his publisher (this relationship has to be nurtured, through listening and helping out on any literary project). The author cannot solely depend on his publisher financially since he or she cannot make a living from his early copyright. So it is not exactly dependency. Publishers depend on authors for their sales and there are some authors who are more important than others in this regard. Therefore, the dependence affects more the publisher-author relationship than vice-versa.

Appendix 4:
Interview with Margaret Jull da Costa, sent by E-mail in April 2005

1. Do you usually decide the authors you are going to translate or are you usually commissioned to do that?
I am always commissioned to translate a book.

2. Are some writers more approachable for foreign markets than others? What are the criteria that could be used to distinguish those who are fit to be translated?
I think British and American publishers do prefer foreign books that approximate to the British/American 'norm'. Having said that though, I translate José Saramago and Javier Marías, neither of whom are exactly easy reads or in the usual mould of British/American fiction. So there is a small place for writers who write in a very 'foreign' style, but only a small one. There is a current vogue in Britain for translated detective fiction, which has always been very much a British speciality, but has now spread all over Europe.

3. What is the translator's target? To translate the book/novel as it is, keeping the 'national feelings' or adapt them to the atmosphere of the country into which the book will be published?
I aim to translate a novel into English without losing any of its 'national feeling'. I certainly don't adapt language or plot or characters in any way. That isn't my job.

4. Several translators of Saramago's novels have won relevant literary prizes. As far as you understand the system, do you believe the choice of the author (more or less well-known) influences the award?
I really don't know what influences the choice of prizewinners. Sometimes it seems to be the author's reputation, sometimes the theme of the book. Like all prizes there is a degree of randomness. I think that, even with translation prizes, the original and the author carry more weight than the translator/translation.

5. Do you think that the choice of translators (with credits) influences the reception of the author in the country into which he is published and, therefore, the reviews he will get?

No, most reviewers don't even notice who the translator is or even that the book has been translated. There are a few honourable exceptions, but not many. A lot of readers don't notice that they're reading a translation either.

6. What does Saramago's novels tell you in terms of Portugal? Is it the modern/European country? Is it its history?

Saramago seems to view Portugal as a country trying to become modern, but still dragged down by its history. His latest novel *Ensaio sobre a cegueira*, however, could probably have been written about any Western European country (he is cagey about where the book is set, but it clearly is Portugal), where voter apathy and political indifference are rife. Obviously, *O ano da morte de Ricardo Reis* described with great vividness Salazar's Portugal, but I think in many of his novels he is concerned with wider issues, not just with Portugal.

7. Do you know the exact figures as far as the percentage of fiction published in the U.K. and what is the percentage in terms of translated fiction within the share of fiction published?

I have come across with some indications, especially in some articles by Giovanni Pontiero, but I am not altogether sure whether the figures are up-to-date and where I could get them. I believe that only 6% of all fiction titles published in the UK are translations. You could try contacting the Society of Authors: www.societyofauthors.net for more detailed information.

Appendix 5:
Reasons for the Purchase of Portuguese Fiction:
Results of a Survey in 2001.

Within the context of my research for my PhD thesis on the Portuguese literary field, I needed to understand what were the motivations that drove the Portuguese people to purchase the Portuguese fiction and how the Portuguese buyers became aware of titles. I wanted to know how far education, age and sex are key variables in the decision of purchase. Moreover, it was also important to know whether the purchase and reading of the Portuguese fiction are also compelled by motivations associated with the attempt to gain social status.

This survey was carried out during the last quarter of 2001 and involved 349 respondents and out of them: 57.6 per cent were women (201) and 42.4 per cent (146) were men; 50.7 per cent (177) were aged between 18-25, 33.5 per cent (117) were aged between 26-29, 12.6 per cent (44) were aged between 40-60 and 3.2 per cent (11) were aged 61 and over; 2.3 per cent (8) attended only Primary school, 32.7 per cent (114) attended secondary school, 6 per cent (21) had professional education and 59 per cent (206) had higher education; 21.5 (75) per cent lived in Greater Lisbon, 11.7 (41) per cent lived in Greater Porto, 19.8 (69) per cent lived in Northern Coastland, 15.8 (55) per cent lived in Southern Coastland, 22.6 per cent lived in Northern Inland and 8.6 (30) per cent lived in Southern Inland. Their answers were analysed through the SPSS (Statistical Programme for Social Sciences).

As far as Motivations that impelled respondents to purchase a fiction book, there is a relevant difference in the variable 'random purchase' according to sex (t=2.14; p=0.03) and, as shown in Table 1, women (F=2.66; SD=1.18) tend to buy fiction more randomly than men (M=2.39; SD=1.22).

Table 1: Average Statistical Data of Group in a 1-5 Scale

	Sex	Mean	Std. Deviation
Advertising	Female	2.33	1.02
	Male	2.28	1.09
Bestsellers' List	Female	2.23	1.09
	Male	2.26	1.07
Reviews	Female	3.12	1.21
	Male	3.00	1.09
Word-of-mouth	Female	3.76	1.01
	Male	3.64	1.00
Publicity	Female	2.89	1.12
	Male	2.78	1.09
Talks	Female	2.67	1.16
	Male	2.47	1.12
Random Purchase	**Female**	**2.66**	**1.18**
	Male	**2.39**	**1.22**

As far as age is concerned, the One-Way ANOVA variance analysis showed that there is a relevant difference in the 'word-of-mouth advertising' (F=6.21;p=0.00), as indicated in Table 2:

Table 2: One Way ANOVA for Age Independent variable

	F	Sig.
Advertising	2.368	.071
Bestsellers' List	1.676	.172
Reviews	1.007	.390
Word-of-mouth	**6.215**	**.000**
Publicity	.629	.597
Talks	.274	.844
Random Purchase	1.208	.307

The Scheffe Test indicated that there is a difference between individuals aged between '18-25 years old' and those aged between '40-60 years old' and also between those aged between 26-39 years old and those aged between '40-60 years old'. As shown in Table 3, the youngest respondents are the most influenced by 'word-of-mouth advertising' (M=3.88; SD=0.86), while the oldest respondents are the least influenced (M=3.18; SD=1.11).

Table 3: Descriptive Table of Motivations according to Age

		N	Mean	Std. Deviation
Word-of-mouth	18-25	177	3.88	. 86
	26-39	117	3.68	1.06
	40-60	44	3.18	1.11
	61 and over	11	3.45	1.44
	Total	349	3.71	1.00

The One-Way ANOVA Test did not indicate any significant differences according to Education but showed relevant differences in the 'word-of-mouth advertising' according to Region:

Table 4: One Way ANOVA Test according to Region

	F	Sig.
Advertising	.906	.477
Bestsellers' List	2.434	.035
Reviews	2.548	.028
Word-of-mouth	**4.643**	**.000**
Publicity	1.459	.203
Talks	.996	.420
Random Purchase	.697	.626

The Test of Post-Hoc comparison showed that the respondents living in the southern Coastland are the most motivated by 'word-of-mouth advertising' (M=4.24; SD=0.72, whereas those living in the southern Inland are the least influenced (M=3.27; SD=1.31), as shown in Table 5:

Table 5: Descriptive Table of Motivations according to Region

		Mean	Std. Deviation	Std. Error
Word-of-Mouth	Lisbon	3.68	. 87	. 10
	Porto	3.61	1.12	. 17
	Northern Coastland	3.65	1.05	. 13
	Southern Coastland	4.24	. 72	9.70E-02
	Northern Inland	3.65	. 93	. 11
	Southern Inland	3.27	1.31	.24
	Total	3.71	1.00	5.37E-02
	Southern Inland	2.43	1.10	. 20
	Total	2.59	1.15	6.14E-02

Table 6 shows average values for the seven motivations in descending order:

Table 6: Average Importance given to Motivation in Descending Order

	Mean	Std. Deviation
Word-of-mouth	3.71	1.00
Reviews	3.07	1.16
Publicity	2.85	1.10
Talks	2.59	1.15
Random Purchase	2.54	1.20
Advertising	2.31	1.05
Bestsellers' List	2.25	1.08

Table 7: Factor Analysis of the Motivations impelling the Purchase of Fiction

	Factor 1 Social Pressures (Unconscious Purchase)	Factor 2 Deliberate Search (Conscious Purchase)
List of Bestsellers	0.83	
Advertising	0.79	
Publicity	0.66	
Random Purchase		0.69
Reviews		0.58
Talks		0.57
Word-of-mouth		0.56
Eigenvalue	2.549	1.130
Total Variance Explained	28.99%	23.5%

Table 7 shows the results of a factor analysis (principal components with Varimax rotation with Kaiser normalisation). There are two major components: the first, Social Pressure, contains the highest percentage of variance explained (28.99%), suggesting that the respondents feel more pressured by advertising and media exposure given to writers and Books than by the desire of keeping up to date with talks about fiction. Nevertheless, when questioned, respondents answered that the motivations included in the second component, Deliberate Search, were the most important.

This survey also showed that there are no significant differences as far as the purchaser's awareness of the Publishing House is concerned. Around eight-six per cent of the respondents answered that it was not important.

As far as Reasons that restrain the purchase of fiction, the Independent-Samples Test revealed that men (M=2.21; SD=1.19) are more likely to buy a book with pictures than women (F=1.95; SD=1.06), as shown in Table 8:

Table 8: Independent-Samples T Test for reasons for buying a book fiction

	Sex	N	Mean	Std. Deviation
Price	Female	201	3.29	1.09
	Male	148	3.23	1.18
Cover	Female	201	2.29	1.17
	Male	146	2.24	1.16
Picture on Cover	Female	200	2.19	1.17
	Male	145	2.18	1.08
Blurb	Female	200	2.28	1.14
	Male	146	2.32	1.16
Font	Female	200	2.66	1.27
	Male	146	2.54	1.28
Number of Pages	Female	200	1.97	1.10
	Male	146	2.12	1.16
Pictures/Drawings	**Female**	**200**	**1.95**	**1.06**
	Male	147	2.21	1.19

One-Way ANOVA Tests and Post-Hoc comparisons showed that the respondents aged between 26-39 (M=2.34) were the least concerned with the 'font', whereas those aged 60 and over (M=3.27) were the most influenced; The respondents aged 60 and over were also the most influenced by 'pictures or drawings'(M=3.36). There were also significant differences in 'pictures or drawings' according to Education (F=3.27;p=0.00): the respondents with primary education (M=3.13) were the most influenced by this variable and those with higher education (M=1.96) were the least influenced. There were no differences according to Region.

Table 9 shows the average importance given to several reasons for buying fiction in descending order:

Table 9: Average Importance to Reasons why people buy a particular book in Descending Order

	Mean	Std. Deviation
Price	3.27	1.13
Font	2.61	1.28
Blurb	2.29	1.15
Cover	2.27	1.17
Picture on Cover	2.19	1.13
Pictures/Drawings	2.06	1.12
Number of Pages	2.03	1.12

Table 10: Bi-Factorial Matrix of Reasons for buying a particular Book

	Factor 1 Aspect of the Book	Factor 2 Price and Contents
Cover	0.60	
Picture on the cover	0.76	
Blurb	0.76	
Font	0.68	
Price		0.71
Number of pages		0.76
Pictures or Drawings		0.61
Eigenvalue	2.872	1.023
Total Variance Explained	41.03%	14.61%

The factor analysis of principal components indicated a bi-factorial matrix, in which the respondents are more influenced by the variables concerning the Aspect Of The Book, as a commercial product. The difference of total variance explained is much higher in factor 1 than in factor, despite the 'price' being answered the most important variable.

As far as the Points Of Sale are concerned, Table 11 shows the average given to the points of sale in descending order:

Table 11: Points of Sale in Descending Order

	Mean	Std. Deviation
Bookshop	3.96	1.14
Book Fairs	3.38	1.29
Hyper/Supermarket	2.71	1.31
Book Club	1.80	1.20
Postal	1.68	1.07
Newsagent's	1.56	.99
Second-Hand Book	1.48	.96
Internet	1.34	.84
Airport	1.30	.76
Personal Selling	1.17	.57

Table 12: Factor Analysis of Points of Sale

	Factor1 Occasional	Factor 2 Traditional	Factor 3 Alternative
Book Clubs	0.49		
Postal	0.62		
Door-to-door	0.44		
Airport	0.55		
Internet	0.63		
Bookshops		0.71	
Second-Hand Books		0.44	
Book Fairs		0.70	
Newsagent's			0.66
Hyper/Supermarket			0.79
Eigenvalue	2.122	1.249	1.054
Total Variance Explained	18.61%	13%	12%

Table 12 shows a factor analysis of principal components with Varimax rotation that obtained a 3-factorial matrix. The second and third components show balance scores but it is the first component that accounts for the highest percentage of variance explained. The respondents buy more on Occasional Points of Sale, enticed by the aspect of the book or its media exposure.

Conclusions

The results of this questionnaire show that the Portuguese do not have ingrained reading habits of fiction. This has been confirmed by the annual reports on reading habits published by the Portuguese Association of Publishers and Booksellers. According to the report published in 2001, around eighty-two per cent of the Portuguese population read books and magazines, out of them only eighty per cent read newspapers and magazines and forty-five per cent read books. This report does not discriminate between fiction and schoolbooks, poetry, essays, etc. This APEL's report showed that around nineteen per cent of the Portuguese population bought between five and six books annually and an equal percentage bought between seven and ten books annually. If we consider the results of this research, in which, thirty-one and a half per cent of the respondents buy between three and five books every year, we can conclude that roughly half of the books bought by the Portuguese every year are fiction. The percentage is reasonably satisfactory, despite the fact that it is still a low score. In other words, although it is true that the Portuguese buy fiction, the fact is that they buy few fiction books. If we add to this the fact that, according to the Association's report, only thirty per cent of the Portuguese read between three and five books every year, we can conclude that reading reaches low scores.

As regards the points of sale, the results are not very different from those published by the Association. In this report, the bookshops and the newsagent's (merged variables) were the most often visited point of sale, followed by the hypermarkets and the supermarkets, and the book fairs. In my questionnaire, the bookshop and the newsagent's are autonomous variables and the bookshop is the variable with the highest score, followed by the book fair and by the hypermarkets and supermarkets. Book fairs are points of sale usually related to sales promotions and discounts. Moreover, the variable price was considered the most important. It is easier to encourage a habit of purchase at the traditional points of sale of fiction, also associated with safe and reliable purchase, than at alternative or occasional points of sales, such as the Internet, often regarded as an unreliable medium as far as payment is concerned.

I can also conclude that the customers of fiction are mainly women. Women buy more fiction and read it thoroughly more often. Men prefer reading aided by visual supports. Nevertheless, commercial issues, such as the exposure and outlook of the book, primarily influence both sexes. The book is mainly regarded as a commercial product.

Finally, the Portuguese customers of fiction can be divided into two major types: the innovator and the conservative. The former is younger and open to advertising in its manifold ways: media advertising, the appearance of the book and word-of-mouth. The latter is older, resistant to word-of-mouth on new books and alternative points of sale.

Appendix 6: The Nobel Prizewinners for Literature (1947-2004).

Year	Nobel Laureate	Origin Country	Language	Genre	Original Publisher	Translations	Publishers of Translations
1947	André Gide	France	French	Fiction	Gallimard	U.K.	Martin Secker & Warburg Ltd
1948	T.S. Eliot	U.K.	English	Fiction	Faber, Methuen	France	Éditions de Várenne
1949	William Faulkner	U.S.	English	Fiction		U.K.	Chatto & Windus, Penguin
1950	Bertrand Russel	U.K.	English	Essay	Allen & Unwin		
1951	Pär Lagerkvist	Sweden	Swedish	Poetry	Bonniers	U.S.	Princeton University Press
1952	François Mauriac	France	French	Fiction	Bernard Grasset, Flammarion	U.K.	Eyre & Spottiswoode
1953	Winston Churchill	U.K.	English	History	Cassell	U.S., Switzerland	Macmillan Co., Alfred Scherz
1954	Ernest Hemingway	U.S.	English	Fiction	Scribner's	U.K., France	Cape, Jonathan Cape, Three Mountains Press, Arrow
1955	Halldór Laxness	Iceland	Icelandic	Fiction		U.S., Sweden	
1956	Juan Ramón Jiménez	Spain	Spanish	Poetry		U.S.	Dolphin Book Co
1957	Albert Camus	France	French	Fiction	Gallimard	U.K., Netherlands	Hamish Hamilton, De Bezige Bij

Year	Nobel Laureate	Origin Country	Language	Genre	Original Publisher	Translations	Publishers of Translations
1958	Boris Pasternak	U.S.S.R.	Russian	Fiction	Sovetskii pisatel	U.S., U.K., Italy, France	Feltrinelli, S. Fischer, Collins, Pantheon, Gallimard
1959	Salvatore Quasimodo	Italy	Italian	Fiction	Editzioni di Corrente	U.S.,	
1960	Saint-John Perse	France	French	Poetry	Gallimard	U.S., U.K.	Harcourt Brace & Company, Faber
1961	Ivo Andric	Yugoslavia	Serbo-Croat	Fiction			
1962	John Steinbeck	U.S.	English	Fiction	Viking	U.K., Netherlands	Mandarin, Heinmann, Viking Press, Penguin, De Bezige Bij
1963	Giorgos Seferis	Greece	Greek	Poetry			
1964	Jean-Paul Sartre	France	French	Fiction/ Ess./Poetry	Gallimard		
1965	Mikhail Sholokhov	U.S.S.R.	Russian	Fiction		U.K., U.S., France	Putnam, Four Square Books, Random House, Methuen,
1966	Samuel Agnon, Nelly Sachs	Israel, Sweden		Fiction			
1967	Miguel Angel Asturias	Guatemala	Spanish	Fiction		Argentina, U.S.	Losada, Delacorte Press, Goyanarre
1968	Yasunari Kawabata	Japan	Japanese	Fiction		U.K.	Penguin, Secker & Warburg
1969	Samuel Beckett	U.K.	Irish	Drama	Picador	U.S., Germany	Suhrkamp verlag, Grove Press

Year	Nobel Laureate	Origin Country	Language	Genre	Original Publisher	Translations	Publishers of Translations
1970	Alexandr Solzhenitsyn	U.S.S.R.	Russian	Fiction		U.S., U.K., Germany	Praeger, Dutton,Collins, Harvill, Bodley Head, Farrar, Straus & Giroux, Possev verlag, Flegon press
1971	Pablo Neruda	Chile	Spanish	Poetry		U.K., U.S., Spain, Argentina	G.Massa, Grosman Publisher & Cape Goliard Press, Editorial Lumen, Losada, Rapp & Whiting
1972	Heinrich Böll	Germany	German	Fiction	Verlag Kiepenheuer & Witsch	U.K.	Methuen
1973	Patrick White	Australia	English	Fiction	Currency Press	U.K.	Cape, Routledge & Kegan Paul, Eyre & Spottiswoode, Penguin
1974	Eyvind Johnson, Harry Martinson	Sweden	Swedish	Fiction	Bonniers, Norstedts		
1975	Eugenio Montale	Italy	Italian	Poetry	Mondadori		
1976	Saul Bellow	U.S.	English	Fiction	Viking	Spain, France, U.K.	Seix Barral, Gallimard, Wiedenfeld & Nicolson, Penguin, Secker & Warburg
1977	Vicente Aleixandre	Spain	Spanish	Poetry	Seix Barral		

377

Year	Nobel Laureate	Origin Country	Language	Genre	Original Publisher	Translations	Publishers of Translations
1978	Isaac Bashevis Singer	U.S.	English	Fiction		U.S., U.K.	Harper & Row, Farrar, Straus & Giroux, Penguin, Cape, Secker & Warburg, OPU, Noonday, Owen
1979	Odysseus Elytis	Greece	Greek	Poetry		U.S., France, Italy, Germany	Temple U.P., Univ. Pittsburgh Press, Fata Morgana, Ist Siciliano di Studi Bizantini e Neoellenici, Claasen Verlag, Tschudy Verlag
1980	Czeslaw Milosz	Poland/ U.S.	English	Fiction		U.K., U.S.	University of California Press, Faber, Doubleday, Sidgwick & Jackson
1981	Elias Canetti	U.K.	English	Fiction	Suhrkamp	U.K., Spain, Italy	Cape, Deutsch, Adelphi Edizioni, Ediciones Labor
1982	Gabriel García Marquez	Colombia	Spanish	Fiction	Editorial La Oveja Negra	U.K., U.S., Spain, France, Mexico, Venezuela, Argentina	Cape, Harper & Row, Pan Books, Plaza Y Janés, Ed. Bruguera, Tusquets, Ed, Grasset, Editorial Sudamericana
1983	William Golding	U.K.	English	Fiction		U.K., U.S.	Faber, Lythway Press, Gallimard, Farrar, Straus & Giroux
1984	Jaroslav Seifert	Czechoslovakia	Czech	Poetry	Ceskolovensky spisovatel	France, U.K., U.S., Germany, Sweden	Fripress, London magazine Editions, The Spirit that moves us Press

Year	Nobel Laureate	Origin Country	Language	Genre	Original Publisher	Translations	Publishers of Translations
1985	Claude Simon	France	French	Fiction	Les Éditions de Minuit	U.K.	Cape
1986	Wole Soyinka	Nigeria		Poetry		U.K., U.S.	Methuen & Co, Oxford University Press, Heinemann, Rex Collings, Harper & Row
1987	Joseph Brodsky	U.S.	English	Poetry		U.K., U.S., France, Germany, Italy	Anvil Press Poetry, Harper & Row, Farrar, Straus and Giroux, Gallimard, Autrement, Éditions du Seuil, Mondador
1988	Naguib Mahfouz	Egypt	Arabic	Fiction	American University in Cairo Press	U.K.	Heinemann, Quartet
1989	Camilo Jose Cela	Spain	Spanish	Fiction		U.K., U.S.,	Eyre & Spottiswoode, Little, Brown & Co., Weidenfeld and Nicolson, Abon Books, Bard-Avon, Las Americas, Ecco Press, Cornell, Golancz, Farrar, Straus &, Wisconsin U.P.

Year	Nobel Laureate	Origin Country	Language	Genre	Original Publisher	Translations	Publishers of Translations
1990	Octavio Paz	Mexico	Spanish	Poetry		U.S., U.K., Spain	Seix Barral, Grove Press, Viking Press, Penguin, Cape Goliard, Carcanet, Fabula, Simbad, Españolas, Tenzontle, Fondo de Cultura Economica, Harcourt
1991	Nadine Gordimer	South Africa	English	Fiction		U.S., U.K., France	Farrar Straus Giroux, Viking Press
1992	Derek Walcott	Saint Lucia	English	Poetry		U.S., U.K.,	Cape, Farrar Straus Giroux
1993	Toni Morrison	U.S.	English	Fiction		U.K.	Picador, Penguin, Vintage, Chatto & Windus
1994	Kenzaburo Oe	Japan	Japanese	Poetry		U.S., U.K.,	Grove Press, YMCA Press, Japan Quarterly, Serpent's Tail
1995	Seamus Heaney	U.K.	Irish	Poetry		U.S., U.K.	Faber, Rainbow Press
1996	Wislawa Szymborska	Poland	Polish	Poetry	Wy-dawnictwo Literackie	U.S.,U.K., Sweden, France, Germany, Italy	Forest Books, Harcourt Brace, Princeton U.P.
1997	Dario Fo	Italy	Italian	Drama	Einaudi	U.S.,U.K., France, Sweden, Germany, Spain,	Methuen, Pluto Press, Oberon Books, French

Year	Nobel Laureate	Origin Country	Language	Genre	Original Publisher	Translations	Publishers of Translations
1998	José Saramago	Portugal	Portuguese	Fiction	Caminho	U.S., U.K.,Germany, France,Spain, Italy, Sweden	Random House,Harvill, Harcourt Brace, Feltrinelli, Seix Barral, Alfaguara, Rowholt, Editions du Seuil, Einaudi, Bompiani, Wahlström & Widstrand
1999	Günter Grass	Germany	German	Fiction		U.S., U.K.,	Secker & Warburg, Harcourt Brace, Faber
2000	Gao Xingjian	China	Chinese	Fiction/Drama		France, Sweden, U.S., Hong Kong	University of Chicago,HarperCollins, Chinese U.P., Forum, Atlantis
2001	V.S. Naipaul	Trinidad	English	Fiction		U.K., France, Russia	Deutsch, Viking, Penguin, Heinemann, Minerva, Albin Michel, Bourgois, Raduga
2002	Imre Kertész	Hungary	Hungarian	Fiction		U.S.,Germany, France, Sweden, Austria, Norway, Denmark	Fripress,Norstedt, Actes Sud,Rowohlt,Vintage Internat., Forum, Northwestern University Press, Hydra Books

Year	Nobel Laureate	Origin Country	Language	Genre	Original Publisher	Translations	Publishers of Translations
2003	J.M. Coetzee	South Africa	English	Fiction	Ravan, Secker & Warbugh	U.K.	Secker & Warburg, Minerva, Ravan, Yale University Press, Harvard University Press, Papyrus, Bromberg, Fisher, Hanser, Henssel
2004	Elfriede Jelinek	Austria	German	Fiction/Drama	Sessler	Germany,U.S., U.K.,France, Sweden	Trevi,Forum,Seuil, L'Arche,J.Chambon,Weidenfeld & Nicolson, Serpent's Tail, Rowohlt, Berlin-Verlag, Surkamp,

Appendix 7: The Portuguese Literary Prizes (1978-2004).

CIDADE DE LISBOA – 50,000$00 – Lisbon City Hall

Year	Prizewinner	Panel
1978	Maria Velho da Costa, *Casas Pardas*, Moraes	Ana Hatherly, Fernando Castelo Branco, Maria de Lourdes Belchior, Jacinto do Prado Coelho, Maria Alzira Seixo
1979	Carlos de Oliveira, *Finisterra*, Sá da Costa	Maria Alzira Seixo, Fernando Castelo Branco, Manuel Gusmão, Urbano Tavares Rodrigues
1980	Augusto Abelaira, *Sem Tecto entre Ruínas*, Bertrand	Maria Lúcia Lepecki, Fernando Castelo Branco, David Mourão Ferreira, Jacinto do P. Coelho, Agustina Bessa Luís
1981	José Saramago, *Levantado do Chão*, Caminho	Manuel Gusmão, Fernando C.Branco Mª Lúcia Lepecki, Norberto Lopes, David Mourão Ferreira
1982	Mário de Carvalho, *O Livro Grande de Tebas, Navio e Mariana*, Veja	Salete Salvado, Júlio Conrado, Norberto Lopes, Paula Morão, Manuel Frias Martins

MUNICÍPIO DE LISBOA – 100,000$00 – Lisbon City Hall

Year	Prizewinner	Panel
1983	Lídia Jorge, *Cais das Merendas*. Europa-América/ José Saramago, *Memorial do Convento*, Caminho	Clotilde Guedes da Silva, António Alçada Baptista, João Rui de Sousa, Adolfo Norberto Lopes, Mª Lourdes Belchior, M Duarte, Ivo Cruz, Teresa Rita Lopes, Justino Mendes de Almeida
1984	Vergílio Ferreira, *Para Sempre*, Bertrand	Manuel Pinto Machado, Alçada, Baptista, José Correia Tavares, José, Hermano Saraiva, Víctor Viçoso, Ivo Cruz, Eduardo Prado Coelho, Justino Mendes de Almeida
1985	Lídia Jorge, *Notícias da Cidade Silvestre*, D.Quixote	Víctor Reis, Alçada Baptista, Fernando Assis Pacheco, J. Hermano Saraiva, Mª Lúcia Lepecki, Ivo Cruz, Clara Rocha

Year	Prizewinner	Panel
1986	António Alçada Baptista, *Os Nós e os Laços*, Presença/ Mário Ventura Henriques *Vida e Morte dos Santiagos*, D.Quixote	Víctor Reis, Fausto L. de Carvalho, José Correia Tavares, José H. Saraiva, Mª Lúcia Lepecki, Ivo Cruz, Álvaro Machado, Romeu Correia
1987	David Mourão Ferreira, *Um Amor Feliz*, Presença	Orlando Capitão, Alçada Baptista, José C.Tavares, Fernando C. Branco, Mª de L.Cidraes, Ivo Cruz, Ana Hatherly, Eugénio de Melo e Castro
1988	Baptista Bastos *A Colina de Cristal*, O Jornal	Orlando Capitão, José Correia Tavares, Fernando C. Branco, Urbano T. Rodrigues, D. Ivo Cruz, Salvato Menezes

EÇA DE QUEIRÓS (100,000$00, Lisbon City Hall)

Year	Prizewinner	Panel
1989	João de Melo, *Gente Feliz com Lágrimas*, D.Quixote	Víctor Reis, Urbano Tavares Rodrigues, José Correia Tavares, Alexandre Babo, Ivo Cruz, Fernando Pinto do Amaral, Silvina Lopes
1990	Paulo Castilho, *Fora de Horas*, Contexto	Manuel Barão da Cunha, Luís Forjaz Trigueiros, José Correia Tavares, Maria Augusta Babo, Alexandre Babo
1991	Fernanda Botelho, *Festa em Casa de Flores*, s/n,s/l	Manuel Barão da Cunha, Fernando C. Branco, José Correia Tavares, João Rui de Sousa, Fernando Cristovão, Fernando Martinho, Mª Augusta Babo
1992	Maria Ondina Braga, *Nocturno em Macau*, Caminho	Isabel Rodrigues, Agustina Bessa Luís, Luiz Fagundes Duartes, Alexandre Babo, Fernando Cristovão, Álvaro Machado
1993	Rodrigo Guedes de Carvalho, *Daqui a nada*, Contexto	Salette Salvado, Urbano Tavares Rodrigues, Fernando Bernardes, Alexandre Babo, José Júlio Pinheiro, Álvaro Machado
1994	Seomara da Veiga Ferreira, *Memórias de Agripina*, Presença	Salette Salvado, Fernando Castelo Branco, Luís Rosa, Júlio Conrado, Álvaro Machado
1995	Agustina Bessa Luís, *As Letras do Risco*, Guimarães	Salette Salvado,Fernando Bernardes, Alexandre Babo, José Júlio Pinheiro, Fernando Castelo Branco, Silvina Lopes
1996	Fernando Campos, *A Esmeralda Partida*, Difel	Salette Salvado, Justino Mendes de Almeida, José do Carmo Francisco, Alexandre Babo, José Júlio Pinheiro, Silvina Lopes

D.DINIS – €7.500 – Fundação Casa de Mateus/IPLB and Caixa Geral de Depósitos

Year	Prizewinner	Panel
1980	Agustina Bessa Luís, *O Mosteiro*, Guimarães/ Almeida Faria, *Lusitânia*, Edições 70	Vasco Graça Moura, Mª Alzira Seixo, Ricardo Carballo Calero, Alonso Zamora Vicente
1981	Pedro Tamen, *Horácio e Coriácio*, Moraes/ Virgílio Ferreira, *Conta Corrente I e II*, Bertrand	Vasco Graça Moura, Mª Alzira Seixo, Ricardo Carballo Calero, Alonso Zamora Vicente
1982	Fernando Namora, *Resposta a Matilde*, Bertrand	Vasco Graça Moura, Mª Alzira Seixo, Ricardo Carballo Calero, Alonso Zamora Vicente
1983	Maria Velho da Costa, *Lúcialima*, O Jornal/Camilo José Cela, *Mazurca para los Muertos*	Vasco Graça Moura, Mª Alzira Seixo, Ricardo Carballo Calero, Alonso Zamora Vicente
1984	José Saramago, *O Ano da Morte de Ricardo Reis*, Caminho	Vasco Graça Moura, Mª Alzira Seixo, Ricardo Carballo Calero, Alonso Zamora Vicente
1985	Maria Gabriel Llansol, *Falcão no Punho*, Rolim/ Fernando Guimarães, *Casa: O Seu Desenho*, IN-CM	Vasco Graça Moura, Mª Alzira Seixo Ricardo Carballo Calero, Alonso Zamora Vicente
1986	David Mourão Ferreira, *Um Amor Feliz*, Presença/ Mário de Carvalho, *A Paixão do Conde Fróis*, Rolim	Vasco Graça Moura, Mª Alzira Seixo Pedro Tamen
1987	Eugénio de Andrade, *Vertentes do Olhar*, Limiar	Vasco Graça Moura, Mª Alzira Seixo Pedro Tamen
1988	Luísa Costa Gomes, *Pequeno Mundo*, Quetzal	Vasco Graça Moura, Mª Alzira Seixo Pedro Tamen
1989	Sophia Mello Breyner, *Ilhas*, Texto Editora	Vasco Graça Moura, Mª Alzira Seixo Pedro Tamen
1990	Nuno Júdice, *As Regras da Perspectiva*, Quetzal	Vasco Graça Moura, Mª Alzira Seixo Pedro Tamen
1991	M.S.Lourenço, *Os Degraus do Parnaso*, O Independente	Vasco Graça Moura, Pedro Tamen, Fernando Pinto do Amaral
1992	José Bento, *Silabário*, Relógio d'Água	Vasco Graça Moura, Pedro Tamen, Fernando Pinto do Amaral
1993	Joaquim Manuel Magalhães, *Poeira Levada Pelo Vento*, Presença	Vasco Graça Moura, Pedro Tamen, Fernando Pinto do Amaral

Year	Prizewinner	Panel
1994	Luís Filipe Mendes, *O Jogo de Fazer Versos*, Quetzal	Vasco Graça Moura, Pedro Tamen, Fernando Pinto do Amaral
1995	Eduardo Lourenço, *O Canto do Signo*, Presença	Vasco Graça Moura, Pedro Tamen, Fernando Pinto do Amaral
1996	Fiama Hasse Pais Brandão, *Epístolas e Memorandos*, Relógio d'Água	Vasco Graça Moura, Pedro Tamen, Fernando Pinto do Amaral
1997	José Cardoso Pires, *De Profundis, Valsa Lenta*, D.Quixote	Vasco G. Moura, Fernando P. do Amaral, Nuno Júdice
1998	Lídia Jorge, *O Vale da Paixão*, D.Quixote	Vasco G. Moura, Fernando P. do Amaral, Nuno Júdice
1999	António Lobo Antunes, *Exortação aos crocodilos*, D. Quixote	Vasco G. Moura, Fernando P. do Amaral, Nuno Júdice
2000	Gastão Cruz, *Crateras*, Assírio e Alvim	Vasco G. Moura, Fernando P. do Amaral, Nuno Júdice
2001	Hélia Correia, *Lillias Fraser*, Relógio d'Água; Marcello Duarte Mathias, *A Memória dos Outros*,Gótica	Vasco G. Moura, Fernando P. do Amaral, Nuno Júdice
2002	António Franco Alexandre, *Duende*, Assírio e Alvim	Vasco G. Moura, Fernando P. do Amaral, Nuno Júdice
2003	Frederico Lourenço, *Odisseia*, Cotovia	Vasco G. Moura, Fernando P. do Amaral, Nuno Júdice
2004	Manuel Gusmão, *Migrações do Fogo*, Caminho	Vasco G. Moura, Fernando P. do Amaral, Nuno Júdice

PEN CLUB – €5.000 – PEN CLUB/IPLB

Year	Prizewinner	Panel
1980	Agustina B. Luís, *O Mosteiro*, Guimarães	
1981	Teolinda Gersão, *O Silêncio*, Bertrand; Eduarda Dionísio, *Histórias, Memórias e Mitos de Uma Geração Curiosa*, Círculo de Leitores	Isabel da Nóbrega, Almeida Faria, Casimiro de Brito
1982	José Saramago, *Memorial do Convento*, Caminho	
1983	Vergílio Ferreira, *Para Sempre*, Bertrand	

386

Year	Prizewinner	Panel
1984	José Saramago, *O Ano da Morte de Ricardo Reis*, Caminho	
1985	António Alçada Baptista, *Os Nós e os Laços*, Presença; Mário Ventura, *Vida e Morte dos Santiagos*, D.Quixote	Clara Rocha, Marcelo Duarte Mathias, Yvette Centeno
1986	David Mourão Ferreira, *Um Amor Feliz*, Presença	Clara Rocha, Arnaldo Saraiva Mª Lúcia Lepecki
1987	Baptista Bastos *A Colina de Cristal*, O Jornal	Manuel Ferreira, Casimiro de Brito Clara Ferreira Alves
1988	Maria Velho da Costa, *Missa in Albis*, D.Quixote	José Nobre da Silveira, Teresa Salema, Isabel da Nóbrega
1989	Paulo Castilho, *Fora de Horas*, Contexto; Teolinda Gersão, *Cavalo de Sol*, D.Quixote	Annabela Rita, Casimiro de Brito, Isabel da Nóbrega
1990	Vergílio Ferreira, *Em nome da Terra*, Bertrand	Teolinda Gersão, José Nobre da Silveira, Miguel Viqueira
1991	Mário Ventura, *Évora e os Dias da Guerra*, Caminho	Fernando Dacosta, Mª Lúcia Lepecki, José Nobre da Silveira
1992	Rui Nunes, *Osculatriz*, Relógio d'Água; Teresa Veiga, *A Bela Fria*, Cotovia	Annabela Rita, José Nobre da Silveira, Wanda Ramos
1993	Maria Isabel Barreno, *Os Sensos Incomuns*, Caminho; Júlio Moreira, *A Barragem*, Quetzal	Armando Silva Carvalho, Júlio Conrado, Wanda Ramos
1994	Fernanda Botelho, *Dramaticamente vestida de negro*, Presença	Annabela Rita, Luiz Fagundes Duarte, Wanda Ramos
1995	Luís Felipe Castro Mendes, *Correspondência Secreta*, Quetzal; Mª Judite Carvalho, *Seta Despedida*, Europa-América	Annabela Rita, Helena Barbas, Teresa Salema
1996	Augusto Abelaira, *Outrora Agora*, Presença	Clara Rocha, Annabela Rita, Manuel Frias Martins
1997	Mário Cláudio, *O Pórtico da Glória*, D.Quixote; Teresa Salema, *Benamonte*, Europa-América	Júlio Conrado, Abel Barros Barros Baptista, Annabela Rita
1998	Lídia Jorge, *O Vale da Paixão*, D.Quixote	Ernesto José Rodrigues, Fernando J.B.Martinho

Year	Prizewinner	Panel
1999	Nuno Júdice, *Por todos os Séculos, Quetzal*; Pedro Rosa Mendes, *Baía dos Tigres*, D.Quixote	Manuel Frias Martins, Helena Barbas, Teresa Salema
2000	Ascêncio de Freitas, *O Canto do Sangardata*, Ed.Notícias	Casimiro de Brito, Francisco Belard, Manuel Frias Martins
2001	Hélia Correia, *Lilias Fraser*, Relógio d'Água	
2002	Mafalda Ivo Cruz, *O Rapaz de Botticelli*, Dom Quixote	
2003	Mário de Carvalho, *Fantasia para dois Coronéis e uma Piscina*, Caminho	
2004	Ana Teresa Pereira, *Se nos Encontrarmos de Novo*, Relógio d'Água; Rui Zink, *Dádiva Divina*, Dom Quixote	

GRANDE PRÉMIO DE NOVELA – €14.900 – A.P. E.

Year	Prizewinner	Panel
1982	José C. Pires, *Balada da Praia dos Cães*, O Jornal	Álvaro Salema, Mª Lúcia Lepecki, Jacinto Prado Coelho, Mª Glória Padrão, Óscar Lopes
1983	Agustina Bessa Luís, *Os Meninos de Ouro*, Guimarães	José Palla e Carmo, Mª Glória Padrão, Óscar Lopes, David Mourão Ferreira, Álvaro Salema
1984	Mário Claúdio, *Amadeo*, IN-CM	Eduardo Prado Coelho, Maria Alzira Seixo, Mª Lúcia Lepecki, Diogo P. Aurélio, Carlos Reis
1985	António Lobo Antunes, *Auto dos Danados*, D.Quixote	Álvaro Salema, Paula Morão, Manuel Gusmão, Mª Gloria Padrão Carlos Reis
1986	David Mourão Ferreira, *Um Amor Feliz*, Presença	Óscar Lopes, Arnaldo Saraiva, Luís Forjaz Trigueiros, Joana Varela, Fernando J.B. Martinho
1987	Vergílio Ferreira, *Até ao Fim*, Bertrand	António Quadros, Arnaldo Saraiva, Cristina Almeida Ribeiro, Teresa Rita Lopes, Carlos Reis
1988	João de Melo, *Gente Feliz com Lágrimas*, D.Quixote	Urbano Tavares Rodrigues, Luís Fagundes Duarte Manuel Gusmão, Teresa Rita Lopes, Liberto Cruz

Year	Prizewinner	Panel
1989	Paulo Castilho, *Fora de Horas*, Contexto	Liberto Cruz, Óscar Lopes, Silvina Rodrigues Lopes, António Quadros, Isabel Pires de Lima
1990	Maria Gabriela Llansol, *Um Beijo dado mais Tarde*, Rolim	António Guerreiro, Fernando Dacosta, Helena Buescu, Manuel Gusmão, Mª Fernanda Abreu
1991	José Saramago, *O Evangelho Segundo Jesus Cristo*, Caminho	Mª Lúcia Lepecki, Salvato Trigo Fernando Dacosta, Fausto Lopo de Carvalho, Víctor Viçoso
1992	Helena Marques, *O Último Cais*, D.Quixote	Júlio Conrado, Francisco Belard E. Melo e Castro, Clara Rocha, Carlos Reis
1993	Vergílio Ferreira, *Na Tua Face*, Bertrand	Armando Silva Carvalho, Liberto Cruz, Isabel Pires de Lima, Mª Isabel Barreno, Silvina Rodrigues Lopes
1994	Mário de Carvalho, *Um Deus passeando pela Brisa da Tarde*, Caminho	Fernando J.B.Martinho, Manuel Frias Martins, João Rui de Sousa Margarida Braga Neves, Teolinda Gersão
1995	Teolinda Gersão, *A Casa da Cabeça de Cavalo*, D.Quixote	Ernesto José Rodrigues, Salvato Telles de Menezes, José Carlos Seabra Pereira, Regina Louro, Silvina Rodrigues Lopes
1996	Augusto Abelaira, *Outrora Agora*, Presença	Américo Guerreiro de Sousa, Helena Buescu, Júlio Conrado, Maria Estela Guedes, Paula Morão
1997	Rui Nunes, *Grito*, Relógio d'Água	Cristina Almeida Ribeiro, Fernando Dacosta, Luísa Mellid-Franco, Manuel Frias Martins, Américo G. de Sousa
1998	Fernanda Botelho, *As Contadoras de Histórias*, Presença	Regina Louro, Fernando D Dacosta, Helena Barbas, Teolinda Gersão, Júlio Conrado
1999	António Lobo Antunes, *Exortação aos crocodilos*, D.Quixote	Carlos Figueiredo Lopes, Cristina Robalo Cordeiro, Isabel Pires de Lima, Luiz Fagundes Duarte, Vergílio Alberto Vieira
2000	Maria Velho da Costa, *Irene ou o Contrato Social*, D.Quixote	Eduardo Prado Coelho, Vergílio Alberto Vieira, Yvette Centeno, Clara Rocha, Cristina Robalo Cordeiro
2001	Agustina Bessa Luís, *O Princípio da Incerteza I – Jóia de Família*, Guimarães Editores	Yvette Centeno, António Cândido Franco, Baptista-Bastos, Liberto Cruz Joana Varela

Year	Prizewinner	Panel
2002	Lídia Jorge, *O Vento assobiando nas Gruas*, Dom Quixote	Américo Guerreiro de Sousa, Cristina Robalo Cordeiro, Eunice Silva, Fernando J. B. Martinho Joana Varela
2003	Mafalda Ivo Cruz, *Vermelho*, Dom Quixote	Margarida Braga Neves, Maria Isabel Barreno, Eduardo Prado Coelho, José Carlos Seabra Pereira, Júlio Moreira
2004	Vasco Graça Moura, *Por detrás da magnólia*, Quetzal	José Correia Tavares, Teresa Martins Marques, Fernando Campos, Vergílio Alberto Vieira, Serafina Martins, Teolinda Gersão

CRÍTICA CP/AICL – AICL

Year	Prizewinner	Panel
1980	José Saramago, *A Noite*, Caminho	David Mourão Ferreira, Maria Alzira Seixo, Duarte Faria
1981	Saúl Dias; António Ramos Rosa	
1982	David Mourão Ferreira, *As Quatro Estações*, Presença	Guilherme de Castilho, João Rui de Sousa, Maria da Glória Padrão
1983	Mário Dionísio, *Terceira Idade*; Alexandre O'Neill, *Poesia Completa*, Guimarães	Jacinto do Prado Coelho, António Ramos Rosa, Maria da Glória Padrão
1984	Sophia de Mello Breyner, *Navegações*	Álvaro Salema, João Palma Ferreira, Teolinda Gersão
1985	Vergílio Ferreira, *Para Sempre*, Bertrand	Luís Forjaz Trigueiros, António António Ramos Rosa, Fernando Martinho
1986	José Saramago, *O Ano da Morte de Ricardo Reis*, Camnho; Eugénio de Andrade, *Branco no Branco*, Limiar	Fernando Martinho, Guilherme de Castilho, Manuel Gusmão
1987	Urbano Tavares Rodrigues, *A Vaga de Calor*, Europa-América	
1988	Fernanda Botelho, *Esta Noite Sonhei com Brueghel*, Contexto	Álvaro Salema, Fernando Martinho, Júlio Conrado
1989	Herberto Helder, *Última Ciência*	David Pinto Correia, Álvaro Salema, José Nobre da Silveira
1990	José Blanc de Portugal, *Eneadas – 9 Novenas*	João Rui de Sousa, Fernando Martinho, Helder Godinho

Year	Prizewinner	Panel
1991	Maria Gabriela Llansol, *Um Beijo dado mais Tarde*	Fernando Pinto do Amaral, Luíz Fagundes Duarte, Teresa Amado
1992	Pedro Tamen, *Tábuas das Matérias*, Tertúlia	Ana Hatherly, Isabel Pires de Lima, Urbano Tavares Rodrigues
1993	Agustina Bessa Luís, *Ordens Menores*, Guimarães	João Barrento, José Palla e Carmo Maria Estela Guedes
1994	Miguel Torga – *XVIº Volume*	Yvette Centeno, Casimiro de Brito, José Nobre da Silveira
1995	Maria Velho da Costa, *Dores*, D.Quixote	Fernando Pinto do Amaral, Luíz Fagundes Duarte, Carlos Figueiredo Jorge
1997	José Cardoso Pires, *De Profunddis Valsa Lenta*, D.Quixote	
1998	Manuel Alegre, Caminho	
2001	Manuel António Pina,	Maria Helena Serôdio,
	Atropelamento e Fuga; Rui Nunes, *Rostos*	Paula Morão, Manuel Frias Martins
2002	João Rui de Sousa, *Obra Poética 1960-2002;* Baptista Bastos, *No Interior da Tua Ausência*	Manuel Simões, Maria Fernanda de Abreu, Ernesto Rodrigues
2003	Ana Hatherly, *O Pavão Negro*	Carlos Jorge Figueiredo Jorge, Manuel Simões, José Fernando Tavares
2004	Vítor Aguiar e Silva, *Camões: Labirintos e Fascínios,* Livros Cotovia	

CAMÕES REWARD – 100.000€ – IPLB

Year	Prizewinner	Panel
1989	Miguel Torga	Mª Lourdes Belchior, Eduardo Lourenço, Víctor A. e Silva, Afrânio Coutinho, António Houaiss, Herberto Sales
1990	João M.Cabral Neto	Mª Lourdes Belchior, Eduardo Lourenço, Víctor A. e Silva, Afrânio Coutinho, António Houaiss, Herberto Sales
1991	Craveirinha	David Mourão Ferreira, Arnaldo Saraiva Luís Forjaz Trigueiros, Afonso R. Sant'Anna, Márcio de Sousa, Jorge Fernandes da Silveira

Year	Prizewinner	Panel
1992	Vergílio Ferreira	Fernando Cristovão, Aníbal Pinto de Castro, Ivo de Castro, Cleonice Berardinelli, Jorge Fernandes da Silveira, Márcio de Sousa
1993	Rachel de Queiroz	Carlos Reis, Fernando Guimarães, Idalina Regina Rodrigues, João Escatimburgo, Arnallo Niskier, Óscar Dias Correia
1994	Jorge Amado	Carlos Reis, Idalina Regina Rodrigues, Urbano Tavares Rodrigues, Afonso R. De Sant'Anna, Cleonice Berardinelli, João Ubaldo Ribeiro
1995	José Saramago	Carlos Reis, Idalina Regina Rodrigues, Urbano Tavares Rodrigues, Afonso R. De Sant'Anna, António Torres, Márcio de Sousa
1996	Eduardo Lourenço	Carlos Reis, Urbano Tavares Rodrigues, Idalina Regina Rodrigues, Eduardo Portella, Cleonice Berardinelli, Afonso R. De Sant'Anna
1997	Pepetela	Fernando J.B.Martinho, Óscar Lopes, António Alçada Baptista, Eduardo Portella, Nelida Piñon, Carlos Nejar
1998	Eduardo de C. Mello e Sousa	Fernando J.B.Martinho, António Alçada Baptista, Mª Alzira Seixo, Eduardo Portella Fábio Lucas, Moacyr Seliar
1999	Sophia de Mello Breyner	António Alçada Baptista, Mª Alzira Seixo, Mª Irene Ramalho Santos, Leila Perrone Moisés, Luís Costa Lima, Elmer Correia Barbosa
2000	Autran Dourado	Maria Alzira Seixo, José Manuel Mendes, Irene Ramalho Santos, Mário Chamie, Silviano Santiago, César Leal
2001	Eugénio de Andrade	Maria Irene Ramalho, Isabel Allegro de Magalhães, Alberto Silva, José Manuel Mendes, Carlos Cony, Dionysio Toledo
2002	Maria Velho da Costa	Isabel Pires de Lima Isabel Allegro de Magalhães, Alberto Silva, Alfredo Bosi, José Craveirinha, Artur Pestana (Pepetela)
2003	Ruben Fonseca	Isabel Pires de Lima, Eduardo Prado Coelho, Heloísa Buarque de Holanda, Zuenir Ventura, Lourenço do Rosário, Artur Pestana (Pepetela)
2004	Agustina Bessa Luís	Vasco Graça Moura, Eduardo Prado Coelho, Heloísa Buarque de Holanda, Zuenir Ventura, Lourenço do Rosário, Germano de Almeida

VIDA LITERÁRIA – A.P. E.

Year	Prizewinner
1992	Miguel Torga
1993	José Saramago
1994	Sophia de Mello Breyner
1996	Óscar Lopes
1998	José Cardoso Pires
2000	Eugénio de Andrade
2003	Urbano Tavares Rodrigues

CONSAGRAÇÃO CARREIRA – SPA

Year	Prizewinner
1994	Fernando Lopes Graça/ Carlos Paredes
1995	Manoel de Oliveira/ José Saramago
1996	David Mourão Ferreira
1997	Lagoa Henriques
1998	Jaime Gralheiros/ Jaime Salazar Sampaio
1999	Artur Ramos
2000	Urbano Tavares Rodrigues
2001	José de Guimarães; Carlos do Carmo
2002	Jorge Palma
2003	Matilde Rosa Araújo
2004	Igrejas Caeiro

GRANDE PRÉMIO DO CONTO CAMILO CASTELO BRANCO
– APE/VILA NOVA DE FAMALICÃO CITY HALL

Year	Prizewinner
1992	Mário de Carvalho, *Quatrocentos Mil Sestércios seguido de Conde Jano*
1993	Teresa Veiga, *História da Bela Fria*
1994	Maria Isabel Barreno, *Os Sensos Incomuns*
1995	Maria Velho da Costa, *Dores*, D.Quixote

PESSOA REWARD – 42.900€ – UNYSIS

Year	Prizewinner
1987	José Mattoso
1988	António Ramos Rosa
1989	Maria João Pires
1990	Menez
1991	Claúdio Torres
1992	António e Hanna Damásio
1993	Fernando Gil
1994	Herberto Helder
1995	Vasco Graça Moura
1996	João Lobo Antunes
1997	José Cardoso Pires
1998	Eduardo Souto Moura
1999	Manuel Alegre / José Manuel Rodrigues
2000	Emmanuel Nunes
2001	João Bénard da Costa
2002	Manuel Sobrinho Simões
2003	José Gomes Canotilho
2004	Mário Claúdio